Temperament

Infancy through Adolescence

The Fullerton Longitudinal Study

LONGITUDINAL RESEARCH IN THE SOCIAL AND BEHAVIORAL SCIENCES

An Interdisciplinary Series

Series Editors:

Howard B. Kaplan, *Texas A&M University, College Station, Texas*
Adele Eskeles Gottfried, *California State University, Northridge, California*
Allen W. Gottfried, *California State University, Fullerton, California*

THE ADDICTION-PRONE PERSONALITY
Gordon E. Barnes, Robert P. Murray, David Patton, Peter M. Bentler, and Robert E. Anderson

DRUG USE AND ETHNICITY IN EARLY ADOLESCENCE
William A. Vega, Andres G. Gil, and Associates

DRUGS, CRIME, AND OTHER DEVIANT ADAPTATIONS
Longitudinal Studies
Edited by Howard B. Kaplan

PREMARITAL PREDICTION OF MARITAL QUALITY OR BREAKUP
Research, Theory, and Practice
Thomas B. Holman and Associates

RESILIENCE AND DEVELOPMENT
Positive Life Adaptations
Edited by Meyer D. Glantz and Jeannette L. Johnson

TAKING STOCK OF DELINQUENCY
An Overview of Findings from Contemporary Longitudinal Studies
Edited by Terence P. Thornberry and Marvin D. Krohn

TEMPERAMENT
Infancy through Adolescence
Diana Wright Guerin, Allen W. Gottfried, Pamella H. Oliver, and Craig W. Thomas

---

Temperament
Infancy through Adolescence
The Fullerton Longitudinal Study

Diana Wright Guerin
California State University, Fullerton, California

Allen W. Gottfried
California State University, Fullerton, California

Pamella H. Oliver
California State University, Fullerton, California

and

Craig W. Thomas
Claremont Graduate University, Claremont, California

Kluwer Academic / Plenum Publishers
New York, Boston, Dordrecht, London, Moscow

Library of Congress Cataloging-in-Publication Data

Temperament: infancy through adolescence/by Diana Wright Guerin ... [et al.].
   p.   cm. — (Longitudinal research in the social and behavioral sciences)
   Includes bibliographical references and index.
   ISBN 0-306-47688-6
   1. Temperament in children—Longitudinal studies.   I. Guerin, Diana Wright.   II. Series.

BF798 .T465 2003
155.4′18—dc21

2002042768

ISBN 0-306-47688-6

©2003 Kluwer Academic/Plenum Publishers, New York
233 Spring Street, New York, New York 10013

http://www.wkap.nl/

10 9 8 7 6 5 4 3 2 1

A C.I.P. record for this book is available from the Library of Congress

*To those whose persistent support, positive mood,
and never-ending flexibility made the completion
of this book possible*

Keith, Jon, Ali
Adele, Michael, Jeffrey
Biff, Kristin, Kelly, Jessica, Nate
Audey

and
*to the "children" and families participating
in the Fullerton Longitudinal Study*

Preface

"Your good nature will bring you much happiness."

                                           —Peking Noodle Co.

We began this book with the belief that there are individual differences in temperament that impact the trajectory of the course of development. At a particular point in time, the impact may be small, but over time the effect of these small tweaks may come to be associated with significant and meaningful differences in our individual destinations. In this book, we examined the relations between temperament and various domains of development as well as the home and family environment to document the short- and long-term sequelae of various temperamental characteristics to test this belief.

It takes a certain temperamental profile to complete a collaborative longitudinal research project spanning two decades. Especially during the project's early years, when we were directly assessing the development of over 100 children twice yearly and visiting their homes, high *activity level* was required. Our *biological rhythms* were constantly disrupted as we worked to complete data coding (we used punch cards then!) and checking before the next wave of assessments began. We learned to *approach* new problems and tasks with *intensity*, to be *adaptable* when appointments had to be rescheduled, to be *sensitive* to changes in our study families' situations, and that a *positive mood* is essential. We were not easily *distracted* from our goal of following the study participants through high school completion, and our *persistence* has made all the difference.

The Fullerton Longitudinal Study is the product of a wonderful collaboration among an increasing number of dedicated colleagues, and we thank our co-investigators Adele Eskeles Gottfried, Kay Bathurst, and Jacqueline K. Coffman for their significant contributions and helpful insights to the project. However, we take full responsibility for the analyses presented and interpretations expressed herein.

For over two decades, graduate and undergraduate students at California State University, Fullerton have made valuable contributions to the study, and we thank them for their dedication and fine efforts. Particularly instrumental and longstanding in their support of the project were the following: Ann Barter, Rachel Mason, Makeba Parramore, Michelle Ramos, Colleen Killian, Judit Au, Catherine Lussier, June Havlena, Connie Meyer, Leigh Hobson, Shelli Wynants, Juan Carlos Bojorquez, Gigi Nordquist, Jeff Wisdom, and Kathleen Ellenberger. More recently, we are indebted to Phil Morris, Ewelina Szewczyk, Emily Cheng, Susanne M. Valdez, Clayton Cook, and Vivienne Ganga.

We also thank those who provided financial support at various points during the course of investigation. These include the Spencer Foundation, Thrasher Research Fund, and California State Universities at Fullerton and Northridge.

We are especially grateful to the "children" and families participating in the Fullerton Longitudinal Study. Their continuing commitment and participation has made this project a rewarding and enriching enterprise for the science of human development and for us as professionals and individuals.

Diana Wright Guerin
Allen W. Gottfried
Pamella H. Oliver
Craig W. Thomas

Contents

1

Introduction and Overview

> "(Name) has been described by his kindergarten teacher as being very active and impulsive in class. Some part of his body is always in motion. He is quick to retaliate on the playground if hit or bumped."
> —Parent of Child #16, Difficult Infant Temperament Group, Age 6

The history of temperament is a long one, reaching back to the ancient Greeks and Romans (Garrison & Earls, 1987; Kagan, 1994; Rothbart & Bates, 1998; Strelau, 1998). Although a construct with ancient roots, Alexander Thomas, Stella Chess, and their research colleagues can be credited for stimulating the current surge of research on temperament in the United States, particularly research focusing on the role of temperament in children's development and adjustment. Findings from their longitudinal study and their accompanying conceptualization of temperament have served to stimulate thousands of studies, including the temperament component in the research project detailed herein, the Fullerton Longitudinal Study. In this book, we present an overview of our findings to date concerning the continuity and stability of temperament from infancy through adolescence and its relation to behavioral and emotional adjustment; intelligence, the school context; and the home environment and family relationships.

Pervasiveness of the Temperament Construct

Why has the construct of temperament captured the interest of such a wide audience, including, for example, developmental and personality research psychologists, psychiatrists, pediatricians, nurses and other medical professionals, family and child therapists, teachers, parent educators, and parents?

For many, the construct of temperament offered a conceptually appealing individual difference variable representing the contribution of individuals to the course of their development in opposition to the environmentalism paradigm prevailing throughout most of the first half of the twentieth century. As statistical methods to study behavioral genetics flourished, many researchers became interested in investigating heritable influences on various aspects of temperament

1

(Goldsmith & Gottesman, 1981; Matheny, 1980). Currently, the role of biology in determining temperamental style is a topic of increasing interest, further expanding the temperament audience (Bates & Wachs, 1994).

The finding that certain clusters of temperament dimensions predicted behavior problems (Thomas, Chess, & Birch, 1968) was a major catalyst in generating interest in the concept of temperament. The possible role of this individual difference variable in making some children vulnerable and others resilient to risk factors spurred considerable interest and research activity. Its role as one of many factors determining children's vulnerability and resilience to stress is now recognized:

> ...there is no single source of resilience or vulnerability. Rather, many interacting factors come into play. They include not only individual genetic predispositions, which express themselves in enduring aspects of temperament, personality, and intelligence, but also qualities such as social skills and self-esteem. These, in turn, are shaped by a variety of environmental influences (Basic Behavioral Science Task Force of the National Advisory Mental Health Council, 1996, p. 22).

Accumulating evidence that temperament is stable across extended periods of childhood and adolescence, along with increasing acceptance of the "Big Five" factors of adult personality, has renewed interest in the possibility that certain aspects of temperament represent early developing (Buss & Plomin, 1984) or are precursors of adult personality (Ahadi & Rothbart, 1994; Martin, Wisenbaker, & Huttunen, 1994; Rothbart, 1989). However, this hypothesis has yet to be documented empirically with long-term longitudinal research ranging from infancy through early adulthood (cf., Angleitner & Ostendorf, 1994; Caspi, 1998; Martin et al., 1994; Wachs, 1994).

The application of temperament concepts in clinical and therapeutic settings has also contributed to its popularity as a construct. Although Thomas and Chess have written extensively about the application of temperament in clinical practice (Chess & Thomas, 1984, 1986, 1996), recent years have seen a proliferation of books directed toward parents (e.g., Carey, 1997; Kurcinka, 1991; Neville & Johnson, 1997; Turecki & Tonner, 1989) and, more recently, teachers (Keogh, 2003). Additionally, programs employing temperament as a preventive strategy (Cameron, Hansen, & Rosen, 1991; Cameron & Rice, 1986; McClowry, 1998) and as part of parent education/training (Mettetal, 1996; Sheeber & Johnson, 1994; Sheeber & McDevitt, 1998) have been implemented and evaluated.

Contemporary Interest in the Concept of Temperament

Results from searches of computerized databases of the psychological and educational research literature through 1999 provide testament to the continuing

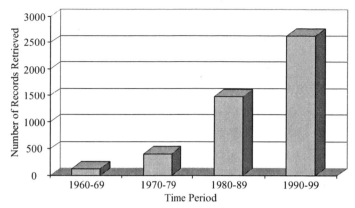

Figure 1.01. Number of records retrieved by decade using free text search (temperament* with human population) in SilverPlatter PsycINFO database, 1960–1999.

popularity and durability of the temperament concept. A free-text search of the database focusing on educational issues (ERIC SilverPlatter) for published articles with the root word "temperament" yielded 49 records for publication years 1970–1979, 180 for 1980–1989, and 240 for 1990–1999. Results from a similar search of the psychological literature using SilverPlatter PsycINFO are displayed in Figure 1.01. As shown in Figure 1.01, records including the root "temperament" (and human population) increased from 123 with publication years 1960–1969 to 2635 for 1990–1999. Although these data no doubt also reflect increasing opportunities to publish due to proliferation of increasingly specialized journals, they also suggest that research including the temperament concept has increased dramatically over the past 30 years in both educational and psychological journals and continues strong.

Another indication of interest in the temperament construct can be gleaned from a perusal of the range of topics of recently published scholarly research that includes temperament as a variable. Much of the research pertains to temperament with respect to developmental risk throughout the life span. For example, research on children includes the relation of temperament to stuttering (Lewis & Goldberg, 1997), slow expressive language development (Paul & Kellogg, 1997), attention deficit hyperactivity disorder (McIntosh & Cole-Love, 1996), child neglect/abuse (Harrington, Black, Starr, & Dubowitz, 1998), and accidental injuries (Plumert & Schwebel, 1997).

Focusing on temperament during adolescence and/or adulthood, researchers have examined its relation to developmental risks such as substance use/abuse (Wills, Windle, & Cleary, 1998), criminal conviction or conduct disorder (Henry, Caspi, Moffitt, & Silva, 1996), health-risk behaviors in young adulthood (Caspi, et al., 1997), eating disorders (Bulik, Sullivan, Carter, & Joyce, 1997), anxiety or phobic disorders (Bernstein, Borchardt, & Perwien, 1996; Sellman & Joyce, 1996), postpartum depression (Beck, 1996), and suicide (Nordstroem, Gustavsson, Edman, & Asberg, 1996).

In the domain of social development and adjustment, temperament has been examined with respect to the mother-infant relationship (Kochanska, 1998), child-rearing stress (Honjo, et al., 1998), child-rearing attitudes (Katainen, Raeikkoenen, & Keltikangas-Jaervinen, 1997), peer relationships (Fabes, Shepard, Guthrie, & Martin, 1997), conscience (Kochanska, 1997), empathy (Miller & Jansen-op-de-Haar, 1997), adolescent-parent relationships (Kawaguchi, Welsh, Powers, & Rostosky, 1998), coping with stress (Eisenberg, Shepard, Fabes, Murphy, & Guthrie, 1998), marital satisfaction (Blum & Mehrabian, 1999), and adult interpersonal functioning (Newman, Caspi, Moffitt, & Silva, 1997).

Recent basic research on temperament has also examined relations to physiological/biochemical measures (see Bates & Wachs, 1994), and fetal antecedents (DiPietro, Hodgson, Costigan, & Johnson, 1996). This cursory scan of recent research including or focusing on the temperament construct shows the pervasiveness of temperament in educational, psychological, clinical, health, and developmental research arenas.

Uniqueness of the Fullerton Longitudinal Study for Investigating Temperament

The FLS is uniquely suited for investigating the developmental aspects of temperament from infancy through adolescence for several reasons, which we have conceptualized into five categories: age span covered, breadth of developmental measures, frequency of temperament measures, cross-context/cross-informant methodology, and nature of the FLS sample. Each of these strengths will be elaborated in the pages that follow.

Long-Term Prospective Study Spanning Infancy through Adolescence

The FLS is a long-term, contemporary investigation of children's development from infancy onward. Thus far, the study cohort has been followed through adolescence. In developmental psychology, such studies are not commonplace. In the temperament literature, there are relatively few long-term longitudinal studies. Prominent examples include the New York Longitudinal Study by Thomas and Chess (Chess & Thomas, 1984; Thomas & Chess, 1977), Australian Temperament Project (Prior, Sanson, & Oberklaid, 1989); Dunedin (New Zealand) Multidisciplinary Health and Development Study (Silva, 1990); Louisville Twin

Study (Matheny, 1989), Bloomington Longitudinal Study (Pettit & Bates, 1984), and the study in Quebec, Canada by Maziade and colleagues (Maziade, Cote, Bernier, Boutin, & Thivierge, 1989a, 1989b). When taking into account the scope (or duration) of investigation in conjunction with the breadth of developmental domains assessed and frequency of assessment waves, the FLS is indeed unique. The FLS is not just a longitudinal study; it is an investment into the understanding of the developmental aspects of temperament throughout childhood and adolescence.

Comprehensive Data Base

The FLS comprises over 16,000 variables collected to assess a comprehensive array of conceptually-derived measures appraising various developmental domains. The extensive breadth of measures has been collected systematically, rigorously, and contemporaneously across time, so as to yield a scientific history of children's development. Measures were chosen based on a preconceived foundation so as to address issues and answer questions in various research themes running through this longitudinal project. These themes include, for example, home and family environment (e.g., A. W. Gottfried & Gottfried, 1984; A. E. Gottfried & Gottfried, 1994); intellectual development (e.g., A. E. Gottfried & Gottfried, 1996; A. W. Gottfried, Gottfried, Bathurst, & Guerin, 1994); parental employment (e.g., A. E. Gottfried, Bathurst, & Gottfried, 1994; A. E. Gottfried, Gottfried, & Bathurst, 1988, 1995, 2002; A. E. Gottfried, Gottfried, Bathurst, & Killian, 1999); academic intrinsic motivation (e.g., A. E. Gottfried, 1990; A. E. Gottfried, Fleming, & Gottfried, 1994, 2001), developmental screening and assessment (e.g., Bathurst & Gottfried, 1987; Guerin & Gottfried, 1987; Guerin, Griffin, Gottfried, & Christenson, 1993a, 1993b), and, of course, temperament (Guerin & Gottfried, 1994a; Guerin & Gottfried, 1994b; Guerin, Gottfried, Oliver, & Thomas, 1994; Guerin, Gottfried, & Thomas, 1997). Hence, we have the opportunity to study both the nomological and differential network of temperament to these domains within a given cohort across time. In this book, temperament will be examined in relation to many of these themes/developmental domains.

Frequency and Continuity of Temperament Assessments

In formulating and executing a longitudinal study, researchers must balance between having a very large sample size with less frequent assessments and fewer measures or having a relatively smaller sample size with more frequent testing periods and a greater number of measures. Because our interest is developmental psychology, we opted for the latter approach. By no means is our sample size small with respect to the psychological literature. The sample size is relatively large given its ratio to the comprehensiveness of developmental assessments. The frequency of assessment waves in the FLS is intensive, comprising 19 laboratory assessments from age 1 through 17 years plus three direct home visits (infancy, preschool, middle childhood). With respect to temperament, we have conducted 10 assessment waves at designated and regular intervals from infancy (beginning 1.5 years) through adolescence (16 years). To our knowledge, there is no other study on temperament of its kind.

By having multiple cross-time assessments of temperament, we are in the position to treat temperament as an antecedent, precursor, or predictor variable as well as a consequence, outcome, or criterion variable. Thus we can conduct forward- and reverse-contingency analyses (A. W. Gottfried, 1973; A. W. Gottfried et al., 1994), examine the relationship of temperament to other domains concurrently and across time, and are in the unique position of aggregating temperament measures. The latter enhances measurement reliability (Epstein, 1979) and at the same time provides a more consolidated approach to data analysis.

We employed temperament scales of known psychometric qualities and utilized them repeatedly within and across developmental periods, permitting us to study issues of both stability and continuity. Aside from the extensive ongoing assessment of temperament during childhood, we incorporated a major contemporary measure of personality at our final lab assessment at age 17. Hence, we are in a position to address the issue of whether various temperament dimensions are antecedents to personality factors.

Cross Context, Cross Informant Methodology

Our comprehensive database derives from information collected across settings and persons. Concurrent with laboratory assessments, data were gathered from home assessments; even within the database on home environment, we had both direct observations as well as indirect (questionnaire) sources of information. For example, with respect to behavioral functioning we gathered cross-informant data from the parent, teacher, and child. We applied this assessment strategy to the realm of temperament as well. Throughout the course of investigation, we assessed parents' perceptions of their children's temperament. Within the chronology of our investigation, we incorporated psychometric self-report assessments of children's temperament when they became available. Then we gathered cross time information on this measure as well. The purpose of our cross-context cross-informant approach was to allow us to examine content variance as well as appraise the construct validity and generalizability of our findings. This approach sheds light on the issue of discriminative validity, as well.

Nature of the Sample

The characteristics of the sample will be described in Chapter 2. Our longitudinal investigation was designed from the outset to study a relatively large sample of children from infancy onward. It is not an intervention study designed to evaluate the effects of a given treatment or experimental manipulation. Furthermore, advice, consultation, or other parental guidance pertaining to events in the course of the children's development was not provided. Succinctly, the FLS tracked and mapped the natural course of development of a relatively large sample of children and their families from infancy into adulthood.

At the outset, our sample represented a range of healthy infants by virtue of the fact that they were not selected because of any risk or clinical factors. This puts us in accord with other major longitudinal studies including the full range of variability rather than building a sample comprising extreme temperament groups. Although comparing qualitatively or quantitatively distinct groups contributes to our fund of knowledge about the nature of temperament, dealing with extremes without the inclusion of the full body of data also sets limits on the full range of possible outcomes that may be observed. First, by comparing the two extremes, nonlinear relationships cannot be detected. Second, it is well known that when only dealing with the extremes at the outset, regression toward the mean is probable. Our approach has been to avoid ascertainment bias (Guerin et al., 1993b) and to take into account the entire range of variance, particularly when examining cross-time relationships. However, we were in the position to conduct analyses with the entire sample range as well as with the extremes.

Throughout the span of the FLS, a high rate of subject and family participation was maintained. For example, the number of subjects completing the 17-year laboratory assessment was 109 of the original 130 at age 1 year. This yields a return rate of 84%, which reduces the probability of sample bias resulting from mortality or selective attrition. Our sample represents an intact sample of normal healthy infants through their course of development from infancy through adolescence.

The NYLS Framework

The framework developed by Alexander Thomas, Stella Chess, and their colleagues based on the observations from their research project, the New York Longitudinal Study (NYLS), provides the theoretical foundation for the FLS; therefore, a review of their approach is in order. At the inception of the FLS in the late 1970's, several books on the NYLS project were available (*Behavioral Individuality in Early Childhood*, *Temperament and Behavior Disorders in Children*, and *Temperament and Development* published in 1963, 1968, and 1977, respectively). Additionally, questionnaires suitable for use in a study such as the FLS incorporating the NYLS concepts were also appearing in the literature, such as the Infant Characteristics Questionnaire (e.g., Bates, Freeland, & Lounsbury, 1979) and the Behavioral Style Questionnaire (McDevitt & Carey, 1978). Hence, the confluence of these fortuitous events with the initiation of the FLS set the stage for our long-term investigation of temperament and development from a behavioral style perspective.

In the behavioral style perspective put forth by the NYLS research team, temperament is defined as follows:

> Temperament may best be viewed as a general term referring to the how of behavior. It differs from ability, which is concerned with the what and how well of behaving, and from motivation, which seeks to account for why a person does what he is doing. When we refer to temperament, we are concerned with the way in which an individual behaves (Thomas et al., 1968, p. 4).

Thomas and Chess's model is an interactionist one; a central tenet of this approach is the concept of "goodness of fit" (Thomas et al., 1968; Thomas & Chess, 1977). This tenet holds that the individual's optimal development will be achieved when the environment and expectations within the environment are consonant with the individual's capacities, characteristics, and style of behaving. When discrepancies exist between environmental demands and the individual's characteristics, development is compromised and distorted or maladaptive functioning occurs. Also related to the interactionist approach is the issue of mutability. Thomas and Chess noted that temperament is not immutable:

> ... Like any other characteristic of the organism—whether it be height, weight, intellectual competence, perceptual skills—temperament is influenced by environmental factors in its expression and even in its nature as development proceeds (1977, p. 9).

The framework includes nine categories or dimensions of temperament, which were derived from parent interviews and child observations in the early years of the NYLS. In addition, direct observation data were collected from a subsample of the NYLS to test the validity of the temperament measures based on ratings of parental interview protocols. The nine dimensions in the NYLS model are displayed with brief descriptions in Table 1.01. As analyses in chapters 3 through 7 are focused on these nine dimensions, each dimension will be described in greater detail in the paragraphs that follow. In the FLS, parent report inventories were used to assess the child's temperament throughout the infant and childhood years, and both parent and child reports were gathered during adolescence. To illustrate the types of items used to assess each dimension, items similar to those included on the various parent report measures used in the FLS will be provided.

Table 1.01.   Brief Descriptions of Nine Temperament Dimensions
Included in the NYLS Model

Dimension	Definition
Activity Level	The level, tempo, and frequency of the motor component in the child's functioning.
Rhythmicity	The degree of regularity of repetitive biological functions, such as sleeping and waking, feeding, or elimination.
Approach/Withdrawal	The nature of the initial response to a new stimulus, such as new food, toys, or people.
Adaptability	The sequential course of the child's responses to new stimuli or altered situations.
Intensity of Reaction	The energy level of response, regardless of quality or direction.
Quality of Mood	The amount of pleasant, joyful, friendly behavior as contrasted with unpleasant, crying, unfriendly behavior.
Persistence/Attention Span	The continuation of an activity in the face of obstacles to its continuation and length of time a particular activity is pursued.
Distractibility	The effectiveness of extraneous environmental stimuli in interfering with or altering the direction of ongoing behavior.
Threshold of Responsiveness	The level of extrinsic stimulation necessary to evoke a noticeable response, regardless of the nature of the response.

Compiled from Thomas et al. (1968)

The Nine NYLS Temperament Dimensions

Activity Level

Ranging from low to high, activity level relates to "the level, tempo, and frequency with which a motor component is present in the child's functioning" (Thomas et al., 1968, p. 20). Items assessing this dimension might include "The child squirms during quiet activities, such as when looking at story books" (toddler), "The child runs ahead when shopping with the parent" (preschool), or "Fidgets when he/she has rides in the car" (middle childhood). During the adolescent period, the measure used assessed general activity level separately from activity level during sleep. A sample item for the former might be "Even when I am supposed to be still, I get very restless after a few minutes." A sample item for the latter might be "I move around a lot in my sleep."

Biological Rhythmicity

This dimension relates to "the degree of rhythmicity or regularity of repetitive biological functions . . . rest and activity, sleeping and waking, eating and appetite, and bowel and bladder function . . ." (Thomas et al., 1968, p. 20). On this dimension, children may be described as those with biological rhythms that are predictable or regular or those whose functioning varies from day to day and are therefore irregular or unpredictable. In the FLS, parents rated their children on items similar to "The child takes daytime naps at varying times from day to day" (toddler) and "The child is tired at his/her bedtime" (preschool). During middle childhood, the measure of temperament used in the FLS changed its focus from biological predictability to social predictability, including an item such as "Keeps her/his things neat and orderly." The measure during adolescence delineated three separate aspects of regularity, including rhythmicity of sleeping, eating, and daily habits.

Approach/Withdrawal

Thomas et al. (1968) defined the dimension of approach/withdrawal as "the child's initial reaction to any new stimulus, be it food, people, places, toys, or procedures" (p. 21). Items during the toddler years were similar to the following: "The child's initial reaction to a new caregiver is rejection (crying, clinging to mother, etc.)," and "The child approaches and plays with unfamiliar pets (small dogs, cats)." During the preschool years, a typical item might be "The child is friendly with strangers when introduced." In middle childhood, the parent rated items comparable to "Outgoing to children her/his age who she/he doesn't know." Items on the adolescent measure might be similar to "I can make myself comfortable anywhere."

Adaptability

Adaptability ranges from slow (unadaptable) to fast (adaptable) and is defined as "the sequential course of responses a child makes to new or altered situations ... emphasis is on the ease or difficulty with which the initial pattern of response can be modified in the direction desired by the parents or others" (Thomas et al., 1968, p. 21). In the FLS, parents responded to items such as "The child is still cautious of strangers after 15 minutes" (toddler), "Changes in plans trouble child" (preschool), or "Settles disagreements with playmates within a few minutes" (middle childhood). In adolescence, the measure employed in the FLS labeled this dimension of behavioral style "flexibility/rigidity," and assessed it with items such as "It takes me a long time to get used to new schedules."

Intensity of Reaction

Intensity of reaction ranges from mild to intense and is defined as "the energy content of the response, irrespective of its direction" (Thomas et al., 1968, p. 21). In the FLS, parents responded to items similar to "The child is easily excited by approval" (toddler) and "The child shows strong responses to both positive and negative things" (preschool). During the middle childhood years, parents rated their children's intensity of reaction using items such as "Shouts, laughs loudly, squeals, etc., when happy." This dimension was not assessed during the adolescent period in the FLS.

Quality of Mood

Thomas et al. (1968) defined quality of mood as "the amount of pleasant, joyful, friendly behavior as contrasted with unpleasant, crying, unfriendly behavior" (p. 23). Mood ranges from positive to negative in quality through middle childhood and from negative to positive during adolescence. Sample items used in the FLS to assess quality of mood resembled "The child has grumpy or 'off' days when he/she is fussy all day" (toddler), "The child smiles while playing" (preschool), and "Remains agreeable even when tired" (middle childhood). During the adolescent assessments, items were similar to the following: "I laugh often during the day," and "Generally, I am cheerful."

Persistence/Attention Span

Thomas et al. characterized this dimension as "two subcategories which are related. By attention span is meant the length of time a particular activity is pursued . . . By persistence, we mean the child's maintaining of an activity in the face of obstacles to its continuation" (1968, p. 24). In the FLS, this dimension was assessed by parent responses to items similar to "The child quickly becomes bored with a new toy" (toddler), "The child pays attention from start to finish when being shown a new activity" (preschool), and "Stays with homework until completed" (middle childhood). During the adolescent years, this dimension was labeled "task orientation" and characterized by items such as the following: "I stay at a task until it's finished," and "Once I start a new hobby or activity, I stay with it."

Distractibility

Distractibility was defined by Thomas et al. as "the effectiveness of extraneous environmental stimuli in interfering with, or in altering the direction of, the ongoing behavior" (1968, p. 23). A sample item assessing this dimension during the toddler years might include "The child stops playing and looks up when a person walks by." In later assessments, sample items resembled "The child seems not to hear when involved in a desired activity" (preschool) and "Looks up right away from play when telephone rings; distracted by routine noises" (middle childhood). In the measure used in the FLS during adolescence, distractibility was a component of the task orientation dimension described in the previous paragraph.

Threshold of Responsiveness

This dimension was defined as "the level of extrinsic stimulation that is necessary to evoke a discernible response" (Thomas et al., 1968, p. 22). An item assessing this dimension during the toddler years was similar to "The child notices soiled clothing, and wants to be changed right away." Typical items from subsequent assessments were similar to "The child notices minor changes in parent's clothing or hairstyle (preschool)" and "Comments on texture of clothing, upholstery, etc." (middle childhood). This dimension was not assessed during adolescence in the measure employed in the FLS.

As previously noted, analyses in chapters 3 through 7 examined the relation of each of these nine temperament traits to aspects of children's development and/or environment from infancy through adolescence. Each of the nine dimensions was treated as a continuous variable.

The Concept of Difficult Temperament

In addition to these nine dimensions of temperament, the NYLS team also identified three temperamental constellations that showed practical significance with respect to children's development and adjustment: easy, difficult, and slow-to-warm-up temperament (Thomas & Chess, 1977). These constellations all represent variations within the normal range of behavioral style. Most of the ensuing research based on the NYLS model of temperament has used the dimensions rather than the constellations as predictor variables, a practice we follow in chapters 3 through 7 herein. Nonetheless, the concept of difficult temperament has played a dominant role in both conceptual and applied work in the field (Bates, 1980; Putnam, Sanson, & Rothbart, 2002). Putnam et al. noted that subsequent research has shown that the dimensions hypothesized to comprise difficult temperament have failed to cluster together, leading to the development of measures of difficult temperament. In chapter 8, we utilized a widely-used measure of difficult infant temperament to study the short- and long-term developmental and environmental sequelae of not only difficult temperament, but also easy temperament, using an extreme groups approach.

Other Child-Focused Models of Temperament

The model proposed by Thomas, Chess and colleagues has certainly generated much research activity. However, numerous conceptualizations of temperament have been proposed. Delineating a precise list of temperament models is complicated by numerous factors, including, for example, whether a distinction between temperament and personality is made, whether research focusing on single attributes qualifies as an approach, and whether one includes models focusing on children, adults, or both. Strelau (1998) provided a compehensive review of additional temperament theories from an international perspective pertaining to children and/or adults. Goldsmith et al. (1987) organized a roundtable discussion of four approaches to temperament. Included in this discussion were researchers with approaches focusing on infancy and childhood developmental eras: the behavior-genetics approach of Buss and Plomin, Thomas and Chess's behavioral style approach, Rothbart and Derryberry's developmental model, and the emotion-oriented approach of Goldsmith and Campos. More recently, Kagan (1994) has proposed a psychobiological model of temperament. Time and the accumulation of empirical data will determine the utility of these numerous conceptualizations in furthering our understanding of this family of individual differences in children and adults.

Introduction to Issues Investigated

For almost two decades, data assessing temperament and several research themes have been systematically collected to detail the development of the cohort of children and their families participating in the FLS. In this book, we present our findings to date concerning the relation of temperament from infancy through adolescence to variables in each of the research themes. The format or structure of the book is delineated in the ensuing paragraphs.

In chapter 2, the methodology employed in conducting the FLS is detailed. The sample characteristics at the onset of the study are provided. The rationale for selecting the parent report inventory to assess temperament is furnished, along with descriptions of the measures of temperament used at ten assessment periods ranging from 1.5 to 16 years. Decisions guiding our data analytic strategy are discussed. Chapter 2 concludes with an overview of the measures employed in each of the research strands during the infancy, preschool years, middle childhood, and adolescent development eras.

In chapters 3 through 8, we provide a systematic analysis of the temperament data collected during the course of investigation. In spite of our desire to provide a comprehensive and detailed analysis of all the temperament data collected, we realized that at best we can provide a broad overview of, in most cases, the "main effects" of temperament with respect to the many domains of development assessed in the FLS. The book concludes in chapter 9 with an integration of the findings from the previous chapters, in particular addressing the significance of temperament and individual dimensions of temperament to children's development in specific domains. Additionally, the implications of findings from the FLS with respect to the NYLS temperament model are discussed.

We now conclude chapter 1 with a review of literature relevant to the issues addressed in chapters 3 through 8: stability and continuity of temperament and relation to personality; behavioral and emotional adjustment; intelligence; the school context; home and family environment; and the long-term developmental significance of extreme temperament during infancy.

Consistency and Change in Temperament

A major contribution of the FLS is the insight that can be gained from its repeated longitudinal assessment of temperament from infancy through adolescence. Data regarding consistency and change in temperament in the FLS cohort are presented in chapter 3. A view held by many researchers and theorists is that temperament represents early developing personality traits. Empirical data addressing this contention conclude chapter 3, with findings from the FLS on the cross-time relation between childhood temperament and the "Big Five" personality traits assessed at age 17.

Age-Related Changes in Temperament

With respect to developmental change at the group level (i.e., continuity, or changes in group means across age), several researchers have reported changes during specific developmental eras. For example, focusing on the first five years of life, Thomas and Chess (1986) found significant changes in means on four of the nine NYLS dimensions (rhythmicity, mood, adaptability, and intensity); parents reported a developmental pattern toward greater biological regularity, faster adaptability, milder intensity of reaction, and more positive mood at age 5 compared to earlier years.

Data from the FLS at ages 3, 3.5, and 5 years using parent reports (Guerin & Gottfried, 1994a) corroborated the NYLS findings; additionally, we observed a developmental pattern toward lower activity level, greater persistence, and increasing sensitivity/reactivity at age 5 years. Our findings on persistence and threshold are in line with those of Fullard, McDevitt, and Carey (1984), who found children were more persistent and more reactive to sensory stimuli with increasing age from 1 to 3 years. Fullard et al. also reported faster adaptability with increasing age.

There is also evidence of significant change in mean levels during the middle childhood period. Consistent with findings by Hegvik, McDevitt, and Carey (1982), we found that children were rated as less active with increasing age (ages 8, 10, and 12 years). Additionally, parents reported greater approach, milder intensity, and less reactivity with increasing age during the later elementary school years

(Guerin & Gottfried, 1994a). No mean changes were observed in the remaining five dimensions in the FLS or in the Hegvik et al. study.

Thus, data from the FLS and other longitudinal studies provide evidence of developmental progression in many temperament dimensions within both the preschool and middle childhood periods. In the FLS, shifting occurred in more dimensions during the preschool period than during the middle childhood period, despite the fact that the latter was twice the time interval of the former. Three dimensions showed significant changes during both periods. Namely, activity and intensity showed similar progressions across both periods; that is, there was a shift toward less activity and less intensity during the preschool period, which was also evident during the middle childhood period. Threshold also showed mean changes during both periods, but in different directions; during the preschool there was a shift toward greater reactivity, while during the middle childhood period there was a drop in sensitivity at 10 years compared to 8 or 12 years.

In chapter 3, we complete our study of temperamental continuity/discontinuity in the FLS by analyzing the last set of temperament measures collected across multiple ages, parent and adolescent self-reported temperament on the Revised Dimensions of Temperament Survey at the 14- and 16-year assessments.

Temperamental Sequelae of Challenging Infant Temperament

In the FLS, the first assessment of temperament was made at 1.5 years using the Infant Characteristics Questionnaire (ICQ) developed by Bates et al. (1979). The ICQ was designed specifically to assess aspects of temperament found challenging by parents during infancy, with the ultimate goal being the longitudinal study of difficult infants. As described in chapter 2, the ICQ assesses four aspects of infant temperament: fussy/difficult/demanding, unadaptability, resistance to control, and unsociability.

We have previously published findings from the FLS documenting the temperamental sequelae of the fussy/difficult/demanding factor of the ICQ from ages 2 through 12 (Guerin & Gottfried, 1994b). Significant correlations of moderate magnitude were evident between the fussy/difficult/demanding factor of the ICQ and several of the NYLS dimensions through age 12. In particular, babies viewed as more fussy at 1.5 years were subsequently reported by parents to be slower to adapt, more negative in mood, and more active at every assessment period through age 12. During the preschool years, babies who were fussy as infants were viewed as more withdrawing/less approaching to novel people, places, and things; commencing in the middle childhood period, a consistent sequel of fussy infant temperament was shorter attention span and less persistence.

Further examination of these data using canonical correlation analyses demonstrated considerable overlap between the four ICQ factors of challenging temperament at 1.5 years and the nine NYLS temperament dimensions throughout childhood (Guerin & Gottfried, 1994b). In the canonical correlation analysis, a linear combination of each set of variables is produced so as to maximize the correlation between the two predicted values. Canonical correlation coefficients between the four ICQ factors and the nine NYLS dimensions ranged from .5 to .6 in magnitude on seven occasions when NYLS dimensions of temperament were measured in the FLS (2, 3, 3.5, 5, 8, 10, and 12) with little cross-time diminution. Hence, data from the FLS demonstrate empirical evidence that infant fussiness correlates significantly with specific dimensions across the childhood period, with bivariate and canonical correlation coefficients ranging to moderate levels of magnitude, even over an interval exceeding a decade.

In chapter 3, we continue our examination of the temperamental sequelae of infant temperament. First, canonical correlation coefficients are examined to determine the extent of overlap between the set of factors assessing difficult infant temperament on the ICQ and the subsequent sets of variables assessing temperament during the developmental eras designated in chapter 2 (toddler, preschool, middle childhood, adolescence). Next, Pearson correlation coefficients between the four ICQ factors and the nine dimensions of the TTS, BSQ, MCTQ, and DOTS-R are examined to determine whether or not unique temperamental sequelae of the various facets of difficult infant temperament are evident. These analyses allow us to determine the extent to which parent perceptions of their children's temperament show systematic relations from infancy at 1.5 years through adolescence, and whether or not there are unique temperamental sequelae of the four aspects of challenging infant temperament.

Stability of Temperament from Infancy

We turn now to the issue of stability, or the maintenance of the relative rank ordering of individuals on aspects of temperament across time. Many contemporary conceptualizations of temperament contain the central tenet that temperament shows consistency across time (c.f., Bates, 1989; Goldsmith et al., 1987; Strelau & Angleitner, 1991).

Data from the New York Longitudinal Study and a limited number of subsequent longitudinal studies spanning several developmental eras have reported findings pertaining to stability of some or all of the NYLS dimensions. Thomas and Chess (1977), using ratings of parental interview protocols, found significant year-to-year correlation coefficients ranging to .52 in magnitude. For intervals of two years, correlations reached a maximum of .37. With three-year intervals (for example, correlations between ages 1 and 4 or 2 and 5), the maximum correlation dropped to .29; correlations were significant for either of these two intervals for only three of the nine dimensions: activity level, rhythmicity, and adaptability.

On the four-year interval from 1 to 5 years, again only three dimensions revealed significant correlation coefficients: activity, rhythmicity, and threshold. The maximum correlation observed across this longest interval was .22.

Thomas and Chess (1986) subsequently reported correlations between temperament ratings in the first five years and temperament ratings based on interviews of the study sample between ages 17 and 24 ("young adulthood"). Correlations for each year during the first five years of life and early adulthood failed to reveal a consistent pattern. Hence, ratings of parental interview protocols in the NYLS reveal evidence of moderate stability over one and two year intervals during early childhood, but low or non-significant stability for intervals spanning three years or longer.

Subsequent longitudinal investigators, benefiting from the conceptual framework provided by the NYLS and the development of numerous instruments to assess temperament via parent report, found stronger evidence of developmental stability in temperament characteristics. Huttunen and Nyman (1982) administered translated versions of the scales developed by Carey and colleagues to parents in Helsinki. The first wave of data was collected when children were 6 to 8 months old; a second wave was collected when children were 5 years. Significant correlations, ranging from .21 to .32, were observed for seven of the nine dimensions (all except intensity and distractibility).

Hegvik et al. (1982) reported correlations between ratings over a 4.5- year interval spanning preschool and middle childhood. Correlations were significant for all nine dimensions; for all except rhythmicity, coefficients ranged from .40 to .59 with a median of .42. Hegvik et al. concluded that children's temperament was more stable during this period compared to infancy.

Maziade, Cote, Boudreault, Thivierge, and Boutin (1986) correlated parent ratings of their children's temperament at 7 and 12 years in a Canadian sample. Temperament at age 7 was measured with a French translation of the Parent Temperament Questionnaire; when children were age 12, parents compeleted a French translation of the Middle Childhood Temperament Questionnaire. Significant cross-time Spearman correlation coefficients were observed for seven of the nine temperament dimensions: activity (.62), adaptability (.72), approach/withdrawal (.58), mood (.62), rhythmicity/predictability (.44), threshold (.43), and intensity (.36). Cross-time coefficients for distractibility and persistence were not significant.

Thus far, we have reported data on the stability of parental reports of temperament on the nine NYLS dimensions from age 2 through 12 years in the FLS (Guerin & Gottfried, 1994b). Age-to-age correlation coefficients for each of the nine NYLS dimensions for each of the seven assessment waves collected from 2 through 12 years can be found in that publication. To summarize those findings, data revealed an impressive level of stability in temperament both within and between periods of childhood as well as across the preschool and middle childhood periods.

Activity level was among the most stable of the temperament characteristics, correlating significantly across every age interval examined and ranging from moderate to high in magnitude (r's $= .38$ to .75). These findings were particularly noteworthy given that the average ratings of activity level on both the preschool BSQ and the middle childhood MCTQ showed significant declines reflecting mean changes during both the preschool and middle childhood periods. Thus, even though as a group children became less active across these age periods, the children tended to retain their relative standing within the cohort.

Another temperament dimension that demonstrated significant levels of stability across every interval in the FLS from ages 2 through 12 years was approach/withdrawal, with correlations ranging from .36 to .77 in magnitude. These results were in accord with those of Kagan, Reznick, and Snidman (1989), who found a moderately high correlation ($r = .67$) between measures of behavioral inhibition (a construct similar to approach/withdrawal) taken at 21 months and 7.5 years in one cohort and a correlation of .61 between measures taken at 43 months and 7.5 years in a second cohort.

In the FLS, stability coefficients of the dimensions of adaptability and intensity during childhood provided an interesting juxtaposition and suggest that particular points in development may provide more insight into subsequent development than others. Stability coefficients for adaptability from age 2 years to subsequent ages were low or non-significant, although from age 3 years onward they were almost exclusively moderate at every age interval (approximately .4 to .7). On the other hand, the pattern of stability coefficients for intensity was generally higher from the 2-year measure (generally moderate in magnitude) than from the 3-year measure to middle childhood (generally low in magnitude when correlated beyond age 5 years). Maziade et al. (1986) reported a similar pattern during the middle childhood period: high stability for adaptability ($r = .72$) and low stability for intensity ($r = .36$). Thus, it may be that the dimensions of temperament have different periods of meaningfulness with respect to anticipating subsequent development; age 2 years appears more meaningful for intensity in terms of stability, whereas age 3 years may represent the lower bound at which adaptability has cross-time consistency.

Significant cross-time stability was also observed for parent reports of the remaining five dimensions of temperament in the FLS between ages 2 and 12. Stability coefficients for distractibility were significant at every time interval studied and were generally moderate in value. Persistence, threshold, rhythmicity, and quality of mood showed significant but low to moderate cross-time stabilities (r's $= .24$ to 43). Stability was generally related to the size of the age interval considered; across the shortest interval with different measures (ages 2 to 3), correlations ranged from .22 to .51 (median $r = .39$) in magnitude. Across the longest interval (ages 2 to 12 years), correlations ranged from .00 to .42 (median $r = .23$).

In chapter 3, the stability of temperament across ages 2 through 16 will be examined using the developmental eras specified in chapter 2: toddler (2 years), preschool (3–5 years averaged), middle childhood (8–12 years averaged) and adolescence (14–16 years averaged).

Early Temperament and Personality in Adolescence

The hypothesis that temperament represents early developing personality traits has been proposed (Buss & Plomin, 1984). The past decade, in particular, has witnessed increasing interest in examining the relation between temperament and personality, especially with respect to the "Big Five" factors of personality. It has been suggested by some that the two constructs overlap such that temperament is a subset of personality (Angleitner & Reimann, 1991; Hofstee, 1991), that temperament represents early developing personality (Buss & Plomin, 1984), or that temperament is a precursor to personality (Martin et al., 1994).

In the absence of empirical data from long term longitudinal studies examining possible relations between early temperament using the NYLS model and personality (c.f., Angleitner & Ostendorf, 1994; Caspi, 1998; Martin et al., 1994), speculations about linkages between specific temperament dimensions and the Big Five personality factors have been advanced. The Big Five personality factors are neuroticism, extraversion, openness to experience, agreeableness, and conscientiousness. In Table 1.02, predicted temperament-personality connections appearing in the literature are displayed. Neuroticism, the personality dimension ranging from emotional instability to adjusted, has been predicted to relate to a variety of temperament characteristics, with multiple researchers suggesting a linkage to characteristics involving emotionality and inhibition. Extraversion, the personality factor relating to the quality and intensity of interpersonal attraction, has been hypothesized to connect with temperamental activity level and approach/withdrawal by numerous researchers. Openness to experience, relating to a preference for novel experiences, has been speculated to relate to temperamental persistence by Caspi (1998). Agreeableness, the factor assessing interpersonal orientation ranging from good-natured to irritable, has been postulated to relate to numerous temperament dimensions including activity, adaptability, negative mood, and persistence. Finally, conscientiousness, relating to one's orientation toward goal-directed behavior, has been proposed to link to activity level and task persistence.

Some shorter-term longitudinal studies examining temperament-personality linkages have been reported. Hagekull and Bohlin (1998) investigated the relations between temperament measured during the preschool years and personality traits in middle childhood in a Swedish sample. Mother and father ratings of temperament when children were 28 months to 4 years were averaged to derive a broad description of child temperament. The personality measure, collected when children were 8 to 9 years old, was based on the five factor model; parent and teacher

Table 1.02.   Predicted Linkages between "Big Five" Personality
Factors and Dimensions of Temperament

Neuroticism
- Activity level: John (1990)
- Adaptability: Martin et al. (1994)
- Biological rhythmicity: Martin et al. (1994)
- Emotionality: Angleitner & Ostendorf (1994); Hagekull (1994); John (1989)
- Negative emotionality: Caspi (1998); Martin et al. (1994)
- Social inhibition: Caspi (1998); Martin et al. (1994)
- Threshold: Martin et al. (1994)

Extraversion
- Activity: Angleitner & Ostendorf (1994); Caspi (1998); Eaton (1994);
  Hagekull (1994); John (1989); Martin et al. (1994)
- Approach/Withdrawal: Ahadi & Rothbart (1994); Caspi (1998); Prior (1992)
- Emotionality: John (1990)
- Intensity: Hagekull (1994)
- Positive affect: Caspi (1998)
- Social inhibition/Shyness: Hagekull, 1994; Martin et al. (1994)

Openness to experience
- Persistence: Caspi (1998)

Agreeableness
- Activity level: Caspi (1998)
- Adaptability: Martin et al. (1994)
- Intensity: Hagekull (1994)
- Negative emotionality: Martin et al. (1994)
- Negative mood: Caspi (1998)
- Persistence: Caspi (1998)
- Sociability: Angleitner & Ostendorf (1994); Hagekull (1994); John (1989)

Conscientiousness
- Activity level: Caspi (1998); Eaton (1994)
- Task persistence: Caspi (1998); Hagekull (1994); Martin et al. (1994)

ratings for each child were averaged to yield scores for neuroticism, extraversion, openness to experience, agreeableness, and conscientiousness.

Hagekull and Bohlin found that preschool temperament features were predictive of personality measured during the middle childhood period, although all correlation coefficients were in the low range of magnitude (e.g., less than .40). Significant Pearson correlations were observed between extraversion and preschool activity level, sociability, and shyness. Agreeableness was predicted by impulsivity and activity level. Conscientiousness was presaged by shyness during the preschool years, neuroticism by impulsivity and activity level, and openness to experience by preschool shyness, activity, and sociability. Hence, these data provide evidence of temperament-personality linkages across the early and middle childhood years.

Our final focus in chapter 3 provides empirical evidence regarding the long-term cross-time relation between temperament in childhood and subsequent personality. When FLS participants were 17 years old, they completed a widely used and standardized assessment of personality, the NEO-FFI (Costa & McCrae, 1989). The NEO-FFI yields scores reflecting the Big Five personality dimensions. We examined the extent to which the childhood temperament measures presaged personality assessed via the NEO in two ways. First, bivariate correlation coefficients were computed between temperament dimensions during each of the delineated developmental eras (infancy, toddler, preschool, middle childhood) and the five personality dimensions of the NEO. Second, multiple regression analyses between the set of temperament dimensions and each of the five NEO factors were conducted to assess the amount of variance in each personality dimension explained by temperament dimensions.

Behavioral and Emotional Adjustment at Home and School

Experts in the fields of child psychiatry, child development, personality, education, and clinical psychology have had a long standing interest in understanding the role of temperament in predicting child psychopathology (Bates et al., 1979; Thomas et al., 1968). Reasons for this wide interest originated from the pioneering work of Thomas et al. (1963, 1968), who identified temperamental difficultness as a potential risk factor for the development of social and behavioral problems.

Thomas et al. (1968) identified a profile of characteristics they called "difficult temperament" consisting of five of the nine dimensions in their model: initial aversion (low approach), slow adaptability to environmental changes, irregular biological rhythmicity, high intensity in emotional expression, and frequent negative mood. Data collected by Thomas, Chess, and their colleagues in the New York Longitudinal Study showed that children displaying the difficult temperament constellation during the preschool years (i.e., at 3 years) were at elevated risk for subsequent behavior disorders. In their book, *Temperament and Behavior Disorders in Children*, they elaborated the relevance of early emerging temperament to later behavior problems.

In chapter 4, we present findings from the FLS examining the link between temperamental characteristics and concurrent and subsequent behavioral disorders. We place these findings in the context of existing literature, an endeavor that is challenging due to the wide range of measures of both temperament and behavior problems that have been employed.

Several limitations of the extant research regarding temperament and behavioral adjustment have been noted (e.g., Caspi, Henry, McGee, Moffitt, & Silva, 1995; Guerin et al., 1997). First, it has been observed that some studies are based on small or unrepresentative samples (such as clinical referrals), thereby making generalizability to the general population questionable. Second, most of the studies have been relatively short in time span, thus limiting our ability to understand the implications (if any) of early temperament with respect to the developmental outcomes of ultimate significance (i.e., adult functioning). Third, many studies used reports of temperament and behavioral adjustment from the same informant. Fourth, the initial measurement of temperament in some studies has been beyond the infancy period, thus leading to concerns of some researchers (e.g., Sanson, Prior, & Kyrios, 1990) of method/concept overlap between temperament and behavior problems. However, recent studies (i.e., Lemery, Essex, & Smider, 2002; Lengua, West, & Sandler, 1998; Sheeber, 1995) using differing methodologies, converged to demonstrate that relationships observed between temperament and behavior problems are genuine and not due to overlapping item content across measures of temperament and symptoms of behavior problems. Fifth, many studies were conducted prior to the development of standardized measures with known psychometric properties of either behavioral/emotional adjustment or temperament. Thus, interpretation of findings, particularly in cases of a lack of relationship, may be compromised; does absence of a temperament-behavior correlation indicate a true lack of relation or poor measurement (e.g., poor validity, reliability) of either or both variables? Sixth, Guerin et al. (1997) noted the statistical issue of non-normal distributions of behavior problems when dealing with a non-clinical sample.

Finally, many researchers have not distinguished whether early temperament is related to increased levels of behavior problems in the normal range of development versus increased frequency of behavior problems in the clinical range. The two diagrams displayed in Figure 1.02 contrast these possible outcomes via scatterplots conceptually depicting the temperament-behavior problem relation. This is an important distinction; significant correlation coefficients between temperament and behavior problems in the normal range (see Panel "a" in Figure 1.02) may not be a source of major concern, merely indicating that children with certain temperaments might be viewed as exhibiting behaviors that are annoying or irritating to others (i.e., parents, teachers). On the other hand, if early temperament predicted behavior problem scores in the clinical range as depicted in Panel "b" of Figure 1.02, this would be of critical concern; this outcome indicates that children's potential may be jeopardized or significantly compromised. It is therefore necessary to examine not only possible linear relations between temperament and behavioral adjustment, but also to determine whether certain temperaments predispose children toward behavior problem scores above cut-off levels indicating serious problems of adjustment.

In the temperament literature, the number of studies pertaining to behavior problems is perhaps the most extensive compared to other developmental outcomes. We selected two features to use in organizing our summary and conclusions

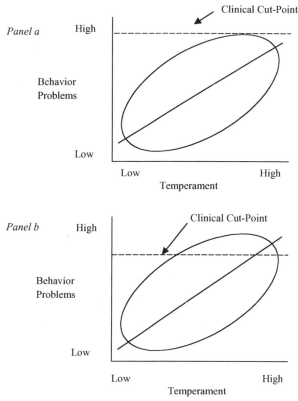

Figure 1.02. Scatterplots contrasting the relation between temperament and behavior problems in the non-clinical range (Panel a) versus clinical range (Panel b).

of this vast literature: (1) the informant for the temperament and behavioral adjustment measures and (2) the temporal relation between the measurement of temperament and the measurement of behavioral adjustment. Figure 1.03 depicts these features and the fourfold table resulting from their intersection. With respect to the informant, we classified studies as using the same informant for both temperament and behavior problems or as using different informants. With respect to the temporal variable, studies were classified as either employing concurrent measures of temperament and behavior problems or as using temperament as an antecedent to behavior problems.

We conceptualized the quality of empirical evidence regarding the temperament-behavior problem relation as ranging in strength from suggestive to compelling. In our view, the least compelling evidence regarding a temperament-behavior problem linkage was that utilizing temperament and behavior problems measured concurrently from a single informant, represented in cell 1 of

Timing of Temperament Measure Compared to Behavior Problem Measure		Informant(s) of Temperament and Behavior Problems	
		Same	Different
	Concurrent	1	2
	Predictive	3	4

Figure 1.03. Matrix depicting conceptualization of temperament-behavior problem research strategies.

Figure 1.03. Many studies falling into this category were among the earliest published, and they served to confirm the overlap between temperament and behavior problems. However, that both measures were collected from the same informant left open the possibility that an unknown portion of the observed relationship between temperament and behavior problems was due to overlapping source variance. Furthermore, many studies utilized the same method of measurement of temperament and behavior problems (questionnaire), thereby creating another possible source of inflation in the estimation of temperament-behavior problem relationship (method variance). Indeed, method overlap is a condition that may characterize studies classified in any cell represented in Figure 1.03.

In our conceptualization, cell 2 represents studies with a possibility of offering more convincing evidence on the validity of temperament as a factor in the development and/or maintenance of behavior problems. These are studies in which concurrent temperament-behavior problem relationships were examined, but with different informants for each variable. For example, parents many have provided information about temperament, but clinicians or teachers may have reported behavior problems. Data from studies such as these provide stronger evidence of a temperament-behavior problem link because they eliminate source variance as a possible explanation for observed relationships. Furthermore, they may also demonstrate that temperament in one setting (such as in the home) is linked to behavior in a different setting (such as school).

However, data collected under the conditions characterized by cells 1 and 2 in Figure 1.03 cannot demonstrate that temperament preceded the onset of behavior problems. This is a strength of the studies meeting the characteristics delineated in cells 3 and 4 of Figure 1.03. Studies meeting the criteria for these cells demonstrate that temperamental characteristics preceded behavior problems, which is a necessary but not sufficient condition to demonstrate a causal relation between temperament and behavior problems. Cell 3 represents studies examining predictive relations between temperament and behavior problem with measures from the same informants (thus again sharing source variance as in Cell 1). Cell 4 represents studies providing the strongest evidence that temperament is a factor in the development and/or maintenance of behavior problems: studies with temperament measured prior to behavior problems and utilizing different informants for each variable.

Concurrent Relations between Temperament and Behavior Problems with Measures by the Same Informant

Earls (1981) studied the relation between parent reports of temperament and parent and clinician assessments of behavior adjustment in 3-year-olds. Parents completed a temperament questionnaire. Behavior problems were assessed via parent ratings and via psychiatric judgments made by two independent clinicians who reviewed collected data. Earls found three temperament dimensions related significantly to overall behavior problem scores: higher behavior problem scores were related to low adaptability, high intensity, and low distractibility. These findings were replicated in the clinical ratings. In a subsequent report, Barron and Earls (1984) also reported significant correlation coefficients between behavior problems and two additional variables: maternal reports of negative parent-child interactions, and high family stress.

Webster-Stratton and Eyberg (1982) examined the relation between mothers' ratings of temperament and behavior problems in 3- to 5-year-olds. Correlation coefficients showed that children who were rated as more active, more fussy, and having shorter attention spans/lower persistence were also rated as exhibiting more behavior problems. Behavior ratings by researchers based on videotapes of mother-child interactions also revealed significant correlation coefficients with child temperament: children rated as more active and with shorter attention spans displayed more behaviors of non-acceptance, including frustration, ignoring, and opposition.

Fagan (1990) measured the relation between teacher reports of temperament and their reports of adjustment for a sample of preschoolers attending publicly-funded urban day care centers. Children rated by teachers as more active, slower to adapt, lower in approach, more intense, more distractible, and less persistent were rated as exhibiting more total behavior problems as well as more hostile-aggressive and anxious/fearful problems; r's ranged from .31 to .62 in magnitude.

Jansen, Fitzgerald, Harn, and Zucker (1995) postulated that the difficult temperament-behavior problem relationship would prosper in the context of an antisocial, alcoholic family environment. They examined the relation between difficult temperament and behavior problems in two groups of 3- to 5-year-old boys; one group clinical (high risk alcoholic, low SES) and the other group non-clinical (comparison group). Jansen et al.'s hypothesis that boys in the clinical group would have significantly more difficult temperaments than boys in the non-clinical group was supported. Boys in the clinical group had significantly higher motor activity levels, poorer attention spans and higher levels of distractibility, were more reactive in their everyday activities, and had more irregular eating and sleeping patterns than boys in the non-clinical behavior problem group. Jansen et al. concluded that boys in the clinical group had more difficulty with self-regulation and self-control than boys in the non-clinical group.

Teglasi and MacMahon (1990) reported concurrent temperament-behavior problem relations during the middle childhood period. Parents completed the Middle Childhood Temperament Questionnaire and a survey of their child's problem behaviors in the home, which had five factors: I. Proneness to angry outbursts and emotional upset; II. Joylessness/apathy; III. Low self-direction; IV. Self-reproach; and V. Oppositionalism/aggression. Each of these common behavior problems was related to one or more temperament dimensions with correlations in excess of .60, especially factors I, II, III, and V. For example, adaptability, intensity, and mood all correlated with Factor I Angry Outbursts; approach related to Factor II Joylessness; lower predictability and persistence related to Factor III Low Self Direction; and higher activity, slower adaptability, and more negative mood related to Factor V Oppositionalism. Teglasi and MacMahon concluded that problem behaviors can be viewed as either direct expressions of temperament or as by-products of the child's temperament and history of environmental demands and supports.

In chapter 4, we examine concurrent relations between temperament and behavior problems assessed in the FLS during the preschool, middle childhood, and adolescent eras, when parents completed assessments of their children's temperament and behavior problems. Given that temperament was assessed repeatedly from toddlerhood through middle childhood using scales based on the nine dimension NYLS model, these analyses allowed us to examine whether the pattern of relation between specific aspects of temperament and internalizing behavior (over-controlled) versus externalizing behavior (undercontrolled) throughout early and middle childhood was global versus differentiated/specific and static/stable versus dynamic. Additionally, within the adolescence era in the FLS, concurrent measures of temperament and behavioral adjustment were collected from the adolescents themselves, hence allowing a similar examination of data using a different informant than parents.

Concurrent Relations between Temperament and Behavior Problems with Measures from Different Informants

Looking at the role of temperament with respect to social adjustment in three-year-olds, Earls (1981) examined the relation between parent reports of temperament and behavior assessed during a 1-hour observation of children's play in a home-based, standardized procedure. High approach was significantly related to several aspects of play, including imaginative play, vitality, ability to adapt and cope, language development, happiness, play involvement, and trust in examiner (all r's ranged from .28 to .39).

Rende and Plomin (1992) studied 164 first graders participating as control subjects in the Colorado Adoption Study. Temperament was measured via parental reports. Internalizing and externalizing behavior problems were assessed via teacher reports. Significant but weak (e.g., $r = .20$) negative correlation coefficients showed that children viewed as less active and less sociable by parents had more internalizing (overcontrolled) behavior problems as rated by their teachers. No significant Pearson correlation coefficients were observed between temperament and externalizing behavior problems.

Analyzing data from the FLS, Guerin et al. (1994) examined concurrent relations between parent reports of temperament and teacher ratings of classroom adjustment in 10-year-olds. Parent ratings of temperament correlated with teacher reports of behavior problems (internalizing, externalizing), with correlation coefficients ranging to .52 in magnitude. Teacher ratings of internalizing behaviors were related to only one temperament dimension, persistence, ($r = -.24$; less persistent, more internalizing problems). Higher externalizing behavior problem ratings by teachers were related to eight of the nine parent-reported NYLS dimensions: lower persistence, lower predictability, slower adaptability, greater distractibility (r's ranged from = .32 to .52 in magnitude), and more frequent negative mood, higher activity level, more intensity, and more sensitivity (r's ranged from .22 to .29 in magnitude).

In the FLS, additional cross-informant ratings of temperament and behavior problems were collected during the middle childhood and adolescent eras. Findings from analyses of these additional data will be presented in chapter 4. During middle childhood, parent ratings of temperament were aggregated across ages 8, 10, and 12; behavior problems were assessed via reports from classroom teachers annually from 6 to 11 years and aggregated. During the adolescent assessment period, both parents and their children completed measures of temperament and behavior problems.

Predictive Relations between Temperament and Behavior Problems with Measures from Same Informants

Relations between difficult infant temperament and subsequent behavior problems have been reported by two research teams. Pettit and Bates (1989) examined relations between temperamental difficultness summed across 6, 13, and 24 months and maternal reports on the social withdrawal, aggression, and total behavior problem scales of the Child Behavior Checklist at 4 years. Temperamental difficultness measured during the first two years significantly predicted 4-year aggression scores ($r = .39$) and total behavior problem scores ($r = .31$), but not social withdrawal scores. Guerin et al. (1997) examined relations between infant temperament at 1.5 years and behavior problems through age 12 years. Significant Pearson correlations were evident between infant temperament and behavior problems through age 12. Difficult infant temperament was related most strongly and pervasively to externalizing as opposed to internalizing types of behavior problems. A greater percentage of infants deemed temperamentally difficult by their mothers subsequently presented elevated problem scores, particularly attention problems, aggressive behavior, and thought problems through age 12. In chapter 4, these data will be re-analyzed using the developmental eras delineated in chapter 2 and extended using additional behavior problem measures collected subsequently (ages 13 – 17). Additionally, developmental outcomes and concomitants of extreme temperament in infancy will be examined in chapter 8.

In another context, Martin and his associates have shown that temperamental factors in the early school years related to the ways that teachers evaluate child behavior and academic performance (Martin, Nagle, & Paget, 1983). Martin et al. correlated teacher reports of temperament collected at the beginning of first grade with teachers' rankings of their pupils' social adjustment at the end of the school year. Students viewed by teachers as slower to adapt, lower in approach, and lower in persistence were subsequently rated as poorer in social adjustment. Using all temperament dimensions to predict social adjustment, Martin et al. found a multiple correlation of .54 in predicting social adjustment rank scores.

Predictive Relations between Temperament and Behavior Problems with Measures from Different Informants

The following eight studies provide the strongest test of temperament-behavior problem relations, demonstrating links between temperament and behavior problems when they are assessed across informants and across time. Measures of temperament or behavioral style collected as early as 1.5 years have been found to predict behavioral adjustment across several years and also across informants and contexts. Perhaps the study with temperament measured at the youngest age is that of Maziade et al. (1989a), who assessed temperament via parental report when babies were 4 and 8 months of age. Behavioral status and temperament were then assessed at age 4 years by two child psychiatrists, based on scores resulting from a structured parent interview. Results showed that infant temperament was not strongly associated with behavioral outcome, although temperament at four years was significantly related to behavioral outcomes. Maziade et al. posited that extreme infant temperament might have an indirect effect on clinical outcome through its significant stability. Over time with development from infancy to childhood, the youngsters' temperament may lead to enhanced propensity for increasing disciplinary conflict with parents in the preschool years, and an abrasive parent-child relationship may develop, which then results in child behavior problems. Assessing temperament during infancy at 1.5 years, Guerin et al. (1997) found that parent ratings of fussy/difficult/demanding infant temperament correlated with teacher ratings of externalizing behavior problems aggregated across ages 6 through 8, albeit at a very low level, $r = .22$.

Garrison, Earls, and Kindlon (1984) examined the relationship of preschool temperament and adjustment soon after school entry. Maternal ratings of their child's temperament were collected when children were 3 years old; approximately three years later, the children's teachers and mothers completed measures of children's adjustment. Additionally, judgments of maladjustment made by two clinical psychologists who independently reviewed the children's files were used. Temperament characteristics were predictive of maladjustment classification; Garrison et al. characterized the behavioral styles of 3-year-olds who were subsequently identified as maladjusted in the early school years as one of "stubbornness [sic], oppositionality, and a style of persistence that is not conducive to positive social interaction" (p. 302).

Jewsuwan, Luster, and Kostelnik (1993) examined relations between parents' perceptions of temperament and children's positive behavioral adjustment and social competence in the preschool setting. Studied were 35 children attending a university-operated preschool. Parents independently rated their child's temperament during their child's first week in preschool. After the children had been in the preschool approximately 2 months, the six head teachers rated the children's adjustment and behavior problems. Children viewed as lower on sociability and higher on emotionality by their parents were rated as more anxious by their teachers (r's ranged from .23 to .52 in magnitude). None of the temperament dimensions were related to measures of hostile-aggressive or hyperactive-distractible behaviors. Additionally, children rated lower in emotionality and higher in sociability were rated more favorably by teachers on global adjustment as well as four of five subscales of adjustment: prosocial behavior, positive affect within the school setting, peer competence, and ego strength. Correlation coefficients ranged to .72 in magnitude and generally replicated across parents. Hence, children viewed by parents as sociable and low in emotionality were subsequently rated as being more well-adjusted by their teachers following the transition to preschool.

Findings from even longer-term longitudinal studies have also been reported. For example, Caspi et al. (1995) assessed relations between early temperament and behavior problems across more than a decade in an unselected sample of over 800 children participating in the Dunedin Multidisciplinary Health and Development Study in New Zealand. Behavioral styles were derived from 22 behavior ratings made by the examiner after observing the child in a data-collection session involving a standard set of cognitive and motor tasks. The 22 behavior ratings were reduced statistically to three factors: lack of control (inability to control impulsive expression, lack of persistence, negative reactions), approach (willingness to explore stimuli in new situations), and sluggishness (passive, withdrawing from novelty). Although not mapping directly to the NYLS dimensions, these factors do share conceptual similarity to many of the dimensions. Teacher and parent ratings of internalizing and externalizing behaviors were collected at ages 9 and 11 and combined for analysis; parent reports were collected again when children were 13 and 15 years old.

Pearson correlation coefficients between 3-year behavioral style ratings (lack of control, approach, sluggishness) and subsequent behavior problems at ages 9 through 15 showed significant correlation coefficients in the low range (maximum magnitude = .30). Lack of control was more strongly and pervasively correlated with later externalizing problems such as hyperactivity, inattention, antisocial behavior, whereas approach/withdrawal was significantly associated with only internalizing problems such as anxiety, fearfulness, and withdrawal. Correlation coefficients from age 5 behavioral styles to subsequent behavior problems showed a similar pattern. Hence, a linkage between specific temperamental characteristics and specific subsequent behavior problems was revealed.

Three studies have examined cross-informant temperament-behavior problem relations within the middle childhood period. From a random sample of 980 7-year-old children in Quebec City, Maziade et al. (1985) selected 26 of the most temperamentally difficult children and a comparison group of 16 of the most temperamentally easy children to test the hypothesis that difficult temperament at 7 years would increase the probability of psychiatric and behavior disorders at 12 years. Two psychiatrists, blind to the temperament scores, separately analyzed data collected via direct interview of the child and parents and standardized questionnaires completed by teachers. Children in the difficult temperament group at 7 years were more likely to qualify for a clinical diagnosis at 12 years. Among 24 children with complete information in the difficult temperament group, 12 qualified for a DSM-III diagnosis (9 had an oppositional disorder and 3 had an attention deficit associated with an oppositional disorder) at age 12 compared to only 1 of the 15 children in the easy temperament group. In a sample of 8- to 12-year-olds, Teglasi and MacMahon (1990) observed significant correlations between parent reports of temperament and teacher ratings of classroom behavior such as citizenship and work habits ($r = .35$ maximum); predictability and persistence were most highly related to teacher ratings. Using data from the FLS, Guerin et al. (1994) examined the one-year predictive utility of parent ratings (age 10) in foretelling behavior problems reported by teachers at age 11. Parent ratings did not significantly predict teacher ratings of internalizing behavior problems, but they predicted externalizing behavior problem ratings by teachers. Slow adaptability, intensity, and lower persistence predicted externalizing and/or total behavior problem scores (r's = .25 to .36 in magnitude).

In addition to the analysis of temperament as a predictor of behavior problems, in chapter 4 we also examine behavior problems as precipitants of temperament. We include these analyses to document how the behavioral adjustment of children may presage, for example, either the expression of their temperament or the perceptions/impressions/ interpretations of others rating the child/adolescent's temperament.

Intelligence

The relation of temperament to development in the intellectual domain is examined in chapter 5. A major focus at the initiation of the FLS was to examine early predictors of intelligence. Hence, regular assessments of intelligence were made during the preschool, middle childhood, and adolescent development eras. Given the multiple assessments of both temperament and intelligence across the course of investigation, examination of temperament features as concomitants, predictors, and sequelae of intelligence was possible. In addition to widely used standardized tests of intelligence, we also examine the relation between temperament and parent reports of developmental status on standardized inventories collected during the preschool years.

Both theory and empirical observations converge to suggest an interconnection between these variables as elaborated by Matheny (1989). However, accumulating evidence shows the relation between temperament and intelligence is limited in magnitude. For example, in a review of the literature on this issue, Keogh (1986, p. 99) concluded " . . . with few exceptions, most studies suggest that there are at best only modest and often no significant relationships between temperament and cognitive ability as expressed in IQ's." Subsequently, Martin (1989) questioned whether distractibility and persistence should be considered aspects of temperament or aspects of the cognitive domain, given their overlap with intellectual measures.

Concurrent Relations between Temperament and IQ

Daniels, Plomin, and Greenhalgh (1984) examined temperament-mental development correlations in both adoptive and nonadoptive families participating in the Colorado Adoption Project. Difficult temperament was measured via averaged parental reports on 10 items, comprising one item for each of the nine NYLS temperament dimensions and one item assessing the overall difficultness of the infant. A factor score was derived; the overall difficultness item loaded highest on the factor, followed by the items assessing mood, distractibility, adaptability, and approach. Daniels et al. found no significant relation between the infant difficult temperament factor and scores on the Bayley Mental Development Index at either 12 or 24 months.

Two studies on concurrent temperament-intelligence relations during the school entry years have been reported. Palisin (1986) examined concurrent and longitudinal temperament-cognition relations in 50 children. Mothers completed three temperament inventories when children were between 4 and 5 years. The Stanford-Binet intelligence test was administered when children were 4; the Wechsler Intelligence Scale for Children (Revised) (WISC-R) and Peabody Individual Achievement Test were administered in second grade. Correlations were observed between all three temperament measures and the Stanford-Binet. The most consistent finding was that temperamental persistence/attention span on all three temperament scales correlated significantly with scores on all three intellectual/ achievement tests, with r's ranging in magnitude from .27 to .41. Across all measures, better performance on cognitive tests was observed in children with better attention spans, lower activity levels, and higher approach. Martin and Holbrook (1985) examined correlations between teachers' ratings of their first grade pupils' temperament and IQ. Pupils reported as quicker to adjust, more approaching, and more persistent by teachers scored higher on IQ, with correlations ranging from .34 to .51 in magnitude.

Matheny (1989) reported concurrently collected temperament-intelligence data spanning the ages 1 to 12 years from the Louisville Twin Study. During the early years, temperament was assessed using observations of the children's responses to a series of vignettes presented in the lab, maternal reports, and ratings of the child's behavior during the administration of the Bayley test. These three assessments were reduced through factor analysis procedures to five measures of temperament. First, the lab observations were reduced to a factor called Lab Tractability, which reflects emotional tone, attentiveness, and social orientation. A similar factor emerged from mothers' TTS ratings (TTS Tractability), comprised of adaptability, mood, and approach. Finally, the IBR ratings of the test administrators were reduced to three factors: IBR Task Orientation (object orientation, goal-directedness, and attention span); IBR Test Affect-Extraversion (social-examiner, cooperativeness, fearfulness, emotional tone); and IBR Activity (activity, body motion, energy). Numerous significant correlations between temperament and mental test scores at 1, 1.5, and 2 years emerged. Matheny reported low but significant correlation coefficients between Bayley scores and Lab Tractability at all ages (r's = .27 to .28), TTS Tractibility at 1.5 and 2 (r's = .27 and .28, respectively), IBR Task Orientation (r's = .37 to .54), IBR Test Affect-Extraversion (r's = .28 to .42), and IBR Activity at 1 and 1.5 (r's = .24 and .18, respectively). Thus, temperament-mental test score correlations were low but significant across situations (lab observations, maternal report) and reached moderate magnitudes when assessed within the same situation (Bayley test setting). Infants with higher Bayley test scores were rated as higher in sustaining attention and persistence, more positive in emotion/mood, cooperating with and adapting quicker to ongoing changes, and approaching to unfamiliar people, activities, and objects.

The correlations evident between IBR Activity and Bayley scores at 1 and 1.5 indicated higher Bayley scores for more active infants.

During the preschool period, adaptability and persistence/attention span correlated with cognitive test scores at ages 3 and 4 (r's = .22 to .30). A similar pattern was observed at ages 5 and 6; significant r's ranged from .21 to .46. Children who were quicker to adapt and more persistent tended to score higher on both of these tests of intelligence. During the middle childhood years, children who were less active, more predictable, less intense, and higher on attention span/persistence tended to score higher on the WISC-R; r's were generally low, but ranged to moderate magnitude. At age 12, self-ratings of temperament on three scales correlated with IQ scores: approach, sleep rhythmicity, and distractibility.

In summarizing his findings, Matheny characterized the NYLS dimensions of attention span/persistence, approach/withdrawal, adaptability, and mood as those overlapping most extensively with IQ. The child with higher mental test scores can be characterized as being more attentive to and persistent on tasks, more approaching to the unfamiliar, more adaptable to changes, and more positive in mood. Additionally, he concluded findings showing varying numbers of IQ-temperament correlations over time suggested that there are developmental changes for the overlap of temperament and IQ. For example, the dimension of activity was significantly correlated with mental scores at twelve months, the correlations were non-significant in toddler years and then negative in childhood. Hence, he concluded that the nature of the temperament-environment relationship shifted over the course of childhood.

Temperament, Test-Taking Behaviors, and Intelligence

As just reviewed, numerous researchers have demonstrated linkages between temperament and intellectual development in children through at least 12 years of age. What is the process that brings about this linkage? Figure 1.04 displays one possible model explaining the overlap between temperament and intelligence. That is, the overlap between temperament and intellectual test scores may arise because certain temperament characteristics facilitate children's performance during the testing procedure, thereby leading to superior performance on the test. This possibility is depicted by Paths B and C in Figure 1.04. That is, the temperament-intelligence relation is an indirect one, mediated by the child's behaviors during the testing procedure. Another possible explanation is that certain temperament features directly facilitate children's propensity to learn new things and hence lead to higher intelligence in general. This possibility is delineated by Path A in Figure 1.04.

According to Baron and Kenny (1986), to test the hypothesis that the temperament-intelligence relationship is mediated by test-taking behaviors, measures of each of the three variables depicted in Figure 1.04 are required:

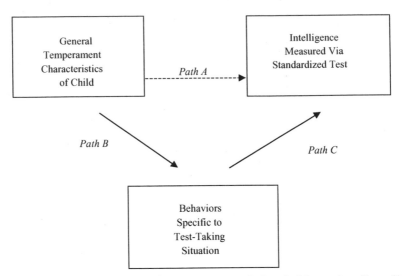

Figure 1.04. Temperament as a direct (dashed arrow) versus indirect (solid arrows) predictor of intelligence test scores.

(1) temperament characteristics in general (that is, outside the testing situation), (2) behaviors during administration of the test, and (3) intelligence test scores. Furthermore, significant bivariate correlations must exist for all paths shown in Figure 1.04. Although prior research has demonstrated these paths exist, an analysis of the direct and indirect hypotheses delineated in Figure 1.04 has not been reported. Hence, in chapter 5, we examine the direct path between temperament dimensions and IQ, as well as the indirect path between temperament and IQ in which the effect of the child's test-taking behaviors are examined as potential mediators of temperament-IQ relations using the procedure recommended by Baron and Kenny (1986). In the FLS, all variables depicted in Figure 1.04 were collected at the following assessment periods: 1.5, 2, 3, 15, and 17 years, thus allowing the possible direct and indirect paths between temperament, test-taking behaviors, and IQ to be examined during the infant/toddler, preschool, and adolescent eras of development.

Parent Reports of Developmental Progress

In previously published research based on FLS data, the validity of parent reports of their children's development on standardized inventories was supported by demonstrating significant and moderate overlap among parent reports and individually-administered, standardized, and widely-used measures of intelligence, achievement, and adaptive functioning (A. W. Gottfried, Guerin, Spencer,

& Meyer, 1983; Guerin & Gottfried, 1987). In chapter 5, we examine how child temperament relates concurrently to these standardized inventories, the Minnesota Child Development Inventory and the Minnesota Preschool Inventory, for two purposes. First, relations were examined to investigate which dimensions of temperament are predictive of developmental progress in a range of developmental domains to determine whether these patterns correspond to those observed between temperament and individually-administered standardized tests. In addition, as a method of potentially replicating the aforementioned analyses, we viewed the use of parent reports as a way of examining temperament-intelligence relations without the potential intervening influence of test-taking behaviors.

Temperament as a Predictor of Intelligence

Evidence relating to the predictive validity of temperament with respect to intellectual development is sparse. Results from three very different types of studies, none of which used the individual NYLS temperament dimensions as predictors, relate to this issue. Maziade, Cote, Boutin, Bernier, and Thivierge (1987) compared three temperamentally different subgroups who were rated at both 4 and 8 months as having difficult (above the 70th percentile), easy (below the 30th percentile), or average (between the 30th and 70th percentiles) temperament. Results revealed that across the entire sample, the Spearman rank order correlation between infant temperament and full scale IQ was significant ($r = -.23$), indicating that difficult temperament was associated with higher IQ scores. Additionally, correlations were higher when only the middle and upper socioeconomic status groups were included in the analysis ($r_S = -.48$, $p < .05$ for full scale IQ). Maziade et al. speculated that infants with difficult temperament might elicit more interactions and opportunities from their parents, whereas infants with easy temperament may be left to themselves more frequently. The increased parental stimulation of infants with difficult temperament would lead to more rapid developmental progress; over the several years between the measures of temperament in infancy and the measure of IQ at age 4.7, the differential parental interaction produced a cumulative and measurable effect on development. Hence, with increasing age temperament may relate to subsequent intelligence. Maziade et al.'s results also suggest that difficult temperament may not always be a disadvantage, nor may easy temperament always be advantageous to the individual.

A different approach to identifying precursors of developmental progress was used by Benson, Cherny, Haith, and Fulker (1993). This approach, called the midtwin-midparent design, is an alternative to the long-term longitudinal design. It employs offspring and their parents to assess potential infant predictors of adult IQ by using the average parental IQ (midparent IQ) as the best estimate of the infants' mature IQ. A regression of the average twin (midtwin) score on average parent IQ (or midparent IQ) captures all of the additive genetic and environmental influences that parents have on their offspring up to the testing age of the offspring. Thus, any relation that is found between the infant and parent measures reflects both genetic and environmental familial influences. Using this approach, Benson et al. found that the task orientation scale from a modified version of the Bayley Infant Behavior Record and affect/extraversion at 9 months predicted parental intellectual functioning. Benson et al. concluded that the degree to which temperamental and motivational factors play a role in the relation between early and later IQ must be considered, and that the ability to stay on-task may very well be a temperamental predisposition that underlies the continuity of intellectual functioning.

More recently, Raine, Reynolds, Venables, and Mednick (2002) investigated the prediction that stimulation-seeking 3-year-olds would have higher IQs in middle childhood. In a sample of children from the island of Mauritius, stimulation seeking-sociability was assessed at age 3 years using four indices: physical exploration away from the mother toward new toys in a laboratory room, verbalizations to the research assistant during cognitive testing, friendliness with the research assistant during cognitive testing, and active social play with other children during free play in a sandbox. Estimates of IQ were obtained at age 11 using six subtests of the WISC-R. Correlations between the measures of stimulation-seeking at age 3 and total estimated IQ at age 11 were .10 (play), .24 (exploration), .30 (verbalizations), and .42 (gregarious). The overall measure of stimulation seeking at 3 years correlated significantly ($r = .25$) with total IQ.

Comparing extreme groups formed on the basis of age 3 stimulation seeking scores (15% highest and 15% lowest) showed that the highest stimulation seekers at age 3 had significantly higher IQs at both 3 and 11 years. Age 3 average IQ scores for high vs. low stimulation seekers were 105.7 versus 85.1, respectively; for age 11, corresponding data were 104.5 versus 92.7. These differences remained significant after controlling for the possible effects of parent education and occupation. Raine et al. hypothesized that stimulation-seeking children create for themselves an enriched environment that in turn stimulates cognitive development. This postulation is in line with Strelau's (1998) analysis of research on temperament and intelligence/giftedness. He concluded that temperament traits set the stage for an interaction between children's environment and their genetically determined intellectual potential: Traits such as sensation-seeking, approach, and activity rather than passivity, for example, increase children's "possibilities and opportunities to make contact with the surrounding world, with unknown and ambiguous stimulation" (p. 355).

Findings from these studies suggest that early temperament will predict subsequent IQ, perhaps due to a cumulative process in which, over time, children actively seek out cognitively-enriching opportunities or elicit them from others. As noted by Scarr and McCartney (1983), individuals may create their own environments and/or select environments that are in line with their interests/characteristics. Hence, with development, correlations between individual differences and environment emerge. In chapter 5, we examine temperament-IQ predictive relations from both directions. That is, antecedent measures of temperament are first used to predict subsequent IQ. Based on the aforementioned research, the dimensions of approach/withdrawal (Benson et al., 1993; Raine et al., 2002) and negative mood (Benson et al.) are expected to predict subsequent IQ. Alternatively, to corroborate the findings by Maziade et al. (1987) that children with more challenging temperament subsequently show superior intellectual development, negative correlations between early measures of adaptability and approach/withdrawal and positive correlations between early measures of intensity, mood, and distractibility with subsequent IQ would be necessary. There is a dearth of research examining intelligence as a predictor of temperament. Hence, we examine these relations in chapter 5 to understand if and how infants' and young children's intellectual development may underlay their behavioral styles throughout childhood and adolescence.

Temperament in the School Context

With increasing age, children spend a larger proportion of their time outside the family home, in the formal education system. Formal education is a virtually universal experience mandated by law for children in the United States, whereby almost all children attend school for five to seven hours per day over approximately nine months per year for more than a decade. Success or failure in school can have far-reaching significance not only for children's immediate intellectual, social, physical, and emotional development, but also for their eventual ability to obtain secure and well-paying employment.

Interestingly, a perusal of current child development textbooks at the time of writing this book revealed no mention of student temperament as a factor related to success in school; indeed, student intelligence was the only individual difference factor discussed in most texts. However, much of the variability in school achievement is not accounted for by cognitive ability (Petrill & Thompson, 1993). Evidence demonstrating both concurrent and predictive relations between temperament and several aspects of school functioning, from academic achievement to classroom adjustment, is accumulating. Many of these studies are reviewed herein.

Keogh has written extensively about the interface of children's temperament and schooling (1982; 1986; 1989). She provided a cogent conceptual framework and comprehensive review of literature on temperament and schooling (1986). Noting that the majority of research on temperament and schooling focused on intellectual/academic achievement outcomes, Keogh admonished readers to keep in mind the full range of children's competencies that influence children's school success and are themselves influenced by what goes on in the school setting. Keogh noted that if one applies the "goodness of fit" concept elaborated by Thomas and Chess (1977) to understand the contribution of temperament to children's school experience, both individual differences in children's temperament and the nature of the demands placed upon the child in the school setting must be considered. She characterized school demands as falling into two major categories: (1) demands that involve academic performance and achievement, and (2) interpersonal demands that relate to socially appropriate and adjusted behavior.

Whether teachers are guided by a traditional or open classroom educational philosophy, it is easy to speculate in which ways children's temperament may facilitate or impede success. In both settings, knowledge acquisition is a primary objective. Certain profiles of temperament characteristics may be particularly compatible with knowledge acquisition because they set the stage for learning. Whether a teacher is delivering the lesson or children are selecting their own learning activities, one would assume that children who are able to focus and maintain their attention and are able to control their activity level would be more apt to learn. Likewise, in either setting, it seems more probable that students who are open to novelty (i.e., high in approach) would make more progress. In a traditional classroom environment where the teacher organizes the daily schedule, children who can adapt quickly from one lesson to the next would be advantaged. To the extent that teaching and learning represent the outcome of interactions between teachers and students or students with each other, the temperamental dimensions of mood and approach/withdrawal may impact learning. Hence, intuitively one could surmise that the temperament dimensions of persistence/attention span, distractibility, activity level, adaptability, approach/withdrawal, and mood would be particularly intertwined with success in the school setting.

Keogh's analysis of the extant data led her to two conclusions. First, significant relationships between children's temperament and their academic competence exist, especially when competence is measured via teacher perceptions, but also when competence is measured via performance on standardized achievement tests. Second, pupils' temperament relates to their behavioral adjustment in the classroom, teacher perceptions of their students' "teachability," and teachers' attitudes toward students. "The social, adjustive aspect of schooling appears to be particularly sensitive to the influence of temperament" (p. 99).

School Entry

The behavioral styles of children may contribute to parents' decisions about whether or not to enroll their child in kindergarten at the earliest possible point in time. Numerous factors undoubtedly play a role in parents' decision-making process (e.g., family resources, characteristics of the school, other individual difference factors within the child). However, parents may be more apt to delay kindergarten entry for children who demonstrate certain temperament profiles. For example, parents' decisions may be related to their assessment of the child's readiness to learn in the academic setting. Schoen and Nagle (1994) demonstrated that teacher-rated temperament scores made a significant contribution to predicting readiness for school. Children who were rated by teachers as higher in persistence, lower in activity, and lower in distractibility scored higher on reading readiness tests. Perhaps children who are lower in persistence or higher in distractibility and activity level (e.g., the factors linked to reading readiness identified by Schoen and Nagle, 1994) may be viewed by parents as less "ready" for school entry.

At the time our sample turned 5, California law allowed parents to decide whether to enroll their children with fall birth dates in kindergarten as they turned 5 or to wait until the following year when the children would be turning 6. To test the possibility that temperament characteristics differentiated children whose kindergarten entry was on-time versus delayed, the temperament characteristics of these two groups prior to and at school entry were compared.

Grade Repetition

Beginning as early as the kindergarten year, grade repetition was experienced by some of the children participating in the FLS. Although little previous research has addressed the issue of the association between temperament and school retention, Maziade, Cote, Boutin, Boudreault, and Thivierge (1986b), in a Canadian sample, found no difference between two extreme temperament groups (most difficult vs. most easy) in the incidence of grade repetition. In chapter 6, we investigate possible links between being retained in a grade and child temperament by comparing the temperament characteristics of children who had repeated a grade to those who had not. Given our past research on temperament and schooling during the transition to middle school (Guerin et al., 1994), we expected that the dimension of persistence would be particularly likely to differentiate these groups, given that it related to both of the areas delineated by Keogh (academic and social/adjustive competencies).

Academic Achievement

Research on temperament and school functioning focusing on preschool and primary grade children has shown that, even after controlling for intelligence, aspects of temperament such as persistence/attention span, distractibility, adaptability, approach/withdrawal and/or activity level are predictive of academic success as measured by standardized achievement tests and teacher-assigned grades (Martin, Drew, Gaddis, & Moseley, 1988; Martin & Holbrook, 1985; Martin et al., 1983; Palisin, 1986).

Martin and his colleagues have conducted an impressive series of studies examining the relation of teacher reports of temperament to both teacher-assigned grades and standardized achievement test scores. Martin et al. (1983) examined correlations between teacher ratings of pupil temperament (assessed November through February of first grade) and first grade reading and math letter grades at the end of the year. They found significant multiple correlations of .65 and .76 between dimensions of temperament and grades for reading and math, respectively. Significant Pearson correlations were evident between reading and math grades and the temperament dimensions of persistence, adaptability, distractibility, and approach, with magnitudes ranging from .50 to .69. Hence, teacher ratings of temperament collected over the early part of the academic year predicted student achievement in reading and math at the end of the same academic year.

Martin and Holbrook (1985) subsequently examined the relation between temperament and achievement in first graders. In this study, reading and math achievement were measured using two methods: (1) teacher-assigned grades and (2) standardized test scores. Correlations between temperament and teacher-assigned grades were significant and in the moderate range, reaching .65 in magnitude. A similar pattern was observed for the standardized test scores, although correlations were somewhat lower in magnitude, reaching .49. Students who were less active, less distractible, more persistent, quicker to adapt, and more approaching tended to demonstrate higher achievement levels in both math and reading. Correlation coefficients were highest for persistence, followed by adaptability. Hence, teachers' temperament ratings of their students predicted achievement measured not only via teacher-assigned grades, but also via a standardized test.

Martin et al. (1988) reported cross-time correlations between teacher temperament ratings assessed during the last three months of the kindergarten year and achievement measured near the end of first grade via teacher-assigned grades and two standardized achievement tests. Kindergarten teacher ratings of temperament predicted first grade achievement test scores, with significant correlations ranging from .26 to .31 in magnitude. Kindergartners who were less active, more adaptable, more approaching, less distractible, and more persistent demonstrated higher total test scores the following year. Similar results were obtained on the second standardized achievement test administered at the end of first grade, with correlations ranging from .28 to .68. Furthermore, the large majority of correlations remained significant even after controlling for scholastic ability. Thus, temperament ratings added significantly to the prediction of academic achievement beyond its best predictor (intelligence) and also predicted achievement across academic years.

Martin et al. (1988) also examined the long-term utility of temperament in predicting academic achievement. They collected teacher assessments in first grade and then examined the children's achievement levels four years later via teacher-assigned grades and via standardized test scores. Even across this four-year span, significant correlations ranging from .30 to .48 were evident. Children viewed as less active, less distractible, and more persistent by their first grade teachers demonstrated higher reading and math achievement performance four years hence in grade 5.

Martin et al. (1988) also reported data collected in a small sample of children evaluated in a clinic setting. Preschool teachers rated children's temperament, and achievement was assessed via standardized test and teacher ratings. Children reported as less active, more approaching, less distractible, and more persistent by their preschool teachers were assigned higher grades by their first grade teachers (correlations ranged from .35 to .72 in magnitude). The strongest temperamental predictors of achievement, whether achievement was measured via test scores or teacher-assigned grades, were the dimensions of distractibility, persistence, and activity.

Hence, these numerous studies by Martin and colleagues demonstrate a link between temperament and academic achievement during the early primary years. These relations exist both concurrently and across time, whether temperament is assessed via teacher or parent reports, across at least two subject areas (reading, math), across two methods of measuring achievement (teacher-assigned grades, standardized tests), and when studied in intact classes, in a clinic setting, or in a community sample. Higher persistence, approach, and adaptability and lower activity level and distractibility were the temperament dimensions found to correlate with academic achievement.

Three studies have examined temperament-school relations beyond the transition to elementary school. Lerner, Lerner, and Zabski (1985) studied fourth grade level teachers and pupils in nine classes, using children's ratings of their own temperament, teachers' expectations regarding their students, teachers' judgments of student academic achievement and adjustment, and scores on standardized tests of achievement. Across teachers, there was little variation in what they expected or demanded from students; they expected from their students "... a relatively low activity level, high attention (and therefore low distractibility), high adaptability and approach (and therefore low withdrawal), relatively high rhythmicity and quite low reactivity" (p. 129). Although finding no relation between temperament and teacher-rated adjustment, Lerner et al. found low but statistically reliable correlations (r's $= .15$ to $.20$) between temperament and achievement. Activity level and adaptability/approach-withdrawal correlated positively with standardized test scores and teacher ratings of ability: students who reported themselves as more active or more adaptable/approaching also scored higher on achievement and were viewed as higher in ability. These data demonstrated that children's self ratings of temperament also related to achievement.

Talwar, Schwab, and Lerner (1989) assessed temperament via adolescent self reports; a factor analysis of the nine temperament variables yielded three factors: Task Rhythmicity (task orientation, rhythmicity in eating, sleeping, daily habits), Activity (general and sleep activity), and Adaptation (flexibility, approach, positive mood). Academic competence was measured via standardized achievement test scores, grade point average across academic subjects, adolescent self appraisals, and teacher ratings of scholastic competence. They found significant correlations ($p < .001$) between the temperament factor Adaptation and all measures of scholastic competence (teacher ratings, student self appraisals, grade point average concurrently and one year later, standardized achievement test scores). Coefficients ranged from .26 to .38 in magnitude and indicated that students who were more flexible, more approaching to new experiences, and more positive in mood demonstrated higher scholastic competence. Student-rated scholastic competence also correlated significantly with the Activity factor; higher activity related to lower scholastic competence. Using structural equation modeling, Talwar et al. concluded that the data supported a developmental-contextual model rather than a direct effects model between temperament and scholastic competence. Temperament related to teacher ratings of academic competence, which related to student self ratings of competence, which then related to actual scholastic competence.

We have previously published data from the FLS on the relation between temperament assessed at 10 years of age using the Middle Childhood Temperament Questionnaire and achievement at ages 10 and 11 (Guerin et al., 1994). Achievement was assessed in two ways: (1) teacher ratings of reading, math, and total learning, and (2) percentile scores based on grade level on the reading and math clusters of the Woodcock-Johnson Psycho-Educational Battery (an individually-administered achievement test). Unlike many other studies of temperament in the school setting, temperament was assessed by parental report rather than teacher or student reports. Parent-reported persistence and distractibility correlated with teacher ratings of reading and math performance at both 10 and 11 years (r's $= .39$ to .41 in magnitude). Correlations between temperament and teacher appraisals of total learning were also significant at ages 10 and 11; most notably, persistence/attention span, distractibility, predictability, and adaptability correlated at both 10 and 11 with teacher ratings of total learning (magnitude of r's ranged from $= .29$ to .47). Standardized test reading scores revealed a similar pattern of significant correlations with temperament dimensions as did teacher ratings of achievement.

Classroom Behavior

Researchers have also examined the relation between children's temperament and their adjustment to and social functioning in the school setting. For example, Martin et al. (1983) examined the relation between temperament ratings and observations of classroom behaviors in two first grade class rooms. Temperament was rated by teachers during the months of November through February; classroom observations were conducted by investigators during the months of January through March (both during the same first grade year). Results showed that the highest and most pervasive correlations were observed between temperament and constructive self-directed behavior and gross-motor inappropriate behavior.

Significant correlations were generally in the range of .40 to .50 in magnitude, and ranged to .63.

Also investigating the relation between temperament and classroom behavior, Guerin et al. (1994) reported data from the FLS at ages 10 and 11. Parent reports of temperament at age 10 were correlated with teacher reports of classroom behaviors (working hard and behaving appropriately) at 10 and 11. At age 10, concurrent ratings of children's temperament (rated by parents) and the first item, working hard (rated by teachers) showed that the temperament dimensions of persistence ($r = .55$) and predictability ($r = .45$) correlated most strongly, followed by adaptability, negative mood, distractibility, and intensity. A similar pattern was observed for behaving appropriately. Correlations were also significant to the next academic year at 11.

Academic Self-Concept

Relatively little research has examined the relation of children's temperament to their reports of their own experiences and perspectives. Keogh (1986) noted that children's temperamental qualities may impact the nature of their school experiences, which could result in long term consequences for children's attitudes toward schooling and their own adequacy and competence at school.

Subsequent to Keogh's review, three studies have assessed the relation between adolescents' self-appraisals of academic competence and temperament. As noted previously, Talwar et al. (1989) found temperament correlated with student self-ratings of scholastic competence. Adolescents who perceived themselves as higher in task orientation and biological rhythmicity, and as more flexible, approaching, and positive in mood also reported higher perceptions of scholastic competence.

Findings previously published from the FLS also bear directly on this issue. Using temperament data collected from parents when their children were 10 and 12 years, Guerin et al. (1994) examined the degree to which the children's self appraisals pertaining to school in general and reading and math in particular were predicted by temperament ratings. Preadolescents whose parents viewed them as more predictable, quicker to adapt, less intense in their reactions, more positive in mood, more persistent, and less distractible at 12 subsequently reported higher levels of self-concept in reading, general school, and/or math at 13 years.

In the third study, Klein (1995) reported relations between self-rated temperament and self-perceptions of scholastic competence in a sample of college students. She reported significant but low correlations between perception of scholastic competence and temperament, with higher ratings of competence associated with longer task orientation, more positive mood, more flexibility, approach rather than withdrawal tendencies, more biological regularity, and lower general activity level.

In chapter 6, findings regarding the relation between children's temperament and their scholastic experiences from school entry to high school completion are presented. The methodology of the FLS in addressing the role of temperament in children's academic experiences is explicated to provide a context for interpretation of these data. More specifically, the educational variables examined include kindergarten entrance age, early grade repetition, grade repetition at any point in primary and secondary school, academic achievement measured via individually-administered standardized tests collected annually, parent and teacher reports of achievement, teacher reports of students' classroom behavior, and students' appraisals of their competency in school and academic intrinsic motivation. Finally, the cross-time and concurrent relations between temperament and high school cumulative grade point average are presented. We examined the relation of temperament to this comprehensive indicator of high school performance in comparison to two well-known predictors of academic performance, intelligence and family socioeconomic status.

Temperament in the Family Context

Over the past decade in particular, increasing attention has been focused on the relation between temperament, aspects of family relationships or home environment, and child outcomes. Putnam et al. (2002) provided a cogent and detailed review of recent literature on child temperament and parenting, noting that individual differences in temperament among children within the same family are evident early in life and have "important implications for parent-child interaction" (p. 255). In-depth analysis of the interface between the child and his/her contexts of development, and research approaches to examine this interface, have been provided by Wachs and Plomin (1991) and Wachs and Kohnstamm (2001).

As we considered a data analytic strategy to organize the ponderous collection of home environment and family relationship data collected during the course of the FLS, we identified several factors that mitigate the discovery of strong relations between temperament and home/family environment. First, from a systems theory perspective, there are several relationship systems operating within the family: marital, sibling, parent-child, etc. The effect of one child's temperament in the context of the family may be difficult to isolate, especially if the study child's temperament is not extreme. The FLS families, especially as the study children advanced in age, were quite diverse in terms of family composition. Variations included factors such as the number of parents in the home and/or in close contact with the study child, the number of siblings in the family, birth order of the study child, family socioeconomic status, etc. Additionally, the family is but one part of the larger number of ecosystems that influence development. Within the environment, both social and physical factors may influence or be influenced by individual differences in temperament. From a methodological perspective, another challenge is the imprecision of measurement of both temperament and home environment variables. Although the measures available have adequate psychometric properties in the main, there is still additional theoretical and psychometric work needed before consensus on "marker variables" in these domains is reached (Wachs, 1991). The goodness of fit concept reminds us that temperament-environment relations may not be evident in direct "main effects," but rather detected through careful examination of moderator variables that modify the impact of temperament depending on the context. Finally, the design of the FLS as a non-intervention longitudinal study of development limits the ability to identify causal relationships.

In spite of these challenges, the FLS has much to contribute to the investigation of temperament in context. First, during the course of investigation in the FLS, data across all developmental eras from infancy through adolescence have been collected, allowing us to examine temperament-context relations in infancy, the preschool years, the elementary school years, and adolescence. Second, data have been collected about children's temperament from multiple informants, including parent reports when children were 1.5 through 16 years and self-reports when the study children were 14 and 16 years. A third strength relates to assessment of the environment; multiple methods have been used to collect data about the context of development, including direct observation, interview, and standardized questionnaires or inventories. Fourth, as with temperament, multiple informants have provided information about the environment and/or family relationships, including mothers, fathers, and the study children. Fifth, repeated measures using the same instruments throughout the course of investigation have been collected. For example, the Family Environment Scale was completed by mothers when children were 3, 5, 7, 8, 10, 12, 14, 16, and 17 years. Having repeated measures across development of both home/family environment and temperament allows the examination of temperament as a precursor and as a sequela of development. A sixth strength is that the environment has been assessed at several levels, including social address variables, physical aspects of the home, and relationships within the family. Related to social relationships, data have been collected to assess not only the parents' perspective of family relations, but also the child's perspectives on his/her relationships with parents. Finally, widely used measures of physical and social environment have been utilized, allowing for clear and direct comparisons to extant research.

Researchers examining the relation between infant temperament and home/family environment measures during the early years have reported correlations in the low range, at best. Daniels et al. (1984) found few significant relations between a composite measure of infant difficult temperament based on the EASI Temperament Survey and the Home Observation for the Measurement of the Environment (HOME) or Family Environment Scale (FES). Matheny, Wilson, and

Thoben (1987) reported finding no significant correlations between the HOME scales and temperamental "tractability" and only a few inconsistent and low correlations with scores on the FES. Specifically, across assessment periods at 12, 18, and 24 months, only one finding replicated across multiple periods: family conflict was lower when infants were more tractable, r's $= -.21, -.26, p < .01$. These studies examining temperament-home environment relations during the first few years reveal little evidence that infant temperament relates to the home/family environment.

In a thorough and articulate analysis of studies on the association between infants' temperament and the care they received, Crockenberg (1986) noted contradictory research findings. Of 16 studies reviewed, 9 studies yielded findings showing that more irritable babies experienced less care giving or less stimulating contact with their mothers. To the contrary, 7 of the 16 studies revealed findings that mothers of irritable babies were more engaged with their babies compared to mothers of babies who were less irritable or easy. Crockenberg concluded that the weak relations observed and contradictory findings may be indicative of a lack of direct relation between infants' temperament and the care they receive. However, her preference was to consider the possibility that infant temperament and care are related, but that other characteristics of the caregiver and/or the care-giving environment interact to determine the nature of the relation.

In a subsequent review of the literature on child temperament and parenting, Putnam et al. (2002) reviewed findings from studies examining potential moderating variables between temperament and parenting, including age of child, sex of child, maternal psychological and social characteristics, and social and cultural factors. They concluded that variability in results, even to the point of contradictory findings as observed by Crockenberg (1986), was still common. They encouraged researchers to examine how child outcomes differ as a function of specific combinations of child temperament and parenting, using outcomes such as cognitive development, behavioral adjustment, school achievement, and self-esteem, for example. In their view, concepts such as "goodness of fit" (Thomas et al., 1968), "effective experience" (Escalona, 1968), and "organismic specificity" (Wachs & Gruen, 1982) have in common the notion that similar parenting behaviors may have different consequences for children with different temperament. Thus, congruent with these conceptualizations, examining the impact of specific temperament-parenting configurations on children's developmental outcomes will be important contributions of future research.

In chapter 7, data collected during the course of the FLS will first be examined to ascertain the degree of relation between temperament dimensions and proximal variables in the home and family environment. Although research on the temperament-home/family environment relation conducted during the first two years of life has yielded weak correlations at best, the relation of these variables as the parent-child relationship develops over time has not been reported. Hence, we examine concurrent temperament-home/family environment relations across the preschool, middle childhood, and adolescent eras. Our primary interest in examining the temperament-environment relations across development is in developing a description of the relation between child characteristics and home and family environment variables over time that may help elucidate how children's temperament comes to be related to other aspects of their development. As recommended by Wachs and Kohnstamm (2001), we examined the relation between early home environment and temperament during middle childhood and adolescence to determine whether child temperament (or its expression) may be influenced by family climate. In addition to examining the home and family environment from the vantage of researchers (conducting the HOME inventory) and parents, the views of the study children regarding their family environment were assessed at two ages (8 and 17 years), and their perceptions of their relationship with their parents were assessed across the ages from 10 to 16. Finally, following the recommendation of Wachs and Kohnstamm (2001) and Putnam et al. (2002), we examine how infant temperament and family environment interact in predicting children's behavioral adjustment in middle childhood.

Temperament in the Extremes: Developmental Trajectories of Three Infant Temperament Groups

In chapters 3 through 7, we examined the relation of challenging aspects of infants' temperament to subsequent temperament (chapter 3), behavioral adjustment (chapter 4), intelligence (chapter 5), school functioning (chapter 6), and home environment/family relationships (chapter 7). Using the four dimensions of the ICQ as continuous variables, we appraised concurrent and cross-time relations with respect to the other domains investigated in the FLS to help elucidate the significance of challenging temperament to development during infancy and beyond. Previewing the findings presented in these chapters, there is evidence that the aspects of challenging infant temperament assessed by the ICQ (fussy/difficult/demanding, unadaptability, resistant to control, and unsociability) relate across-time to numerous aspects of development spanning intervals reaching approximately 15 years. Generally, correlations are in the low range of magnitude, typically less than .40. Nevertheless, given the dramatic changes in human development between infancy and late adolescence, even correlation coefficients in the magnitude of those observed may be considered by some to be quite impressive.

Buss and Plomin have been credited with the suggestion that "children with extreme temperaments are more likely to influence their context, whereas children with more moderate levels of a given temperament are more likely to be influenced by their context" (Wachs & Kohnstamm, 2001, p. 216). Recently, several researchers have recommended employing an extreme groups approach in the study of temperament (e.g., Kagan, Snidman, & Arcus, 1998). For example,

Radke-Yarrow (1998) commented that "...renewed attention to subgroups of children at the extremes in the samples for whom we assess central tendencies can bring a new level of insight into the nature of individual functioning" (p. 82). Putnam et al. (2002, p. 269) noted that "Observations of parenting in extreme temperament groups may be a useful starting point..." for testing hypotheses concerning specific combinations of temperament characteristics and parenting behaviors. Wachs (1991) also discussed the use of extreme groups, particularly to uncover Organism X Environment interactions, over a decade ago.

We have previously noted that the construct of difficult temperament has been a central focus in the study of temperament (Bates, 1980; Putnam et al., 2002). Most often (but not always), difficult temperament has been ascribed to the category of developmental risk factors, perhaps due to recurring findings of its relation to compromised behavioral adjustment. The focus on temperament as a risk factor is understandable, given our discipline's commitment to preventing or intervening when children's development is jeopardized. However, we are also interested in understanding whether having certain temperamental dispositions may protect children from adversity, or even serve as a catalyst in facilitating their development in comparison to other children with more typical or average temperament dispositions. Consider the domain of intelligence. Our understanding of development in this domain and its implications for children's development in other domains would obviously be lacking should we limit our examination only to children in the lower end of the distribution. Hence, our interest in examining both extremes of temperament, "difficult" and "easy." Our goal in comparing the developmental outcomes of infants scoring in the lowest quartile, intermediate two quartiles, and highest quartile for each of the four IQC temperament factors was to use the extensive data of the FLS to document how variations in early temperament may guide or direct the course of human development in five important domains: temperament, behavioral adjustment, intelligence, achievement, and home/family environment.

Findings of relations between parent-reported temperament and child outcomes based on data collected across informants and contexts, especially findings replicated by multiple researchers, can demonstrate that parent perceptions such as those assessed on the ICQ have meaning outside the context of the parent-child relationship. Hence, in this chapter are included several outcome variables assessed using different methods and different informants than parent reports on questionnaires in an effort to assess the external generalizability of parent perceptions of their infants' temperament.

As with any longitudinal study in which the development of individuals is charted across time in the absence of intervention, causal links between variables are impossible to establish. Bates (1989) pointed out that the earlier the measure of temperament and its hypothesized outcomes are measured, the more confident one can be that the association observed reflects the process of a constitutional characteristic shaping the child's development. With increasing age and increasing intervals between the measurement of temperament and its hypothesized outcomes, the potential for confounding between child constitution and environment increases. Hence, we do not assert that developmental sequelae of infant temperament characteristics reported herein solely reflect the impact of that temperament factor. Rather, findings of significant differences in developmental outcomes among the infant temperament groups, especially long-term sequelae, are interpreted as reflecting the result of accumulated interactions that are bidirectional and transactional in nature between children and the contexts of their development over time.

Four Aspects of Challenging Infant Temperament

Turning to the four factors of the ICQ and their possible bearing on children's developmental trajectories, we now examine each of the four factors. Bates (1980; 1989) characterized the fussy/difficult/demanding factor as primarily reflecting negative emotionality. He observed that children rated high on this factor are seen as socially demanding and either unable or unwilling to entertain themselves. According to Bates, infant fussiness/difficultness is actually made up of two overlapping components. First, the child has a need for high levels of stimulation, and second, the child possesses a high sensitivity to aversive stimuli. According to Bates, the aspect of high sensitivity in the fussy/difficult infant creates an overlap with the next ICQ factor, unadaptability. Bates (1989) defined the second ICQ factor, unadaptability, as the infant's initial and/or eventual reactions to new things, new events, and new people. Unadaptability reflects the infant's anxiety tendencies to new people and situations.

The third ICQ factor, originally designated as persistence but more recently labeled resistance to control, relates conceptually to very early unmanageability. Bates, Pettit, Dodge, and Ridge (1998) posited resistance to control comprises two central elements: first, a relatively strong attraction to rewarding stimuli that is accompanied by excitement, and second, a relatively weak level of basic social agreeableness. Bates and McFadyen-Ketchum (2000) observed that resistance to control, on a conceptual level, may reflect an "active ignoring or openly uncooperative stance" (p. 182), difficulties in processing inhibitory cues, and/or problems in inhibiting responses, especially to rewarding stimuli.

Compared to the other three ICQ factors, the fourth factor, unsociability, has been least thoroughly addressed. Originally labeled "dull," (Bates, et al., 1979), unsociability has to do with the infant's tendency to withdraw from social interactions versus to enjoy meeting and being with people (Bates, 1989). Bates, Maslin, and Frankel (1985) noted that sociability, or extraversion, reflected the individual's tendency to have "an open versus timid approach to new people and novel experiences" (p. 169).

Research on Developmental Sequelae of Challenging Infant Temperament

More extensive literature reviews on the concomitants and consequences of various dimensions of infant temperament with respect to temperament during childhood and adolescence, behavioral adjustment, intelligence, achievement, and home environment/family relations have been provided in earlier sections of this chapter. In the following section, studies using the ICQ in particular are reviewed.

Temperament and Personality Sequelae

Lee and Bates (1985) reported cross-time correlations for ICQ difficultness. The correlation between maternal ratings of difficultness at 6 and at 24 months was .57; between 13 and 24 months the correlation was .71, both p's < .001. However, they noted limited stability of membership in the extreme temperament groups between 6 and 24 months; comparing classifications at 24 months to those at 6 months, consistent classifications were 50%, 69%, and 50% for the difficult, intermediate, and easy groups.

Guerin and Gottfried (1994b) also, based on the FLS data, demonstrated significant cross-time correlations between the fussy/difficult/demanding factor and NYLS temperament dimensions through at least childhood (i.e., age 12). Childhood temperamental sequelae of fussy/difficult/demanding infant temperament included slower adaptability to changes, more frequent or intense negative mood, and higher activity level.

Lanthier and Bates (1997) reported significant correlations between temperament measured during infancy on the ICQ and personality measured at age 17. Infant difficultness predicted lower extraversion, and infant unadaptability predicted higher neuroticism, r's = −.19 and .25, respectively. Higher correlation coefficients were observed for unsociability, which predicted neuroticism and openness (r's = .30 and .21, respectively). Resistance to control in infancy presaged lower agreeableness ($r = −.43$) and lower conscientiousness ($r = −.19$) at 17 years.

Behavioral and Emotional Adjustment

Bates et al. (1985) examined temperament assessed at 6, 13, and/or 24 months as predictors of three kinds of behavior problems in 3-year-olds: anxiety, hostility, and hyperactivity. Behavior problems were assessed via maternal report using the Preschool Behavior Questionnaire. Difficultness aggregated across 6, 13, and 24 months predicted all three types of behavior problems. Resistance to control assessed at 13 months entered into the prediction of hostility and hyperactivity, but not anxiety. A measure of infant sociability at 24 months was predictive of anxiety problems at 3 years.

Andersson and Sommerfelt (1999), in a Norweigian sample, examined relations between factors of the ICQ assessed at 6 and 13 months with behavioral adjustment at age 5. All ICQ factors correlated at significant but low levels (maximum $r = .24$) with a global behavior problem score.

Summarizing across his longitudinal research program using the ICQ, Bates (1989) reported a pattern of differentiated predictiveness for temperament in foretelling behavior problems. Specifically, he reported that ICQ fussy/difficultness predicted both internalizing and externalizing types of behavior problems at 3 and 6 years. On the other hand, unadaptability was more predictive of later internalizing types of behavior problems compared to externalizing problems, and resistance to control predicted externalizing behavior problems better than internalizing problems. Bates and McFadyen-Ketchum (2000) demonstrated that resistance to control interacted with maternal restrictive control in relation to the development of behavior problems. That is, the relationship between children's resistance to control and behavior problems depended upon the type of parenting they experienced. Children high in resistance to control who experienced high levels of maternal control exhibited fewer behavior problems than those who experienced low levels of maternal control.

Infant Temperament and Intellectual Development

Two studies have examined the relation between infant temperament assessed via the ICQ at 6 and 13 months (Andersson & Sommerfelt, 1999; Olson, Bates, & Kaskie, 1992) and 24 months (Olson et al., 1992) and subsequent cognitive development. Both failed to demonstrate significant relations between temperament and cognitive development at ages 5 through 8.

Infant Temperament and Home Environment/Family Relationships

Lee and Bates (1985), using direct observations of naturally occurring interactions in the home, examined the relation between perceived difficultness and the nature of interactions between mothers and their 2-year-olds. The major categories of parent and child behaviors coded included affection, maturity demands, communication, interpersonal control, and child trouble behaviors. They predicted that conflict-like events would be more frequent in dyads in which the child was perceived as difficult in temperament. Their hypothesis was confirmed; mothers who rated their children as more difficult in temperament were more likely to have toddlers who essentially pushed the limits (i.e., broke household rules, caused mild damage to persons/property); the mothers of toddlers rated as temperamentally difficult were more likely to use an intrusive discipline style and negatively reinforce undesirable child behavior. Specifically, Lee and Bates found that mothers who rated their toddlers as more difficult were more likely to restrain or remove their children, give in to their toddler after initially resisting, and less likely to make maturity demands or give their children choices between alternative behaviors.

Additional analyses comparing extreme groups on the difficultness factor replicated these general findings and demonstrated that the difficult group differed significantly from both the easy and intermediate groups (easy and intermediate groups did not differ from each other). Lee and Bates interpreted these findings as evidence of an emerging coercive parent-child interactive style and proposed that this parenting style provides a linkage between early difficult temperament and later behavior disorders.

In chapter 8, findings regarding short- and long-term developmental and environmental sequelae of the four aspects of challenging infant temperament assessed on the ICQ are presented. Findings in chapter 8 provide necessary but not sufficient evidence to establish that early individual differences in temperament shape the course of developmental trajectories throughout childhood and adolescence. A major goal of chapter 8 is to examine the FLS data for evidence that certain temperamental characteristics may actually facilitate or advance children's development, acting as catalysts or assets rather than as liabilities or risk factors.

In chapter 9, the developmental course and implications of temperament from infancy through adolescence are explicated. The comparative developmental significance of each of the nine NYLS dimensions is examined with respect to behavioral, intellectual, scholastic, and family relationships. Implications of findings from the FLS with respect to child development theory and practice are elucidated.

2

Methodology of the Fullerton Longitudinal Study and Data Analytic Strategy

> "(Name) is a very well adjusted mature kindergarten student. He interacts well with his peer group and teachers. (Name) tries hard in all areas of the curriculum and does above average work. Sometimes (Name) has exhibited a negative response to suggested activities—such as music or a game activity. He becomes immediately involved, though, and seems to like the activity suggested. I attribute this negative attitude to trying to "act" older. He seems to be embarrassed to show excitement about things. This seems to be a part of his personality, as I've noticed this response around his parents, also.
> —Teacher of Child 17, Easy Infant Temperament Group, Age 6

FLS Assessment Waves

The Fullerton Longitudinal Study (FLS) is a contemporary investigation of 130 infants and their families. Children were 1 year old at the initiation of the project; they were tested every 6 months from 1 year through 3.5 years and at yearly intervals from 5 through 17 years thus far, as displayed in Table 2.01. Thus, across the span of investigation covered in this book, participants visited our lab for 19 assessments and FLS researchers made 3 direct in-home assessments. Subject retention has been excellent, with 109 (84%) returning for assessment at age 17.

Participants

When the study was launched in 1979, the FLS staff recruited families listed in birth notifications provided by hospitals in the communities surrounding California State University, Fullerton. These lists were mailed directly to our lab by the hospital staff and included all babies born at each site. All children were born during the period between late August and early December 1978. To participate in

Table 2.01.   Data Assessment Waves in the Fullerton Longitudinal Study

Developmental era	Age in years
Assessments in laboratory	
Infancy	1, 1.5
Toddler/Preschool Years	2, 2.5, 3, 3.5, 5
Middle Childhood	6, 7, 8, 9, 10, 11, 12
Adolescence	13, 14, 15, 16, 17
Home visits	
Infancy	1.5
Preschool Years	3.25
Middle Childhood	8

the FLS, infants were required to be free of visual and neurological abnormalities, full term at birth, and of normal birth weight. Birth weights ranged from 85 to 172 oz ($M = 124.62$, $SD = 16.3$). All families spoke English.

Demographic characteristics of the FLS sample at 1 and 17 years are displayed in Table 2.02. To characterize the demographics of the sample shown in Table 2.02, the FLS study group comprised approximately equal proportions of boys and girls and first- and later-borns and was primarily Caucasian. Paternal full-time employment was high at both the early and later years; however, dramatic changes in maternal employment are evident between the early and later data collection periods.

Table 2.02.   Demographic Characteristics of the FLS Sample at 1 and 17 Years (Percentages)

	Age (years)	
Demographic variable	1	17
Sex		
Male	52.3	56.0
Female	47.7	44.0
Ethnicity		
Caucasian	90.0	90.8
Other	10.0	9.2
Birth order		
First born	54.6	49.5
Second or later born	55.5	50.5
Maternal Employment Status		
Not employed	63.8	18.2
Employed full-time	20.0	62.6
Paternal Employment Status		
Not employed	0.0	10.1
Employed full-time	99.0	87.6
Marital Status of Mother		
Married	93.1	76.8

Near the onset of the investigation, over 60% of mothers were not employed outside the home; at the time of their children's 17-year visit, over 60% of mothers were employed full-time. (Additional details concerning maternal work history are available in A.E. Gottfried et al., 1988, 1995). Maternal marital status also showed appreciable change, falling from over 90% married at the 1.5 assessment to approximately 75% when children were 17 (although mothers were not necessarily married to the same person [i.e., the study child's natural father] at the 17-year follow-up).

The families participating in the FLS represented a wide range of middle-class socioeconomic status as measured by the Hollingshead Four Factor Index of Social Status (Hollingshead, 1975; see also A. W. Gottfried, 1985; A. W. Gottfried Gottfried, Bathurst, Guerin, & Parramore, 2003). The mean Hollingshead Social Status Index was 45.6 ($SD = 11.9$) at the initiation of the FLS and 48.6 ($SD = 11.4$) at the 17-year assessment. The occupations of mothers and fathers showed a wide range, varying from semi-skilled workers to professionals. Additional details concerning the characteristics of this sample at various stages of the investigation have been previously published (A. E. Gottfried, et al., 1988; A. W. Gottfried et al., 1994).

Delineation of Developmental Eras

Presently, the FLS database contains over 16,000 variables chronicling the development of our study population and their families for 17 years. Given the magnitude of the FLS database, a major task for us was to develop a data analytic plan that would guide us in systematically addressing the issues of concern. Given our interest in documenting the relations between temperament and development in the various domains assessed in the FLS, we conceptualized the longitudinal aspect of the data as four developmental eras across which we would examine temperament-development relations. These eras correspond to commonly used delineations in developmental psychology: infancy (through 1.5 years), toddler/preschool years (2 to 5 years), middle childhood (6 to 12 years), and adolescence (13 to 17 years). These age boundaries are also consistent with those of the temperament measures used in the FLS: the Infant Characteristics Questionnaire for infancy, the Toddler Temperament Scale and Behavior Style Questionnaire for toddler/preschool years, the Middle Childhood Temperament Questionnaire for middle childhood, and the Dimensions of Temperament Scale-Revised for adolescence. As our first data reduction strategy, then, our decision was to average across ages to yield a single measure when repeated measures were available within a developmental era. For example, the Middle Childhood Temperament Questionnaire (MCTQ) was administered three times (at ages 8, 10, and 12 years). These measures were averaged by dimension across age to yield a single measure of the nine MCTQ dimensions to represent the middle childhood era. In addition to increasing the reliability of the measures (see Epstein, 1979; Rushton, Brainerd, & Pressley, 1983), this procedure also maximized the available sample size; participants who would have been excluded due to missing data at a particular age were included because their data were averaged across their extant data. In addition, our examination of cross-time stability coefficients showed moderate to high stability for temperament and most aspects of development. Hence, averaging across measures was deemed an appropriate and desirable data reduction method.

Tests for Attrition Bias

In any longitudinal study, but especially one spanning almost two decades, attrition bias or participant mortality (i.e., differential drop out of participants) is a potential concern. The possibility of attrition bias in the FLS was investigated by conducting comparisons of the 109 children continuing through the entire study (to age 17 thus far) to those dropping out during the course of investigation ($n = 21$) on several key variables: infant temperament, socioeconomic status, developmental progress, and home environment. These analyses revealed no evidence of attrition bias.

In the area of infant temperament, comparisons were conducted with respect to the four aspects of difficult infant temperament assessed at 1.5 years using the Infant Characteristics Questionnaire. All comparisons between those dropping out and those continuing in the study were nonsignificant: fussy/difficult/demanding (t [121] $= 1.06$, $p = .29$), unadaptable (t [121] $= 0.19$, $p = .85$), resistant to control (t [121] $= 1.27, p = .21$, and unsociable (t [121] $= 1.29, p = .20$). Nor did these groups differ on their 1-year index of socioeconomic status (t [124] $= 1.55$, $p = .12$), developmental progress as measured via the mental development index of the Bayley Scales of Infant Development at 1 year (t [128] $= 1.45, p = .15$), or on the total score of the Home Observation for Measurement of the Environment conducted at 1.25 years (t [127] $= 1.75, p = .08$). Hence, those dropping out of the study did not differ from those continuing through high school completion on these key indicators.

Use of Parent Report Measures

Several methods are currently used to assess temperament, including observer ratings in the home, classroom, or other natural setting; structured observations in the research setting; parent interviews; self-reports for older children and adolescents; and parent or teacher reports on standardized questionnaires, for example. However, at the outset of the FLS in the late 1970's, measurement options were much more limited. Indeed, it was not until 1982 that Hubert, Wachs, Peters-Martin, and Gandour (1982) provided the first systematic integration of empirical findings relating to the psychometric properties of instruments assessing children's temperament.

Our selection of parent reports on standardized questionnaires to assess the temperament of the FLS study children was based on several considerations. First, given that the theoretical framework of the New York Longitudinal researchers was the dominant orientation addressing children's temperament in the late 1970's, we sought measures based on this conceptualization of temperament. We wanted to be able to compare findings from the FLS with the accumulating corpus of research literature on children's temperament based on this orientation. Second, because of our longitudinal design, we wanted a set of measures that could be used to assess temperament across the several developmental eras that our investigation would eventually span. Carey and his colleagues were then in the process of developing questionnaires that would meet our needs for several years. Third, we wanted measures with established and acceptable psychometric qualities, including both reliability and validity. In addition, the items on the parent report measures of children's temperament had face validity. The items tapped aspects of children's unique behavioral styles that parents would generally have the most opportunities to observe and thus parents would have the best database upon which to draw. For example, parents were likely in the best position to observe infrequently occurring behavior that may be useful in measuring a particular dimension, such as the child's intensity of reaction to noxious stimuli (for instance accidental injuries, medical procedures), surprises, etc. The utility of parent reports on standardized inventories to assess characteristics such as behavioral functioning (Achenbach, 1991a) and cognitive development (A. W. Gottfried et al., 1983, 1984; Guerin & Gottfried, 1987) also bolstered our confidence in parents as informants. Finally, efficiency was an important consideration, given that the FLS was designed to investigate multiple themes, many of which were quite demanding in terms of participant and staff time (including, for example, individually administered tests of developmental/ intellectual status, direct assessments of home environment). After consideration of all of these factors, we decided to employ parental report measures throughout this study. The scales selected and ages of administration are displayed in Table 2.03.

Table 2.03. Temperament and Personality Measures Collected in the Fullerton Longitudinal Study

Developmental era	Measure	Age(s) administered (years)
Infancy	● Infant Characteristics Questionnaire	1.5
Toddler/Preschool	● Toddler Temperament Scale	2
	● Behavioral Style Questionnaire	3, 3.5, 5
Middle Childhood	● Middle Childhood Temperament Questionnaire	8, 10, 12
Adolescence	● Revised Dimensions of Temperament Survey	14, 16
	● NEO Five Factor Inventory	17

Temperament Measures Used in the FLS

The earliest measure of temperament collected in the FLS was the Infant Characteristics Questionnaire (ICQ) developed by Bates et al. (1979). The ICQ was designed to assess aspects of temperament found difficult or challenging by parents. By the late 1970's, the constellation of difficult temperament was considered by some to be the most widely used construct in the temperament literature (cf. Bates, 1980), primarily due, perhaps, to the demonstrated linkage between difficult temperament and subsequent behavior problems (Thomas et al., 1968). We next selected the family of inventories developed by Carey and colleagues to assess temperament from the toddler period and throughout childhood: Toddler Temperament Scale (Fullard et al., 1984), Behavioral Style Questionnaire (McDevitt & Carey, 1978), and Middle Childhood Temperament Questionnaire (Hegvik et al., 1982). All of these instruments were based on the NYLS theoretical foundation and yielded scores on each of the nine NYLS dimensions, allowing for study of the contribution or role of variation on specific behavioral dimensions in children's development. Our final measure of temperament was selected as the participants reached adolescence. At that time, our examination of the available measures led us to select the Revised Dimensions of Temperament Survey developed by Windle and Lerner (1986). This inventory was also based on the NYLS orientation, although not assessing all of the nine dimensions. In addition to sharing the same theoretical foundation as our previous measures, we selected this scale because it had versions for the parents and adolescents to complete.

The family of questionnaires used by the FLS to chart the temperament of our population has shown to be a fortuitous selection. In their comprehensive review of questionnaire measures of children's temperament, Slabach, Morrow, and Wachs (1991) characterized the questionnaires used in the FLS during infancy and childhood as being in active use since the previous review of measures by Hubert et al. (1982) and noted that the revision of the Dimensions of Temperament Survey suggested it was also a vital measure.

Infant Characteristics Questionnaire (ICQ)

This instrument was designed specifically to assess difficult temperament, with the ultimate goal being the longitudinal study of difficult infants (Bates et al., 1979). The version of the ICQ utilized in the FLS consists of 32 items, each of which is rated by the parent on a scale from 1 (optimal temperament trait) to 7 (difficult temperament trait). Using a factor analytic approach, Bates et al. identified the four factors: (a) fussy/difficult/demanding; (b) unadaptable; (c) persistent (subsequently labeled "resistant to control"); and (d) unsociable. In their extensive review of temperament instruments, Hubert et al. (1982) recommended the ICQ for use when the major goal of the study was to investigate the correlates of difficult temperament. The ICQ possesses satisfactory test-retest reliability for the fussy/difficult/demanding factor, an acceptable level of internal consistency, and moderate stability (Slabach et al., 1991). In the FLS, internal reliability coefficients for the four factors were .82, .67, 59, and .53 for fussy/difficult/demanding, unadaptable, resistant to control, and unsociable factors, respectively. Mothers completed the ICQ when participants were 1.5 years old.

Toddler Temperament Scale (TTS)

The TTS was designed to assess temperament in 1- to 3-year-old children (Fullard et al., 1984). For each of 97 items, the parent indicates how often the child exhibits a given behavior using a scale from 1 ("almost never") to 6 ("almost always"). The TTS yields nine scores corresponding to the nine NYLS temperament dimensions (activity level, biological rhythmicity, approach/withdrawal, adaptability, intensity, negative mood, persistence/attention span, distractibility, threshold of responsiveness). According to Fullard et al. (1984), standardization research demonstrated satisfactory reliability for the TTS; coefficient alphas ranged from .53 to .84 with a median of .72 for the nine dimensions (2-year-olds); test-retest reliability over a 1-month interval ranged from .69 to .89 (median $r = .81$). More recently, Slabach et al. (1991) characterized the test-retest reliability of the TTS as satisfactory (excluding biological rhythmicity dimension) and its stability as moderate. In the FLS, coefficient alphas ranged from .48 to .86 (median $r = .64$). For the aforementioned scales of the TTS, the coefficient alphas in the FLS were .62, .64, .86, .64, .64, 58, .68, .75, and .48, respectively. The TTS was administered at age 2.

Behavioral Style Questionnaire (BSQ)

This 100-item questionnaire was designed to assess temperament in 3- to 7-year-olds (McDevitt & Carey, 1978). Like the TTS, parents respond using a rating scale from 1 to 6. In the standardization sample, coefficient alphas ranged from .47 to .84 for the nine temperament dimensions (total instrument alpha $= .84$). Test-retest reliability over a 1-month interval ranged from .67 to .93 for the nine dimensions ($r = .89$ for the entire scale). Although Slabach et al. (1991) characterized the test-retest reliability of the BSQ as questionable, research based on the FLS sample (Guerin & Gottfried, 1994a) showed correlation coefficients across a six month interval ranging from .54 (adaptability) to .77 (approach), with a median r of .69. Especially in view of the fact that these data are based on a six-month test-retest interval, which exceeds the 3-month test-retest interval adopted by Slabach et al. as a criteria for the maximum allowable gap in their review, these data support the acceptability of the test-retest reliability of the BSQ. Coefficient alphas averaged separately for each of the nine dimensions across the three assessment ages in the FLS (3, 3.5, 5 years) ranged from .46 to .81 (median = .70; mean = .67). More specifically, for the nine dimensions (activity level, biological rhythmicity, approach/withdrawal, adaptability, intensity, negative mood, persistence/attention span, distractibility, threshold of responsiveness), coefficient alphas in the FLS were as follows: .72, .57, .81, .74, .73, .69, 63, .70, .46.

Middle Childhood Temperament Questionnaire (MCTQ)

Designed to assess temperament in 8- to 12-year-olds, this instrument follows the same format as the TTS and BSQ. The 99 items assess the nine NYLS temperament dimensions, however, the dimension of biological rhythmicity on the TTS and BSQ is replaced by a dimension labeled predictability/quality of organization on the MCTQ (Hegvik et al., 1982). Given that both the biological rhythmicity and the predictability/quality of organization dimensions assess regularity of behavior, there is conceptual overlap (Hegvik et al., 1982, p. 198). However, predictability/ quality of social organization deals with task performance and social behavior rather than biological functioning.

Slabach et al. (1991) concluded that the MCTQ showed internal consistency coefficients among the highest of all scales examined in their review of temperament inventories. Furthermore, they characterized the test-retest reliability of the MCTQ as satisfactory. Coefficient alphas ranged from .71 to .87 with a median of .81 for the nine dimensions; over an average of 75 days, test-retest reliability was $r = .88$ (Hegvik, et al., 1982). Across the three assessment periods in our sample at ages 8, 10, and 12, coefficient alphas averaged separately for the nine dimensions had a median value of .82, a mean value of .79, and ranged from .68 to .84. More specifically, for activity level, predictability/quality of organization, approach/withdrawal, adaptability, intensity, negative mood, persistence/attention span, distractibility, and threshold of responsiveness, coefficient alphas averaged across ages 8, 10, and 12 were .84, .68, .83, .77, .83, .82, .82, .80, and .69, respectively.

Dimensions of Temperament Survey – Revised (DOTS-R)

Two versions of the Revised Dimensions of Temperament Survey (Windle & Lerner, 1986) were administered when participants were 14 and 16 years. Parents completed the DOTS-R Child and adolescents completed the DOTS-R Child (Self). The DOTS-R Child version is designed for the respondent to be the parent (describing the child), whereas the DOTS-R Child (Self) version is completed by the adolescents to describe their own temperament. Although differing slightly in the wording of instructions and items (pronouns vary to reflect the person who is providing the ratings, the adolescent or parent), both versions comprise

54 items and yield scores for nine temperament characteristics derived through factor analysis: activity-general, activity-sleep, approach, flexibility, positive mood, rhythmicity-sleep, rhythmicity-eating, rhythmicity-daily habits, and task orientation.

Slabach et al. (1991) described the internal consistency of the DOTS-R factors as highly satisfactory. Cronbach's alpha reliability coefficients for the nine dimensions ranged from .54 (rhythmicity-daily habits) to .81 (activity-sleep) in a sample of elementary students (Windle & Lerner, 1986). In our sample, coefficient alphas for each of the nine dimensions averaged across the two assessment ages ranged from .61 to .90 (median = .78) for adolescent self reports and from .50 to .91 (median = .81) for parent reports. For the activity-general, activity-sleep, approach, flexibility, positive mood, rhythmicity-sleep, rhythmicity-eating, rhythmicity-daily habits, and task orientation dimensions, coefficient alphas for adolescent self reports were .90, .88, .72, .70, .87, .66, .78, .61, and .83, respectively; for parent reports the corresponding values were .91, .89, .80, .79, .86, .62, .81, .50, and .83.

Measures Collected in Other Developmental Domains and the Environment

As described in chapter 1, the FLS methodology was conceptualized to address numerous themes throughout the entire course of investigation: temperament and personality, behavioral problems and competencies, intellectual development, academic functioning, and home and family environment. Tables 2.03 through 2.07 display the specific measures collected in each thematic strand during the infancy, toddler/preschool, middle childhood, and adolescent periods. Table 2.03 summarizes the temperament and personality measures employed in the FLS, which are examined in chapter 3. Chapter 4 addresses the relation between temperament and behavioral adjustment; specific measures assessed during each developmental era in the FLS are listed in Table 2.04. In chapter 5, the relation of temperament to intelligence is examined; Table 2.05 displays the intellectual measures employed. Chapter 6 addresses the relation between temperament and the variety of educational measures listed in Table 2.06. Detailed home visits and repeated assessments of family functioning were conducted during the FLS; in chapter 7 we present our findings based on the measures listed in Table 2.07. A detailed description of each of the measures employed in the FLS will be provided in the ensuing chapters.

Intercorrelations Among Temperament Dimension Scores

Although concerns have been raised about the factor structure and internal consistency coefficients of some dimensions on the Toddler Temperament Scale

Table 2.04. Behavior and Adjustment Measures Collected in the Fullerton Longitudinal Study

Developmental era	Measure	Age(s) administered (years)
Infancy	• None	—
Toddler/Preschool	• Eyberg Child Behavior Inventory	3.25
	• Preschool Behavior Questionnaire	3.5
	• Child Behavior Checklist	4, 5
Middle Childhood	• Child Behavior Checklist	6, 7, 8, 9, 10, 11, 12
	• Teacher Report Form	6, 7, 8, 9, 10, 11
Adolescence	• Child Behavior Checklist	13, 14, 15, 16, 17
	• Youth Self Report	17

and Behavior Style Questionnaire (Gibbs, Reeves, & Cunningham, 1987; Slabach et al., 1991) and the dimensionality of the NYLS model (Slabach et al., 1991), we opted to use the extant measures (that is, the TTS and BSQ) and all nine NYLS dimensions in our analyses. This decision was based on the desire to facilitate comparison of findings from the FLS with the existing literature based on these scales and to provide empirical data on the usefulness of the various dimensions in understanding development across the developmental eras examined herein (infancy, preschool, middle childhood, and adolescence).

Examination of the intercorrelations among dimensions on the temperament scales employed in the FLS showed that interdependence among some scales was quite high. These intercorrelations were conceptually feasible and to a certain extent reflected commonsense notions or experience about the nature of children's temperament. For example, some of the highest correlations were observed

Table 2.05. Intellectual Measures Collected in the Fullerton Longitudinal Study

Developmental era	Measure	Age(s) administered (years)
Infancy	• Bayley Scales of Infant Development	1, 1.5
Toddler/Preschool	• Bayley Scales of Infant Development	2
	• McCarthy Scales of Children's Abilities	2.5, 3, 3.5
	• Minnesota Child Development Inventory	2.5
	• Kaufman Assessment Battery for Children	5
	• Minnesota Preschool Inventory	5
Middle Childhood	• Wechsler Intelligence Scale for Children – Revised	6, 7, 8, 12
Adolescence	• Wechsler Intelligence Scale for Children – III	15
	• Wechsler Adult Intelligence Scale – Revised	17

Table 2.06.   School-Related Measures Collected in the Fullerton Longitudinal Study

Developmental era	Measure	Age(s) administered (years)
Infancy	• None	
Toddler/Preschool	• Kaufman Assessment Battery for Children Achievement Scale	5
Middle Childhood	• Wide Range Achievement Test-Revised	6
	• Teacher Report Form	6, 7, 8, 9, 10, 11
	• Woodcock-Johnson Psycho-Educational Battery	7, 8, 9, 10, 11, 12
	• Young Children's Academic Intrinsic Motivation Inventory	7, 8
	• Self Description Questionnaire – I	10
	• Children's Academic Intrinsic Motivation Inventory	9, 10
	• Self Description Questionnaire – II	12
Adolescence	• Woodcock-Johnson Psycho-Educational Battery	13, 14, 15, 16, 17
	• Self Description Questionnaire – II	14, 16
	• Children's Academic Intrinsic Motivation Inventory	13
	• Children's Academic Intrinsic Motivation Inventory – High School	16, 17

between the adaptability and negative mood dimensions. When children have a hard time adapting to changes in plans, they often object and pout to express their displeasure or frustration. Intercorrelations among the dimensions must be considered when interpreting findings, however. In correlation analyses, dimensions

Table 2.07.   Home Environment and Family Relationship Measures Collected in the Fullerton Longitudinal Study

Developmental era	Measure	Age(s) administered (years)
Infancy	• Home Observation for the Measurement of the Environment (HOME) – Infant version	1.25
Toddler/Preschool	• HOME – Preschool version	3.25
	• Family Environment Scale	3, 5
Middle Childhood	• HOME – Elementary School version	8
	• Family Environment Scale	7, 8, 10, 12
	• Self Description Questionnaire – I	10
	• Self Description Questionnaire – II	12
Adolescence	• Family Environment Scale	14, 16, 17
	• Self Description Questionnaire – II	14, 16
	• Parent-Child Relationship Inventory	15, 16

Table 2.08. Intercorrelations Among Temperament Dimensions on the Toddler Temperament Scale

Temperament dimension	Temperament dimension ($N = 112$)								
	1	2	3	4	5	6	7	8	9
1. Activity Level	1.00								
2. Rhythmicity[a]	.03	1.00							
3. Approach[a]	.04	.05	1.00						
4. Adaptability[a]	−.46***	.00	.38***	1.00					
5. Intensity	.45***	−.14	−.10	−.41***	1.00				
6. Negative Mood	.17	.00	−.44***	−.51***	.46***	1.00			
7. Persistence[a]	−.21*	.04	.11	.18	−.05	−.08	1.00		
8. Distractibility	.30**	−.21*	−.14	−.40***	.33*	.24*	−.19*	1.00	
9. Threshold	.07	−.14	.01	−.05	.14	.14	.18	.14	1.00

[a] Signs of coefficients were reversed to facilitate interpretation.
*$p < .05$. **$p < .01$. ***$p < .001$.

showing high intercorrelations will likely cluster together in predicting outcomes. In multiple correlation analyses, dimensions showing high intercorrelations are less likely to both enter as predictors of the same criterion; the variance explained by the second variable would likely already be explained by the first highly correlated dimension. Thus, we present the intercorrelations among dimensions in the ICQ, TTS, BSQ, MCTQ, and DOTS-R so that the intercorrelations among dimensions can be considered in interpreting the findings reported herein.

In a prior publication, we noted that significant correlations existed among some factors of the ICQ (Guerin & Gottfried, 1994b). Strongest intercorrelations were observed between the fussy/difficult/demanding factor and unadaptability ($r = .48$) and unsociable ($r = .48$). Additionally, resistance to control correlated significantly with unadaptable ($r = .41$). Hence, aspects of temperament that parents find challenging are not independent; infants who fuss and cry more also tend to be viewed as slower to adapt and less sociable. Likewise, those who are viewed as less manageable (higher in resistant to control) tend to be viewed as slower to adapt.

As shown in Table 2.08, numerous intercorrelations among TTS dimensions of similar magnitude to those observed among ICQ factors were evident. Negative mood related at moderate levels with approach, adaptability, and intensity, indicating that toddlers who were withdrawing (low approach), slower to adapt, and more intense tended to be viewed as negative in mood. Also in the moderate range, toddlers higher in activity tended to be rated as less adaptable and more intense.

Intercorrelations among the dimensions of the BSQ and MCTQ ranged to a higher magnitude than those in the TTS, however. As shown in Table 2.09, of particular note was the strong correlation of $r = -.69$ between adaptability and

Table 2.09. Intercorrelations Among Temperament Dimensions on the Behavioral Style Questionnaire

Temperament dimension	Temperament dimension ($N = 118$)								
	1	2	3	4	5	6	7	8	9
1. Activity Level	1.00								
2. Rhythmicity[a]	.05	1.00							
3. Approach[a]	.19*	.21*	1.00						
4. Adaptability[a]	−.30**	.25**	.53***	1.00					
5. Intensity	.34***	.16	−.06	−.14	1.00				
6. Negative Mood	.27**	−.13	−.45***	−.69***	.48***	1.00			
7. Persistence[a]	−.39***	.13	.16	.49***	−.02	−.33***	1.00		
8. Distractibility	.27**	.02	.00	−.12	.49***	.22*	−.12	1.00	
9. Threshold	.18*	.01	.03	−.04	.61***	.28**	−.08	.57***	1.00

[a] Signs of coefficients were reversed to facilitate interpretation.
*$p < .05$. **$p < .01$. ***$p < .001$.

negative mood on the BSQ. A correlation of even higher magnitude was observed between negative mood and adaptability on the MCTQ, as shown in Table 2.10. The high correlation between MCTQ persistence/attention span and predictability should also be noted. We expect that these dimensions will show similar patterns of correlation in subsequent Pearson correlation analyses, and this assumption will be examined as we evaluate the pattern of findings between temperament and behavior problems, intelligence, school functioning, and home/family environment in chapters 4 through 7, respectively.

Table 2.10. Intercorrelations Among Temperament Dimensions on the Middle Childhood Temperament Questionnaire

Temperament dimension	Temperament dimension ($N = 107$)								
	1	2	3	4	5	6	7	8	9
1. Activity Level	1.00								
2. Predictability[a]	−.39***	1.00							
3. Approach[a]	.09	.12	1.00						
4. Adaptability[a]	−.53***	.52***	.22*	1.00					
5. Intensity	.58***	−.34***	−.01	−.58***	1.00				
6. Negative Mood	.54***	−.51***	−.17	−.78***	.57***	1.00			
7. Persistence[a]	−.47***	.70***	−.17	.62***	−.30**	−.57***	1.00		
8. Distractibility	.34***	−.21*	−.01	−.29**	.26**	.30**	−.36***	1.00	
9. Threshold	.21*	−.12	−.02	−.30**	.36***	.28**	−.12	.57***	1.00

[a] Signs of coefficients were reversed to facilitate interpretation.
*$p < .05$. **$p < .01$. ***$p < .001$.

Table 2.11.   Intercorrelations Among Temperament Dimensions on the Revised Dimensions of Temperament Survey (Parent Informants Below Diagonal, $N = 105$; Adolescent Informants above Diagonal, $N = 111$)

Temperament dimension	Temperament dimension								
	1	2	3	4	5	6	7	8	9
1. Activity – General	1.00	.35***	.21*	−.25**	.18	−.10	−.24*	.00	−.20*
2. Activity – Sleep	.38***	1.00	−.10	−.31**	.01	−.19*	−.16	−.03	−.26**
3. Approach	.01	.02	1.00	.41***	.35***	.17	.23*	.19*	.33***
4. Flexibility	−.25*	.01	.48***	1.00	.16	.10	.15	.09	.19*
5. Positive Mood	−.09	.06	.35***	.31**	1.00	.13	.15	.10	.26**
6. Rhythmicity – Sleep	−.14	−.28**	.28**	.16	.21*	1.00	.54***	.47***	.29**
7. Rhythmicity – Eating	−.17	−.08	.27**	.23*	.21*	.62***	1.00	.41***	.37***
8. Rhythmicity – Habits	−.05	.13	.16	.11	.15	.50***	.63***	1.00	.31**
9. Task Orientation	−.49***	−.19	.22*	.18	.16	.27**	.16	.11	1.00

$^*p < .05.$ $^{**}p < .01.$ $^{***}p < .001.$

Intercorrelations among the dimensions of the DOTS-R were limited and focused. Table 2.11 displays intercorrelations among DOTS-R dimensions for parent respondents (below main diagonal) and adolescent informants (above main diagonal). As might be expected, the three scales assessing regularity of functioning were correlated at moderate magnitudes. These were the strongest intercorrelations evident across both informants.

Use of Extreme Temperament Groups

In chapter 8, we employ an extreme groups categorical approach to examine the developmental trajectories of three infant temperament groups formed within each temperament factor of the ICQ. Wachs (1991) noted that the comparison of qualitatively different groups has been used to study temperamentally easy versus temperamentally difficult children by researchers such as Gordon (1981), Maziade, et al. (1985), and Wachs and Gandour (1983). We agree with Bates (1989), who noted that the field has only begun the process of determining what the main effects of temperament are, particularly beyond the earliest years of development, and that further research on the main effects model is needed, especially to support the investigation of more complex person-by-environment interaction models that will eventually make possible effective clinical application of temperament research.

Our use of three groups based on quartile scores is quite deliberate. First and foremost, although there has been extensive focus in the extant literature on the developmental liability or risk associated with various temperamental characteristics (particularly difficult temperament), substantially less attention has been paid to temperament as a personal asset that may afford developmental advantage.

Although we have in mind most particularly the potential developmental advantages of possessing "easier" temperament, it is also possible that the development of children with more difficult temperament may be advantaged, for example, by evoking or eliciting attention or other resources from caregivers (Bates, 1989; DeVries, 1984; Maziade et al., 1985; Putnam et al., 2002). Lee and Bates (1985, p. 1320) used an extreme groups approach with three groups "as a way of testing the meaning of extreme scores" of infant difficultness.

Using the middle two quartiles as a baseline comparison group, in chapter 8 we investigated whether short and long-term outcomes of infants in the low and high extreme quartiles differed significantly from (1) each other and/or from (2) the baseline intermediate temperament group. We interpreted extreme temperament as representing a personal asset or developmental advantage when the outcomes of infants in an extreme (either low or high) temperament group were significantly superior compared to outcomes of infants in the intermediate temperament group. Likewise, extreme temperament was deigned a developmental liability when outcomes showed that infants in an extreme temperament group subsequently scored significantly poorer on outcomes compared to the intermediate group.

Figure 2.01 displays a sampling of the potential outcomes that may result from the longitudinal comparison of developmental outcomes of the three aforementioned infant temperament groups. In these graphs, low, intermediate, and high temperament groups are plotted along the abscissa. To facilitate this description of potential outcomes, we use the term "challenging temperament" to indicate any of the four ICQ factors (fussy/difficult/demanding, unadaptable, resistant to control, unsociable). Thus, by "low challenging infant temperament group" we mean infants scored in the lowest quartile on a given ICQ factor and thus showing dispositions parents find least challenging (such as easygoing/positive mood, quick adaptability, easy manageability, and sociable, respectively). Those scored in the highest quartile comprise the "high" challenging infant temperament group whose scores suggested they were, as infants, more fussy, slower to adapt/inflexible, hard to manage/resistant to control, and socially reticent. On the ordinate, the average developmental outcome is represented; for the purpose of this explication, assume that higher scores represent a more positive outcome (versus, for example, behavior problems, in which case lower scores would indicate a preferred outcome).

Graph (a) depicts findings that support the null hypothesis: no group differences in developmental outcome occur as a function of infant temperament group. Graphs (b) and (c) depict statistically significant differences among all three infant temperament groups (low, intermediate, and high), with (b) illustrating low challenging temperament as a developmental asset and high as a liability; (c) represents the opposite. Graph (d) illustrates an outcome in which infants high in challenging temperament subsequently showed compromised development compared to the intermediate and low infant temperament groups, which did not differ from each other; being in the low temperament group in scenario (d) would not be interpreted

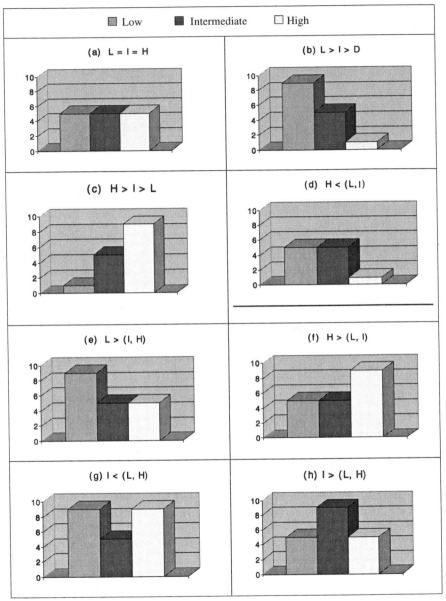

Figure 2.01. A sample of possible outcomes resulting from comparisons of the developmental outcomes of three groups differing on degree of challenging infant temperament (low, intermediate, and high).

as a developmental asset, given that the outcomes for that group were not different from those of the intermediate group, however, having high challenging temperament would be interpreted as evidence of a potential developmental liability. In Graph (e) evidence of low challenging temperament being an asset is shown, however, high challenging temperament would not be interpreted as a liability because the developmental outcome was not significantly poorer than the intermediate group. Graph (f) shows results that would support the notion that having infant temperament that parents rated as highly challenging facilitated subsequent development, although being lower than average on challenging temperament had no impact. Graphs (g) and (h) represent the possibility that having an extreme temperament, whether easy or challenging, impacts developmental outcome in a similar way; in situation (g), having extreme temperament facilitates the developmental outcome, and in situation (h), having extreme temperament impedes or negatively impacts developmental outcome.

When Pearson correlations are used to assess the degree of association between temperament characteristics and developmental outcomes measured as continuous variables, resulting coefficients may be attenuated, perhaps even zero, if the relation between the variables is not a linear relation, such as those depicted in graphs (d) through (h) in Figure 2.01. By employing three infant temperament groups, the detection of nonlinear relations is possible (Lee & Bates, 1985), and a more precise description of the impact of extreme temperament characteristics on development can be provided.

3

Consistency and Change in Temperament

"(Name) has always been a very happy easy going child. He maintains a positive outlook, does very well in school, and is looking forward to college. I not only love my son, I like him."
—Parent of Child #4, Easy Infant Temperament Group, Age 17

Issues Investigated

In this chapter, we address two central issues in the study of development: change and consistency. The longitudinal research methodology is best suited to address the nature of temperament with advancement in age during childhood, as it allows examination of both the consistency of the individual's rank position compared to others (i.e., stability) as well as change/consistency in the dimensions of temperament across individuals as a function of age (i.e., continuity). As noted in chapter 1, a particularly unique aspect of the Fullerton Longitudinal Study (FLS) is the frequency and continuity of temperament assessments; 10 assessment waves were conducted at designated and regular intervals from infancy (1.5 years) through adolescence (16 years). The temperament measures used during each developmental era and dimensions assessed on each measure are summarized in Table 3.01. These longitudinal data allowed us to examine the following questions about constancy and change in temperament measured via parent reports:

1. *Is there evidence of systematic change in average ratings of temperament across age?* In a prior publication, Guerin and Gottfried (1994a) noted significant changes in mean ratings of several dimensions of temperament assessed repeatedly across the preschool and middle childhood eras. Since that publication, additional temperament assessments have been conducted in the FLS as the children progressed through adolescence. More specifically, when participants were 14 and 16 years, a parent and the adolescent completed the Dimensions of Temperament Survey – Revised (DOTS-R);

Table 3.01.   Temperament Measures and Dimensions Used in the FLS during Each Developmental Era

Infancy	Toddler/preschool years	Middle childhood	Adolescence
ICQ	TTS, BSQ	MCTQ	DOTS-R
• Fussy/Difficult/Demanding	• Activity Level	• Activity Level	• Activity – General
• Unadaptable	• Rhythmicity	• Predictability	• Activity – Sleeping
• Resistant to Control	• Approach	• Approach	• Approach
• Unsociable	• Adaptability	• Adaptability	• Flexibility
	• Intensity	• Intensity	• Positive Mood
	• Negative Mood	• Negative Mood	• Rhythmicity – Sleep
	• Persistence	• Persistence	• Rhythmicity – Eating
	• Distractibility	• Distractibility	• Rhythmicity – Daily Habits
	• Threshold	• Threshold	• Task Orientation

Note: ICQ = Infant Characteristics Questionnaire; TTS = Toddler Temperament Scale; BSQ = Behavioral Style Questionnaire; MCTQ = Middle Childhood Temperament Questionnaire; DOTS-R = Dimensions of Temperament Survey – Revised.

both rated their perception of the temperament of the adolescent. Hence, we examined these additional data for evidence of age-related changes in temperament during adolescence.

2. *To what extent does temperament in infancy presage temperament during childhood and adolescence?* That is, if a baby displays a particular temperament, to what extent is that same behavioral style evident across childhood and adolescence? The earliest measure of temperament in the FLS was collected at 1.5 years with the administration of the Infant Characteristics Questionnaire (ICQ). Guerin and Gottfried (1994b) examined the degree of overlap between infant temperament and temperament during childhood using canonical correlation coefficients and reported moderate and significant canonical correlation coefficients throughout age 12. In this section, we continued these analyses by examining canonical correlation coefficients between the ICQ and temperament measured via the DOTS-R during adolescence. Additionally, canonical correlation analyses using the aggregated temperament variables on the Behavioral Style Questionnaire (BSQ) for preschool and Middle Childhood Temperament Questionnaire (MCTQ) for school-aged children are reported.

3. *Are there specific and unique temperamental sequelae of various aspects of infant difficult temperament?* In the third section of this chapter, the specific temperamental sequelae of all four factors of the ICQ (fussy/difficult/demanding, unadaptable, resistant to control, unsociability) are examined at age from age 2 through 16 to determine whether unique or

similar patterns of sequelae emerge for the four aspects of temperament assessed on the ICQ and also over which developmental eras, if any, specific temperamental sequelae are evident for the four ICQ factors.

4. *What is the pattern of stability across the nine dimensions of temperament across the preschool, school-age, and adolescent years?* In this section, we investigate the stability of the nine NYLS dimensions from ages 2 through adolescence, thus extending the findings of Guerin and Gottfried (1994a). Additionally, stability is examined across the preschool, middle childhood, and adolescence eras using the aggregated temperament scores derived from repeated measures on the BSQ, MCTQ, and DOTS-R, respectively.

5. *Does childhood temperament predict personality as the adolescents approach early adulthood?* In the final section, the evidence from the FLS regarding temperament – measured as early as 1.5 years – as a predictor of personality is examined. Following the approaches previously described to evaluate the stability of temperament, we began by examining Pearson correlation coefficients between the aforementioned temperament measures and the "Big Five" personality traits. Second, canonical correlation analyses between the set of temperament dimensions during each era and the set of personality factors on the NEO were conducted.

Description of Measures Used in the FLS

Temperament

The measures of temperament used during the course of the FLS were described in detail in chapter 2. To review briefly, standardized inventories were administered to one parent, almost exclusively the mother, when children were ages 1.5 (ICQ), 2 (TTS), 3, 3.5, 5 (BSQ), 8, 10, 12 (MCTQ), 14 and 16 years (DOTS-R). At ages 14 and 16, both adolescent self-reports and parent ratings of the temperament of the adolescent were collected. The temperament scales for each developmental era and their dimensions are displayed in Table 3.01.

Personality

The NEO Five-Factor Inventory (NEO-FFI; Costa & McCrae, 1989) was administered to adolescents at their 17-year assessment. This inventory is a shortened version of the standardized NEO Personality Inventory self-report measure designed to assess five dimensions of normal adult personality and is based on the five-factor model of personality. The dimensions measured are neuroticism (N), extroversion (E), openness to experience (O), agreeableness (A), and conscientiousness (C). The NEO-FFI consists of 60 items, 12 for each dimension. For each item, the adolescent indicates one of five answers (*strongly disagree, disagree, neutral, agree, strongly agree*). As no cut-off points delineating the presence or absence of these traits exist, a dimensional interpretation of the scores is used; high scores indicate higher levels of the labeled characteristic.

Costa and McCrae (1985) described the five NEO factors as follows. Neuroticism refers to the adjustment of individuals. Those who score high on this scale are described as worrying, nervous, and emotional, whereas those scoring low are calm, relaxed, and unemotional. Extraversion assesses the quantity/intensity of interpersonal attraction. High scorers are sociable, active, and person-oriented; low scorers are reserved, aloof, and task-oriented. Openness refers to the degree to which individuals seek out and appreciate a variety of experiences or tolerate unfamiliarity. Those scoring high on this trait are described as curious, imaginative, and have broad interests; low scorers are conventional and have narrow interests. Agreeableness assesses whether one is characterized by compassion versus antagonism in thoughts, feelings, and behaviors. High scorers are typified as good-natured, helpful, forgiving, and gullible, and low scorers as suspicious, uncooperative, cynical, and irritable. Finally, Costa and McCrae described conscientiousness as reflecting the individual's degree of organization, persistence, and motivation in goal-directed behavior. High scores on conscientiousness indicate individuals who are more organized and hard-working; low scores indicate laziness and aimlessness.

NEO-FFI scores demonstrate high correlations with scores based on the longer version, the NEO Personality Inventory; according to Costa and McCrae (1989), correlations ranged from .75 for conscientiousness to .89 for neuroticism. Coefficient alphas assessing internal consistency of the NEO-FFI scales based on the FLS data are .89, .79, .76, .74, and .84 for the N, E, O, A, and C scales, respectively. All data analyses were based on NEO *T* scores.

Findings and Discussion

Developmental Changes in Parent Ratings of Children's Temperament

Preschool and Middle Childhood

Developmental changes in children's temperament within the preschool and middle childhood eras were previously examined using data from the FLS (Guerin & Gottfried, 1994a). To summarize, the BSQ and MCTQ were each administered three times during the FLS in the preschool and middle childhood developmental eras, respectively; the dimension averages on these scales were examined using a multivariate analysis of variance (MANOVA) with age as a within-subjects variable and gender as a between-subjects variable. The results revealed that parents described children's temperament as becoming more biologically regular or predictable, less intense, more positive in mood, more persistent, and more reactive with increasing age during the preschool period (ages 3, 3.5, and 5) (for more detail, interested readers are referred to Table 1, Guerin & Gottfried, 1994a). On the MCTQ, Guerin and Gottfried (1994a) reported that four dimensions showed age-related changes in mean ratings: activity, approach/withdrawal, intensity, and threshold. Children were perceived as less active, more approaching, less intense, and less reactive with increasing age from 8 to 12 years. Hence, parent perceptions of their children's temperament revealed age-related significant changes in mean levels on seven of the nine dimensions during the preschool or middle childhood years: biological rhythmicity, mood, persistence, reactivity (threshold), approach, intensity, and activity level. Changes in group averages reflect developmental shifts in the direction of greater attentional, behavioral, and emotional self-regulation with increasing age during childhood.

Adolescence

To check for developmentally-related changes during adolescence on the DOTS-R, a doubly multivariate analysis of variance (Sex X Age X Temperament Dimension) was conducted on the parent ratings and on the adolescent self-reports on the DOTS-R. Analyses of the parent ratings showed no overall sex differences, $F(9, 80) = 1.19, p > .05$; nor was there evidence of significant Gender X Age interactions, $F(9,80) = 1.23, p > .05$. Finally, there was no evidence of age-related changes in mean temperament ratings of their adolescents' temperament from 14 to 16 years in the parent ratings, $F(9,80) = 1.36, p > .05$. Similar overall results were obtained when adolescent self-reports on the DOTS-R were examined: $F(9, 97) = 1.19, p > .05$ (gender differences), $F(9, 97) = 0.69, p > .05$ (Gender X Age interaction), and $F(9, 97) = 1.76, p > .05$ (age differences). Mean temperament ratings given by parents and adolescents for the nine DOTS-R dimensions are displayed in Table 3.02, along with univariate F test results for age-related changes. Univariate tests also reveal little evidence of age-related changes in temperament during adolescence; only 1 of 18 tests was significant.

Hence, there is little evidence of age or gender differences in temperament during the mid-adolescent period, especially when considered with respect to the age differences detected previously on the BSQ (3, 3.5, and 5 years) and the MCTQ (8, 10, and 12 years). As with the gender comparisons previously reported regarding FLS analyses of the ICQ, TTS, BSQ, and MCTQ (Guerin & Gottfried, 1994a, 1994b), these findings are in accord with Chess and Thomas's assessment: "Overall, the findings from the NYLS and from other centers abroad are consistent in the absence of striking sex differences in temperament" (1984, p. 94). These findings, however, do not preclude the possibility that temperament may differ in

Table 3.02. Average Temperament Ratings at 14 and 16 Years and Statistical Test Results for Age-Related Mean Changes on the Dimensions of Temperament Survey (Revised) for Parent and Adolescent Informants

	Parent ($N = 90$)			Adolescent ($N = 107$)		
	14	16	F_{Age}	14	16	F_{Age}
Activity-General	1.92	1.92	0.00	2.63	2.69	0.92
Activity-Sleeping	2.25	2.23	0.10	2.82	2.68	2.42
Approach	3.07	3.08	0.01	2.92	2.93	0.11
Flexibility	3.33	3.40	1.96	3.04	2.98	1.22
Positive Mood	3.60	3.52	3.75	3.50	3.56	1.41
Rhythmicity-Sleeping	2.93	2.92	0.03	2.51	2.50	0.00
Rhythmicity-Eating	3.44	3.34	3.90	2.86	2.89	0.22
Rhythmicity-Daily Habits	2.88	2.90	0.14	2.41	2.60	10.11*
Task Orientation	2.79	2.79	0.00	2.76	2.69	1.35

*$p < .05$.

its functional significance for boys versus girls. That is, individual differences in temperament may differentially moderate the relation observed between variables for boys versus girls. Putnam et al. (2002), for example, review several studies showing gender-by-temperament interactions in parenting behavior. Although conflicting findings are not uncommon, Putnam et al. characterized the preponderance of findings as showing that parents are less accepting of irritability and negative affect in girls than boys. Thus, although gender differences in temperament variables are not striking, child gender may certainly moderate the impact of the child's temperament on the behavior of others. Putnam et al. suggest that, in the case of parenting behavior, differential beliefs held by parents about what constitute desirable behavioral styles for girls versus boys may explain why child temperament impacts parenting behaviors differently depending on child gender.

Stability of Temperament from Infancy Through Adolescence

Aspects of temperament that parents find challenging during the infancy period were measured using the ICQ at 1.5 years. The ICQ assesses four aspects of difficult temperament: fussy/difficult/demanding, unadaptability, resistance to control, and unsociability. As summarized in Table 3.01, temperament measures administered subsequently during the preschool, middle childhood, and adolescence periods yielded scores for several dimensions of temperament, including either all nine NYLS dimensions (TTS, BSQ, MCTQ) or a subset of them (DOTS-R).

To examine the extent to which mothers' reports of challenging temperament during infancy portended subsequent temperament, we conducted two sets of analyses. First, canonical correlation analyses were conducted to assess the degree of overlap among the four ICQ factors and the subsequent sets of temperament variables: the nine dimensions of the TTS, BSQ, MCTQ, and DOTS-R, in turn. The canonical correlation analysis produces a linear combination of each set of variables so as to maximize the correlation between the two predicted values. More specifically, the canonical correlation coefficient (r_c) represents the degree of correspondence between the four factors of the infant difficultness on the ICQ and the nine dimensions of the TTS, BSQ, MCTQ, and the DOTS-R, respectively. Given that there was a significant degree of overlap among the two sets of temperament measures during each developmental era, a second set of analyses using bivariate correlation coefficients was conducted to examine the specific temperamental sequelae the four ICQ factors during childhood and adolescence.

With respect to the canonical correlation analyses, parent perceptions of temperament showed significant cross-time relations from infancy through adolescence, with magnitudes in the moderate range. The results of canonical correlation analyses computed between the set of ICQ factors and the nine NYLS dimensions of the TTS (2 years), BSQ (3–5 years) and the MCTQ (8–12 years) are displayed in Table 3.03; results for the DOTS-R parent reports (14–16 years) are shown in Table 3.04. In each table, the zero-order correlations or loadings between the variables and the canonical variates, canonical correlation coefficients, and squared canonical correlations are listed.

As shown in Tables 3.03 and 3.04, canonical correlation coefficients between infant difficult temperament measured at 1.5 years and temperament assessed during the toddler, preschool, middle childhood, and adolescent years were in the moderately high range (r_c's = .61 to .64) across all developmental eras. Given that these coefficients are derived from analyses involving four different temperament questionnaires administered across periods spanning over 15 years, these results suggest an impressive degree of consistency. At all ages, the ICQ fussy/difficult/demanding factor loaded most heavily on the variate representing the four ICQ factors (correlations with variates ranged from .87 to .98 for this factor), as shown in the top portion of Tables 3.03 and 3.04. As shown in the middle portion of Table 3.03, among the variables during the childhood eras loading most heavily on NYLS variate were negative mood (TTS, BSQ, MCTQ), adaptability (BSQ, MCTQ), intensity (TTS), and activity level (MCTQ). As shown in Table 3.04, general activity level loaded most strongly in forming the DOTS-R variate followed by flexibility, rhythmicity, and task orientation.

These canonical correlation analyses indicated a substantial degree of overlap between parental perceptions of their children's temperament in infancy and each developmental era through adolescence. Challenging infant temperament, most strongly defined by fussy/difficult/demanding temperament, correlated at a consistently moderate level with temperament during the toddler, preschool, middle childhood, and adolescent years. The variates representing temperament

Table 3.03.   Results of Canonical Correlation Analysis between Infant and Childhood Temperament: Zero-Order Correlations of Variables and Variates, Canonical Correlations, and Squared Correlation Coefficients

	Temperament measure		
	TTS (N = 110)	BSQ (N = 114)	MCTQ (N = 103)
ICQ Set (Infancy)			
Fussy/Difficult/Demanding	.87	.93	.98
Unadaptable	.57	.65	.55
Resistant to Control	.73	.65	.59
Unsociable			
Childhood Set			
Rhythmicity[a]	.33	.37	.48
Approach	.53	.61	.34
Adaptability	.49	.81	.92
Intensity	.60	.38	.64
Negative Mood	.69	.74	.79
Activity Level	.52	.54	.77
Persistence		.37	.61
Distractibility	.35		.37
Threshold			.38
Canonical r	.64***	.64***	.61***
Squared canonical r	.42	.41	.37

Note: Loadings less than .30 in magnitude are not shown. TTS = Toddler Temperament Scale, BSQ = Behavioral Style Questionnaire, MCTQ = Middle Childhood Temperament Questionnaire.
[a] Biological rhythmicity dimension of TTS and BSQ replaced by the dimension of predictability/quality of organization on the MCTQ.
*** $p < .001$.

across the childhood and adolescent period were defined most strongly by the dimensions of adaptability/flexibility, negative mood, and activity level, although at least seven of the nine dimensions showed loadings of .30 or higher in every analysis. Canonical correlation coefficients showed no diminution with increasing age, ranging from .61 to .64, even though the age spans between assessments ranged from 6 months for the TTS to approximately 15 years for the DOTS-R.

In summary, these canonical correlation analyses revealed that parent reports of their children's characteristic behavioral style show a moderate, indeed impressive, degree of stability from infancy through adolescence. The amount of shared variance between maternal ratings on the ICQ at 1.5 years and temperament ratings during the toddler, preschool, middle childhood, and adolescent eras ranged from 37 to 42 percent. Although not indelible, parent perceptions of their children's temperament at least from 1.5 years reveal a core behavioral style that persists across the childhood and adolescence eras.

**Table 3.04. Results of Canonical Correlation
Analysis between Infant and Adolescent
Temperament: Zero-Order Correlations
of Variables and Variates, Canonical
Correlations, and Squared Correlation
Coefficients ($N = 99$)**

ICQ Set (Infancy)	
Fussy/Difficult/Demanding	.90
Unadaptable	.46
Resistant to Control	.61
Unsociable	.47
DOTS-R Set (Adolescence)	
Activity – General	.81
Activity – Sleeping	
Approach	−.30
Flexibility	−.51
Positive Mood	−.44
Rhythmicity – Sleeping	−.40
Rhythmicity – Eating	−.51
Rhythmicity – Daily Habits	−.52
Task Orientation	−.49
Canonical r	.63***
Squared canonical r	.40

Note: Loadings less than .30 in magnitude are not shown. DOTS-R =
Revised Dimensions of Temperament Scale.
***$p < .001$.

Specific Sequelae of Aspects of Infant Temperament that Parents Find Challenging

The next set of analyses was conducted to determine whether or not there were unique temperamental sequelae of the four aspects of infant temperament assessed by the ICQ (fussy/difficult/demanding, unadaptability, resistance to control, and unsociability). In the Thomas and Chess model, the "difficult" temperament constellation is defined by five of the nine dimensions, including biological irregularity, withdrawal or low approach, slow adaptability, high intensity, and negative mood (Thomas et al., 1968). In the next section, we examined the sequelae of all four aspects of challenging temperament assessed by the ICQ to ascertain the overlap of these two conceptualizations of difficult temperament.

There was evidence of unique patterns of temperamental sequelae for the four ICQ factors that persist across the toddler, preschool, middle childhood, and adolescent developmental eras. Table 3.05 displays Pearson correlation coefficients between the specific aspects of challenging infant temperament on the ICQ and the

Table 3.05. Pearson Correlation Coefficients between Infant Characteristics Questionnaire Factors and Temperament Dimensions from Age 2 Years through Middle Childhood

Infant characteristics questionnaire	Temperament dimension								
	Activity level	Rhythm[a]	Approach[a]	Adapt[a]	Intensity	Neg mood	Persist[a]	Distract	Threshold
Toddler temperament scale (N = 110)									
Fussy/Difficult	.28**	−.22*	−.29**	−.25**	.33***	.43***	−.16	.19*	.02
Unadaptable	.03	−.07	−.46***	−.09	.11	.31***	−.09	−.03	.10
Resistant to Control	.39***	−.16	−.12	−.32***	.35***	.31***	−.02	.23*	.03
Unsociable	−.08	.01	−.14	.06	−.11	.09	−.29**	−.14	−.24*
Behavioral style questionnaire (N = 114)									
Fussy/Difficult	.31**	−.23*	−.37***	−.49***	.20*	.44***	−.21*	.15	.11
Unadaptable	.05	−.22*	−.41***	−.33***	.10	.35***	−.14	.10	.02
Resistant to Control	.39***	−.09	−.10	−.35***	.21*	.28**	−.23*	.11	.13
Unsociable	−.14	−.19*	−.26**	−.18	−.20*	.16	−.18	−.10	−.26**
Middle childhood temperament questionnaire (N = 103)									
Fussy/Difficult	.46***	−.28**	−.19	−.55***	.37***	.46***	−.37***	.23*	.25*
Unadaptable	.14	−.13	−.27**	−.32**	.22*	.26**	−.12	.09	.19
Resistant to Control	.40***	−.23*	−.06	−.29**	.26**	.34***	−.24*	.11	.01
Unsociable	−.02	−.07	−.17	−.22*	.13	.08	−.09	.02	.00

[a]Signs of coefficients were reversed to facilitate interpretation.
*$p < .05$. **$p < .01$. ***$p < .001$.

Table 3.06. Pearson Correlation Coefficients between Infant Characteristics Questionnaire Factors and Dimensions of Adolescent Temperament (Parent Report)

Infant characteristics questionnaire	Revised dimensions of temperament survey ($N = 99$)								
	Activity – general	Activity – sleeping	App	Flex	Positive mood	Rhythm-sleeping	Rhythm-eating	Rhythm-habits	Task orient
Fussy/Difficult	.48***	.05	−.11	−.27**	−.24*	−.23*	−.27**	−.29**	−.24*
Unadaptable	.18	.01	−.16	−.36***	−.21*	−.07	−.17	−.13	.03
Resistant to Control	.46***	.26**	−.05	−.14	−.08	−.20*	−.18	−.08	−.28**
Unsociable	.08	−.17	−.27**	−.30**	−.25*	−.06	−.21*	−.26**	−.08

*$p < .05$. **$p < .01$. ***$p < .001$.

dimensions of temperament assessed by the TTS, BSQ, and MCTQ in successive panels, respectively; results for the DOTS-R are displayed in Table 3.06.

Examining first the specific temperamental sequelae of the fussy/difficult/ demanding aspect of infant temperament, significant correlations reaching moderate magnitudes overlap considerably with the difficult temperament cluster conceptualized by Thomas et al.: babies rated as challenging by parents on this dimension were subsequently rated during the toddler and preschool years as less regular in terms of biological functioning, withdrawing rather than approaching to novel experiences, slower to adapt to changes in their environment, more intense in their reactions, and more negative in mood. Slow adaptability and negative mood were particularly prominent consequences that show significant correlations with the fussy/difficult/demanding factor at every development era from toddlerhood through adolescence (as indicated by correlations showing less flexibility and less positive mood on the DOTS-R). Biological irregularity was another temperamental consequence of fussy/difficult/demanding temperament; although correlations across the developmental eras were in the low range, they were significant at every age period, including the adolescent period on all three dimensions of rhythmicity (eating, sleeping, and daily habits). Although intensity is not measured on the DOTS-R during adolescence, it was a significant correlate of fussy/difficult/demanding infant temperament during the toddler, preschool, and middle childhood years.

Both the Bates and Thomas et al. conceptualizations of difficult temperament are derived from observations focusing primarily on infant temperament. Strelau (1998) suggested that the pattern of characteristics comprising difficult temperament may be age-specific. Although the temperamental sequelae of the ICQ fussy/difficult/demanding factor corresponded closely to the difficult cluster described by Thomas et al., examining the temperamental sequelae across the developmental eras revealed three patterns that diverged from their conceptualization. First, approach/withdrawal was not a consistent consequent. With increasing age, the dimension of approach/withdrawal ceased to correlate with the ICQ fussy/difficult/demanding factor, as can be seen in Table 3.05 during the middle childhood years and on Table 3.06 during adolescence. This may be an example of an age-related change in difficult temperament. Possible explanations for age-related changes in difficult temperament may be postulated. For example, as infants accrue an expanding set of experiences with the environment, their exposure to novel experiences may occur less frequently as more things become familiar. Children may also gain more control over the types of experiences they have and avoid novelty, for example, by choosing activities with which they are familiar. Alternatively, they may acquire skills or learn strategies to facilitate their overt response to, if not their subjective experience of, novelty. Hence, the lack of correlation with approach during middle childhood and adolescence may represent successful adaptation or accommodation to novelty in the environment.

A second interesting pattern of results was that activity level consistently and at moderate magnitude correlated with the ICQ fussy/difficult/demanding factor. As shown in Tables 3.05 and 3.06, a tendency toward higher levels of activity, with correlations of .28, .31, .46, and .48 across four different measures of temperament from 2 years through adolescence, was evident. This pattern has been noted in another large longitudinal study. Canadian researchers reported that activity level also clustered with other dimensions of the NYLS difficult temperament in their longitudinal study in middle childhood (Maziade, Boutin, Cote, & Thivierge, 1986c). Additionally, Buss (1991, p. 59) commented that highly active children may cause problems for adults and thus be considered "difficult children." Interestingly, Carey and McDevitt (1995) found that high activity level was one of the characteristics that parents found hardest to manage in children aged 1 through 12 years.

Finally, at every age there is a consistent, albeit low, correlation between infant fussy/difficult/demanding temperament and either low persistence/attention span, high distractibility, or both of these dimensions. Infants rated as more fussy/difficult/demanding were subsequently more distractible and/or shorter in persistence/attention span, and this trend was more evident during middle childhood. Parents may be particularly sensitive to variations in persistence/attention span during the middle childhood years as the child must adjust to demands and expectations required to negotiate successfully the formal education process.

Next, we examined the temperamental consequences of the second factor of the ICQ, unadaptability. This aspect of challenging infant temperament also portended higher ratings of negative mood at every developmental era from toddlerhood through adolescence (see less positive mood on the DOTS-R, Table 3.06). A second temperamental consequence of slow infant adaptability was a tendency to withdraw from new experiences during the early and middle childhood eras (indicated by inverse correlations with approach on Table 3.05). A third and final temperamental sequela to slow adaptability during infancy was slower adaptability during the preschool, middle childhood, and adolescent (see negative correlation with flexibility in Table 3.06) eras. Hence, infants higher on this factor subsequently showed three of the same sequelae as those scoring higher on the fussy/difficult/demanding factor (viz., negative mood, withdrawal, slower adaptability), but did not evidence tendencies toward intensity, biological irregularity, higher activity level, or shorter attention span/persistence as they developed.

Moving now to the sequelae of resistance to control during infancy, one temperamental outcome clearly emerged as the strongest and most consistent correlate: activity level. Across developmental eras from toddlerhood to adolescence investigated in the FLS, the magnitude of the correlation coefficient did not diminish, ranging from .39 on the TTS (Table 3.05) to .46 on the DOTS-R (Table 3.06). Across childhood, infants who were more resistant to control also tended to be rated as slower to adapt and more negative in mood. Albeit at low magnitudes, this aspect of infant temperament was accompanied by shorter attention span/persistence during childhood and adolescence.

The final ICQ factor, unsociability, failed to show a consistent pattern of temperamental sequelae. Across the four developmental eras examined, correlations showed little specificity/differentiation across the dimensions of temperament assessed, nor was there replication of trends across time.

To sum up results of the bivariate correlation analyses, the fussy/difficult/demanding factor of the ICQ showed a strong degree of overlap with the difficult temperament cluster proposed by Thomas, Chess, and colleagues over four decades ago. Infants viewed as more fussy/difficult/demanding at 1.5 years showed a consistent pattern of temperament that persisted almost intact throughout at least adolescence. They tended toward temperament characterized by more negative mood, slower adaptability to change, more irregularity in biological rhythms, and also higher levels of activity. Their childhoods were marked by more intense reactions and withdrawal tendencies when faced with new people, places, and experiences. Persistence/attention span was also shorter, particularly during middle childhood but also during other developmental eras. ICQ unadaptability portended more challenging temperament patterns across development, marked particularly by negative mood, a tendency to withdraw when faced with novelty, and slower adaptability. Resistance to control also presaged long-term challenging behavioral style marked most strongly by higher levels of activity and shorter persistence/attention span through adolescence.

What these three aspects of challenging infant temperament with long-lasting temperamental consequences share, at virtually every developmental era, is a tendency toward negative mood, which Bates (1980, 1989) considered as the core of difficult temperament. The significance of these early patterns of temperament and their temperamental sequelae will be explored in chapters 4 through 7, where we examine the behavioral/emotional adjustment, intellectual development, academic experiences, and home/family functioning of our population as a function of temperament. In chapter 8, we analyze the home/family environment and developmental outcomes across childhood and adolescence associated with low and high extreme group membership on these aspects of challenging infant temperament. One goal of the analyses in chapter 8 is to determine the extent to which sequelae of challenging infant temperament support the notion that difficult temperament is a developmental liability, that easy temperament is a developmental asset, or that both of these mechanisms may be operating.

Considering both the canonical and Pearson correlation analyses, evidence from the FLS suggests that parents form a stable impression of their children's behavioral style as early as 1.5 years, and this impression continues through at least mid-adolescence. None of the four aspects of difficult temperament assessed by the ICQ showed a perfect correspondence to Thomas and Chess's difficult temperament constellation. However, it is clear that the ICQ, particularly the fussy/difficult/demanding factor, assesses aspects of behavioral style that overlap with this construct. Negative mood and slow adaptability were salient sequelae of at least three of the four ICQ factors. In subsequent chapters, the long-term behavioral intellectual, academic, and social consequents of challenging infant temperaments are examined.

Stability of Specific Temperament Dimensions from Childhood through Adolescence

Toddler Years Onward

Parent reports of the nine NYLS temperament traits were assessed throughout childhood using the family of scales developed by Carey and colleagues: the TTS, BSQ, and MCTQ. Pearson correlation coefficients assessing stability of dimensions of children's temperament from age 2 throughout the preschool and middle childhood years are displayed in Table 3.07. Three basic patterns were revealed. First, activity level, approach/withdrawal, intensity, and distractibility showed moderate stability through the preschool and middle childhood years. Stability coefficients were moderate (e.g., .40 or higher) magnitudes, ranging to .55 on both the BSQ and MCTQ. Second, the dimensions of rhythmicity-predictability, negative mood, and threshold showed significant correlations from age 2, but correlations were of lower magnitude on the MCTQ. Finally, adaptability and persistence showed low but significant stability from the age 2 to the preschool years, but not to middle childhood.

Although the DOTS-R does not measure all nine NYLS dimensions, several overlap conceptually. In addition to the dimensions bearing the same labels, (activity, rhythmicity, and approach), these include the following pairs: TTS persistence and DOTS-R task orientation, TTS adaptability and DOTS-R flexibility, and finally,

Table 3.07.   Cross-Time Stability of Toddler
Temperament: Pearson Correlation Coefficients
between Temperament at Age 2 and Dimensions
of the Behavioral Style Questionnaire and Middle
Childhood Temperament Questionnaire

Toddler temperament scale	BSQ ($N = 107$)	MCTQ ($N = 98$)
Activity Level	.55***	.49***
Rhythmicity/Predictability[a,b]	.44***	.22*
Approach[a]	.49***	.50***
Adaptability[a]	.30**	.04
Intensity	.55***	.46***
Negative Mood	.44***	.21*
Persistence[a]	.51***	.19
Distractibility	.46***	.41***
Threshold	.38***	.28**

[a] Signs of coefficients were reversed to facilitate interpretation.
[b] Biological Rhythmicity dimension of BSQ replaced by the dimension
of Predictability/Quality of Organization on MCTQ.
*$p < .05$. **$p < .01$. ***$p < .001$.

TTS negative mood and DOTS-R positive mood. Bivariate correlation coefficients between parent ratings on the TTS and DOTS-R provided evidence of significant cross-time stability for four of these six dimensions from toddlerhood through adolescence.

Most impressive was the correlation between TTS and DOTS-R general activity level, $r = .41, p < .001$. In conjunction with the correlations observed between the toddler and childhood years (r's = .55 and .49 with the BSQ and MCTQ, respectively), these data illustrated a consistent and moderate degree of cross-time stability for activity level from age 2 through 16 years. These findings are in accord with and extend the conclusions of Hubert et al. (1982) and Slabach et al. (1991); after an extensive review of the psychometric properties of temperament questionnaires, they concluded that the evidence showed that activity level was among the most stable of temperament dimensions. Showing discriminant validity, no other dimensions of temperament on the DOTS-R correlated with TTS activity level.

Biological rhythmicity at 2 years was related to all three aspects of rhythmicity assessed on the DOTS-R: sleeping ($r = .38, p < .001$), eating ($r = .35, p < .001$), and daily habits ($r = .28, p < .01$). Again, in conjunction with the data reported in Table 3.07, these bivariate correlation analyses indicated that parent perceptions of children's biological regularity (BSQ, DOTS-R) and the conceptually-related predictability/organization (MCTQ; Hegvik et al., 1982) were stable across childhood and adolescence. Without information about daily patterns from additional family

members, however, it is difficult to ascertain if these significant cross-time correlations reflect more about the child's temperament or the regularity/predictability
of the family's/parents' routines. However, parent ratings of rhythmicity on the
DOTS-R were, as observed with activity level, quite specific in that these were
the only dimensions of the DOTS-R to show significant correlations with TTS
rhythmicity.

The third DOTS-R dimension showing significant stability with ratings on
the TTS at age 2 was approach, ($r = .31, p < .01$). Thus, along with the significant correlations of .49 (BSQ) and .50 (MCTQ), these results indicate that the
tendency to approach or withdraw from new people, places, experiences, et cetera,
is moderately stable from age 2 through adolescence. These results demonstrate
that toddler's initial reaction to approach or withdraw from novelty showed notable
stability, especially given that multiple measures of temperament spanning over a
decade of development were employed.

Although not as striking in magnitude, the dimension of persistence/attention
span showed significant stability from age 2 through early childhood, middle
childhood (see Table 3.07), and adolescence, where the correlation with task orientation was observed to be .22, ($p < .05$). Although quite low in magnitude,
the finding of any cross-time pattern over these ages is particularly noteworthy; the types of tasks available for parents to observe the toddler's persistence/
attention span are quite different from those used once children enter school,
when these behaviors may involve more independent and/or academic pursuits
rather than interactions with toys or self-help activities. The remaining two dimensions, DOTS-R flexibility and positive mood, did not show significant cross-time
stability.

Preschool Years Onward

Looking forward from the preschool years, ages 3 to 5, to middle childhood
and adolescence revealed even stronger stability coefficients. Examining correlation coefficients between the temperament dimensions aggregated across age on
the BSQ, MCTQ, and DOTS-R, we observed that, almost without exception, every
coefficient was significant and moderate to high in magnitude. Pearson correlation
coefficients between ratings averaged across the preschool years on the BSQ and
those averaged across the middle childhood years on the MCTQ ranged from .26
to .69. The strongest cross-time correlation on these scales was for the dimension
of approach ($r = .69$), followed by the dimensions of adaptability ($r = .58$), activity level ($r = .54$), distractibility ($r = .54$), negative mood ($r = .48$), persistence
($r = .44$), threshold ($r = .42$), and intensity ($r = .37$, all p's $< .001$). The correlation of lowest magnitude was between BSQ rhythmicity and MCTQ predictabil-
ity/quality of organization, $r = .26, p < .01$. The stability of this dimension may

Table 3.08. **Pearson Correlation Coefficients between Preschool-Age Temperament on the Behavioral Style Questionnaire and Adolescent Temperament on the Revised Dimensions of Temperament Survey (Parent Report)**

Behavioral style questionnaire	Revised dimensions of temperament survey ($N = 102$)								
	Activity – general	Activity – sleeping	Approach	Flex	Positive mood	Rhythm – sleep	Rhythm – eating	Rhythm – habits	Task orient
Activity Level	.46***	.01	.17	−.04	.05	.02	−.05	.04	−.29**
Rhythmicity[a]	−.13	−.17	.13	.05	.00	.37***	.42***	.44***	.22*
Approach[a]	−.11	.07	.46***	.28**	.07	.17	.12	.14	.14
Adaptability[a]	−.37***	.01	.31**	.36***	.09	.25*	.24*	.14	.23*
Intensity	.32**	.16	.03	−.24*	.13	−.02	.00	.09	.03
Negative Mood	.37***	.04	−.28**	−.39***	−.03	−.27**	−.23*	−.14	−.11
Persistence[a]	−.29**	.02	.10	.13	−.02	.04	.14	.08	.33**
Distractibility	.11	.01	.04	−.08	.04	.02	.09	.11	−.07
Threshold	.21*	.19	.13	−.08	.08	.07	.01	.10	.09

[a] Signs of coefficients were reversed to facilitate interpretation.
*$p < .05$. **$p < .01$. ***$p < .001$.

be attenuated because, according to Hegvik et al. (1982), measures during the toddle and preschool years compared to that during middle childhood differ in focus between biological and social predictability.

During the span from preschool through adolescence, five of the six temperament dimensions assessed on both the BSQ and DOTS-R showed significant cross-time stability; correlation coefficients are displayed in Table 3.08. Parent reports of activity level and approach showed moderate stability (both r's $= .46$); correlations for rhythmicity/predictability, adaptability/flexibility, and persistence/task orientation were all statistically significant, ranging from .33 to .44 across all ages. As with the TTS and DOTS-R, the correlation between BSQ negative mood and DOTS-R positive mood was not significant. The pattern of significant correlations between the dimensions of the BSQ and DOTS-R did not show the same strength of differentiation nor specificity as was observed between the TTS and DOTS-R, where correlations tended to be significant only among dimensions that were conceptually similar.

Middle Childhood Years Onward

Finally, as shown in Table 3.09, examination of the correlations between the MCTQ and the DOTS-R revealed impressive cross-time correlation coefficients for several of the dimensions measured by both scales and significant coefficients for all six dimensions. Particularly striking were the cross-time correlation

Table 3.09.   Pearson Correlation Coefficients between Middle Childhood
Temperament Questionnaire and Adolescent Temperament on the Revised
Dimensions of Temperament Survey (Parent Report)

Middle childhood temperament questionnaire	Revised dimensions of temperament survey ($N = 99$)								
	Activity-general	Activity-sleep	Approach	Flexibility	Positive mood	Rhythm-sleep	Rhythm-eating	Rhythm-habits	Task orient
Activity Level	.74***	.27**	.11	−.14	−.08	−.16	−.18	.00	−.43***
Predictability[a]	−.32**	−.05	.08	.24*	.14	.34**	.40***	.25*	.39***
Approach[a]	−.01	.16	.68***	.36***	.15	.16	.14	.09	.08
Adaptability[a]	−.49***	.00	.18	.53***	.24*	.18	.26**	.20	.35***
Intensity	.48***	.14	−.01	−.26*	.04	−.05	−.15	−.04	−.24*
Negative Mood	.50***	.11	−.15	−.35***	−.21*	−.23*	−.19	−.05	−.28**
Persistence[a]	−.47***	−.03	.15	.30**	.26**	.23*	.30**	.13	.59***
Distractibility	.34***	.08	.07	−.15	.06	.00	−.12	.04	−.31*
Threshold	.18	−.09	.06	−.23*	.00	.09	−.06	−.07	−.05

[a] Signs of coefficients were reversed to facilitate interpretation.
*$p < .05$. **$p < .01$. ***$p < .001$.

coefficients for activity level and approach, r's $= .74$ and .68, respectively. Also in the moderately high range (exceeding .50) were the stability coefficients of persistence/task orientation and adaptability/flexibility. Although different in emphasis, the cross-time correlation of predictability to three three types of rhythmicity on the DOTS-R ranged from .25 to .40. Finally, albeit in the low range, negative mood during the middle childhood years correlated with DOTS-R positive mood.

Stability of Specific Temperament Dimensions during Adolescence

For readers interested in stability within the adolescent years, we diverged from our developmental era aggregation strategy and provide the analyses in Table 3.10. Correlation coefficients in the left column represent stability across the ages of 14 and 16 from ratings provided by parents of their adolescents' temperament; those in the right column represent the same analysis based on adolescent self-ratings. Coefficients tended to be higher for parent informants (range $= .50$ to .77) compared to adolescent self-reports (range $= .32$ to .65). Although not a measure of stability, for those interested we also report the cross-informant correlations of the parent and adolescent reports aggregated across ages 14 and 16 years. Following the order displayed in Table 3.10, the correlation coefficients between parent and self-ratings were .42, .38, .27, .36, .24, .28, .22, .41, and .36, respectively (all p's $< .05$). These results show low to moderate correlations across informants.

Table 3.10.   Stability of Adolescent Temperament from 14 to
16 Years on the Revised Dimensions of Temperament Survey
for Parent and Adolescent Informants

Temperament dimension	Parent ($N = 90$)	Adolescent ($N = 107$)
Activity – General	.77***	.65***
Activity – Sleep	.61***	.41***
Approach	.63***	.56***
Flexibility	.66***	.48***
Positive Mood	.54**	.47***
Rhythmicity – Sleeping	.51***	.46***
Rhythmicity – Eating	.54***	.32**
Rhythmicity – Daily Habits	.50**	.44***
Task Orientation	.56***	.43***

*$p < .05.$ **$p < .01.$ ***$p < .001.$

Hence, within-informant ratings across a two-year interval were generally higher than cross-informant ratings assessed at the same ages. These correlations are in line with those reported in other studies examining inter-rater and inter-parent agreement (c.f., Slabach et al., 1991, pp. 212–213).

Continuity and Stability of Specific Temperament Dimensions from Toddlerhood through Adolescence: Integration with Prior Findings

Continuity of Temperament

Evidence from three longitudinal studies with respect to mean changes in the NYLS temperament dimensions reveal differences on 7 of the 9 dimensions. The developmental changes show that, with increasing age during this period, children's behavioral style shifts toward quicker adaptability (Fullard et al., 1984; Guerin & Gottfried, 1994a; Thomas & Chess, 1986), milder intensity of reaction (Guerin & Gottfried, 1994a; Thomas & Chess, 1986), more predictability in biological rhythmicity (Guerin & Gottfried, 1994a; Thomas & Chess, 1986), more positive mood (Guerin & Gottfried, 1994a; Thomas & Chess, 1986), longer persistence/attention span (Fullard et al., 1984; Guerin & Gottfried, 1994a), more sensitivity to changes in the environment (threshold; Fullard et al., 1984; Guerin & Gottfried, 1994a), and lower activity level (Guerin & Gottfried, 1994a). These studies compared temperament across the first 5 years (Thomas & Chess, 1986), ages 1 through 3 (Fullard et al., 1984), or ages 3 through 5 (Guerin & Gottfried, 1994a) and reflect a trend toward increasing organization and self-regulation.

During middle childhood and adolescence, evidence suggests increasing continuity in behavioral style. During middle childhood, results from two longitudinal studies show age-related changes were detected on only 4 of the 9 NYLS dimensions. Hegvik et al. (1982) reported lower activity level across this era, as also found in the FLS (Guerin & Gottfried, 1994a). Additionally, FLS data revealed higher approach, milder intensity of reaction, and less sensitivity to changes (threshold) across the ages from 8 to 12 years (Guerin & Gottfried, 1994a). Hence, thus far the data suggest increasing continuity in temperament during the middle childhood compared to the preschool years. During adolescence, FLS data across the ages of 14 and 16 years showed no age-related changes in either parent assessments of the adolescents' temperament or the adolescents' own self-ratings across the nine dimensions of the DOTS-R, dimensions somewhat comparable, but not identical to, the NYLS dimensions. Hence, age-related changes were most pronounced during the preschool period, continued at a lower frequency during the middle childhood era, but were not evident during the adolescent era. Although the span of years examined in the FLS during the adolescent era was only two years (from age 14 to 16), this span is equivalent to that examined in the FLS during the preschool era (ages 3 to 5); hence, the increasing continuity during adolescence cannot be completely attributed to the relatively short age span examined.

Stability of Temperament

Results from prior longitudinal studies show that during the first five years, stability coefficients decreased dramatically with increasing age intervals between assessments. For example, data from the NYLS showed maximum correlations of .52, .37, .29, and .22 for 1-, 2-, 3-, and 4-year age intervals, respectively (Thomas & Chess, 1986). Huttenan and Nyman (1982) found correlations in the .2 to .3 range for the interval between infancy and 5 years.

Data from the FLS revealed significant and moderate levels of stability in behavioral style from 1.5 years onward. Although not directly measuring the NYLS dimensions, the ICQ administered at 1.5 years showed significant correlations with NYLS dimensions across the childhood and adolescent eras. Maximum correlations observed between the ICQ factors and the dimensions assessed during the toddler, preschool, middle childhood, and adolescence eras were .46, .49, .55, and .48. Hence, even across intervals exceeding a decade, evidence of moderate stability was revealed. Cross-time correlations of the TTS dimensions assessed at age 2 with the BSQ administered during the preschool years were significant for all 9 dimensions and ranged from .30 to .55. Six of the nine TTS dimensions also correlated significantly with their corresponding assessment on the MCTQ during middle childhood with coefficients in the moderate to high range (i.e., .4 to .7). For the six conceptually similar scales assessed by the TTS at age 2 and the DOTS-R during adolescence, stability coefficients were significant for four; however, coefficients were in the low range, .2 to .4. Hence, compared to prior longitudinal studies examining the stability of temperament from the early years, results from the FLS showed more evidence of stability, with coefficients reaching moderate levels over intervals exceeding five years and more. Reasons for the comparatively higher stability coefficients in the FLS may include (1) improvements in measurement instruments compared to those employed in earlier studies, (2) initial temperament measures in the FLS during the second year rather than the first year, and (3) use of aggregated measures in the FLS during the preschool, middle childhood, and adolescent temperament eras.

As to stability of temperament during childhood, results from previous studies reveal moderate stability from the preschool to middle childhood period (Hegvik et al., 1984) and from age 7 to 12 years (Maziade, Cote, Boudreault, Thivierge, & Boutin, 1986a). Both of these research teams reported stability for most temperament dimensions (at least 7 of 9) in the moderate to high range (i.e., .4 to .7). Results from the FLS corroborated and extended these findings. In the FLS, eight of the nine dimensions assessed in the preschool era on the BSQ showed stability coefficients with the MCTQ in middle childhood ranging from .37 to .69; during adolescence, five of the six conceptually similar dimensions assessed both scales showed significant stability coefficients ranging from .33 to .46.

Stability data from middle childhood to adolescence in the FLS show significant stability for all six conceptually-similar dimensions common to the MCTQ and DOTS-R, with coefficients ranging from .21 to .74. Coefficients were in the moderate to high range for four of the six dimensions (activity level, approach, persistence/task orientation, adaptability/flexibility) and in the low to moderate range for rhythmicity and mood. Chapter 9 contains an integrative summation of continuity and stability findings for each dimension in turn.

Childhood Temperament and Personality during Adolescence

To determine the extent to which earlier temperament measures were precursors of personality in adolescence, we conducted bivariate correlation and multiple regression analyses. Through these analyses, we sought to determine if a direct mapping of temperament dimensions assessed longitudinally in the infant, preschool, middle childhood, or adolescent eras to the Big Five temperament traits assessed at age 17 years was evident.

Bivariate Correlations

Using bivariate correlation analyses, the evidence that early temperament (i.e, from infancy, todderhood, preschool years, middle childhood) is linked directly to personality traits assessed in adolescence was modest at best. Pearson correlation coefficients computed between dimensions of the temperament scales administered during the infancy, preschool, and childhood eras (ICQ, TTS, BSQ, MCTQ) and the NEO-FFI revealed few significant correlations, and those that were present were not replicated across developmental eras. Of 155 correlations, 12 were significant at the .05 level. These will be discussed in the larger context of temperamental precursors to each of the five personality factors in the following paragraphs.

Table 3.11 displays Pearson correlation coefficients between the NEO-FFI factors and adolescent temperament as rated by a parent (top panel) and the adolescent (bottom panel) on the DOTS-R averaged across ages 14 and 16. As would

Table 3.11. Pearson Correlation Coefficients between Adolescent Personality on the NEO and Adolescent Temperament as Reported on the Revised Dimensions of Temperament Survey by Parents (Upper Panel) and Adolescents (Lower Panel)

Revised dimensions of temperament survey	NEO scale				
	Neuroticism	Extraversion	Openness	Agreeableness	Conscientiousness
Parent report (N = 104)					
Activity – General	.04	.18	−.09	−.09	−.20*
Activity – Sleeping	.05	.04	.01	−.09	−.05
Approach	−.17	.30**	.20*	.24*	−.03
Flexibility	−.24*	.09	.12	.17	.07
Positive Mood	−.07	.04	.00	.12	−.01
Rhythmicity – Sleeping	.01	.11	.09	.11	.19
Rhythmicity – Eating	.01	.04	−.02	.04	.05
Rhythmicity – Habits	−.02	.03	.00	.03	.23*
Task Orientation	−.22*	.16	.04	.17	.38***
Adolescent self-report (N = 110)					
Activity – General	.14	.18	−.14	−.09	−.24*
Activity – Sleeping	.24*	−.02	−.14	−.17	−.20*
Approach	−.37***	.53***	.23*	.24*	.18
Flexibility	−.39***	.24*	.15	.25**	.24*
Positive Mood	−.13	.34***	.11	.23*	.16
Rhythmicity – Sleeping	−.08	.15	−.02	.10	.34***
Rhythmicity – Eating	−.27**	.25**	−.04	.08	.36***
Rhythmicity – Habits	−.07	.12	−.06	.00	.20*
Task Orientation	−.39***	.32**	.13	.34***	.37***

*p < .05. **p < .01. ***p < .001.

be expected due to shared source variance, there were a greater number of significant correlations between adolescents' self-rated temperament and their self-rated personality compared to parents' ratings of temperament and adolescent ratings of personality. Additionally, the magnitude of correlations was higher for adolescent temperament ratings than when parents were informants. As shown in the top panel, the highest correlation between parent-rated temperament and adolescent personality was between task orientation and conscientiousness, reaching .38. As can be seen in the lower panel of Table 3.11, approximately one-half of the correlations between adolescent self-ratings of temperament and the NEO-FFI dimensions of personality were significant, reaching a magnitude of .53.

Looking across the temperament measures in all the developmental eras investigated in the FLS, let us begin by examining cross-time relations with neuroticism at age 17. Costa and McCrae (1985) characterize this dimension as reflecting adjustment versus emotional instability, with high scores indicating worrying, nervousness, and emotionality. Numerous temperament dimensions have been speculated as forerunners of neuroticism, including activity level, adaptability, rhythmicity, emotionality/negative emotionality, social inhibition, and threshold (see Table 1.03 in chapter 1). In the FLS, only one temperament scale prior to the adolescent era predicted neuroticism at 17 years: ICQ unsociability at age 1.5 years ($r = .19, p < .05$). In adolescence, flexibility, task orientation, and approach were the strongest predictors of NEO neuroticism; more favorable adjustment in adolescence (i.e., lower neuroticism scores) was related to greater temperamental flexibility, task orientation, and approach. No evidence supporting the posited linkages to temperamental activity level, emotionality, or threshold (see Table 1.03) was found in any developmental era investigated in the FLS.

Extraversion is characterized by Costa and McCrae as assessing the quantity and intensity of interpersonal attraction. High scorers on the NEO-FFI are described as sociable, active, and person-oriented. Among the temperament measures used in the FLS during the infancy, toddler/preschool, and childhood eras, only one predictor of adolescent extraversion in the FLS was evident: negative mood at 2 years ($r = .20, p < .05$). In adolescence, approach and mood were the strongest predictors of extraversion. Task orientation, rhythmicity (eating), and flexibility were also significantly correlated. In the FLS, there was no evidence of a linkage between activity level or intensity and extraversion in adolescence. Our findings dovetail with those of Hagekull and Bohlin (1998) in terms of sociability/shyness as precursors of extraversion, but fail to replicate the linkage to activity level they observed when extraversion in childhood was the criterion variable.

The third of the five NEO factors is openness to experience. High scores on openness indicate an intrinsic seeking and appreciation of experience and tolerance for the unfamiliar. In the FLS, preschool temperament dimensions of adaptability ($r = .26$), persistence ($r = .23$), and activity level ($r = .23$) correlated with openness in adolescence. This supports Caspi's (1998) speculation that persistence would relate to openness. In middle childhood ($r = .31$) and adolescence, the temperament dimension of approach significantly predicted openness at age 17. The approach dimension on the scales in the FLS is the closest to a measure of sociability, although it also assesses reactions to new places, activities, foods, and so forth. Hagekull and Bohlin found sociability/shyness and activity level to predict openness in childhood.

High scores on the agreeableness factor of the NEO-FFI are indicative of individuals who are good-natured and thoughtful. Activity level, adaptability, intensity, negative emotionality/mood, persistence, and sociability have been hypothesized as temperamental predictors of agreeableness (see Table 1.03). The earliest predictor of 17-year agreeableness observed in the FLS was negative mood during the middle childhood years ($r = -.32$; children rated with with less negative mood by parents subsequently rated themselves as more agreeable at 17 years). During adolescence in the FLS, several dimensions related significantly to NEO-FFI agreeableness: task orientation, flexibility, approach, and mood. Adolescents who were task oriented, flexible, approaching to novelty, and positive in mood tended to score higher on agreeableness. No links between childhood activity level or intensity and agreeableness were observed in the FLS, although predictions of relations with adaptability (flexibility), emotionality/mood, persistence, and sociability were supported.

The last of the five NEO factors is conscientiousness. Conscientiousness is characterized by Costa and McCrae as reflecting the individual's degree of organization, persistence, and motivation in goal-directed behavior. Activity level and task persistence have been suggested to foretell conscientiousness, as shown in Table 1.03. In the FLS, predictors of conscientiousness were evident in several developmental eras. In the infancy period, resistance to control correlated significantly: infants rated lower on resistance to control scored themselves higher on conscientiousness at 17, $r = -.21$. During the toddler period, activity level and adaptability predicted conscientiousness: those rated as less active ($r = -.21$) and faster to adapt ($r = .25$) rated themselves as more conscientious in adolescence. On the MCTQ in middle childhood, there was a tendency toward greater predictability ($r = .29$) and persistence ($r = .25$) among those who subsequently viewed themselves as more conscientious. In adolescence, the correlates of conscientiousness were task orientation, rhythmicity, flexibility, and activity level. Hence, both of Caspi's (1998) predictions were supported. Although Hagekull and Bohlin (1998) found a link between shyness and conscientiousness, data from the FLS failed to demonstrate a significant relation to approach/withdrawal.

Hence, these longitudinal data featuring measures of temperament spanning the developmental eras from infancy, preschool, and middle childhood, show little evidence of direct cross-time linkages between specific temperament dimensions and the Big Five factors of personality in the FLS cohort at age 17.

Wachs (1991) and Ahadi and Rothbart (1994) expressed doubts that a direct mapping of temperament to personality dimensions was likely; these data corroborate their suspicions. Although FLS data revealed an impressive level of stability of temperament dimensions across the preschool, childhood, and adolescent eras, there was little evidence that early temperament explained variability in personality at age 17. As we examined these data we regretted that cross-informant data on adolescent personality (i.e., parent or peer reports) had not been collected. Having parent reports of personality in addition to those of the adolescents would allow the determination of whether or not the absence of early temperament-personality linkages observed in these data are a function of relying on cross-informant data or reflect a true lack of relation.

Multiple Regression Analyses

Using multiple regression analyses with temperament dimensions as predictor variables and personality factors as criterion variables, Hagekull and Bohlin (1998) found that childhood extraversion and agreeableness were the personality factors best predicted by preschool temperament measures, with multiple R's of .50 and .44, respectively. Using a similar procedure with the FLS data proved useful only for the DOTS-R adolescent self-report, as on four of the five NEO-FFI scales only one significant predictor emerged from among the dimensions using DOTS-R parent reports. Multiple regression coefficients ranged from .20 to .30 for N, E, O, and A and reached .42 for C when parent reports of temperament were used as predictors of adolescent ratings of personality on the NEO.

Adolescent self-ratings of temperament resulted in multiple regression coefficients similar to those observed by Hagekull and Bohlin. Results are displayed in Table 3.12; multiple R's for the five factors of the NEO ranged from .30 (openness to experience) to .55 (extraversion). Temperament dimensions accounted for between 7 and 29 percent of the variance in personality scores at 17 years (adjusted for shrinkage).

We also conducted similar multiple regression analyses using both parent and adolescent temperament ratings on the DOTS-R to predict the NEO. Using both parent and adolescent DOTS-R ratings as predictors produced significant but small increments in the amount of variance explained by the adolescent self-reports on the DOTS-R. For the results displayed in Table 3.12, adding parent reports after adolescent self-reports produced significant increments in R^2 on three NEO-FFI factors (3, 3, 6 percent for E, A, and C scales, respectively). Alternatively, using adolescent self-ratings on the DOTS-R in addition to parent reports augmented the amount of variance explained by significant and substantial increments, as shown in Table 3.13. The adolescent self-ratings of temperament increased the amount of variance explained by parent reports by .20, .22, .00, .10, and .09 on the N, E, O, A, and C scales. However, using both the parent

Table 3.12. Multiple Regression Analyses Using Adolescent Temperament Dimensions on the Revised Dimensions of Temperament Survey (Self-Ratings) as Predictors of Adolescent Personality on the NEO

Criterion	Predictor	R	R^2	Adjusted R^2	F_{Equation}[a]
Neuroticism	Flexibility	.39	.15	.15	
	Task Orientation	.51	.26	.24	18.44***
Extraversion	Approach	.53	.28	.27	
	Positive Mood	.55	.31	.29	23.54***
Openness to Experience	Approach	.23	.05	.04	
	Activity – General	.30	.09	.07	5.12*
Agreeableness	Task Orientation	.34	.12	.22	
	Flexibility	.39	.15	.14	9.74***
Conscientiousness	Task Orientation	.37	.14	.13	
	Rhythmicity – Sleeping	.44	.20	.18	13.11***

[a] $df = 2, 107$.
*$p < .05$. **$p < .01$. ***$p < .001$.

Table 3.13. Multiple Regression Analyses Using Adolescent Temperament on the Revised Dimensions of Temperament Survey (Parent and Adolescent Reports) as Predictors of Adolescent Personality on the NEO

Criterion	Predictor and informant	R	R^2	Adjusted R^2	F_{Equation}	df
Neuroticism	Flexibility (Parent)	.24	.05	.06		
	Task Orientation (Adolescent)	.43	.17	.13		
	Flexibility (Adolescent)	.52	.25	.09	12.55***	3,103
Extraversion	Approach (Parent)	.30	.08	.09		
	Approach (Adolescent)	.53	.27	.19		
	Positive Mood (Adolescent)	.56	.30	.03	15.46***	3,103
Openness	Approach (Parent)	.20	.03	.04	4.44*	1,103
Agreeableness	Approach (Parent)	.24	.05	.06		
	Task Orientation (Adolescent)	.41	.15	.11	10.11***	2,103
Conscientiousness	Task Orientation (Parent)	.38	.14	.14		
	Rhythmicity – Daily Habits (Parent)	.42	.16	.17		
	Rhythmicity – Eating (Adolescent)	.50	.23	.07		
	Task Orientation (Adolescent)	.53	.25	.03	9.72***	4,103

*$p < .05$. **$p < .01$. ***$p < .001$.

and adolescent ratings of temperament to predict the NEO did not improve the multiple correlations by meaningful amounts beyond those observed when using the adolescent self-reports on the DOTS-R displayed in Table 3.12.

Summary and Conclusions

1. *Is there evidence of systematic change in parent reports of temperament as a function of child age within the preschool, middle childhood, and adolescent eras?* There were significant changes in mean ratings of parents during the preschool, middle childhood eras, but not during the adolescent era. During the preschool years from 3 to 5, parents rated their children as increasing in biological regularity, becoming milder in intensity, more frequently positive in mood, having longer persistence/attention spans, and becoming more sensitive or perceptive. During the middle childhood years from 8 to 12, children were rated as decreasing their activity level, becoming more approaching to novel people, places, and things, again becoming milder in intensity, and becoming less sensitive or perceptive. Significant age-related changes in mean ratings did not characterize either parent or adolescent ratings of adolescent temperament.

2. *To what extent does temperament in infancy presage temperament during childhood and adolescence?* Temperamentally challenging infants continued to be rated by parents as temperamentally challenging throughout childhood and adolescence. Canonical correlations between the four aspects of difficult temperament assessed when infants were 1.5 and the sets of subsequent temperament dimensions through at least mid-adolescence were significant and moderately high in magnitude, with little diminution across the approximately 15-year time frame.

3. *Are there specific and unique temperamental sequelae of various aspects of infant difficult temperament?* Although infant fussiness presaged several aspects of childhood temperament including higher activity level, slower adaptability, more negative mood, biological irregularity, and lower persistence/attention span, some specificity of temperamental sequelae was evident in the consequences of unadaptability and resistance to control. In addition to exhibiting slower adaptability and more negative mood, infants who were viewed as less adaptable at 1.5 years were also consistently lower in approach during childhood, whereas those who were viewed as more resistant to control were rated as higher in activity level and lower in persistence/attention span during the preschool, middle childhood, and adolescent eras.

4. *What is the pattern of stability across the nine dimensions of temperament across the preschool, school-age, and adolescent years?* Parents form a

stable impression of their children's behavioral style. Significant cross-time correlations were observed for the majority of dimensions across the toddler, preschool, middle childhood, and adolescent eras of development. The dimensions showing the most impressive and consistent cross-time stability were activity level and approach.

5. *Does childhood temperament predict personality during adolescence?* A direct and linear mapping of infant/childhood temperament dimensions to adolescent personality factors was not evident. Although scattered significant correlation coefficients between early temperament and adolescent personality factors were observed, they were low and not consistent across developmental eras. FLS data demonstrated linkages between adolescent self-reported temperament and personality over a time span of approximately 2 years. Temperament dimensions accounted for the greatest variance in the personality factors of extraversion and neuroticism, explaining approximately 25% of the variance in each.

4

Temperament and Behavioral/ Emotional Adjustment

"He is a quick thinker and bright, but does not use his potential. Has behavior problems because he wants to control people and situations—becomes frustrated when he can't. Does not want to accept responsibility for his actions. Because he doesn't see a separation of his behavior and his personhood—his self esteem is very low. He's always in trouble and that reinforces his negative feelings of self worth."

—Parent of Child #1, Difficult Infant Temperament Group, Age 11

Issues Investigated

The linkage between early temperament and behavior problems during middle childhood found by the NYLS group served as a catalyst for the study of temperament. Data based on the FLS and other longitudinal studies have not only replicated the findings of the NYLS researchers regarding the predictive power of early temperament with respect to behavioral adjustment, but also have extended downward the age at which temperament has been shown to foretell childhood behavior problems. This chapter details results from the FLS data regarding concurrent and predictive relations between temperament and behavior problems using multiple informants (parents, teachers, adolescent self-reports) and state-of-the-art behavior problem measures. Specifically, as reflected in the review of literature in chapter 1, we present results from the FLS in terms of the timing of the measurement of temperament in relation to behavioral adjustment (concurrent vs. cross-time) and in terms of informant on the two measures (same vs. different):

1. *What is the pattern of concurrent temperament-behavior problem relations throughout childhood and adolescence when both are reported by one informant?* Do the same patterns of relation between temperament and behavioral adjustment emerge at each developmental era (preschool, middle childhood, adolescence)? Are the patterns of relation different for

internalizing versus externalizing behavior problems? Is the pattern of results similar when temperament and behavior problems are reported by adolescents compared to parents?

2. *What is the magnitude of relation between concurrent assessments of temperament and behavioral adjustment across different informants?* In this section, we examined the relation between parent reports of temperament and behavior problems assessed by informants other than parents, beginning with teacher reports of internalizing and externalizing behavior problems during middle childhood. During the adolescent era, the relation between parent reports of temperament and adolescent reports of behavioral adjustment was investigated, as well as the relation between adolescent reports of temperament and parent reports of behavioral adjustment.

3. *Within the same informant, across what spans of time do dimensions of temperament forecast behavioral adjustment?* A particular strength of the FLS is the use of multiple measures of temperament and behavioral adjustment. In this section, cross-time relations between temperament and behavioral adjustment are explored, with ages spanning from infancy (i.e., 1.5 years) through adolescence. In addition to the aforementioned correlation analyses, we also examine whether specific aspects of infant temperament are precursors of clinically-elevated behavior problems, and, if so, across which periods of development.

4. *Across different informants, to what extent do dimensions of temperament predict behavioral adjustment?* In these analyses, the degree to which early measures of temperament provided by parents are predictive of subsequent measures of behavior problems as reported by teachers and adolescents is documented.

5. *To what extent do behavior problem scores presage aspects of subsequent temperament?* Again capitalizing on the multiple measures of temperament and behavioral adjustment collected in the FLS, we examined the temperamental sequelae of children's behavioral adjustment. Our purpose was to determine the extent to which specific types of behavioral problems might forecast either the expression of children's temperament or the perception/impression/interpretation of the temperament informant.

6. *To what extent do parent and adolescent reports of adolescent temperament combine to explain behavioral adjustment?* The utility of utilizing both parent and adolescent ratings of temperament to predict behavioral adjustment in adolescence is explored herein.

Description of Measures Used in the FLS

Behavior problems were assessed by parent report when children were 3.25 through 17 years, by teacher report annually from 6 through 11 years, and by the

Table 4.01.   Temperament and Behavior Problem Measures Employed in the FLS during Each Developmental Era

| Developmental era | Temperament | | Behavior problems | |
	Measure	Informant	Measure	Informant
Infancy	Infant Characteristics Question. (ICQ)	Parent	—	—
Toddler	Toddler Temperament Question. (TTS)	Parent	—	—
Preschool	Behavioral Style Questionnaire (BSQ)	Parent	Eyberg Child Behavior Inventory (ECBI); Preschool Behavior Question. (PBQ); Child Behavior Checklist (CBCL)	Parent
Middle Childhood	Middle Childhood Temperament Question. (MCTQ)	Parent	Child Behavior Checklist (CBCL)	Parent
			Teacher Report Form (TRF)	Teacher
Adolescence	Rev. Dimensions of Temperament Survey (DOTS-R)	Parent	Child Behavior Checklist (CBCL)	Parent
	Rev. Dimensions of Temperament Survey (DOTS-R)	Adolescent	Youth Self Report (YSR)	Adolescent

adolescents themselves at 17 years. Table 4.01 summarizes the temperament and behavior problem measures collected during each developmental era and the informant for each measure. The reliability and validity of each of these inventories have been documented in the clinical and/or developmental psychology literature; all scales have been shown to discriminate clinical from non-clinical children in large populations and/or children referred for assessment. In addition, given that our participants represent a wide range of middle class families and that parents and teachers possessed the reading skills necessary to complete these inventories independently, we deemed these inventories suitable for assessing the behavioral adjustment of participants in this study.

Eyberg Child Behavior Inventory (ECBI)

The items on the ECBI assess a wide range of parental concerns (Eyberg, 1980). The parent responds to 36 items by indicating the frequency of occurrence of each behavior on a scale from 1 (*never occurs*) to 7 (*always occurs*). These ratings are summed to yield an overall problem behavior intensity score. The parent also indicates whether the behavior is a problem for the parent per se by circling "*yes*" or "*no*." The "yes" responses are counted to yield the total problem score. Test-retest reliability for a standardized sample of children ranged from .86 to .88 (Robinson, Eyberg, & Ross, 1980). Validity of the ECBI was supported by Burns and Patterson (1990), who demonstrated that the ECBI discriminated between children currently in treatment for learning disability or behavioral problems from children with no treatment history. The ECBI was completed at the 3.25-year assessment.

Preschool Behavior Questionnaire (PBQ)

Consisting of 30 items, this behavior checklist yields a total behavior problem score and scores for three specific behavior scales: hostile-aggressive, anxious, and hyperactive-distractible. For each item, the parent indicates that the behavior "*doesn't apply*," "*applies sometimes*," or "*certainly applies*." Standardized on a large population of children ages 3 to 6 years, this questionnaire has been shown to discriminate clinical from non-clinical subjects (Behar & Stringfield, 1974). The PBQ was completed by a parent (almost exclusively mothers) at the 3.5-year assessment.

Child Behavior Checklist for Ages 4–18 (CBCL), Teacher's Report Form (TRF), Youth Self Report (YSR)

These widely used and well-established instruments were designed to provide a standardized format to obtain reports from parents and teachers of behavioral/emotional problems of children ages 4 through 18 years (Achenbach, 1991a, 1991b). The YRF is similar in purpose and was designed for use with youth between ages 11 and 18 (1991c.). All instruments include 118 specific problem items and two open-ended problem items. The informant uses a three-point scale to respond to each item, describing the child/adolescent currently or within the last six months. Possible responses include 0 (*Not True*), 1 (*Somewhat or Sometimes True*), or 2 (*Very True or Often True*). Items are summed to yield eight syndrome scores (withdrawn, somatic complaints, anxious/depressed, social problems, thought problems, attention problems, delinquent behavior, and aggressive behavior) and two broad-band category scores, internalizing and externalizing problems. Internalizing behavior problems relate to over-controlled behavior and reflect behaviors such as withdrawal, somatic complaints, and anxiety or depression. Externalizing behavior problems, in contrast, relate to under-controlled behaviors such as aggressive and delinquent behavior.

Achenbach (1991a) reported a mean test-retest reliability of $r = .89$ for problem scales of the CBCL over a one-week period. For the TRF, test-retest reliability over a mean interval of 15 days averaged $r = .90$ for problem scales (Achenbach, 1991b). One-week test-retest reliabilities for the YSR averaged $r = .72$ (Achenbach, 1991c). These instruments also demonstrate evidence of content, construct, and criterion-related validity. For correlation and regression analyses, raw scores were analyzed, as recommended by Achenbach (1991a, 1991b, 1991c).

The CBCL was completed annually by one of the parents when children were ages 4 to 17 years. The TRF was administered annually from ages 6 through 11 years, while children were in elementary school and spent all or significant portions of their school day with a single teacher. The YSR was completed by adolescents at the 17-year visit, although two items pertaining to self harm and suicidal thoughts were deleted due to concerns regarding liability. This yielded 14 annual assessments on the CBCL and 6 on the TRF.

To improve reliability, cross-time aggregates of the CBCL and TRF were computed. Scores were aggregated to correspond to the developmental eras described in chapter 2. Specifically, parent reports were aggregated across the preschool era (ages 4, 5), middle childhood era (ages 6, 7, 8, 9, 10, 11, 12), and across the adolescent era (ages 13, 14, 15, 16, 17). Teacher reports were aggregated across the middle childhood years (6, 7, 8, 9, 10, 11). As a check for the comparability of these aggregates, correlation coefficients between teacher and parent reports on the externalizing scale were compared to previous studies. Consistent with results reported in a meta-analysis conducted by Achenbach, Howell, and McConaughy (1987) and the findings of Phares, Compas, and Howell (1989), the average correlation between teacher and parent reports on the externalizing scale in the present study was .36.

Findings and Discussion

Because children participating in this project represented a non-clinical sample (i.e. not selected at the outset for clinical reasons or referral), the distribution of behavior problem scores was expected to be positively skewed (that is, a preponderance of scores at or near zero). When behavior problem data were evaluated for the violation of the assumption of normality and the assumption was violated, data were submitted to square root transformations to correct for positive skewness (Tabachnick & Fidell, 2001). Additionally, analyses using nonparametric statistics were conducted. Results from both of these additional approaches yielded similar conclusions to those using non-transformed data and parametric statistics; therefore, analyses are reported using non-transformed data and parametric analyses for ease of interpretation and discussion.

Concurrent Relations between Temperament and Behavior Problems with Measures by the Same Informant

To examine the within-informant, concurrent relation between the nine NYLS dimensions and behavioral adjustment, Pearson product-moment correlation coefficients were computed between the following measures:

- Preschool era: BSQ and ECBI, PBQ, and CBCL administered at ages 4 and 5;
- Middle childhood era: MCTQ and CBCL aggregated across ages 6–12 years;
- Adolescent era: DOTS-R (parent report) and the CBCL aggregated across ages 13–17 years; and DOTS-R (adolescent self-report) and YSR collected at 17 years.

Preschool Era

Scores on the BSQ were pervasively associated with concurrent measures of preschool behavioral adjustment. Pearson correlation coefficients between the BSQ and ECBI and PBQ, both measured during the third year, are presented in Table 4.02. Evaluating the results by temperament dimension (i.e., horizontally), six of the nine dimensions related pervasively to indices of behavioral adjustment during the third year. These included negative mood, adaptability, approach, activity level, intensity, and persistence/attention span. More behavior problems were associated with temperament characterized as more negative in mood, slower in adaptability to changes, withdrawal from (rather than approaching) novel people, places, and situations, higher activity level, greater intensity of reaction, and less persistence/shorter attention span. Correlations ranged to moderately high magnitude (.65). Three temperament dimensions, biological rhythmicity, distractibility,

Table 4.02. Pearson Correlation Coefficients between Preschool-Age Temperament and Behavior Problems during the Third Year

Behavioral style questionnaire dimension	Eyberg child behavior inventory (N = 113)		Preschool behavior questionnaire scale (N = 104–112)			
	Intensity score	Problem score	Total behavior disturbed	Hostile-aggressive	Anxious	Hyperactive-distractible
Activity Level	.45***	.28**	.20*	.21*	−.08	.54***
Rhythmicity[a]	−.13	−.20*	−.12	−.08	−.16	−.01
Approach[a]	−.29**	−.26**	−.41***	−.30**	−.49***	−.03
Adaptability[a]	−.53***	−.35***	−.60***	−.57***	−.43***	−.33***
Intensity	.29**	.26**	.27***	.30**	.22*	.16
Negative Mood	.55***	.43***	.65***	.61***	.43***	.31**
Persistence[a]	−.49***	−.18	−.29**	−.33**	−.15	−.39***
Distractibility	.14	.17	.10	.24*	−.04	.03
Threshold	.10	.10	.15	.14	.08	.02

[a] Signs of coefficients were reversed to facilitate interpretation.
*p < .05. **p < .01. ***p < .001.

and threshold, failed to show evidence of a systematic relation to any of the behavior scales during the third year.

On the ECBI, informants rated both the frequency/intensity of occurrence for each problem, as well as whether or not the behavior was a problem for them. Temperament characteristics related to the intensity behavior problem score were negative mood, slow adaptability, less persistence, and higher activity level. Although the strength of relation between specific temperament dimensions and problem scores was not as strong as with the intensity score, it is interesting to note that during the preschool period variations in children's persistence/attention span did not significantly relate to the problem score. As will be shown in Table 4.03, this dimension of temperament showed increasingly stronger associations with behavior problem measures throughout the childhood era.

The PBQ provides more detailed assessment of behavioral/emotional problems; along with a composite measure (total behavior disturbed), there are three scale scores: hostile-aggressive, anxious, and hyperactive-distractible. Examining results vertically in Table 4.02 provides some evidence of specificity or differentiation of temperament scales in relation to behavioral and emotional problems during the preschool years. The total behavior disturbed and hostile-aggressive scales were most strongly related to negative mood and slow adaptability. The anxious scale was most strongly correlated with approach, but also to a moderate degree

Table 4.03. Pearson Correlation Coefficients between Concurrent Temperament and Behavior Problem Measures during the Preschool and Middle Childhood Eras

| | Child behavior checklist age (years) and scale | | | |
| | 4 and 5 aggregated[b] ($N = 115$) | | 6–12 aggregated[c] ($N = 107$) | |
Temperament dimension	Internalizing	Externalizing	Internalizing	Externalizing
Activity Level	.11	.37***	.26**	.49***
Rhythm/Predict[ad]	−.24**	−.20*	−.47***	−.52***
Approach[a]	−.50***	−.37***	−.28**	−.04
Adaptability[a]	−.47***	−.55***	−.54***	−.65***
Intensity	.25**	.31**	.30**	.51***
Negative Mood	.46***	.50***	.43***	.55***
Persistence[a]	−.26**	−.37***	−.49***	−.54***
Distractibility	.07	.17	.26**	.30**
Threshold	.08	.10	.27**	.30**

[a] Signs of coefficients were reversed to facilitate interpretation.
[b] Temperament measure = Behavioral Style Questionnaire; Behavior problem measure = Child Behavior Checklist aggregated across ages 4 and 5.
[c] Temperament measure = Middle Childhood Temperament Questionnaire; Behavior problem measure = Child Behavior Checklist aggregated across ages 6–12.
[d] BSQ biological rhythmicity dimension is replaced by predictability/quality of organization on the MCTQ.
*$p < .05$. **$p < .01$. ***$p < .001$.

with negative mood and slow adaptability. Thus, preschoolers viewed as more withdrawing to novel situations, people, and so forth, more negative in mood, and slower to adapt also tended to be rated as more anxious on the PBQ. Not surprisingly, activity level was the strongest temperamental correlate of the hyperactive-distractible scale, followed by persistence with a negative correlation indicating that less persistence/shorter attention span was related to higher scores on this scale.

Several patterns of relation between temperament and behavioral adjustment observed in the behavior problem scales administered during the third year were replicated with different measures of both temperament and behavior problems in subsequent waves of the FLS. Table 4.03 displays two sets of analyses representing concurrent temperament-behavior relations during the preschool and middle childhood eras, respectively. More specifically, Pearson correlation coefficients between dimensions of the BSQ assessed during the preschool years and CBCL internalizing and externalizing scores aggregated across ages 4 and 5 are displayed in columns 2 and 3; results displayed in columns 4 and 5 display concurrent relations during middle childhood using aggregated temperament (MCTQ) and behavior problem (CBCL) scales. Patterns strikingly similar to those observed during the third year were evident. First, the strongest and most pervasive relations were observed between behavior problems and the temperament dimensions of negative mood and adaptability. For these dimensions, correlations were uniformly moderate to high in magnitude for both internalizing and externalizing types of problems during both developmental eras. Second, approach related more strongly and specifically to internalizing types of problems, whereas activity level showed a similar pattern with respect to externalizing problems. Third, the dimensions of distractibility and threshold failed to relate or showed correlations in the low range with both types of problems.

Comparing the patterns across the preschool and middle childhood eras, two different patterns were also apparent. For the temperament dimensions of rhythmicity/predictability and persistence/attention span, correlation coefficients appeared somewhat stronger during the middle childhood as compared to the preschool era. With respect to rhythmicity and predictability/quality of organization, Hegvik et al. (1982) noted a shift in item content from the BSQ to the MCTQ. On the BSQ, rhythmicity is assessed with respect to the regularity of the child's biological functioning, for example, in the areas of sleeping, eating, toileting, and so forth. In contrast, the MCTQ items on this scale relate more to social predictability, such as following through with parental requests. On the scale of persistence/attention span, correlation coefficients during middle childhood are somewhat stronger than in prior assessments. Individual differences among children on this dimension may be more apparent as children encounter the formal educational process during middle childhood.

To reiterate, a strong and pervasive pattern of relationships among concurrent measures of temperament and behavior problems during the preschool and middle childhood eras, with correlation coefficients reaching moderately high (viz., .65) magnitudes, was in evidence. In comparing correlation coefficients of temperament dimensions with internalizing versus externalizing behavior problems during the preschool years, some evidence of differential relations emerged. Low approach tended to relate more strongly with internalizing types of problems such as anxiety and emotional problems, whereas activity level was specifically related more strongly to externalizing problems on the CBCL and the hyperactive scale on the PBQ. However, two dimensions of preschool temperament related consistently and at the strongest levels to all behavior problem indexes: negative mood and slower adaptability. As we noted in chapter 2, we found these two dimensions to be strongly correlated; children low on one of these dimensions tend to be lower on the second, and vice versa for high scorers. With respect to behavior problems, the developmental concomitants of these two dimensions of temperament are quite similar: higher behavior problem scores on both internalizing and externalizing types of problems.

These results corroborate findings of earlier investigators who used different measures of temperament and/or behavior problems during the preschool years with respect to finding higher levels of behavior problems associated with slower adaptability (Earls; 1981; Fagan, 1990), more negative mood (Webster-Stratton & Eyberg, 1982), lower persistence or shorter attention span (Fagan, 1990; Jansen et al., 1995; Webster-Stratton & Eyberg, 1982), higher activity levels (Fagan, 1990; Jansen, et al., 1995; Webster-Stratton & Eyberg, 1982), and lower in approach (Fagan, 1990). Moreover, although we observed a general lack of relation between distractibility and behavior problems during the preschool years, others have found conflicting results. Earls (1981) reported low distractibility predicted higher behavior problem scores, although Fagan (1990) and Jansen et al. (1995) found higher distractibility related to higher behavior problem scores. The results of the middle childhood data revealed a high degree of concordance with those of Teglasi and MacMahon (1990). They reported significant correlations between adaptability, intensity, and negative mood and behaviors that parents reported as causing friction at home, particularly the factors related to angry outbursts and emotional upset and oppositional behaviors. Additionally, consistent with our findings at each developmental era, Teglasi and MacMahon reported that approach related to a factor assessing internalizing types of behavior problems, joylessness and apathy.

Sanson et al. (1990; see also Bates, 1990) raised the concern that linkages between temperament and behavior problems might be inflated due to item overlap between the two measures. Subsequent studies utilizing differing methods to assess and then control item overlap have concluded that, although the measures were confounded, the confounding did not account for relation observed between concurrent and/or cross-time measures of temperament and behavior problems (Lemery et al., 2002; Lengua et al., 1998). In fact, Lemery et al. (2002) reported that associations between "purified" temperament and behavior problem scales (in which items with conceptual or empirical redundancy as determined via expert ratings or factor analysis, respectively, had been eliminated) were equivalent in magnitude to those observed in the original scales. They concluded that "... measurement confounding does not account for the observed relation between temperament and behavior problem symptoms" (p. 880).

Adolescent Era

During the adolescent era, both parents and adolescents reported on temperament and behavioral adjustment measures. Table 4.04 displays correlation coefficients between parent-reported temperament and scales of the CBCL and between adolescent-reported temperament and scales of the YSR. Three major conclusions can be drawn. First, correlation coefficients did not range as high as in previous eras (highest = .49). Second, three scales showed significant temperament-behavior relations across informants: flexibility (related to earlier measures of adaptability), task orientation (persistence), and rhythmicity of eating. Adolescents rated as more flexible, longer in task orientation, and more regular in eating were also reported to have lower behavior problems of both an internalizing and externalizing nature. Third, as in prior eras, differentiation or specificity in temperament-behavior problem relations was evident for the general activity and approach scales: general activity related more strongly with externalizing behavior

Table 4.04. Pearson Correlation Coefficients between Revised Dimensions of Temperament Survey and Behavior Problems during Adolescence (Within Informant)

| | Informant and behavior problem type | | | |
| | Parent[a] ($N = 105$) | | Adolescent[b] ($N = 110$) | |
Temperament dimension	Internalizing	Externalizing	Internalizing	Externalizing
Activity-General	.14	.49***	.20*	.37***
Activity-Sleeping	.12	.12	.27**	.23*
Approach	−.33**	−.11	−.30**	−.01
Flexibility	−.37***	−.32**	−.29*	−.28**
Positive Mood	−.32**	−.31**	−.03	−.02
Rhythmicity-Sleep	−.24*	−.24*	−.21*	−.16
Rhythmicity-Eating	−.24*	−.26**	−.24*	−.22*
Rhythmicity-Habits	−.03	−.12	−.12	−.20*
Task Orientation	−.30**	−.42***	−.31**	−.27**

[a] Child Behavior Checklist aggregated across 13 through 17 years.
[b] Youth Self Report Form at 17 years.
*$p < .05$. **$p < .01$. ***$p < .001$.

problems, whereas approach related specifically to internalizing problems. The remaining temperament dimensions showed inconsistent patterns or non-significant correlations to behavior problems.

In summary, there was much consistency in the pattern of concurrent relations between temperament dimensions and behavior problems assessed during the preschool, middle childhood, and adolescent years. Specifically, adaptability, negative mood, and persistence were consistently associated with measures of concurrent behavioral adjustment, both internalizing and externalizing types of problems. Evidence of specificity of relations between temperament and internalizing versus externalizing broad bands of behavior problems was repeatedly observed for approach and activity level, with low approach relating to internalizing problems and high activity level relating to externalizing problems.

Concurrent Relations between Temperament and Behavior Problems with Measures by Different Informants

Using different informants to assess temperament and behavior problems constitutes a stronger demonstration of temperament-behavior problem relations. To assess if parent reports of temperament were associated with concurrent reports of behavior problems by other informants, we examined the relation between the following informants:

- Parent and teacher: MCTQ and Teacher Report Form administered at ages 6–11;
- Adolescent and parent: DOTS-R (adolescent self-report) and CBCL aggregated across ages 13 to 17 years; and
- Parent and adolescent: DOTS-R (parent report) and Youth Self Report.

Associations between parent reports on the MCTQ and teacher reports on the TRF collected across the middle childhood period were assessed using Pearson correlation coefficients. As shown in Table 4.05, a number of significant correlation coefficients between parent-reported temperament (aggregated across ages 8, 10, and 12) with teacher reports of both internalizing and externalizing behavior problems resulted (11/18, or 61%, were significant). Clearly, more pervasive and stronger relations were observed between temperament and externalizing behavior problems compared to internalizing behavior problems. Temperament accounted for a maximum of about 5 percent of the variance in internalizing problems. However, correlations with externalizing behavior problems reported by teachers reached moderately high magnitude of .49, explaining about 25 percent of the variance. Parent ratings of the temperament dimensions of persistence/attention span, adaptability, predictability, and activity level were most strongly related to teacher ratings of behavior at school.

Table 4.05. Pearson Correlation Coefficients (Cross Informant) between Temperament and Behavior Problems during the Middle Childhood Years

Middle childhood temperament dimension	Teacher report form ($N = 107$)	
	Internalizing	Externalizing
Activity Level	.08	.33**
Predictability[a]	−.25*	−.36***
Approach[a]	−.13	.18
Adaptability[a]	−.15	−.39***
Intensity	.19*	.23*
Negative Mood	.15	.23*
Persistence[a]	−.20*	−.49***
Distractibility	.16	.25**
Threshold	.23*	.14

[a] Signs of coefficients were reversed to facilitate interpretation.
*$p < .05$. **$p < .01$. ***$p < .001$.

Cross-informant concurrent temperament-behavior problem data were also available during the adolescent era. Table 4.06 displays correlation coefficients between adolescent self-ratings of temperament and parent-reported behavior problems on the CBCL (aggregated across ages 13 through 17) in the left two columns of data, and coefficients between parent-rated temperament and adolescent self-reports of behavior problems on the YSR (17 years) in the right two columns of data. Although approximately one-third of correlation coefficients were significant and in the expected direction, coefficients were low in magnitude.

Thus, the association between temperament and behavior problems is not the result of relying on single informants. These results indicated temperament was related to reports of behavior problems from various informants. This relation was not the consequence of common method variance. However, correlation coefficients reached higher magnitudes when parents and teachers were informants rather than when adolescents provided either the temperament or behavior problem measure (cf., Tables 4.05 vs. 4.06). Data based on teacher reports were particularly impressive, given that participants in the FLS were not intact classrooms of students; children attended public or private schools according to the location of their home, parent/child preferences, or other criteria. By the elementary school years, many FLS families had moved to homes in different communities, counties, and states. Therefore, the teachers serving as informants on the TRF were not comparing children in the FLS to each other. These data provide impressive evidence that parent reports of temperament are meaningful outside the parent-child relationship and across diverse settings.

Table 4.06.   Pearson Correlation Coefficients between Revised Dimensions of Temperament Survey and Behavior Problems (Cross Informant)

| | Informant and behavior problem type | | | |
| | Parent (CBCL) | | Adolescent (YSR) | |
Temperament dimension	Internalizing	Externalizing	Internalizing	Externalizing
Activity-General	−.01	.21*	−.08	.16
Activity-Sleeping	.06	.00	.01	.07
Approach	−.20*	.01	−.21*	−.21*
Flexibility	−.22*	−.23*	−.24*	−.21*
Positive Mood	−.21*	−.26**	−.14	−.12
Rhythmicity-Sleep	−.16	−.14	−.07	−.24*
Rhythmicity-Eating	−.11	−.09	−.11	−.21*
Rhythmicity-Habits	−.06	−.01	−.11	−.21*
Task Orientation	−.16	−.13	−.10	−.28**

$N = 111$ for Child Behavior Checklist and $N = 104$ for Youth Self Report.
$*p < .05. **p < .01. ***p < .001.$

Cross-informant temperament-behavior problems relations during adolescence between parent and adolescent is not as impressive, however. In an attempt to understand why parent-adolescent correlations were relatively low compared to parent-teacher correlations, we examined the intercorrelations among the temperament and behavior problem measures, when available. Prior research has shown that correlation coefficients between mothers' and fathers' ratings are moderate (i.e., .40 at best) for aspects of temperament (Slabach et al., 1991) and .4 for behavior problem ratings by parents and teachers (Achenbach et al., 1987; Phares et al., 1989). Hence, some concordance between reports by informants who know the child well is present, but agreement was certainly not high. As documented in chapter 3, in the FLS correlations between parent and adolescent ratings of temperament ranged from .24 to .42 for the dimensions of the DOTS-R aggregated across ages 14 and 16 (median $r = .36$). Parent-adolescent ratings of internalizing and externalizing behavior problems were significant but low, r's = .27 and .24, respectively. To eliminate the possibility that differences in assessment ages between the CBCL (aggregated across ages 13 through 17) and the YSR (age 17) resulted in a diminution of this relation, correlations between the CBCL at age 17 only and the YSR were calculated. The coefficients were equally low (r's = .25 and .24, respectively). For comparison purposes, correlations between parent and teacher reports on the CBCL and TRF (aggregated across age) were examined; the coefficients for internalizing and externalizing problems were .33 and .46, respectively. (No teacher reports of temperament were collected in the FLS.) Thus, it appears that parents' and teachers' ratings of behavior problems were slightly better aligned than those of parents and their adolescents; this may be a factor in the low temperament-behavior problem relation during adolescence across parent and adolescent informants. At the conclusion of this chapter, we examine whether using reports of both parents and adolescents as predictors in multiple regression analyses accounts for additional variance compared to using only one informant in investigating the temperament-behavior problem relation.

Cross-Time Relations between Temperament and Behavior Problems with Measures by the Same Informant

To examine the cross-time relation between temperament and behavioral adjustment assessed throughout each developmental period, Pearson product-moment correlation coefficients were computed. The coefficients between temperament and behavior problems, both assessed from parent informants, were examined as follows:

- Infancy onward: ICQ factors and the summary scores of the ECBI, PBQ, CBCL (aggregated across ages 4–5, 6–12, 13–17 years);
- Toddler years onward: TTS dimensions and summary scores of the ECBI, PBQ, CBCL (aggregated across ages 4–5, 6–12, 13–17 years);
- Preschool years onward: BSQ and CBCL (aggregated across ages 6–12, 13–17 years);
- Middle childhood onward: MCTQ and CBCL (aggregated across ages 13–17 years).

Beginning with the ICQ, parent reports of temperament measured at 1.5 years significantly predicted behavior problems through at least age 17 years. Pearson correlation coefficients between the four factors of the ICQ assessed at 1.5 years and parent reports of behavior problems from 3.25 through 17 years are displayed in Table 4.07. Three major conclusions can be drawn. First, the fussy/difficult/demanding and unadaptable factors of the ICQ correlated positively and pervasively with parent reports of behavior problems across all four inventories administered from age 3.25 through 17 years. Conversely, the resistant to control and unsociable factors demonstrated only a few significant associations. Second, correlation coefficients between the fussy/difficult/demanding and unadaptability factors and behavior problems ranged to moderate magnitudes, even with a decade between the assessment of temperament and the assessment of behavior problems. Third, correlations tended to be higher for the fussy/difficult/demanding factor compared to the unadaptability factor and higher for externalizing as opposed to internalizing behavior problems on the CBCL. Bates has suggested differential predictiveness among the four factors of the ICQ (1989). Data from his longitudinal research indicated that whereas the fussy/demanding/difficult factor related to both internalizing and externalizing behavior problems assessed at 3 to 6 years, the

Table 4.07.   Pearson Correlation Coefficients between Infant Temperament and Behavior Problems during the Preschool, Middle Childhood, and Adolescent Eras

Behavior problem scale	Infant characteristics questionnaire factor			
	Fussy/demand	Unadaptable	Resistant to control	Unsociable
Eyberg child behavior inventory ($N = 110$)				
Intensity Score	.47***	.27**	.36***	.11
Problem Score	.39***	.20*	.31**	.08
Preschool behavior questionnaire ($N = 100–110$)				
Total Behavior Disturbed	.41***	.28**	.18	.19
Hostile-Aggressive	.34***	.21*	.19	.11
Anxious	.35***	.25**	.05	.13
Hyperactive-Distractible	.22*	.13	.18	.08
Child behavior checklist				
4–5 years ($N = 111$)				
Internalizing	.40***	.40***	.17	.26**
Externalizing	.56***	.34***	.30**	.14
6–12 years ($N = 107$)				
Internalizing	.38***	.27**	.14	.23*
Externalizing	.49***	.32**	.28**	.19
13–17 years ($N = 108$)				
Internalizing	.20*	.21*	.05	.28**
Externalizing	.51***	.32**	.24*	.26**

$^*p < .05.$ $^{**}p < .01.$ $^{***}p < .001.$

unadaptability factor related primarily to internalizing behavior problems and the resistant to control factor related principally to externalizing behavior problems. In the FLS, however, differential behavioral sequelae for fussy/difficult/demanding versus unadaptable infant temperament were not consistent across developmental eras or behavior problem measures.

To determine whether infant difficultness predisposes children to subsequent behavior problems in the clinical range, chi-square analyses comparing groups of children high and low on each ICQ factor with clinical cut points on the ECBI, PBQ, CBCL, YSR, and TRF were conducted. These analyses allowed us to determine whether the ICQ factors differentially predicted the more specific narrow-band syndromes of clinically elevated behavior problems during the preschool, middle childhood, and adolescent periods and followed the strategy employed by Guerin et al. (1997).

Specifically, Guerin et al. recoded scores on the ICQ fussy/difficult/ demanding factor to create two categories for each factor: infants rated in the lower 85% and infants rated in the upper 15%. This procedure was also applied to create two groups for the remaining three ICQ factors in this chapter: adapt-able and unadaptable, not resistant to control and resistant to control, and sociable and unsociable. Cut-off points were computed by adding the standard deviation and standard error to the mean of each of the ICQ factors. These computations resulted in cut points of 3.88 for fussy/difficult/demanding, 3.81 for unadaptability, 5.29 for resistant to control; and 2.91 for unsociable. Using these cut points yielded 17 infants (10 boys, 7 girls) with fussy/difficult/demanding temperament, 18 infants (9 boys, 9 girls) with unadaptable temperament, 15 infants (9 boys, 6 girls) with resistant to control temperament, and 19 infants (9 boys, 10 girls) with unsociable temperament at 1.5 years. This represented approximately 15% of the sample, similar to the 10% classified as difficult by Thomas and Chess (1977) in their sample. These lower and upper groups on the four ICQ factors were compared to determine if behavior problem status (clinically elevated vs. not clinically elevated) differed between the two groups.

Scores on the ECBI and PBQ were categorized as normal or clinically-elevated based on established clinical cut points for the respective scales. For the ECBI, scores of 11 on the problem scale and 127 on the intensity scale are the criteria used to select children for treatment (Burns, Patterson, Nussbaum, & Parker, 1991). The PBQ yields scores for three scales (hostile-aggressive, anxious, and hyperactive-distractible) and a total behavior problem score. The clinical cut points for the 95th percentile rank were scores of 10, 6, 6, and 23, respectively (Sattler, 1982). The CBCL, TRF, and YSR each comprise eight behavioral syndromes. For each of the syndromes, children were coded as to whether their score was below versus at or above the clinical borderline. Achenbach (1991a, 1991b) recommends $T = 67$ (95th percentile) as a cut point to represent the bottom of the clinical range. Thus, for each syndrome a dichotomized value of 0 was assigned to scores below the 95th percentile and a value of 1 was assigned to scores at or above the 95th percentile. Chi-square tests with Yates' correction for continuity were used to test whether those categorized with a difficult temperament were at an elevated risk for specific clinical behavior problems during each of the developmental eras.

Behavioral Adjustment during the Preschool Era

By way of review, Guerin et al. (1997) reported that children who were in the high fussy/difficult/demanding temperament group at 1.5 years were at increased risk for clinically-elevated behavior problems during their third year. A significantly greater percentage of children in the upper 15% of the distribution on the fussy/difficult/demanding infant temperament factor were subsequently at or above the 95th percentile on the ECBI intensity score (68.8% vs. 22.3%) as well as on the number of problems score (37.5% vs. 11.7%). A similar pattern emerged on the PBQ; children in the upper 15% group on the fussy/difficult/demanding temperament status group were more frequently above the cut points on the hostile-aggressive (42.8% vs. 12.1%), hyperactive-distractible (31.2% vs. 4.3%), and total behavior disturbed (38.5% vs. 9.2%) scales compared to those falling in the lower

**Table 4.08.   Percentage of Children above Clinical Cut
Points during the Third Year as a Function of Infant
Temperament Status on Unadaptability Factor of the ICQ**

Behavior problem index (age in years)	Infant temperament status		χ^2
	Lower 85%	Upper 15%	
Eyberg child behavior inventory (3.25)[b]			
Intensity Score	27.4	40.0	0.48
Problem Score	11.6	40.0	5.98*
Preschool behavior questionnaire (3.5)[c]			
Hostile-Aggressive	14.6	25.0	.45
Anxious	19.4	56.3	8.09**
Hyperactive-Distractible	6.5	17.6	1.11
Total Behavior Problem	8.2	40.0	8.74**

$*p < .05.$ $**p < .01.$

85% on the distribution on the fussy/difficult/demanding factor. No differences
were detected on the anxious scale of the PBQ.

Not examined by Guerin et al. (1997) was whether or not infant unadaptability
was a risk factor for behavior problems. As shown next in Table 4.08, children in
the upper 15% on the unadaptable factor when they were infants were significantly
more likely than those in the adaptable temperament status group to have elevated
behavior problem scores during their third year on the ECBI problem, PBQ
anxious, and PBQ total behavior problem scales. The remaining two ICQ factors
(resistant to control and unsociable) did not significantly differentiate children
with clinical versus non-clinical behavior problems on the ECBI and PBQ.

Parents also completed the CBCL when children were 4 and 5 years. The
aforementioned infant temperament groups continued to differ in terms of fre-
quencies of elevated behavior problem scores. A significantly greater percentage
of children in the high fussy/demanding/difficult temperament group during infancy were subsequently reported by parents as exhibiting elevated behavior problem scores on the CBCL during the preschool years (ages 4–5). Specifically, a
greater percentage of infants in the fussy/difficult/demanding temperament group
as compared to the remaining infants scored above the clinical cut point on the
social problems scale [18.8% vs. 2.1%; χ^2 $(1, N = 111) = 5.37, p < .05$], aggressive behavior scale [43.8% vs. 5.3%; χ^2 $(1, N = 111) = 17.23, p < .001$], and
externalizing scale [56.3% vs. 22.1%; χ^2 $(1, N = 111) = 6.46, p < .05$]. Children
in the unadaptable temperament group at 1.5 years continued to show elevated
behavior problem scores at ages 4 and 5 on the CBCL compared to the remaining
infants. Significant differences were evident on the narrow band categories of social problems [17.6% vs. 2.1%; χ^2 $(1, N = 111) = 4.86, p < .05$] and aggressive

behavior [29.4% vs. 7.4%; χ^2 (1, $N = 111$) = 5.11, $p < .05$]. The infants in the upper 15% of the distribution on ICQ unsociability showed clinically-elevated behavior problem scores on three narrow band categories: withdrawn [22.2% vs. 4.3%, χ^2 (1, $N = 111$) = 4.81, $p < .05$], thought problems [33.3% vs. 8.6%; χ^2 (1, $N = 111$) = 6.27, $p < .05$], and delinquent behavior [27.8% vs. 7.5%; χ^2 (1, $N = 111$) = 4.48, $p < .05$]. Additionally, a significantly greater percentage of infants in the unsociable temperament group was subsequently above the cut point for internalizing behavior problems [38.9% vs. 14.4%; χ^2 (1, $N = 111$) = 4.56, $p < .05$]. Hence, a significantly higher proportion of infants in the upper 15% of the distribution on aspects of challenging infant temperament (a percentage similar to that reported for difficult temperament in the NYLS) compared to the remaining 85% of the cohort were reported by parents to show clinically-elevated levels of behavior problems across a number of measures during the preschool years.

Behavioral Adjustment during the Middle Childhood Era

Significantly greater percentages of children in the most challenging infant temperament groups continued to show clinically-elevated behavior problems in the middle childhood years. Results of the analyses of the CBCL during middle childhood as a function of temperament status group during infancy are displayed in Table 4.09. Greater proportions of children in the high fussy/difficult/demanding temperament group were reported by parents during middle childhood as displaying elevated behavior problem scores on anxious/depressed, thought problems, attention problems, aggressive behavior, and externalizing scales. As shown the lower panel of Table 4.09, children in the high unadaptable group at 1.5 years were more likely to display elevated problem scores on the syndromes of withdrawn, somatic complaints, and delinquent behaviors, as well as on both broadband scales (internalizing and externalizing). Resistant to control and unsociable temperaments did not significantly differentiate children with clinical levels from non-clinical levels of behavior problems during the middle childhood years.

Similar chi-square analyses using teacher ratings on the TRF yielded no significant differences in the percentages of children with clinically-elevated and non-elevated behavior problem scores comparing groups based on the unadaptable, resistant to control, or unsociable factors. However, as reported by Guerin et al. (1997), children in the fussy/difficult/demanding group were more likely than other children to display a higher frequency of clinically-elevated scores on the attention problems scale of the TRF at ages 6–8 years [14.3% vs. 0.00%; χ^2 (1, $N = 92$) = 5.66, $p < .05$] and on the thought problems scale at ages 9–11 [28.6% vs. 6.4%; χ^2 (1, $N = 92$) = 4.33, $p < .05$]. Thus, dimensions of temperament during infancy, toddlerhood, and the preschool years consistently related to the PBQ hyperactive-distractible scale as well as parent and teacher reports of attention problems during

Table 4.09. Percentage of Children With Clinically-Elevated Behavior Scores during Middle Childhood as a Function of Infant Temperament Status on Fussy/Difficult/Demanding and Unadaptable Factors of the ICQ

Child behavior checklist (6–12 years)	Infant temperament status		χ^2
	Lower 85%	Upper 15%	
Fussy/difficult/demanding			
Withdrawn	9.8	20.0	.52
Somatic Complaints	10.9	20.0	.33
Anxious/Depressed	12.0	40.0	5.64*
Social Problems	13.0	20.0	.10
Thought Problems	6.5	33.3	7.36**
Attention Problems	9.8	40.0	7.42**
Delinquent Behavior	9.8	26.7	2.04
Aggressive Behavior	6.5	40.0	11.35***
Internalizing	32.6	60.0	3.08
Externalizing	19.6	53.3	6.26*
Unadaptability			
Withdrawn	7.6	33.3	6.18*
Somatic Complaints	8.7	33.3	5.21*
Anxious/Depressed	13.0	33.3	2.60
Social Problems	13.0	20.0	.10
Thought Problems	9.8	13.3	.00
Attention Problems	10.9	33.3	3.70
Delinquent Behavior	8.7	33.3	5.21*
Aggressive Behavior	8.7	26.7	2.57
Internalizing	30.4	73.3	8.48**
Externalizing	18.5	60.0	9.94**

$N = 107$.
$*p < .05.$ $**p < .01.$ $***p < .001.$

middle childhood. It is possible that specific aspects of early temperament may provide early signs of attention deficit hyperactive problems.

Behavioral Adjustment during the Adolescent Era

During the adolescent period, the chi-square analyses between the ICQ factors and subsequent behavior problem groups classified on the parent-reported CBCL yielded only two significant differences. A greater percentage of adolescents in the fussy/difficult/demanding infant temperament group had scores in the clinically-elevated range on the aggressive behavior scale [20.0% vs. 3.2%; χ^2 $(1, N = 113) = 4.10, p < .05$]. Additionally, a greater percentage of those in the unsociable temperament group as infants had elevated scores on the somatic complaints scale [33.3% vs. 7.8%; χ^2 $(1, N = 113) = 6.99, p < .01$].

Findings of elevated rates of thought problems among adolescents in the unadaptable and the resistant to control infant temperament groups were evident in the analysis of adolescent self-reports on the YSR. On the thought problem syndrome, 26.7% of children in the high unadaptable temperament group during infancy were rated in the elevated range compared to 4.4% of the children in the low unadaptable group comprising the 85% of the distribution with the lowest scores on the unadaptable factor of the ICQ, χ^2 (1, $N = 105$) = 6.14, $p < .05$. Similarly, 27.3% of the adolescents in the resistant to control temperament group during infancy were rated in the elevated range on thought problems; the comparative figure for the remaining children was 5.3%, χ^2 (1, $N = 105$) = 3.98, $p < .05$.

In summary, a greater percentage of children in the fussy/demanding/difficult or unadaptable infant temperament groups at 1.5 years exhibited behavior problem scores in the clinical range during preschool compared to children who were not deemed as high in fussy/difficult/demanding or unadaptable temperaments. During middle childhood, both the fussy/difficult/ demanding and unadaptable ICQ groups again were over-represented among children with clinically elevated behavioral problem syndromes. However, each of these factors portended a different pattern of syndromes. During the adolescent period, the predictive power of the ICQ factors was diminished with fussy/difficult/demanding and unsociable infant temperaments each relating to only one behavioral outcome. Finally, there was no association between the ICQ factors and teacher reports of clinically elevated behavior problems across the years when teacher reports were aggregated across the entire range from 6 through 11. However, infants in the highest unadaptability and resistant to control infant temperament groups were more likely to have self-reported clinically elevated scores on the YSR thought problems scale.

To determine whether the nine NYLS temperament dimensions showed specificity in cross-time correlations with later behavior problems, correlation coefficients were computed across the developmental periods, using earlier measures of temperament (e.g., TTS, BSQ, and MCTQ) to predict parent reports of subsequent behavioral adjustment measured on the ECBI, PBQ, and CBCL.

Preschool Temperament and Subsequent Behavior Problems

Correlation coefficients between the nine NYLS dimensions measured on the TTS at 2 years and behavior problems assessed via the ECBI and PBQ during the third year are displayed in Table 4.10. Clearly, negative mood at age 2 was the most pervasive and strongest harbinger of behavior problems during the third year. Across both behavior problem inventories, toddlers with negative mood tended to exhibit higher levels behavior problems on all indices with the exception of hyperactive-distractible. Activity level at age 2 related most strongly to the hyperactive-distractible scale on the PBQ. TTS negative mood also correlated significantly with CBCL internalizing and externalizing scales aggregated across ages 4 and 5, r's = .33, .35, $p < .01$. However, correlations with CBCL and YSR

Table 4.10. Pearson Correlation Coefficients between Toddler Temperament Scale and Behavior Problems during the Third Year

TTS temperament dimension	Eyberg child behavior inventory (N = 104)		Preschool behavior questionnaire scale (N = 95–103)			
	Intensity	Problem	Total beh. disturbed	Hostile-aggressive	Anxious	Hyperactive-distractible
Activity Level	.33**	.20*	.12	.11	−.04	.22*
Rhythmicity[a]	−.11	−.21*	−.11	−.14	−.08	.04
Approach[a]	−.19*	−.11	−.22*	−.21*	−.26**	.03
Adaptability[a]	−.38***	−.23*	−.16	−.12	−.11	−.07
Intensity	.37***	.24*	.28**	.28**	.19	.26**
Negative Mood	.47***	.33**	.31**	.27**	.39***	.15
Persistence[a]	−.26**	−.16	−.15	−.18	.00	−.04
Distractibility	.16	.11	.07	.08	.04	.10
Threshold	.06	.03	−.01	.08	.02	.04

[a] Signs of coefficients were reversed to facilitate interpretation.
*p < .05. **p < .01. ***p < .001.

internalizing and externalizing scales during subsequent developmental eras (ages 6–12 and 13–17) revealed only scattered and low coefficients.

Correlation coefficients between the BSQ and the broad band categories of the CBCL aggregated across middle childhood and adolescence are presented in Table 4.11. Three major findings are as follows. First, coefficients were strongest and most pervasive with externalizing behavior problems, with magnitudes in the

Table 4.11. Pearson Correlation Coefficients between Preschool-Age Temperament and Behavior Problems during Middle Childhood and Adolescence on the Child Behavior Checklist

Temperament dimension	Middle childhood (N = 111)		Adolescence (N = 110)	
	Internalizing	Externalizing	Internalizing	Externalizing
Activity Level	.07	.41***	.05	.37***
Rhythmicity[a]	−.17	−.08	−.12	−.09
Approach[a]	−.30**	−.19*	−.12	−.16
Adaptability[a]	−.26**	−.40***	−.07	−.33***
Intensity	.07	.27**	−.02	.23*
Negative Mood	.23*	.40***	.12	.34***
Persistence[a]	−.20*	−.24*	−.05	−.19
Distractibility	.05	.13	.02	.14
Threshold	−.03	.05	−.11	.03

[a] Signs of coefficients were reversed to facilitate interpretation.
*p < .05. **p < .01. ***p < .001.

Table 4.12.   Pearson Correlation Coefficients between
Middle Childhood Temperament and Behavior
Problems during Adolescence

Temperament dimension	Broad-band category	
	Internalizing	Externalizing
Activity Level	.08	.43***
Predictability[a]	−.29**	−.48***
Approach[a]	−.22*	−.06
Adaptability[a]	−.30**	−.60***
Intensity	.16	.43***
Negative Mood	.25*	.57***
Persistence[a]	−.33**	−.54***
Distractibility	.15	.31**
Threshold	.20*	.25*

$N = 106$.
[a] Signs of coefficients were reversed to facilitate interpretation.
*$p < .05$. **$p < .01$. ***$p < .001$.

low moderate range for both developmental eras. Second, preschoolers who were more negative in mood, slower to adapt, and higher activity level exhibited higher levels of externalizing behavior problems during both middle childhood and adolescence. Finally, approach/withdrawal was the strongest correlate of internalizing problems during middle childhood (more withdrawing preschoolers rated higher on internalizing problems), but there were no significant cross-time correlations with internalizing problems during adolescence.

Middle Childhood Temperament and Subsequent Behavior Problems

Although preschool temperament did not show strong cross-time correlations with behavior problems during adolescence, temperament during middle childhood correlated at strong magnitudes with externalizing behavior problems. As shown in Table 4.12, six of the nine temperament dimensions of the MCTQ correlated above .40 with externalizing problems. Cross-time coefficients were strongest (above .50) for adaptability, negative mood, and persistence/attention span. Temperamental characteristics of slow adaptability, negative mood, and lower persistence/attention span presaged higher externalizing or undercontrolled types of problems in adolescence.

Cross-Time, Cross-Informant Relations between Temperament and Behavior Problems

In this section, we examined what we considered to be the strongest test of temperament-behavior problem linkages, those in which the reports of different informants were used to predict behavior problems across time. Beginning with data on the prediction of behavior problems from temperament ratings, we conducted the following analyses:

- Cross-time correlations between ICQ factors at 1.5 years and behavior problem scores reported by teachers (TRF, ages 6–11) and by the study children (YSR at age 17);
- Cross-time correlations between TTS dimensions at 2 years and behavior problems based on teacher ratings (TRF, ages 6–11) and by the study children (YSR at age 17);
- Cross-time correlations between BSQ dimensions aggregated across the preschool years and behavior problems based on teacher ratings (TRF, ages 6–11) and the study children (YSR at age 17);
- Cross-time correlations between MCTQ dimensions during middle childhood and behavior problems based on ratings by the study children (YSR at age 17).

Given that the temperament and behavior problem reports involved behaviors in different settings (for TRF) or across long periods of time (YSR), correlation coefficients observed were expected to be low in magnitude. As a basis for comparison, consider that Achenbach et al. (1987) and Phares et al. (1989) reported the average correlation coefficient between concurrently assessed teacher and parent reports of behavior problems in the range of .30.

ICQ

An examination of the relationship between the ICQ factors during infancy and cross-informant reports of internalizing and externalizing behavior problems yielded few significant correlation coefficients, all of low magnitude. ICQ fussy/difficult/demanding temperament correlated with teacher ratings of externalizing behavior problems, with more behavior problems associated with more fussy/difficult temperament, $r = .22, p < .05$. In the analyses between the ICQ and the YSR, the ICQ unadaptable factor significantly related to adolescents' self-reports of both internalizing problems and externalizing problems (r's $= .21$ to $.23, p < .05$). ICQ unsociability also correlated with externalizing problems, ($r = .20, p < .05$).

TTS

Only 1 of 36 correlation coefficients computed between the TTS and teacher or adolescent self ratings of internalizing and externalizing behavior problems was significant. Hence, there is no evidence that preschool age temperament is predictive of teacher reported behavior problems across the elementary school years. There was little evidence that toddler temperament related to subsequent behavior problems across setting/informant (i.e., in the school by teacher) or across informant in a similar setting across long periods of time.

BSQ

Parent reports on the BSQ in the preschool years related at low levels with teacher ratings of behavior problems on the TRF during elementary school, ages 6 through 11. Preschool-age activity level ($r = .28$, $p < .01$), slow adaptability ($r = .24$, $p < .05$), and low persistence/attention span ($r = .21$, $p < .05$) all correlated with externalizing behavior problems.

Analyses assessing the relation between parent reports of temperament during the preschool years and adolescent reports of behavior problems on the YSR at 17 years failed to demonstrate either strong or meaningful relations.

MCTQ

No significant correlations were observed between parent-reported temperament during middle childhood and adolescent's self-rated behavior problems at 17 years.

Hence, there was scant evidence that earlier ratings of children's temperament by parents revealed any useful information about the child's subsequent behavior across settings and informants (i.e., in elementary school by teacher report) or informant (adolescent self-reports).

Multiple Regression Analyses Between Temperament and Behavior Problems

By way of summarizing the ponderous data from the FLS between temperament and behavior problems, we present Table 4.13, which displays the amount of variance in behavior problems explained by each temperament measure collected across infancy, childhood, and adolescence.

The ICQ in infancy related across time to both internalizing and externalizing behavior problems, explaining as much as 25 to 30 percent of the variance in externalizing behavior problems. For all externalizing measures save the YSR, the fussy/difficult/demanding factor was the sole predictor variable, however. ICQ unsociability and unadaptability were the primary predictors for internalizing behavior problems; the largest amount of variance explained in internalizing problems was 10 to 15 percent.

Regression analyses using the TTS at age 2 to predict behavior problems resulted in lower multiple correlations compared to the ICQ. Moreover, there was no clear pattern of temperament variables entering into the regression equations.

Temperament dimensions during the preschool years showed a stronger pattern of relation with behavior problems, with multiple correlation coefficients ranging to .45 for internalizing and .63 for externalizing problems. Approach entered

Table 4.13. Multiple Regression Analyses between Temperament and Behavior Problems as a Function of Temperament Measure, Informant, and Assessment Timing

Behavior problem inventory and age(s) in years	Informants	Assessment timing (eras)	Internalizing problems			Externalizing problems		
			R	Adj. R^2	F	R	Adj. R^2	F
Infant characteristics questionnaire ($N = 104$–110)								
Child Behavior Check. 4/5	Same	Cross-Era	.39	.10	9.58***	.57	.32	53.62***
Teacher Report Form 6-11	Cross	Cross-Era	—	—	—	.21	.04	5.16*
Child Behavior Check. 6-12	Same	Cross-Era	.39	.13	9.21***	.52	.27	39.35***
Child Behavior Check. 13-17	Same	Cross-Era	.28	.07	8.93**	.51	.25	36.22***
Youth Self Report 17	Cross	Cross-Era	.21	.04	4.78*	.23	.04	5.68*
Toddler temperament scale ($N = 91$–105)								
Child Behavior Check. 4/5	Same	Cross-Era	.33	.10	12.39***	.40	.14	9.77***
Teacher Report Form 6-11	Cross	Cross-Era	—	—	—	—	—	—
Child Behavior Check. 6-12	Same	Cross-Era	.24	.05	6.22*	.30	.08	9.76**
Child Behavior Check. 13-17	Same	Cross-Era	—	—	—	.20	.03	4.11*
Youth Self Report 17	Cross	Cross-Era	—	—	—	.32	.08	5.35**
Behavioral style questionnaire ($N = 107$–114)								
Child Behavior Check. 4/5	Same	Concurrent	.45	.19	14.03***	.63	.37	23.66**
Teacher Report Form 6-11	Cross	Cross-Era	—	—	—	.28	.07	9.09**
Child Behavior Check. 6-12	Same	Cross-Era	.30	.08	10.62***	.50	.24	18.08***
Child Behavior Check. 13-17	Same	Cross-Era	—	—	—	.32	.08	5.35**
Youth Self Report 17	Cross	Cross-Era	.24	.05	6.28*	.20	.03	4.41*
Middle childhood temperament questionnaire ($N = 104$–106)								
Teacher Report Form 6-11	Cross	Concurrent	.33	.09	6.16**	.60	.35	19.68***
Child Behavior Check. 6-12	Same	Concurrent	.57	.31	16.53***	.74	.53	40.82***
Child Behavior Check. 13-17	Same	Cross-Era	.33	.10	12.56**	.66	.41	25.76***
Youth Self Report 17	Cross	Cross-Era	—	—	—	—	—	—
Revised dimensions of temperament survey (parent report; $N = 103$–104)								
Child Behavior Check. 13-17	Same	Concurrent	.48	.21	10.15***	.36	.12	8.18***
Youth Self Report 17	Cross	Concurrent	.24	.05	6.15*	.28	.07	8.37**
Revised dimensions of temperament survey (adolescent self-report; $N = 109$–110)								
Child Behavior Check. 13-17	Cross	Concurrent	.22	.04	5.70*	.36	.12	8.18***
Youth Self Report 17	Same	Concurrent	.39	.14	9.72***	.46	.19	9.25***

*$p < .05$. **$p < .01$. ***$p < .001$.

as the first predictor of internalizing problems at ages 4/5 and 6–12, whereas negative mood and activity level were the most consistent predictors of externalizing problems. Furthermore, temperament during the preschool years significantly predicted externalizing problems across time and informant (i.e., TRF during middle childhood and YSR during adolescence).

Temperament during middle childhood explained 9 and 35 percent of the variance in teacher-reported internalizing and externalizing behavior problems, respectively. The corresponding values for concurrent parent reported behavior problems were 31 and 53 percent, respectively. Temperament during middle childhood also predicted parent reports of behavior problems in adolescence, explaining 10 and 41 percent of the variance in internalizing and externalizing problems, respectively. No clear pattern of predictors for internalizing problems was evident; however, adaptability and predictability were predictors of externalizing problems multiple times.

Adolescent temperament related concurrently to behavior problem ratings both within and across informants. Looking within informants, temperament explained about 15 to 20 percent of the variance in internalizing problems and 15 to 30 percent of the variance in externalizing problems. Cross-informant relations explained about 5 and 10 percent of the variance in internalizing and externalizing problems, respectively. Flexibility entered into the prediction of internalizing problems across numerous equations; activity level, mood, and task orientation related to externalizing problems across numerous equations.

Behavior Problems as Prognosticators of Temperament Using Measures from the Same Informants

Repeated assessments of both temperament and behavior problems allowed us to examine the predictive relation between behavior problems and subsequent temperament. Although the focus in the extant literature has been to examine the reverse temporal sequence (i.e., temperament as a predictor of behavior problems), we were interested in documenting how behavior problems may influence the expression of children's temperament or others' perceptions/impressions/interpretations of their behavioral style. We report analyses for the earliest behavior problem measures collected in the FLS, the Preschool Behavior Questionnaire administered during the third year and the Child Behavior Checklist aggregated across ages 4 and 5. These scales allowed the examination of the temperamental sequelae during middle childhood and adolescence of specific types of preschool-age behavior problems.

Analyses examining the middle childhood temperamental sequelae of behavior problems assessed during the preschool years are displayed in Table 4.14. The results indicated significant stability of behavioral patterns across the preschool and middle childhood eras. Assessments of emotional and behavioral adjustment

Table 4.14. Pearson Correlation Coefficients between Behavior Problems during Preschool Years and Temperament during Middle Childhood

Behavior problem index	Middle childhood temperament questionnaire dimension								
	Activity	Predict[a]	Approach[a]	Adapt[a]	Intensity	Negative mood	Persist[a]	Distract	Threshold
Preschool behavior questionnaire (N = 96–103)									
Total Behavior Problems	.26*	−.41***	−.46***	−.19	.34**	.43***	−.44***	.19	.14
Hostile-Aggressive	.19	−.36***	−.20*	−.36***	.24*	.31**	−.36***	.18	.15
Anxious	.05	−.21*	−.27**	−.21*	.19	.21*	−.23*	.06	.06
Hyperactive-Distractible	.35***	−.32**	.04	−.38***	.24*	.27**	−.41***	.28**	.06
Child behavior checklist at ages 4/5 (N = 106)									
Internalizing	.07	−.23*	−.35***	−.25**	.23*	.20*	−.14	.05	.17
Externalizing	.34***	−.40***	−.22*	−.56***	.42***	.46***	−.45***	.26**	.31**

[a]Signs of coefficients were reversed to facilitate interpretation.
*p < .05. **p < .01. ***p < .001.

at 3.5 years on the PBQ, displayed in the top panel of Table 4.14, showed numerous temperamental sequelae during middle childhood, with correlation coefficients ranging to .46 in magnitude. The strongest and most pervasive temperamental consequences were evident for the total behavior problem scale: preschoolers with higher behavior problem totals during childhood were less predictable/organized, withdrawing, negative in mood, and lower in persistence. A similar pattern was observed for those with hostile-aggressive behaviors, albeit slightly lower. Preschoolers rated higher on hyperactive-distractible problems during childhood were less persistent, more active, slower to adapt, more distractible, and negative in mood. Also showing outcome specificity, anxious behaviors in preschool portended withdrawing temperament during middle childhood.

Moving to the lower panel of Table 4.14, children's scores on the externalizing scale during the preschool era related to all nine NYLS temperament dimensions during middle childhood, with correlations reaching .56 in magnitude. Externalizing behavior problems during preschool presaged temperament characterized as slow adaptability, negative mood, lower persistence/attention span, intense rather than mild reactions, and lower predictability/organization. Preschoolers with higher internalizing scores were less approaching of novelty during middle childhood.

Similar analyses conducted with parent ratings on the DOTS-R during adolescence revealed that both internalizing and externalizing behavior problems during the preschool years foretold lower flexibility in adolescence, r's $= -.34$ and $-.37$, $p < .001$. Preschoolers with higher externalizing problem scores, as adolescents, were higher in activity level ($r = .43, p < .001$), lower in task orientation ($r = -.30$, $p < .01$), and withdrawing ($r = -.23, p < .05$). More overcontrolled behavior during the preschool years portended, in addition to lower flexibility, lower approach ($r = -.32, p < .01$) during adolescence.

Using Combined Adolescent and Parent Temperament Ratings to Predict Adolescent Behavior Problems

In the final set of regression analyses, the utility of including both parent and adolescent self ratings of temperament in predicting behavior problems was examined. As in prior analyses, temperament ratings were aggregated within informant and across ages 14 and 16 years on the DOTS-R. Parent ratings on the CBCL were aggregated across ages 13 through 17 years; adolescent self ratings of behavior problems were collected using the YSR at age 17. On all behavior problem measures, the internalizing and externalizing scales were analyzed. Results are displayed in Table 4.15.

The major conclusion from these analyses is that including temperament ratings from both informants generally failed to improve the amount of variance explained beyond that of the behavior problem informant. On analyses in which

Table 4.15.   Multiple Regression Analyses Comparing Amount of Variance in Behavior Problems during Adolescence Explained by Parent and Adolescent Ratings of Temperament

Behavior inventory and informant	Internalizing problems			Externalizing problems		
	R	Adjusted R^2	F	R	Adjusted R^2	F
Parent ratings of temperament entered first						
Child Behavior Checklist (Parent Informant)						
Parent	.48	.21	10.15***	.59	.32	15.57***
Adolescent	—	—	—	—	—	—
Youth Self Report (Adolescent Informant)						
Parent	.24	.11		.28	.07	
Adolescent	.43	.16	7.36***	.45	.18	8.56***
Adolescent ratings of temperament entered first						
Child Behavior Checklist (Parent Informant)						
Adolescent	.23	.04		.37	.12	
Parent	.49	.21	7.87***	.59	.32	13.17***
Youth Self Report (Adolescent Informant)						
Adolescent	.37	.12	8.24***	.41	.15	
Parent	—	—	—	.45	.18	8.41***

$N = 103–104.$
$^*p < .05.\ ^{**}p < .01.\ ^{***}p < .001.$

the behavior problem and temperament measures were provided by the same informant (i.e., first and fourth sets of analyses in Table 4.15, the including the other informant failed to account for a significant increment in variance explained. In the one instance when the second informant's temperament ratings entered into the equation (final set of analyses for externalizing problems on the YSR), the change in R^2 was 3 percent. Having the second temperament informant led to a significant increment in R^2 only when the behavior problem informant was entered last into the equation (i.e., second and third sets of analyses in Table 4.15). In these analyses, the temperament ratings of the second informant (i.e., the behavior rating informant) increased the variance in behavior problems explained by 5 to over 15 percent.

Summary and Conclusions

1. *What is the pattern of concurrent temperament-behavior problem relations throughout childhood and adolescence, when both are reported by the same informant?* Across childhood and adolescence, adaptability/flexibility consistently related to both internalizing and externalizing behavior problems. During childhood, negative mood was a consistent correlate of

both types of behavior problems, whereas during adolescence task orientation related to both. These aspects of temperament correlated moderately (i.e., .40 to .60) with behavior problems. Specificity in temperament-behavior problem relations was also evident; approach/withdrawal related to internalizing problems and activity level to externalizing problems. Multiple regression analyses showed that temperament explained between 15% to 30% of the variance in internalizing behavior problems when measured concurrently and within informant during the preschool, childhood, and adolescent eras; for externalizing problems, variance explained by child temperament ranged from 10% to over 50%.

2. *What is the magnitude of relation between concurrent assessments of temperament and behavioral adjustment when measured across different informants?* Teacher reports of behavior problems during the middle childhood related to moderate magnitudes with parent-reported temperament. Persistence/attention span and adaptability were related most strongly to teacher-reported behavior problems. Multiple regression analyses showed that parent ratings of child temperament explained 9% of the variance in internalizing problems and 37% of the variance in externalizing problems. However, cross informant ratings of behavior problems and child temperament during adolescence (parent and child rated each) were markedly lower; cross-informant ratings of temperament on the DOTS-R explained approximately 5% of the variance in internalizing problems and approximately 10% of the variance in externalizing problems as measured on the CBCL and YSR.

3. *Within the same informant, across what spans of time do dimensions of temperament predict behavioral adjustment?* Aspects of challenging infant temperament relate across time to internalizing problems in middle childhood and adolescence, explaining approximately 10% of the variance. For externalizing problems, the corresponding value is 25%. Dimensions of preschool temperament explain 8% and 24% of the variance in internalizing and externalizing problems during middle childhood, but 0% and 8%, respectively, during adolescence. Cross time relations between middle childhood temperament and adolescent behavior problems reach moderate magnitudes and explain 10% and 41% of the variance in internalizing and externalizing problems, respectively. Parent reports of infant temperament also related significantly to classifications of behavior problems as normal versus clinically elevated during the preschool, middle childhood, and adolescent eras.

4. *Across different informants, to what extent do dimensions of temperament predict behavioral adjustment measured later in development?* Parent reports of temperament during the infancy and preschool eras relate across time to teacher reports of externalizing problems, explaining

approximately 5% of the variance. Parent reports of temperament during the early years relate at low levels to adolescent reports of behavior problems at 17, explaining at best 4% of the variance in internalizing problems and 8% of the variance in externalizing problems.

5. *Within the same informant, to what extent do early behavior problems predict aspects of subsequent temperament?* Behavior problems assessed during the preschool years related to moderate magnitudes with temperament assessed during middle childhood, and behavior problems in middle childhood predicted temperament during adolescence, also at moderate levels. Preschool externalizing problems related to a greater range of subsequent temperament dimensions, but especially adaptability, negative mood, and persistence in middle childhood and general activity and task orientation in adolescence. Internalizing problems related across time to subsequent approach in middle childhood and approach and flexibility in adolescence. Hence, temperament-behavior problem relations are bidirectional.

6. *Does the combination of child and parent ratings of behavior problems during adolescence improve the prediction of behavior problems?* Generally, the utilizing the cross-informant of temperament did not significantly increase the amount of variance explained beyond that of the behavior problem informant.

5

Temperament and Intelligence

"(Name) is a delightful boy. He is very well adjusted and is really a joy to work with. In general he takes directives well and listens to good and correctional criticisms equally. To some extent, (Name) was not working up to his potential earlier in the year. He was rushing a great deal and to some degree, I believe, felt "being first done was best." This has begun to correct itself. Where his work quality was not up to his potential earlier, it is improving. The work is getting neater and the effort is increasing. If allowed, it seems (Name) would be content with just getting by with "easy B's;" with attention he works for the "A's" and he does aim to please. In many respects, though, his performance and attitude does not reflect the "gifted child" his test scores indicate."
—Teacher of Child #11, Difficult Infant Temperament Group, Age 9

Issues Investigated

In this chapter, we address one of the central themes of development charted in the FLS, intelligence. The interface and overlap between temperament and cognitive ability from infancy though adolescence are examined. As noted in chapter 1, five issues will be addressed:

1. *Which dimensions of temperament correlate with concurrently-administered standardized tests of intelligence?* The temperamental concomitants of intelligence are examined across the infant, preschool, middle childhood, and adolescent eras.
2. *Can the temperament-intelligence relationship be explained by test-taking behaviors during the administration of the intellectual tests?* At three points in time during the FLS, test-taking behavior as a possible mediating variable between temperament and intelligence test scores was examined.
3. *Are the relations evident between temperament and cognitive skills as measured by standardized tests also evident when parent reports of developmental progress are used?* As another approach to explore the possible mediating effect of test taking behavior on the relation between

temperament and intelligence, we examined the relation between temperament and parent reports of developmental progress on standardized inventories of child development.

4. *To what extent do aspects of earlier temperament forecast or predict intellectual development throughout childhood and adolescence?* A necessary but not sufficient observation for temperament to influence children's cognitive/intellectual growth is that earlier temperament relate to subsequent intelligence. In this section, the degree of relation between earlier temperament and intelligence across shorter and longer intervals of time are examined.

5. *To what extent do earlier measures of children's intelligence predict temperament and personality?* In the final section, FLS measures of intelligence are examined as potential predictors of children's behavioral style and personality. Concurrent temperament-intelligence relations do not elucidate whether individual differences in children's ability to process and coordinate information and communicate their needs effectively may impact their behavioral styles. Hence, earlier measures of intelligence as predictors of subsequent temperament are examined to ascertain whether empirical evidence exists to support this possible direction of relation. Furthermore, discussion regarding the intersection between personality and intelligence has been revisited recently (Collis & Messick, 2001). In chapter 3, data from the FLS failed to show direct links between temperament during infancy, preschool years, or middle childhood with personality at age 17. To conclude chapter 5, we examine the extent to which early measures of intelligence foretell personality.

Description of Measures Used in the FLS

Intellectual development and its influences are central strands of the FLS project, and their centrality is demonstrated through ongoing and frequent assessment. Developmental/intelligence tests were administered at each assessment through age 8; intelligence was also appraised at ages 12, 15, and 17. During the infant, preschool, and adolescent years, test administrators completed standardized ratings of the examinees' test-taking behaviors.

Direct Laboratory Assessments of Intelligence

Infancy

At 1, 1.5, and 2 years, infants were tested on the mental scale of the Bayley Scales of Infant Development (Bayley, 1969). The Bayley was selected because it was the most extensively standardized and researched psychometric assessment of sensorimotor intelligence. The Mental Development Index (MDI), aggregated across ages 1, 1.5, and 2 years, was used in all analyses in this chapter, unless otherwise noted.

Preschool

Children were administered the McCarthy Scales of Children's Abilities (McCarthy, 1972) at 2.5, 3, and 3.5 years. The General Cognitive Index, comprising scales assessing verbal, perceptual-performance, and quantitative skills, was analyzed in this chapter. Unless otherwise noted, analyses are based upon scores on the General Cognitive Index aggregated across the three administrations.

At age 5, children were tested using the Kaufman Assessment Battery for Children (KABC; A. S. Kaufman & N. L. Kaufman, 1983). The mental processing composite score was used in all analyses in this chapter.

Middle Childhood

The Wechsler Intelligence Scale for Children-Revised (WISC-R; Wechsler, 1974) was administered at ages 6, 7, 8, and 12 years. This well-known test comprises 10 subtests assessing verbal and performance tasks. Analyses herein used the Full Scale IQ, averaged across the 6-, 7-, 8-, and 12-year assessments.

Adolescence

At 15 years the Wechsler Intelligence Scale for Children – Third Edition (WISC-III; Wechsler, 1991) was administered, and the Wechlser Adult Intelligence Scale-Revised (WAIS-R; Wechsler, 1981) was given at age 17. As with the WISC-R, the WISC III and the WAIS-R comprise ten subtests. All analyses utilized the Full Scale IQ.

Parent Report Measures

Two standardized parent report inventories regarding children's development were administered. When children were 2.5 years old, mothers completed the Minnesota Child Development Inventory (MCDI; Ireton & Thwing, 1972–1974); the Minnesota Preschool Inventory (MPI; Ireton & Thwing, 1979) was administered when children were 5 years. The MCDI comprises 320 empirically derived age-related statements describing children's development that form eight scales: gross motor, fine motor, expressive language, comprehension-conceptual (receptive language skills), situation comprehension, self-help, personal social, and general development. The general development scale is composed of the most discriminating items from the seven other scales.

The MPI consists of 150 items that form seven developmental scales: self help, fine motor, expressive language, comprehension, memory, letter recognition, and number comprehension. For both the MCDI and MPI, the respondent's task is to mark "yes" or "no" to each statement as to whether or not the child has attained the developmental skill described. The scale score, representing the number of "yes" responses for each scale, was analyzed. The MCDI and MPI have shown to be valid measures of children's current and future developmental status in the FLS (A. W. Gottfried, Guerin, Spencer, & Meyer, 1984; Guerin & Gottfried, 1987). Other researchers have supported the screening efficiency of these inventories in both nonclinical and clinical/at-risk samples (e.g., Dean & Steffen, 1984; Ireton & Thwing, 1979; Ireton, Thwing, & Currier, 1977; Saylor & Brandt, 1986; Shoemaker, Saylor, & Erickson, 1993).

Test Taking Behavior

Bayley Infant Behavior Record (IBR)

At the conclusion of the administration of the developmental or intelligence test at 1.5 through 6 years, the examiner rated the child's behavior during the testing session by completing items selected from the IBR (Bayley, 1969). A complete list of all items meeting the FLS criterion of 85% inter-observer reliability has been previously published (A.W. Gottfried et al., 1994). Following Matheny (1980), the average ratings on the following items were computed to yield a task orientation score: object orientation, goal directedness, and attention span. The four items of social orientation to the examiner, cooperativeness, fearfulness, and emotional tone were averaged to yield an affect/extraversion score. Matheny (1980) also described an activity scale, comprising the activity, body motion, and energy items. Only the energy item was available for analysis in the FLS. From the examiner ratings on the IBR, three scores (task orientation, affect/extraversion, and activity) were used as indicators of test taking behavior during the infant, toddler, and preschool years.

Guide to the Assessment of Test Session Behavior (GATSB)

Immediately following administration of the WISC-III at the 15-year assessment and the WAIS-R at the 17-year assessment, the examiner completed the GATSB (Glutting & Oakland, 1992) to describe the adolescent's behavior during the test session. The GATSB comprises 29 items to which the examiner responds *Doesn't apply, Sometimes applies,* or *Usually applies.* Responses are summed across subsets of items to yield three scales: Avoidance, Inattentiveness, and Uncooperative Mood; *T*-scores were analyzed.

Findings and Discussion

Temperament-IQ Relations Assessed Concurrently

Pearson correlation coefficients between the temperament scores and concurrently administered standardized tests of intelligence were computed at each developmental era. Beginning in the infancy period with relations between the ICQ factors and the Bayley Mental Development Index (MDI) aggregated across ages 1, 1.5, and 2 years, only one significant correlation coefficient was observed: ICQ unsociability correlated with the MDI, $r = -.19$, $p < .05$. The more unsociable the infant, the lower the Bayley MDI. Conversely, infants rated as less unsociable in their interactions with people by their mothers scored higher in mental development during the second year.

Concurrent temperament-IQ relations are displayed in Table 5.01 for the toddler, preschool, and middle childhood eras. Beginning in the left-most column, correlation coefficients between the TTS and the Bayley MDI (both administered at age 2 years) are shown; toddlers who were more positive in mood, persistent, less distractible, and more approaching tended to have higher Bayley MDI scores. These findings corroborate those reported by Matheny (1989) regarding the first and second year data of the Louisville Twin Study, who reported higher Bayley scores among infants with longer attention span/persistence, positive mood, and

Table 5.01. **Pearson Correlation Coefficients between Concurrent Measures of Temperament and Intelligence, Toddlerhood through Middle Childhood**[a]

	TTS	Behavioral style questionnaire		MCTQ
	Bayley mental develop index	McCarthy general cognitive index	Kaufman mental processing scale	Wechsler full scale IQ
Activity level[b]	−.05	−.17	−.30**	−.11
Approach[b]	.20*	.33***	.21*	.30**
Adaptability[b]	.16	.34***	.37***	.20*
Negative mood	−.27**	−.25**	−.25**	−.23*
Persistence[b]	.26**	.31***	.36***	.29**
Distractibility	−.23*	−.01	−.04	−.27**

[a]Rhythmicity, intensity, and threshold are omitted, as no correlation coefficients were significant at any of the ages shown.
[b]Signs of coefficients were reversed to facilitate interpretation.
Note: *N*'s = 107–118.
*$p < .05$. **$p < .01$. ***$p < .001$.

tendencies to approach novelty in their environment. Findings from the Fullerton and Louisville studies contrasted those from the Colorado Adoption Study (Daniels et al., 1984), where researchers concluded temperament was unrelated to measures of intellectual development from 1 to 2 years. Perhaps the measures of temperament used in the former studies were more sensitive in assessing temperament than the global temperament measure utilized in the latter.

In the second and third columns of Table 5.01, temperament-IQ linkages during the preschool years are presented. Correlation coefficients between the BSQ and the general cognitive index of the McCarthy Scales and the mental processing scale of the KABC are displayed. On both measures, preschoolers who were quicker to adapt to change, less negative in mood, more persistent, and more approaching rather than withdrawing from novelty scored higher. Additionally, at age 5, more active children scored lower on the KABC mental processing scale. These findings corroborate those of Palisin (1986), Matheny (1989), and Martin and Holbrook (1985). Palisin reported higher intelligence scores associated with temperament characteristics of longer attention span/persistence, the tendency to approach rather than withdraw from new situations, people, etc., and lower activity level. Matheny reported significant temperament-IQ relations at age 3 years (adaptability and persistence/attention span) and 5 years (adaptability, persistence/attention span, approach). In an elementary school setting using teacher reports of temperament, Martin and Holbrook reported higher IQ test scores among first graders rated as more adaptable to changes, approaching to novelty, and persistent. As with findings from the previous researchers with respect to activity level, results from the FLS are inconsistent, sometimes showing a significant albeit low correlation with intelligence and sometimes showing no relation.

Temperament and IQ also correlated significantly during the elementary school years. The final column in Table 5.01 displays correlation coefficients between dimensions of the MCTQ and the full scale IQ of the WISC-R. Children with longer attention span/persistence, lower distractibility, less negative mood, approach rather than withdrawal tendencies, and quicker adaptability tended to score higher on the WISC-R. These findings are in line with those of Matheny with respect to attention span/persistence. Corroboration of these findings also comes from similar measures collected outside the U.S. Czeschlik (1993), comparing temperaments of 10-year-olds in very high intelligence (i.e., top 2%, $n = 150$) to average intelligence ($n = 134$) groups, found that parent ratings of temperament differed on two dimensions: distractibility and intensity; lower scores on each of these dimensions were observed in the high-intelligence group. Teachers rated pupils in the high-intelligence group higher in both task orientation and personal-social flexibility.

Two dimensions of temperament related to full-scale IQ on the WISC-III at 15 years and the WAIS-R at 17 years: approach and flexibility. At ages 14 and 16 years, assessments of the adolescents' temperament were made via teen self-reports and parent reports on the DOTS-R; these were aggregated across age within informant.

Parent ratings of teens' temperament on the DOTS-R related significantly to the 15- and 17-year IQ measures on two dimensions: approach and flexibility with the WISC-III at 15 years (r's = .24 and .22, respectively) and approach on the WAIS-R at 17 years (r = .20). Adolescent self-ratings showed a similar pattern: at age 15, approach and flexibility related to IQ (r's = .23 and .37, respectively); at age 17, flexibility correlated .32 (correlation coefficients with teen self-reported flexibility were significant at the .01 level). No other dimensions on the DOTS-R, by either teen or parent assessment, correlated significantly with adolescent IQ.

Across the developmental eras investigated in the FLS, four temperament dimensions repeatedly emerged as concomitants of intellectual test performance: negative mood and persistence/attention span from the toddler years through middle childhood, and approach/withdrawal and adaptability/flexibility from the preschool years through adolescence. Children who were characterized as less negative in mood, more persistent or with longer attention spans, approaching to new people, places, and objects, and quicker to adapt to changes scored higher on standardized tests of intelligence throughout their early development, childhood, and adolescence. Significant correlation coefficients were of a similar, modest magnitude across the developmental periods. Matheny (1989) identified the same four temperament dimensions (attention span/persistence, approach, adaptability, negative mood) as overlapping with concurrent measures of intelligence using data from the Louisville Twin Study.

To assess whether multiple dimensions of temperament combined would better explain the variance in intelligence, multiple regression analyses to parallel the aforementioned correlation analyses were conducted. The amount of variance explained in the measures of intelligence described herein by concurrent measures of temperament ranged from less than 5% (infancy, toddler years) to 14–19% (preschool, middle childhood). During the adolescent era, only one dimension entered, whether parent or adolescent reports were used. Hence, the amount of variance explained did not exceed that of the bivariate correlations during adolescence. The temperament dimensions of rhythmicity/predictability, intensity, and threshold never related to any measures of intelligence in the FLS in the aforementioned analyses.

Temperament, Test-Taking Behavior, and Intelligence

An issue previously raised was the extent to which the relation between temperament and IQ was due to the child's test-taking behaviors (Matheny, 1989; Strelau, Zawadzki, & Piotrowska, 2001). For example, Matheny (1989, p. 273) noted that "...the positive manner of the child during testing will elicit higher evaluations from the examiner." Strelau et al. noted that temperament characteristics may modify the results of intelligence tests by moderating the "stimulative value" of the testing situation (p. 63). That is, the standardized test environment may be perceived as more or less interesting/engaging depending upon the individual's temperament profile.

To test whether the temperament-IQ relation is completely or partially mediated by behaviors during the testing session, we followed the procedures outlined by Baron and Kenny (1986). According to Baron and Kenny, a variable is considered to be a mediator when four conditions are met. First, the predictor variable (in this case, a temperament dimension) must be associated significantly with the outcome measure, intelligence. This was demonstrated in the first section of this chapter. Second, the predictor variable must be associated significantly with the proposed mediator, test-taking behaviors. Third, the proposed mediator must be related to the criterion variable (in this case, IQ test scores). Finally, the impact of the predictor on the outcome measure must be less when controlling for the mediator. In cases in which the path from the predictor to the criterion (i.e., temperament to IQ) is no longer different from zero, complete mediation has occurred. When the path from the predictor to the criterion is still different from zero after controlling for the effect of the mediator, partial mediation is said to occur. We used the formula delineated by Baron and Kenny (1986) to test the significance of the indirect effect (e.g., paths B and C in Figure 1.04). When a significant mediator was identified following the aforementioned test, we then examined whether partial or complete mediation was indicated.

In the FLS, the examiner rated each examinee's behavior using the Bayley Infant Behavioral Record (IBR) immediately following administration of the Bayley Scales of Infant Development at age 1.5 and 2 years and following administration of the McCarthy Scales at 3 and 3.5 years. Immediately following the administration of the WISC-III (15 years) and the WAIS-R (17 years), the examiner completed the Guide to the Asssessment of Test Session Behavior (GATSB). To ascertain whether behaviors observed by the examiner related to parental ratings of children's temperament across time and other settings (condition 2), bivariate correlation coefficients were computed between the three IBR factors (task orientation, affect/extraversion, and activity) and the temperament dimensions of the ICQ (1.5 years), TTS (2 years), and BSQ (3 and 3.5 years). During adolescence, correlation coefficients were computed between the DOTS-R temperament dimensions and the three factors of the GATSB (avoidance, inattentiveness, uncooperative mood). Because test-taking ratings are based on behaviors during the completion of a specific test, neither IBR nor GATSB scores were aggregated across assessments.

Beginning with the ICQ, no correspondence was observed between examiner ratings on the IBR and parent ratings on the ICQ. At age 2 years, two significant correlation coefficients were observed between examiner ratings on the IBR and parent ratings of temperament on the TTS: IBR activity related to TTS activity level and approach, r's $= .44$ ($p < .001$) and $.26$ ($p < .01$), respectively. During the preschool period, examiner ratings on the IBR at 3 and 3.5 years and parent ratings on the BSQ showed significant correlations that replicated across both test periods for four BSQ dimensions. Youngsters rated by their parent as more approaching to new experiences were rated by the test examiner as higher on IBR task orientation and affect/extraversion, r's $= .22$ to $.28$. Children rated by parents as quicker to adapt to changes were rated by examiners as more task oriented and showing more positive affect/extraversion, r's $= .20$ to $.37$. Children rated by parents as more negative in mood were rated by examiners as lower in task orientation, r's $= .19$ and $.25$. Finally, parent ratings of persistence/attention span related positively to examiner ratings of task orientation at both 3 and 3.5 years, r's $= .31$ and $.33$.

Only four significant correlations emerged between GATSB ratings by test examiners and parent ratings on the DOTS-R averaged across ages 14 and 16 years. Parent ratings of approach related significantly and inversely to examiner ratings of avoidance at both 15 and 17 years, r's $= -.29$ and $-.30$, respectively. Additionally, at 15 years parent ratings of task orientation on the DOTS-R related to examiner ratings of inattentiveness and also uncooperative mood on the GATSB, r's $= -.29$. Hence, examiner ratings of test-taking behavior typically correlated with parent ratings of temperament at low magnitudes (at best) during the toddler, preschool, and adolescent years; however, there was no overlap between test-taking behavior ratings and parent ratings of temperament at 1.5 years. In all developmental eras, other than infancy, test-taking behavior was related to dimensions of temperament and could therefore be assessed as mediators of the temperament-IQ relation using FLS data.

The third required condition for the operation of a mediating variable is that the proposed mediator relate to the criterion variable. Hence, the relation between test-taking behaviors and IQ test scores was examined next. Pearson correlation coefficients between certain test taking behaviors as recorded on the IBR at 1.5, 2, 3, and 3.5 years showed significant correlations with all IQ test scores administered concurrently during the early years, as presented in Table 5.02.

The avoidant scale of the GATSB related inversely to IQ; adolescents who were resistant to the examiner's attempts at rapport, who were less enthusiastic,

Table 5.02.   Pearson Correlation Coefficients between Ratings of Test-Taking Behaviors and IQ

Infant behavior record factor	IQ assessment age			
	1.5	2	3	3.5
Task Orientation	.55***	.54***	.61***	.67***
Affect/Extraversion	.42***	.47***	.46***	.54***
Activity	.15	−.04	.17	.18

N's $= 109–123$.
***$p < .001$.

who persisted less on solving the test items, etc., scored lower IQ scores. The GATSB inattentiveness and uncooperative mood scales also related significantly to IQ at age 17, but not at 15 years. Adolescents who were more inattentive and more uncooperative during testing had lower IQ test scores at 17 years.

We now present the results of the statistical tests to determine whether test-taking behaviors partially or completely mediated the relations observed between temperament and IQ. The first three conditions outlined in prior paragraphs were met for 14 combinations of temperament dimensions, test-taking behaviors, and IQ. The temperament dimensions and test-taking behaviors that both related to IQ are listed in columns 1 and 2 in Table 5.03. In the first panel of Table 5.03, test-taking behaviors (IBR affect-extraversion and task orientation) as potential mediators of the relation between five dimensions of temperament and the General Cognitive Index (GCI) of the McCarthy Scales administered at 3 years were examined. The second panel shows the results of analyses of the relation between preschool temperament and the GCI at 3.5 years. The final panel shows the same results for adolescent temperament and the full scale IQ at 17 years. Moving now across Table 5.03, the third column displays the path coefficient observed for the direct path between temperament and the GCI. The fourth column displays the path coefficient controlling for the effect of the mediator indicated, and the fifth and

Table 5.03.   Summary of Analyses Examining Test-taking Behavior (TTB) as a Mediator of Temperament-IQ Relations

Temperament dimension	Test-taking behavior	Direct path	Path controlling for test-taking behavior	Test of indirect effect	Degree of mediation
McCarthy general cognitive index at 3 years					
Rhythmicity	Affect/Extraversion	.21	−.08	2.08	Complete
Approach	Task Orientation	.25	−.14	2.58	Complete
Approach	Affect/Extraversion	.25	−.15	2.58	Complete
Adaptability	Task Orientation	.32	−.17	3.26	Partial
Adaptability	Affect/Extraversion	.32	−.24	3.00	Partial
Negative Mood	Task Orientation	.20	−.08	2.03	Complete
Persistence	Task Orientation	.31	−.17	3.17	Partial
Persistence	Affect/Extraversion	.31	−.25	2.93	Partial
McCarthy general cognitive index at 3.5 years					
Approach	Task Orientation	.33	−.18	3.46	Partial
Approach	Affect/Extraversion	.33	−.21	3.26	Partial
Adaptability	Task Orientation	.27	.05	2.87	Complete
Adaptability	Affect/Extraversion	.27	−.15	2.76	Complete
Persistence	Task Orientation	.25	−.03	2.61	Complete
WISC-III					
Approach	Avoidant	.28	.12	2.72	Complete

sixth columns display the results and conclusion of the statistical test that the indirect effect is zero. In column 5, scores greater than 1.96 indicate the indirect path (mediator) was significant, $p < .05$.

In every analysis displayed in Table 5.03, test-taking behavior was shown to be a significant mediator of the relation between temperament and IQ. In approximately one-half of the analyses, test-taking behavior was a complete or perfect mediator between temperament and IQ, indicating that the relation between temperament and IQ after controlling for test-taking was diminished to zero in magnitude. In the remaining cases, test-taking behavior was a significant mediator, but a significant (and low magnitude) relation between temperament and IQ remained. There was no discernable pattern as to when partial or complete mediation occurred with respect to the specific temperament dimension, test-taking behavior, or age. What can be concluded from these analyses is that the child's behavior during the testing process, in many cases, explained the relation observed between temperament and IQ test scores. Furthermore, in all situations investigated herein, test-taking behaviors certainly accounted for a significant amount of the relation observed between parent reports of temperament and IQ test scores.

The finding that test-taking behaviors either partially or sometimes completely mediate the relation between temperament and intelligence test scores should not be assumed to signify that temperament is unrelated to intelligence, per se. What these findings show is that when intelligence is measured via individually administered standardized tests, variations in the examinee's temperament are intertwined with the way he/she approaches the test-taking situation. Using alternative methods to measure intelligence may provide a clearer indication of how individual differences in temperament may shape children's intellectual development. These findings underscore the importance of utilizing multiple indicators of the construct of intelligence. For example, in the next section we examine how children's temperament relates to a standardized inventory utilizing maternal reports of their children's developmental progress. In chapter 6, the relation of children's temperament to their cumulative high school grade point average is examined. By using these multiple indicators related to cognitive ability, we believe a clearer understanding of the role of temperament in children's intellectual development will be gained.

Temperament and Standardized Parental Reports of Child Development

In addition to individually-administered intelligence tests, standardized inventories of developmental progress were collected when participants were 2.5 and 5 years of age using the MCDI and MPI, respectively. Using parent reports on standardized inventories comprising items assessing children's developmental and cognitive accomplishments in real life situations provided an assessment of cognitive functioning independent of the test-taking situation. Based on the data observed between temperament and the children's performance on the standardized tests during the preschool years, we were particularly interested in whether the dimensions of approach/withdrawal, adaptability, persistence/attention span, and negative mood (see Table 5.01) would also predict parent reports of development.

Pearson correlation coefficients showed that preschool BSQ approach/withdrawal and persistence/attention span correlated consistently and significantly with the MCDI general development, expressive language, and comprehension-conceptual scales (r's $= .22$ to $.32$), but that BSQ adaptability and negative mood did not. Approach/withdrawal, adaptability, and persistence correlated consistently and significantly with the MPI scales of expressive language, comprehension, memory, and letter recognition, r's $= .25$ to $.33$. Negative mood correlated significantly with MPI memory and letter recognition (r's $= -.23$, $-.25$, respectively), but not expressive language or comprehension. Hence, approach/withdrawal and persistence/attention span related significantly and pervasively to cognitive skills, whether cognitive skills were measured via individually-administered standardized intelligence tests or via parent reports on standardized child development inventories.

Temperament as a Predictor of Intelligence

The FLS data present a unique opportunity to examine the extent to which early temperament features were predictive of subsequent intelligence through late adolescence. Pearson correlation coefficients between temperament measured during the toddler, preschool, and middle childhood development eras and subsequent intelligence are displayed in Table 5.04. Three of the four factors of the infancy measure of temperament (ICQ) correlated with the McCarthy General Cognitive Index (GCI), the WISC-R full scale IQ, the WISC-III full scale IQ, or the WAIS full scale IQ. Unsociability was related to intelligence scores only through preschool, whereas unadaptability presaged IQ at multiple ages. The fussy/difficult/demanding factor significantly correlated during every developmental stage from elementary school through late adolescence, although at a low magnitude (r's $= -.20$). More difficult and fussy infants scored lower on intelligence tests through at least adolescence. To ascertain whether the factors of the ICQ would combine to explain subsequent intelligence, stepwise multiple regression analyses were examined. In no analysis did multiple ICQ factors combine to explain variation in subsequent intelligence.

As shown in the second panel of Table 5.04, dimensions of temperament assessed at 2 years via the TTS correlated significantly with the McCarthy GCI,

Table 5.04. Pearson Correlation Coefficients Assessing Temperament Dimensions as Predictors of Intelligence from Preschool through Adolescence

Temperament dimension	Intelligence scale				
	McCarthy GCI	KABC MPS	Full scale IQ 6–12	Full scale IQ 15	Full scale IQ 17
	Infant characteristics questionnaire at 1.5 years				
Fussy/Difficult	−.12	−.32**	−.20*	−.21*	−.21*
Unadaptable	−.23*	−.21*	−.19	−.14	−.21*
Resistant to Control	−.10	−.17	−.14	−.06	−.04
Unsociable	−.26**	−.10	−.13	−.13	−.11
	Toddler temperament scale at 2 years[b]				
Activity Level	−.01	−.18	−.02	−.08	−.04
Approach[a]	.18	.30**	.34**	.25*	.29**
Adaptability[a]	.13	.17	.11	.08	.06
Intensity	−.01	−.17	−.13	−.23*	−.14
Negative Mood	−.21*	−.32**	−.31**	−.28**	−.25*
Persistence[a]	.04	.08	.07	.07	−.01
Distractibility	.01	−.12	−.07	−.05	−.10
	Behavioral style questionnaire (3, 3.5, 5 years aggregated)[b]				
Activity Level		−.30**	−.12	−.09	−.07
Approach[a]		.21*	.33***	.24*	.26**
Adaptability[a]		.37***	.30**	.31**	.20*
Intensity		−.17	−.09	−.09	−.15
Negative Mood		−.25**	−.14	−.15	−.14
Persistence[a]		.36***	.32**	.32**	.13
Distractibility		−.04	.00	−.01	−.04
	Middle childhood temperament questionnaire (8, 10, 12 years aggregated)[b]				
Activity Level				−.10	.01
Approach[a]				.25*	.31**
Adaptability[a]				.28**	.16
Intensity				−.17	−.05
Negative Mood				−.22*	−.18
Persistence[a]				.21*	.11
Distractibility				−.25*	−.24*

[a]Signs of coefficients were reversed to facilitate interpretation.
[b]Rhythmicity and threshold are omitted, as no correlation coefficients were significant at any of the ages shown.
Note: N's = 102–118 on ICQ; N's = 97–111 on TTS; N's = 105–111 on BSQ; N's = 102 on MCTQ analyses.
*$p < .05$. **$p < .01$. ***$p < .001$.

the WISC-R Full Scale IQ, the WISC-III Full Scale IQ, and the WAIS Full Scale IQ. Approach and negative mood, with significant correlations ranging to .34, demonstrated a consistent pattern of association with intelligence through age 17. Children who were negative in mood scored lower on subsequent intellectual tests, whereas more socially outgoing children scored higher on standardized measures of IQ. Toddler temperament dimensions combined to predict IQ at only one age in the series of stepwise multiple correlation analyses conducted on the five IQ criterion variables shown in Table 5.04. On the full scale IQ during middle childhood, negative mood and approach combined to explain 16% of the variance (adjusted for shrinkage) in the IQ scores aggregated across ages 6 to 12 years, $R = .42$, $F(2, 91) = 9.37, p < .001$.

In the next panel of Table 5.04, correlation coefficients between preschool-age temperament dimensions measured via the BSQ and subsequent measures of IQ on the Wechsler tests revealed significant relations ranging to .37 in magnitude. The temperament dimensions repeatedly relating to intelligence were approach, adaptability, and persistence. Preschoolers who were more sociable, interested in new toys and activities, adapted easily to new situations, and persistent in their goal-directed activities subsequently scored higher on IQ tests through adolescence. Stepwise multiple regression analyses conducted to determine whether temperament dimensions combined to explain subsequent intelligence showed significant multiple predictors for IQ at two ages. First, on the KABC at age 5, preschool temperament dimensions of approach and persistence combined to explain 18.7% of the variance (adjusted for shrinkage) in MPS scores, $R = .45$, $F (2, 98) = 12.29$, $p < .001$. Also, 15-year IQ was predicted by the same combination of preschool temperament variables. Approach and persistence combined accounted for 19.3% of the variance (adjusted for shrinkage) in full scale IQ at 15 years, $R = .46$, $F(2, 98) = 12.72, p < .001$.

The final panel in Table 5.04 displays correlation coefficients appraising the relation between temperament during the elementary school years and IQ during adolescence. On the MCTQ during middle childhood, dimensions that correlated consistently with IQ in adolescence were approach and distractibility, with higher approach and lower distractibility related to of higher IQ scores at ages 15 and 17. At both 15 and 17 years, stepwise multiple regression analyses showed that the dimensions of approach and distractibility during middle childhood combined to predict IQ. At age 15, these temperament characteristics combined to explain 9.2% of the variance in IQ, $R = .33$, $F(2, 99) = 6.04$, $p < .01$. At age 17, 14.1% of the variance in full scale IQ was explained, $R = .40$, $F (2, 99) = 9.14$, $p < .001$. However, it must be noted that these relations, as was the case with the concurrent relations, are possibly mediated by test-taking behavior.

Approach/Withdrawal and Intelligence Across Childhood/Adolescence

In the FLS, the dimension of approach was associated with intelligence scores across all developmental eras as well as being the most consistently related concurrently to all measures of intelligence. This finding corroborates findings of prior researchers (Benson et al., 1993; Raine et al., 2002) who demonstrated that children who negotiate their social and physical environments forthrightly experience intellectual advantage, perhaps by evoking or creating for themselves a "... more potent and continuous environmental enrichment ... " (Raine, et al, 2002, p. 672). In fact, Raine et al. reported significant and developmentally meaningful differences in subsequent IQ among groups formed based on age 3 stimulation-seeking measures. Raine et al. reported an average IQ difference of 12 points between the lowest and highest approach groups (age 3) was evident at age 11; they concluded that "Future studies need to replicate the nature of this longitudinal relationship in Western societies to assess cross-cultural generalizability ... " (2002, p. 672). Given the multiple domains prospectively assessed during the course of investigation of the FLS, including temperament, intelligence, and family/home environment, in the next several paragraphs we present analyses to corroborate the findings of Raine et al. with respect to early temperament and subsequent IQ as well as to test their proposed mechanism leading to more efficacious cognitive functioning (enriched environment).

The aforementioned prospective relations between early temperamental approach/withdrawal and subsequent intelligence (displayed in Table 5.04) replicate, in a Western sample comprising children from a wide range of middle-class families, Raine et al.'s primary finding of a linkage between the early tendency to approach novelty and higher intellectual functioning during middle childhood. In point of fact, findings from the FLS extend those of Raine et al. in that approach/withdrawal measured at age 2 (rather than 3 years) was found to be prospectively linked to higher IQ scores, not only through the middle childhood years as found by Raine et al., but also through at least age 17. Correlations are similar in magnitude to that reported by Raine et al. ($r = .25$ between age 3 stimulation seeking and age 11 estimate of IQ). In the FLS, 2-year approach/withdrawal correlated .30, .34, .25, and .29, respectively, with full scale IQ measured on four different intellectual tests: the KABC at age 5, WISC-R during middle childhood, the WISC-III at 15, and the WAIS-R at age 17.

Raine et al. created extreme groups based on stimulation seeking scores at age 3, comparing groups comprising the top 15% and bottom 15% of the sample. Using the same cutpoints in the FLS data on TTS approach/withdrawal measured at age 2 years, two extreme groups were formed. Scores of exactly 2.0 and 4.0 demarcated the most and least approaching toddlers in the FLS, respectively, and yielded group sizes of 17 in both extremes and 78 in the intermediate group. Analysis of variance was used to compare the average IQ scores of the three toddler approach groups from infancy through adolescence. As shown in Figure 5.01, results replicate those of Raine et al. in showing that toddlers with stronger tendencies to approach novel people, places, and experiences, over time, showed higher IQs than toddlers with the opposite proclivities.

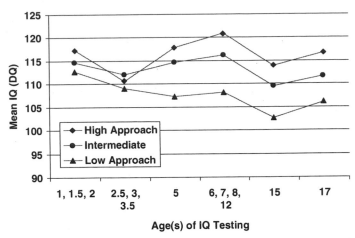

Figure 5.01. Mean DQ or IQ across developmental eras as a function of temperamental approach/withdrawal group membership at age 2.

Even more interesting, these data support the notion that youngsters differing in approach tendencies, over time, diverge in IQ. Although group differences were not evident during the infancy or preschool periods, significant differences emerged at age 5 [$F(2, 101) = 3.58$, $p < .05$)] and continued through middle childhood [$F(2, 100) = 4.75, p < .05$)]. Group differences at ages 15 and 16 approached statistical significance, $F(2, 97) = 2.85$, $p = .06$ and $F(2, 96) = 2.82$, $p = .06$, respectively. Furthermore, we note that none of the other eight temperament dimensions assessed at age 2 yielded the pervasive pattern of differences observed with respect to IQ across the childhood and adolescent development eras when extreme groups were compared using the procedure delineated above for approach/withdrawal.

Strelau (1998) and Raine et al. (2002) both postulated that youngsters with exploratory, stimulation seeking, approaching tendencies experience more enriched and continuous environmental stimulation, perhaps through niche-picking or active/evocative gene-environment interactions (Scarr & McCartney, 1983). To ascertain whether FLS data supported the proposed mechanism of environmental enrichment, we compared the three approach/withdrawal groups to determine whether they differed in experiencing or evoking an enriched environment as measured on the (1) Home Observation and Measurement of the Environment (HOME) at 1.25, 3.25, and 8 years; (2) Intellectual-Cultural Orientation scale of the Family Environment Scale at 3, 5, 8, 10, 12, 14, 16, and 17 years; (3) child's requests to participate in lessons, sports, hobbies, clubs, and courses during middle childhood and adolescence; and (4) academic intrinsic motivation at ages 7, 8, 9, 10, 13,

16, and 17 (total or general school scales). Results for each will be discussed in turn.

Home Observation for the Measurement of the Environment (HOME)

To test the mechanism of a more enriched or continuously stimulating environment, we first determined whether the three approach/withdrawal groups (low, intermediate or high) differed in the quality and/or quantity of proximal home environment. The scales of the HOME (see chapter 7) administered during the infant, preschool, and elementary school years were analyzed. Although the items of the HOME focus on provisions made for the child or responses to the child's behavior and verbalizations, the directionality or source of impetus for the environmental qualities is not attributed. Nonetheless, we reasoned that differences in variables such as verbal responsivity, provision of learning materials, or variety of opportunities among the groups, for example, would at least provide evidence that environmental enrichment might serve as the mechanism by which, over time, the three approach/withdrawal groups came to differ on IQ. That is, differences on variables such as these, if discovered, would provide necessary but not sufficient evidence that children were eliciting from their environment different levels of stimulation. However, of 22 scales on the three versions of the HOME, only 1 significant difference among groups was detected. Hence, data from the direct observation and semistructured interviews of mothers in the infancy, preschool, and elementary school years failed to support the notion that more approaching children experienced enriched environments.

Family Environment Scale (FES)

Next, we examined mothers' reports on the Intellectual-Cultural Orientation scale of the FES. The FES is described more fully in chapter 7. R. H. Moos and Moos (1986) conceptualized intellectual-cultural orientation as the interest a family shows in political, social, intellectual, and cultural activities. A. W. Gottfried and Gottfried (1984) reported that this scale was positively related to early cognitive functioning. Average scores on the intellectual-cultural orientation scale for the three groups are displayed in Figure 5.02. Significant group differences favoring children in the high approach/withdrawal group emerged at age 5 [F (2, 100) = 18.14, $p < .01$] and were also evident at age 7 [F (2, 98) = 4.66, $p < .05$], 10 [F (2, 92) = 6.79, $p < .01$], and 12 [F (2, 90) = 7.80, $p < .01$], but not thereafter at ages 14, 16, and 17. Although these data do not signify that the study children themselves evoked or requested these kinds of activities, they do

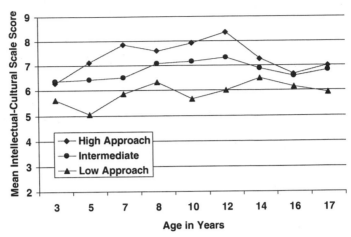

Figure 5.02. Mean Intellectual-Cultural scale score across age as a function of approach/withdrawal group membership at age 2.

document that mothers of toddlers rated as approaching to novelty subsequently rated their family environment as significantly stronger in this intellectually stimulating orientation during the middle childhood years than did the mothers who rated their toddlers as more withdrawing to novelty. The onset of these differences parallels the onset of differences in IQ scores among the three approach groups.

Children's Requests for Activities

The final two sets of variables more directly address whether the children who were high in approach as toddlers subsequently initiated or played an active role in creating an intellectually stimulating environment for themselves. When children were 8 years of age, mothers were asked whether or not the child had requested to participate in extracurricular lessons, sports, hobby activities, clubs, or courses (for additional details, see chapter 6 in A. W. Gottfried et al., 1994). Points were awarded for each type of activity requested: 0 points if no request had been made and the child was not involved in any of the designated activities, 1 point if the child was involved in an activity at the parents' decision, 2 points for activities in which the parent and child jointly decided the child would participate, and 3 points if the child had originated the request for a specific activity. These data were collected multiple times during middle childhood (8, 9, 12 years) and adolescence (annually from 13–17 years). Using the developmental era designations

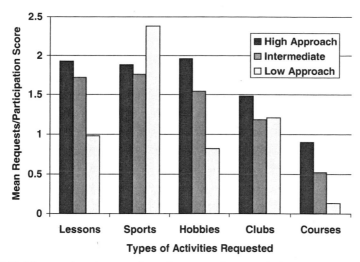

Figure 5.03. Mean number of requests for various types of extracurricular activities during middle childhood as a function of approach/withdrawal group membership at age 2.

previously established, averages were computed for each type of extracurricular activity during the years 8, 9, and 12 (middle childhood era), and ages 13 through 17 (adolescent era).

Significant differences in the degree to which children requested and partici-pated in extracurricular activities were evident on four of the five categories during middle childhood, but none of the categories during adolescence. Results for the middle childhood era are displayed in Figure 5.03, which shows the mean partici-pation/requests scores during middle childhood for the low, intermediate, and high approach temperament groups. Toddlers who were more approaching as opposed to more withdrawing were significantly more likely to participate in/request extracur-ricular lessons [F (2, 98) = 5.20, $p < .01$], and hobbies [F (2, 97) = 5.89, $p < .01$], and also tended to participate in/request more courses [F (2, 94) = 2.86, $p = .06$]. On the other hand, toddlers who were low in approach were significantly more likely to participate in/request extracurricular sports activities, F (2, 97) = 3.13, $p < .05$. No group differences were evident for the category of extracurricular clubs. The requests of the high approach toddlers were qualitatively different from those of low approach toddlers; low approach toddlers subsequently requested more participation in sports than high approach toddlers. Interestingly, these findings mirror the results reported by A. W. Gottfried et al. (1994) concerning gifted chil-dren. This pattern of participation and engagement in which children elicit more activities and engage in more activities was found to be a marker of children who eventually became gifted.

That group differences were not evident during the adolescent years may be attributable to manifold explanations, including, for example, the greater independence of adolescents in making decisions about participation in extracurricular activities, the availability of publicly-supported activities (e.g., band, choir, art courses in high schools), or changes in the expression of early approach proclivities due to development in other domains, such as cognitive development.

Academic Intrinsic Motivation

Finally, FLS data on children's academic intrinsic motivation allowed testing of Strelau's and Raine et al.'s assertions that high approach toddlers more actively influenced/interacted with their environment. A. E. Gottfried (1985, 1986, 1990) has written extensively about children's academic intrinsic motivation, which she characterizes as "an orientation toward mastery, curiosity, persistence, task endogeny, and the learning of challenging, difficult, and novel tasks" (A. W. Gottfried et al., 1994, p. 12). We hypothesized that children in the high-approach group of toddler temperament would exhibit higher levels of academic intrinsic motivation. In the FLS, academic intrinsic motivation was assessed via child reports on the Young Children's Academic Intrinsic Motivation Inventory (Y-CAIMI) or on the CAIMI (as age appropriate) at the 7-, 8-, 9-, 10-, 13-, 16-, and 17-year lab visits. Results of comparisons of the low, intermediate, and high approach groups across these ages are displayed in Figure 5.04 in terms of mean z-scores; data were transformed to z-scores to compensate for scaling differences on the YCAIMI and CAIMI. Differences among the groups favoring the high approach group emerged during early adolescence at the 13-year assessment [$F(2, 97) = 3.69, p < .05$] and continued in the 15-year [$F(2, 98) = 4.99, p < .01$] and 17-year [$F(2, 98) = 3.81$, $p < .05$] assessments. From the middle childhood years through late adolescence, children who had been high in temperamental approach as toddlers showed a progression toward increasing academic intrinsic motivation, whereas those in the low approach group as toddlers became increasingly less so.

Hence, data from the FLS corroborate and extend those of Raine et al. in that toddlers who were low versus high in approach when coming into contact with novel people, experiences, and so forth, although not differing in intelligence during the early years, did show significantly different levels of intelligence from age 5 through 17 years. As shown in Figure 5.01, the eventual differences in IQ between those toddlers who were lowest versus highest in temperamental approach were large in magnitude, exceeding 10 IQ points, and consistent across childhood and adolescence. The FLS data also provided evidence in support of the mechanism proposed by Raine et al. through which temperament and intelligence might be linked, that of environmental enrichment. Examination of this proposed mechanism showed that differences in the family orientation to intellectual-cultural

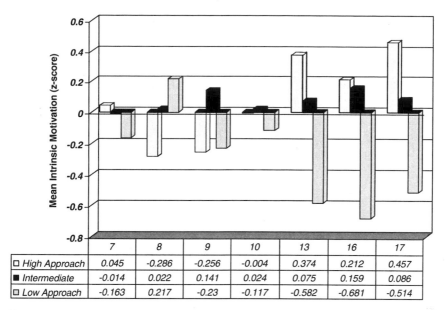

	7	8	9	10	13	16	17
☐ High Approach	0.045	-0.286	-0.256	-0.004	0.374	0.212	0.457
■ Intermediate	-0.014	0.022	0.141	0.024	0.075	0.159	0.086
☐ Low Approach	-0.163	0.217	-0.23	-0.117	-0.582	-0.681	-0.514

Figure 5.04. Mean intrinsic motivation z-scores across age as a function of approach/withdrawal group membership at age 2.

pursuits coincided with the emergence of differences in IQ. Additionally, the high-approach toddlers requested and participated in more extracurricular activities such as lessons, hobbies, and courses, but were less inclined to participate in extracurricular sports, during the middle childhood years. In adolescence, but not before, the toddlers who were high in approach showed higher levels of academic intrinsic motivation, that is, enjoyment of and curiosity about the learning of challenging, difficult, and novel tasks. Thus, converging evidence from two extensive longitudinal studies conducted in multiple cultures indicates that approach/withdrawal is an individual characteristic that is prospectively linked to higher scores on intelligence tests. In addition, data from the FLS provide empirical evidence that at least one of the mechanisms through which this link is established is through children experiencing and seeking enriched and varied stimulating environments.

Intelligence as a Predictor of Temperament and Personality

Examination of concurrent temperament-IQ relations show that a relatively limited set of temperamental characteristics, namely negative mood and persistence from the toddler years through middle childhood, and approach/withdrawal and adaptability/flexibility from the preschool years through adolescence, were concomitants of higher intellectual performance. In part, the relation between intelligence and these temperament dimensions is mediated by the child's behavior during the testing situation. We have also shown that different temperamental characteristics from an early age were related to differences in the environment experienced and/or produced during childhood and adolescence. In this section, we examine our longitudinal data from the opposite direction to see the extent to which intelligence from the earliest ages is predictive of the subsequent behavioral styles of children as perceived by parents throughout childhood and adolescence. For example, one might predict that higher levels of intellectual performance during the earlier developmental eras would presage quicker adaptation to changes, more positive mood, or more persistence/greater task orientation because these individuals are able to cope more effectively with environmental demands by processing information more quickly or staying with a task until it is solved. They may also experience less frustration as a result of their superior intellectual development, thereby leading to more positive mood.

To investigate these predictions, Pearson correlation coefficients were computed using the aforementioned aggregated IQ scores to predict temperament characteristics during each developmental era. The results are presented in Tables 5.05 (childhood) and 5.06 (adolescence). Across both tables, it can be seen that exactly one temperament dimension was predicted by IQ test scores at every developmental era: persistence/attention span (task orientation in adolescence). Higher IQ test scores from infancy, preschool, and middle childhood predicted higher levels of attention span/persistence or task orientation at every age. Although other temperamental outcomes of IQ were replicated across development, such as quicker adaptability/greater flexibility, for example, none shows the strength and consistency of relation shown by persistence/attention span/task orientation. Hence, aspects of temperament were precursors of intelligence, and intelligence was also a precursor of temperament, especially persistence/task orientation.

In chapter 3, we examined whether individual differences in temperament during early development might represent personality in its nascence, particularly personality as conceptualized in the "Big Five" model. Recall that in chapter 3 the evidence examining linkages between early temperament characteristics and these five dimensions of personality assessed at age 17 was limited. Differentiated and consistent cross-time patterns of relation between dimensions of temperament and personality were not evident for any of the five NEO factors, leading us to conclude that findings from the FLS did not strongly support the notion that early temperament represents the origins of personality, at least personality assessed in late adolescence. However, as shown in Table 5.07, consistent and differentiated patterns of relation did emerge between early measures of intelligence and three

Table 5.05. **Pearson Correlation Coefficients Assessing IQ as a Predictor of Temperament during the Preschool and Middle Childhood Years**

Intelligence measure	Temperament dimension								
	Activity level	Rhythm[a]	Approach[a]	Adapt[a]	Intensity	Negative mood	Persistence[a]	Distract	Threshold
	Behavioral style questionnaire (3, 3.5, 5 years, aggregated)								
Bayley MDI	−.16	.08	.19*	.25**	.01	−.12	.39***	−.16	.14
	Middle childhood temperament questionnaire (8, 10, 12 years, aggregated)								
Bayley MDI	−.10	.05	.17	.14	−.11	−.09	.25*	−.22*	.00
McCarthy GCI	−.10	.14	.33**	.20*	−.14	−.18	.29**	−.20	−.05
KABC MPS	−.19	.13	.16	.28**	−.14	−.31**	.37***	−.23*	−.08

[a]Signs of coefficients were reversed to facilitate interpretation.
Note: $N = 18$ on BSQ; N's $= 105–107$ on MCTQ analyses.
*$p < .05$. **$p < .01$. ***$p < .001$.

Table 5.06. Pearson Correlation Coefficients Assessing Intelligence as a Predictor of Temperament during Adolescence

Intelligence measure	Dimension of temperament								
	Activity-general	Activity-sleeping	Approach	Flexibility	Positive mood	Rhythm – eating	Rhythm – sleep	Rhythm – habits	Task orientation
Bayley MDI	−.10	.00	.11	.11	−.09	.10	.07	−.01	.31**
McCarthy GCI	−.23*	−.04	.27**	.22*	.02	.18	.16	.04	.35***
KABC MPS	−.33**	−.09	.07	.16	.03	.05	−.03	−.10	.35***
WISC-R IQ	−.19	.00	.19	.22*	.07	.05	−.03	−.10	.25*

N's = 99 to 105.
*p < .05. **p < .01. ***p < .001.

of the five NEO factors, particularly openness. Openness, which is indicative of an intrinsic seeking and appreciation of experience and tolerance for the unfamiliar, was predicted by intelligence/developmental index scores at every developmental era from infancy through adolescence in the FLS. Infants/toddlers, preschoolers, children, and adolescents scoring higher on tests of intellectual development tend to view themselves, at age 17, as more open to experiences, curious, and tolerant of the unfamiliar. These results are in line with those of John, Caspi, Robins, Moffitt, and Stouthammer-Loeber (1994), who found a correlation coefficient of .39 between openness and WISC-R full scale IQ measured concurrently in a sample of boys aged 12 to 13 years. They concluded that intellectual performance was most closely aligned with openness from among the factors comprising the five factor model, at least in early adolescence. These data, using a different measure of openness than that used by John et al., showed that intelligence measured as early as the second year of life and throughout the preschool, middle childhood, and adolescent developmental eras was a significant precursor of openness at age 17. In fact, the correlation of .36 observed in the FLS between IQ at 15 years and

Table 5.07. Pearson Correlation Coefficients between Earlier Measures of Intelligence and Personality at 17 Years

Intelligence measure	NEO-FFI				
	Neuroticism	Extraversion	Openness	Agreeableness	Conscientiousness
Bayley MDI	−.15	.04	.22*	.06	.17
McCarthy GCI	−.26**	.06	.31**	.20*	.15
KABC MPS	−.25**	−.04	.23*	.35***	.28**
WISC-R Full IQ	−.22*	.04	.26**	.27**	.15
WISC-III Full IQ	−.15	.16	.36***	.34***	.15

N = 105–111.
*p < .05. **p < .01. ***p < .001.

openness at 17 years is comparable to that reported by John et al. Although John et al. reported that controversy exists regarding the meaning and composition of the openness factor, if it is one of the "Big Five" factors then our efforts to identify the origins and early predictors of personality clearly must extend beyond aspects of development generally included under the rubric of temperament.

These consistent patterns of relation between intelligence and aspects of personality at age 17 suggest that early intelligence tells as much, if not more, than early measures of temperament about future aspects of people's personality (i.e., openness) as they move from high school into the larger world. Differences in the psychometric qualities of intelligence versus temperament measures may certainly account for the stronger pattern of relations observed between early intelligence and personality compared to early temperament and personality. Furthermore, these data support recent calls to examine again the empirical and conceptual interrelations between the domains of personality and ability (i.e., Collis & Messick, 2001).

Summary and Conclusions

1. *Which dimensions of temperament correlate with concurrently-administered standardized tests of intelligence? Does each temperament dimension show a similar pattern of relation to intelligence across the developmental eras investigated?* Three major findings emerged from the assessment of concurrent temperament-intelligence relations. First, relative to the other temperament dimensions, four aspects of temperament correlated consistently and significantly with intellectual performance across multiple eras of development: negative mood and persistence/attention span (toddler, preschool, and middle childhood eras) and approach/withdrawal and adaptability (preschool, middle childhood, and adolescent eras). However, these correlations did not exceed .40 in magnitude. Second, multiple regression analyses showed that the combination of temperament dimensions accounted for approximately 15 to 20% of the variance in IQ scores during the preschool and middle childhood eras. Finally, three NYLS temperament dimensions failed to relate significantly to intelligence: rhythmicity/predictability, intensity, and threshold.

2. *Can the temperament-intelligence relationship be explained by test-taking behaviors during the administration of the intellectual tests, or is there a direct link between temperament and intelligence test scores?* In every instance in which it was possible to ascertain whether test-taking behavior mediated the relation observed between temperament characteristics and IQ, test-taking behavior was found to be a significant mediator. In

approximately one-half of these cases, test-taking behavior was a perfect or complete mediator, reducing the temperament-IQ relation to zero. Hence, test-taking behavior is certainly an important contributor to the temperament-IQ link. However, that some of the relationships remained even after removing the effects of test-taking behavior also suggest that certain temperament characteristics may facilitate children's accomplishments in the intellectual arena.

3. *Are the relations evident between temperament and intellectual development as measured by standardized tests also evident when parent reports of developmental progress are used?* Data from parent reports on standardized inventories of children's development also provide evidence that children's temperamental characteristics have a bearing on their developmental progress. Many of the temperament-development linkages observed between parent reports of temperament and standardized intelligence tests were replicated when parent reports of developmental progress were examined. These data extend the scope of the measurement of intelligence to real life, day to day situations, assessing the developmental status of children via parent reports on standardized inventories.

4. *To what extent do aspects of earlier temperament forecast or predict intellectual development throughout childhood and adolescence?* Significant correlations were observed over long time spans, although the magnitudes of the relations were in the low range (that is, less than .40). For example, ICQ fussy/difficult scores related significantly to IQ measures at ages 5 through 17; TTS approach/withdrawal, and negative mood consistently were associated with IQ through age 17; BSQ adaptability, approach/withdrawal, and persistence/attention span were prospectively linked to IQ during middle childhood and adolescence; as were MCTQ approach/withdrawal and adaptability in adolescence.

5. *To what extent do earlier measures of children's intelligence predict temperament and personality?* Children with higher IQ are subsequently rated as more persistent and having longer attention spans/task orientation at every stage of development from preschool through adolescence. This is the clearest temperament consequence of high intellectual test scores. In terms of personality, higher IQ test scores were, from infancy, consistent precursors of the personality characteristic of openness, which relates to curiosity, learning new things, and thinking about concepts and ideas, and also, from the preschool years, agreeableness.

6

Temperament in the School Context

"(Name) has much potential and has spurts of greatness. But if the task generally does not come easily at first, she has a tendency to give up. For instance, in reading she has a large sight vocabulary, but when she gets a word that is unfamiliar she refuses to use any word attack skills to figure it out. (Name) is a happy, fanciful child with a vivid imagination. At times she can drift into a world of her own and not complete given academic tasks. She is small and very cute, and often uses these to her utmost advantage."
—Teacher of Child #8, Easy Infant Temperament Group, Age 6

Issues Investigated

The Fullerton Longitudinal Study is somewhat unique in terms of methodology in comparison to much of the extant research on the relation of temperament to various aspects of children's experiences in the school context. Much, if not most, prior research on temperament in the school context uses intact classrooms of students, often utilizing teacher reports of temperament based on their observations of the children's behavior in the classroom environment. This arrangement provides numerous research advantages, including, for example, temperament ratings of children based in somewhat standard settings with somewhat consistent demands/stressors and expectations, temperament ratings by teachers who are experienced and knowledgeable observers of behavior who have had a wealth of opportunity to observe the range of behavioral styles present in most classrooms, and access to regularly-collected indicators of academic performance (grade reports, standardized tests, etc.). In contrast, the FLS is not restricted to a single, isolated classroom, school district, or region. The FLS sample is comprised of children attending a variety of types of schools (e.g., private non-sectarian, private with religious affiliation, public) across a broad geographic region spanning not only Southern California, where all study children were born, but, as the study progressed, increasingly diverse geographic locations. Indeed, as the study participants advanced through their formal education, they were living in states as varied as California, Oregon, Washington, Arizona, Texas, Ohio, and Minnesota, for example. Not only was there diversity of school type and geographic location, but there was also variation in grade level from the time of school entry onward. California's age cut-off for kindergarten was in early December when the study children were entering school, and because the birth dates of the children in the FLS were all in the fall months, approximately two-thirds of the study participants entered kindergarten as they were turning 5 years and the remaining one-third a year later. Additionally, some students were retained in grade at various points during the course of investigation. These variations, reflecting the true nature of children's school experiences in the real world, are mirrored in the FLS database.

Given these methodological differences with many other studies of temperament and school processes or outcomes, we expected that the magnitude of relation between temperament and outcome variables would be lower than those observed in intact classrooms. Additionally, in the FLS, temperament ratings were provided by parents based on their observations of children during their daily lives in a variety of settings, which may include the classroom setting, but generally, we assumed, did not. This, also, we expected to diminish the degree of relation observed between temperament and school variables. We provide these comments because we believe they are important contextual factors for readers to understand as they interpret and evaluate the findings presented herein. Although potentially increasing the error or unexplained variance into the research design and findings, these methodological features enhance the external validity or generalizability of the findings.

In this chapter, we examine the relation between temperament and four general spheres of academic outcomes: academic achievement, behavior in the classroom, and the children's/adolescents' self-perceptions or appraisals of their general performance in school and academic intrinsic motivation. As indicators of academic achievement, we examined progress through grades, performance on standardized and individually-administered tests, ratings of achievement from three sources (parents, teachers, self-reports by adolescents), and cumulative high school grade point average. Behavior in the classroom was based on teacher ratings, as noted above, from teachers in classrooms of numerous schools that vary in geographic location, type, and grade. Finally, we included the children's/adolescents' own perspectives regarding their performance, competence, and motivation toward school to ascertain if their temperament related to these self-appraisals.

The specific issues addressed in this chapter include the following:

1. *Do children with delayed school entry differ in temperament from children who entered on time?* The FLS sample comprised children born during the months when parents had the option of entering them into kindergarten or allowing the children another year before entering the formal educational

system. Thus, we began our investigation of temperament-school relations by examining if individual differences in children's temperament related to this early educational decision made by parents.

2. *Do children who repeat a grade differ in temperament from those who move through their school experience with no grade repetitions?* Following their kindergarten or first grade years, just over 10 percent of children in the FLS cohort were retained in grade; during the course of investigation, approximately 15 percent of the children were eventually retained in grade. The temperament characteristics of the retained and non-retained groups were examined to ascertain if specific temperament characteristics might place children at risk for grade retention.

3. *Which dimensions of temperament relate to students' academic achievement? Are the dimensions similar across various indicators of academic achievement and across the elementary and secondary school periods?* Academic achievement was assessed annually in the FLS via individually-administered standardized tests and/or via parent and teacher ratings. In these analyses, the temperamental correlates of achievement in reading and math subject areas across primary and secondary school years were examined.

4. *In what ways does children's temperament relate to teachers' appraisals of their pupils' classroom competence?* During the elementary school years, teachers provided ratings of their students' behavior in the classroom. These ratings were correlated with parent reports of temperament to ascertain the extent to which children's behavioral styles related to teacher assessments of their students' competence.

5. *Do aspects of children's temperament relate to their academic intrinsic motivation and academic self-concept?* As children develop, they receive feedback regarding their academic prowess, which may eventually influence self-appraisals of their interest and competence in academic pursuits. In this section, the relation of children's temperament to their self-appraisals of academic self competence and academic intrinsic motivation is investigated.

6. *Does temperament contribute to the prediction of high school cumulative grade point average? Does temperament relate to cumulative grade point average after considering two major correlates of academic achievement, intelligence and family socioeconomic status?* Cumulative academic records of all study participants were collected at the end of their high school experience, allowing examination of their academic achievement across secondary school. Concurrent and cross-time relations between temperament and the cumulative grade point average were investigated, as well as the amount of variance in this important index explained by temperament after controlling for intelligence and SES.

Description of Measures Used in the FLS

Educational History

Beginning with the 5-year assessment, information regarding children's educational progress was collected annually through a questionnaire completed by the parent who accompanied the child to the research center, usually the mother. Commencing at the 5-year assessment, we included items assessing whether children had enrolled in kindergarten; thereafter, we annually assessed the children's grade level. From these data we were able to follow the children's progress and determine when children were retained in a grade.

Academic Achievement

Academic achievement was assessed annually from ages 5 through 17 years. At age 5, children were tested using the Kaufman Assessment Battery for Children (KABC; A. S. Kaufman & Kaufman, 1983). The KABC contains an achievement scale assessing children's knowledge of well-known places and faces, arithmetic, riddles, and reading/decoding. Standard scores ($M = 100$, $SD = 15$) on the achievement scale were analyzed.

At 6 years, the Wide Range Achievement Test-Revised (WRAT-R; Jastak & Wilkinson, 1984) was used. The WRAT-R appraises academic performance in the areas of reading, arithmetic, and spelling. In keeping with subsequent analyses in which reading and math achievement areas are examined, the standard scores ($M = 100$, $SD = 15$) for reading and arithmetic were analyzed.

At ages 7 through 10, the Woodcock-Johnson Psycho-Educational Battery was given (Woodcock & Johnson, 1977). At ages 11 through 17, the Woodcock-Johnson Psycho-Educational Battery – Revised (Woodcock & Johnson, 1989) was administered. Across the entire age span of the FLS, achievement in reading and math was assessed. Unless otherwise noted, percentile scores comparing children with their appropriate grade population were analyzed for these two basic achievement areas.

In addition to these direct, objective assessments of achievement using standardized tests, ratings of achievement in math and reading were assessed via parent, teacher, and self-reports on the Child Behavior Checklist, Teacher Report Form, and Youth Report Form, respectively (Achenbach, 1991a, 1991b, 1991c). Parents' ratings were on a 4-point scale (1 = *"failing"* to 4 = *"above average"*) and were collected from ages 6 through 17. Teachers' ratings were on a 5-point scale (1 = *"far below grade level"* to 5 = *"far above grade level"*) and were collected at ages 6 through 11. Self-ratings were measured on a 4-point scale (1 = *"failing"* to

4 = "*above average*") at age 17. Thus, for all informants, higher ratings indicated superior academic achievement.

Classroom Competence

Teacher reports of classroom competence were collected during the elementary school years, when students primarily were taught by the same teacher throughout the entire school day, so that teachers would have sufficient opportunity to become familiar with the student. Using the Teacher Report Form (TRF, Achenbach, 1991b), teachers rated children at ages 6 through 11 on the sufficiency of their classroom functioning in four areas: how hard the child is working, the degree to which the child is behaving appropriately, how much the child is learning, and how happy the child is. On the TRF, teachers are directed to rate the child in comparison to typical children of the same age. All ratings utilize a scale ranging from 1 ("*much less*") to 7 ("*much more*"). (Findings concerning temperament and teacher ratings of behavior problems on broad band categories (internalizing, externalizing) are presented in chapter 4.)

Academic Self-Concept

Academic self-concept was assessed at age 10 using the Self Description Questionnaire I (SDQ I; Marsh, 1988), and at ages 12, 14, and 16 with the SDQ II (Marsh, 1990). In completing the SDQ I, children respond to 76 positively worded declarative sentences [e.g., "I'm good at _____ (subject area)"] with one of five responses: *false, mostly false, sometimes false/sometimes true, mostly true, true*. The SDQ-II is similar in format; however, both positively and negatively worded items are included among the 102 items, and there are six response options rather than five. Scores on the general school category were examined; Marsh (1988, 1990) reports internal reliability coefficients in excess of .85.

Academic Intrinsic Motivation

Throughout the course of the FLS, repeated assessments of academic intrinsic motivation were collected. Academic intrinsic motivation is defined as "enjoyment of school learning characterized by an orientation toward mastery; curiosity; persistence, task endogeny; and the learning of challenging, difficult, and novel tasks" (A. E. Gottfried, 1985, p. 632). During the middle childhood era, academic intrinsic motivation was assessed at ages 9 and 10 using the Children's Academic Intrinsic

Motivation Inventory (CAIMI; A. E. Gottfried, 1986) and at ages 13, 16, and 17 using the high school version of the CAIMI (A. E. Gottfried et al., 2001). In all analyses, the scores on the general school scale were analyzed. Reliability of the CAIMI for the general school scale ranged from .67 to .83 (A. E. Gottfried, 1985); for the high school version, internal consistency for this scale was .91 (A. E. Gottfried, et al., 2001).

Findings and Discussion

School Entrance Age

All FLS participants were born in the months from late August through early December. With the exception of one child, all were eligible to be enrolled in public kindergarten programs when they were approximately 4.75 years of age (that is, they would turn five in the first few months of their kindergarten year in school and be among the youngest students in the class). Alternatively, parents could enroll their child the following year, after their child had attained the age of 5, therefore making their child among the oldest in the class. At the 5-year visit to the lab, 68% (75) of the children were enrolled in kindergarten, and 32% (35) were not. Prior studies have shown the rate of voluntarily delaying entry to kindergarten varies widely across time and location (Guerin, Sandwell, & Lovil, 1998). In this section, we examine if children entering kindergarten as they turned 5 (and were therefore among the youngest in the class) differed from those whose parents delayed their entry until the following year.

BSQ scores of children who entered kindergarten as they turned 5 and those held out were compared. Only one of the nine dimensions differentiated the two groups: adaptability. Children whose kindergarten entry was voluntarily delayed by parents were described as slower to adapt ($M = 2.73$) than those whose parents entered into kindergarten ($M = 2.41$), $t(108) = 2.87$, $p < .05$ (on the BSQ, higher scores indicate slower adaptability).

Martin et al. (1983) noted that some temperament theorists consider adaptability to be the most general temperament variable. They found that pupils rated by teachers as slow to adapt at the start of first grade were subsequently observed by independent raters to participate in more gross-motor inappropriate behaviors, more non-constructive self-directed activities, and fewer constructive self-directed activities. Our finding that children whose kindergarten entry was voluntarily delayed by parents differed solely on adaptability among the nine NYLS dimensions suggests that adaptability is a salient dimension to parents, as well. Children who whose kindergarten entry was voluntarily delayed were seen by their parents across a variety of situations assessed on the BSQ as slower to adapt to changes. Some may view this accommodation as an example supporting the notion of goodness of fit, in that parents adjusted their child's educational experience to accommodate to perceived differences in the child's ability to adapt to the demands of the school setting.

Progress through Grades

Three temperament dimensions were found to differentiate children who at some time experienced grade repetition during the course of their kindergarten through high school educational history: adaptability, persistence/attention span, and threshold of responsiveness.

Retention during the School Entry Years

Of the 110 children for whom data were available at age 7, 13 (11.8%) had repeated either kindergarten or first grade. No differences between children who repeated kindergarten or first grade ("repeaters") and those who had not ("non-repeaters") were observed in temperament during the infancy (ICQ) or toddler (TTS) periods. On the BSQ during the preschool years, repeaters were rated as less sensitive to changes in environment on the threshold dimension ($M = 3.69$) than non-repeaters ($M = 3.87$), $t(109) = 2.10$, $p < .05$. Additionally, repeaters were rated as slower to adapt ($M = 2.81$) during the preschool years than non-repeaters ($M = 2.46$), $t(109) = 2.19$, $p < .05$. Subsequently during the elementary school years on the MCTQ, pupils who repeated kindergarten or first grade were rated as slower to adapt ($M = 2.77$) compared to non-repeaters ($M = 2.40$), $t(104) = 2.15$, $p < .05$ (lower scores indicate quicker adaptability on the BSQ and MCTQ).

Retention at Any Time during Primary and Secondary School

By 17 years, 17 (15.9%) of the 107 FLS participants had repeated a grade. As with the kindergarten/first grade repeaters, no differences were observed in the infancy (ICQ) or toddler (TTS) measures. However, students who had repeated a grade at any time during their school career had been rated as less persistent or having a shorter attention span ($M = 3.20$) than non-repeaters ($M = 2.89$) during the preschool years, $t(104) = 2.20$, $p < .05$. During the elementary school years from 8 to 12, repeaters had been rated as less persistent ($M = 2.76$) than non-repeaters ($M = 2.37$), $t(100) = 2.35$, $p < .05$ (lower scores indicate more persistence/longer attention span on the BSQ and MCTQ). No repeater/non-repeater differences were observed on the DOTS-R ratings by parents.

Hence, during the preschool years, slow adaptability and less sensitivity to environmental changes characterized children who would repeat a grade early in their educational experience, whereas those who would repeat a grade at any point during their educational experience evinced shorter persistence/attention span during the preschool and middle childhood years. The aspects of temperament differentiating children who progressed through grades unretained and those who repeated a grade were those that involved detecting changes in their environment, the ease or difficulty with which they typically adjusted to changes, and their ability to sustain or modulate their attention as needed.

Temperament and Academic Achievement during the Elementary Grades

A second important indicator of success in school is academic achievement. To evaluate the relation between temperament and academic achievement, Pearson correlation coefficients were computed between parent-rated temperament scores aggregated within developmental periods and a variety of comprehensive measures of academic achievement. These measures included yearly, objective, standardized achievement tests, as well as teacher-rated, parent-rated, and pupil self-rated academic standings.

We digress briefly to comment on these indicators of achievement in school. An important methodological note regarding the assessment of achievement in the FLS is that all tests were administered individually; group tests were not employed at any time. In the process of appropriately administering a standardized test, whether it is an intelligence test, achievement test, or test of another cognitive capacity, the examiner's role is to engage and maintain rapport with the examinee. Hence, individual differences on specific dimensions of temperament, such as persistence/attention span, distractibility, approach/withdrawal, and others, may be reduced or attenuated as a result of the testing procedure as the examiner engages and guides the examinee throughout the testing procedure. With this in mind, we examined parent, teacher, and self reports as indicators of academic achievement as well.

In the final section of this chapter, we examine the relation between temperament and cumulative grade point average in high school as a third indicator of academic achievement. Cumulative high school grade point average is a global index of academic performance that is the result of a multitude of factors, some of which are generally under the control of the individual student (assignment completion and quality, courses selected, attendance, etc.) and some of which are generally beyond the control of the individual student (specific courses required to graduate, family resources, peers to whom they are compared, etc.). In summary, as we examined the relation of individual differences in temperament to academic achievement, we were particularly interested in determining the dimensions of temperament (if any) that evinced relations with academic achievement across method, across source or informant, as well as across development. Based on the analyses thus far presented on progression through grades, as well as prior research, the dimensions of adaptability (flexibility on the DOTS-R) and persistence/attention span (task orientation on the DOTS-R) were expected to be particularly intertwined with academic achievement measures.

School Entry Years

Parent-rated temperament characteristics of preschool children assessed on the BSQ were correlated with standardized tests when the children were five and six years old to determine if children's temperament was related to these early measures of academic achievement. As shown in Table 6.01, temperament dimensions that correlated significantly and in a positive direction with the achievement scale of the Kaufman Assessment Battery for Children were persistence/attention span, adaptability, and approach/withdrawal, whereas negative mood correlated inversely with achievement. When the children were six years old, they were administered the Wide Range Achievement Test. The math and reading achievement scores correlated significantly with a similar cluster of temperament dimensions: persistence/attention span, adaptability, approach/withdrawal, and negative mood. The pattern and magnitude of the correlation coefficients were similar for both reading and arithmetic. Findings during the school entry years in the FLS are consistent with previous research demonstrating teacher ratings of children's temperament dimensions of persistence/attention span, adaptability, distractibility, approach,

Table 6.01. Pearson Correlations between Preschool Temperament and Standardized Achievement Scales

Behavioral style questionnaire (3, 3.5, 5 years)	Kaufman assessment battery for children	Wide range achievement test-revised	
	Achievement scale	Reading	Arithmetic
Activity Level	−.18	−.23*	−.03
Rhythmicity[a]	.16	.13	.08
Approach[a]	.31***	.31***	.40***
Adaptability[a]	.37***	.43***	.39***
Intensity	−.03	−.12	.05
Negative Mood	−.22*	−.31***	−.22*
Persistence[a]	.38***	.42***	.31***
Distractibility	−.03	.04	.08
Threshold	.17	.14	.26**

$N = 106–111$.
[a] Signs of coefficients were reversed to facilitate interpretation.
*$p < .05$. **$p < .01$. ***$p < .001$.

and activity relate to standardized achievement measures as well as to teachers' ratings of academic achievement.

Middle Childhood

Throughout the elementary school years, repeated measures of achievement were administered annually. Beginning at age 7, participants were individually given the Woodcock-Johnson standardized tests for reading and math; scores for each subject area were aggregated across ages 7 through 12 years in the analyses next reported. In addition, parent and teacher ratings of reading and math achievement were assessed via the CBCL (ages 6–12) and TRF (ages 6–11), respectively; in the following analyses, these were averaged across the years shown. Correlations between MCTQ dimensions and the aforementioned achievement measures are presented in Table 6.02. Although several temperament dimensions related to achievement, the most consistent patterns of relation across subject area and informant were with the dimensions of persistence/attention span and distractibility.

Data from the FLS during the transition to school corroborate and extend findings of Palisin (1986) and Schoen and Nagle (1994) as well as the family of studies by Lerner et al. (1985) and Martin and his colleagues on the elementary school years (Martin et al., 1983; Martin et al., 1988; Martin & Holbrook, 1985). Across these studies, the temperament dimensions of persistence/attention span, adaptability, distractibility, and/or approach/withdrawal related significantly to concurrent and cross-time measures of achievement.

Table 6.02. Pearson Correlations between Temperament and Reading and Arithmetic Aggregates during Middle Childhood

Temperament dimension	Woodcock-Johnson		Parent ratings		Teacher ratings	
	Reading	Arithmetic	Reading	Arithmetic	Reading	Arithmetic
Activity Level	−.09	−.09	−.24*	−.20*	−.26**	−.23*
Predictability[a]	.25**	.14	.30**	.12	.29**	.26**
Approach[a]	.24*	.17	.12	.11	.20*	.11
Adaptability[a]	.23*	.14	.29**	.09	.29**	.19
Intensity	−.13	−.14	−.18	−.15	−.19*	−.20*
Negative Mood	−.16	−.18	−.22*	−.11	−.21*	−.21*
Persistence[a]	.27**	.17	.38***	.25*	.43***	.36***
Distractibility	−.27**	−.24*	−.27**	−.30**	−.35***	−.33***
Threshold	−.05	−.04	−.05	−.06	−.04	−.01

$N = 107$.
[a]Signs of coefficients were reversed to facilitate interpretation.
*$p < .05$. **$p < .01$. ***$p < .001$.

Temperament and Academic Achievement during the Adolescent Years

During the adolescent years, temperament was assessed by both the study children (adolescents) themselves and a parent utilizing the DOTS-R. Ratings for each dimension were aggregated within informant across ages 14 and 16. As previously noted, although the dimensions assessed by the DOTS-R do not comprise the nine NYLS dimensions, there is considerable conceptual overlap. For example, besides dimensions sharing the same label on both measures, the DOTS-R task orientation dimension represents an aggregate of persistence and (lack of) distractibility and MCTQ adaptability is related to DOTS-R flexibility. As during middle childhood, achievement was measured via individually-administered standardized tests (reading and math tests of the Woodcock-Johnson) and also via parent ratings on the CBCL. Achievement test scores were aggregated across ages 13 through 17 years, as were parent ratings of achievement. At age 17, self-ratings of achievement were assessed using the Youth Self Report Form. Correlation analyses between temperament and these three measures of achievement revealed only three dimensions of temperament related significantly to achievement that were replicated across informant, method, and/or subject area: task orientation, flexibility, and general activity level.

During adolescence, parent ratings of task orientation on the DOTS-R correlated significantly and positively with Woodcock-Johnson math achievement ($r = .24$, $p < .05$), parent ratings of reading and math (r's $= .50$ and $.42$, $p < .001$, respectively), and youth self-ratings of reading achievement ($r = .45$, $p < .001$). Parent ratings of flexibility correlated with Woodcock-Johnson reading scores and youth self-rated math, (r's $= .23$ and $.25$, $p < .05$, respectively). Finally, parent reported general activity level related inversely to Woodcock-Johnson math scores and parent ratings of reading and math performance, r's $= -.21$ ($p < .05$), $-.32$, and $-.26$ (p's $< .01$), respectively. No other correlations were significant between parent-rated temperament and achievement as measured during adolescence via the Woodcock-Johnson, parent ratings, or self-ratings.

Two dimensions of the DOTS-R completed by adolescents to assess their own temperament related significantly to measures of achievement: task orientation and flexibility. Task orientation related to math performance on the Woodcock-Johnson during adolescence, parent ratings of math achievement, and self-reported reading achievement, r's $= .22$, $.19$ (p's $< .05$), and $.29$ ($p < .01$), respectively. Flexibility related significantly to four of the six achievement measures: Woodcock-Johnson reading ($r = .23$, $p < .05$), math ($r = .39$, $p < .001$), parent ratings of math ($r = .29$, $p < .01$), and adolescent self-ratings of math ($r = .25$, $p < .05$). No other significant correlations were observed between adolescent self-rated temperament and these measures of achievement.

Taken together, findings from the FLS data on the relation between achievement and parent and adolescent self-ratings of temperament on the DOTS-R during adolescence coincide nicely with those of Talwar et al. (1989). They reported low to moderate positive correlations between higher scholastic competence and the temperament dimensions of flexibility, approach, positive mood, and low activity level in adolescents. The current findings also extend those reported by Guerin et al. (1994) on the FLS sample during the transition to junior high school.

Thus, individual differences in temperament related to academic achievement at school entry, during middle childhood, and during adolescence and replicated across method, source, and/or subject area (math, reading). Across these three periods, the dimensions of persistence/attention span (task orientation during adolescence) and adaptability (flexibility during adolescence) were repeatedly found to correlate with academic achievement, with magnitudes reaching moderate to high. Approach and mood correlated during school entry and middle childhood, but not during adolescence, and at lower magnitudes. Hence, these data provide empirical confirmation that students who achieved well in school across their academic careers were those who were persistent and stayed on task and could accommodate to changing environmental conditions. In elementary school, they were more positive in mood and also more approaching of novel tasks and experiences. These temperament dimensions that characterized children's typical approach to life outside the classroom as reported by parents and the adolescents themselves, however, seemed particularly conducive to academic performance. Given the distinctive research environment afforded by the FLS in comparison to many other studies of temperament and academic achievement detailed at the beginning of this chapter, we believe these results are particularly impressive.

Intelligence is a potent predictor of academic achievement. In the next set of analyses, we examined whether temperament dimensions contributed to the prediction of achievement after variance attributable to intelligence was removed. In chapter 5 the relation between temperament and intelligence was documented, with results showing low to moderate relations. To determine the extent of the independent relation between temperament and academic achievement over and above the shared relation with intelligence, stepwise multiple regressions entering intelligence in the first step and parent ratings of temperament in the second were conducted. Results are displayed in Table 6.03. In these analyses, intelligence was measured via aggregated measures across middle childhood (ages 6, 7, 8, and 12) and adolescence (ages 15 and 17). Measures of math and reading achievement and temperament as previously described were used in these analyses.

Parent ratings of temperament contributed to the prediction of academic achievement beyond that explained by intelligence, especially with respect to reading. For reading achievement, parent ratings of temperament accounted for significant increments in the amount of variance explained by intelligence in five of the six measures. The increment in R^2 was fairly small in middle childhood,

Table 6.03. Multiple Regression Analyses Examining the Increment in Variance in Achievement Explained by Temperament during Middle Childhood and Adolescence After Controlling Intelligence

Achievement measure	Reading			Math		
	R	Adjusted R^2	F	R	Adjusted R^2	F
	Middle childhood ($N = 106$)					
Parent Ratings						
IQ	.58	.33		.57	.32	51.10***
Temperament	.64	.40	35.86***	—	—	—
Teacher Ratings						
IQ	.67	.44		.66	.43	
Temperament	.72	.51	55.72***	.70	.48	49.20***
Woodcock-Johnson						
IQ	.60	.36		.67	.45	86.95***
Temperament	.64	.40	36.40***	—	—	—
	Adolescence ($N = 86$–103)					
Parent Ratings						
IQ	.46	.21		.53	.28	
Temperament	.64	.39	34.46***	.63	.39	33.66***
Adolescent Self-Ratings						
IQ	.35	.11		.44	.18	20.31***
Temperament	.53	.26	16.00***	—	—	—
Woodcock-Johnson						
IQ	.65	.41	72.80***	.74	.55	124.17***
Temperament	—	—	—	—	—	—

$^*p < .05.$ $^{**}p < .01.$ $^{***}p < .001.$

ranging from 4% on the Woodcock-Johnson to 7% on parent and teacher ratings. In adolescence, however, the contribution of temperament was quite striking in predicting the achievement rating measures, increasing the amount of variance in reading achievement explained by temperament on the parent and youth ratings by 18% and 15%, respectively. For math achievement, temperament increased the amount of variance explained by intelligence on only two of the six measures, teacher ratings during middle childhood and parent ratings during adolescence. In virtually all analyses when temperament entered after intelligence to explain academic achievement, the criterion variable was measured via informant ratings. Conversely, on only one of the four situations in which the Woodcock-Johnson was the criterion variable did temperament contribute beyond intelligence. One explanation for this pattern of results is that the ratings of the informants were influenced by the child/adolescent's temperament more so than the standardized individually-administered intelligence test. As suggested earlier in the discussion of the findings on Table 6.02, perhaps the testing procedure on standardized tests reduced the impact of individual differences in temperament on the characteristic being tested. More subjective appraisals, such as those collected via informant ratings on the CBCL, TRF, and YSR, may be influenced by children's/adolescents' full range of behaviors evident every day in the classroom or home setting. For example, informants may take into account the extent to which the student completed extracurricular tasks, homework assignments, in-class assignments, etc., or the student's difficulty in completing tasks on time and use this information in making their appraisal. Additionally, the student's temperamental persistence/attention span or task orientation may influence his/her ability to complete assignments, thus impacting the actual grade earned. In the one-to-one interactions that take place during the standardized test situation, individual differences in persistence/attention span may be attenuated. We will examine the relation of temperament to students' cumulative grade point average from high school in the final section of this chapter. We viewed the cumulative high school grade point average as a global indicator of achievement that reflected the collective and cumulative impact of individual differences in not only IQ, but also temperament and opportunity. Hence, we will conclude this chapter with an examination of this important global indicator of academic achievement and how IQ, SES, and temperament are related to it. Before that, however, the relation between temperament and two other aspects related to the school context, classroom behavior and student self-appraisals, are examined.

Teachers' Appraisals of Pupils' Classroom Behavior

Previous research has shown teachers' ratings of children's temperament are related to observed classroom behavior (Martin et al., 1983). Children who were rated by teachers as more active, more distractible, slower to adapt, and less persistent engaged in more inappropriate behaviors during classroom observations as coded by researchers. The first question we addressed concerning classroom behavior was whether parents' ratings of their preschool children's temperament presaged teachers' appraisal of pupils' behavior across the elementary years. Pearson correlation coefficients were computed between aggregated scores of parents' reports on the BSQ when the children were 3, 3.5 and 5 years of age and teachers' ratings of children's classroom behavior on the TRF across the entire elementary school period from ages 6 to 11. Teachers evaluated children's classroom behavior through four items on the TRF in which they were asked to rate the extent to which the child was working hard, behaving appropriately, learning, and happy compared to typical pupils of the same age.

Parent ratings of their children's temperament during the preschool years related significantly to teacher ratings of classroom behavior during the elementary school years, r's $= .20$ to $.40$ in magnitude. With respect to elementary school teachers' estimations of how much their pupils were learning compared to others of the same age, five of the nine BSQ dimensions were significantly related: persistence/attention span and adaptability, activity level, negative mood, and approach/withdrawal. Preschoolers rated by their parents as more persistent and longer in attention span, quicker to adapt, lower in activity level, more positive in mood, and more approaching to novel experiences and people were, during the elementary school years, rated by their teachers as learning more in their classrooms. Teacher ratings of how hard the child was working in their classroom were also predicted by parent ratings of preschool-age temperament, specifically persistence/attention span, activity level, and adaptability; children viewed as more persistent, less active, and quicker to adapt were subsequently rated by teachers as working harder. Teacher ratings of children's happiness in the school context were correlated with parent ratings of preschool-age approach/withdrawal and adaptability. Finally, higher activity level presaged teacher ratings of less appropriate behavior during the elementary school years.

Parent ratings of higher activity level and slower adaptability during the preschool years foretold less positive ratings from classroom teachers during the elementary school years on three of the four TRF ratings: working hard, behaving appropriately; and learning for activity level and working hard, learning, and happiness for adaptability. Thus, parent reports of their children's temperament during the preschool years were predictive of teachers' ratings of classroom functioning during the elementary years, particularly teacher estimates of how much the child was learning and how hard the child was working, and explained up to about 10 percent of the variance in these indicators of classroom competence.

When using concurrent measures of temperament and classroom behavior, the pattern of relationships observed in the FLS was more pervasive than with the cross-time measures of temperament. Seven of the nine temperament dimensions measured on the MCTQ during middle childhood correlated with at least three of the measures of classroom behavior; significant correlations ranged to .49. These correlation coefficients are reported in Table 6.04. These findings are consistent with aforementioned research demonstrating that temperament characteristics salient in the classroom are persistence/attention span, adaptability, distractibility, and activity level. Persistence/attention span, adaptability, and distractibility correlated with all four measures of classroom behavior at a moderate level, reaching $r = .49$. Activity level correlated significantly and negatively with behaving appropriately, learning, and happy. In addition, predictability/quality of organization was related to all four measures of classroom behavior, with correlations reaching a magnitude of .40. The two dimensions that did not relate to teacher ratings of classroom behavior were approach/withdrawal and threshold. In the context of a familiar classroom, individual differences in approach/withdrawal, relating to

Table 6.04. Pearson Correlations between Middle Childhood Temperament and Teacher Ratings of Children's Classroom Behavior

Middle childhood temperament questionnaire	Teacher report form (6–11 years)			
	Hard working	Behaving appropriately	Learning	Happy
Activity	−.18	.30**	−.25**	−.22*
Predictability[a]	.40***	.36***	.37***	.40***
Approach[a]	−.01	−.09	.12	.04
Adaptability[a]	.29**	.38***	.33***	.33***
Intensity	−.17	−.24*	−.23*	−.25**
Negative Mood	−.19*	−.22*	−.26**	−.24*
Persistence[a]	.49***	.42***	.48***	.41***
Distractibility	−.34***	−.23*	−.36***	−.27**
Threshold	−.11	−.11	−.09	−.15

$N = 107$.
[a] Signs of coefficients were reversed to facilitate interpretation.
$*p < .05. **p < .01. ***p < .001$.

how easily children approach new people and events, and threshold, which relates to how sensitive children are to environmental stimuli, may not be as salient to teachers as they appraise classroom behavior compared to the students' ability to complete assignments and stay on task. These findings and those previously reported on the BSQ and teacher ratings support the validity of parent reports of children's temperament, in that they demonstrate that parent reports of temperament predict their children's functioning across time, in different contexts, and as viewed by a different informant. These findings are particularly remarkable in view of the circumstances under which the data were collected (as detailed in the opening paragraph of this chapter).

In the next analyses we examine the relation between temperament and classroom conduct after controlling for the contribution made by the child's intelligence. The results of the regression analyses are presented in Table 6.05. After entering children's full scale IQ score aggregated over the elementary years, the aggregated MCTQ temperament dimensions were entered in the regression equation as a block. The temperament dimensions added to the variance explained over and above IQ for all four of the criterion variables, accounting for an additional 26% of the variance in teacher ratings of working hard, an additional 27% of the variance of teachers' appraisals of how appropriately the student is behaving, an additional 17% of the variance in how much the student is learning, and an additional 20% of the variance in teachers' assessments of how happy the student is in comparison to other students.

Table 6.05. **Multiple Regression Analyses Using Intelligence and Temperament as Predictors of Classroom Competence**

Child behavior checklist, teacher report form	Significant predictors	Multiple R	R^2	R^2 Change	F	df
Hard Working	IQ	.45	.21		27.12***	10, 96
	Temperament	.68	.47	.26	8.41***	
Behaving Appropriately	IQ	.30	.09		10.28**	10, 96
	Temperament	.60	.36	.27	5.45***	
Learning	IQ	.64	.41		72.47***	10, 96
	Temperament	.76	.58	.17	13.35***	
Happy	IQ	.31	.09		10.85***	10, 96
	Temperament	.54	.29	.20	3.94***	

*$p < .05$. **$p < .01$. ***$p < .001$.

Self-Concept and Academic Intrinsic Motivation

We next examined whether students' temperament related to their appraisals of their school competence or academic self-concept. There was no demonstrably strong relation between temperament and general school academic self-concept in the elementary school years. No temperament dimensions related to general school self-concept at age 10; at the 12 year assessment, correlations between the SDQ II and the temperament ratings aggregated across the middle childhood years produced two significant correlations: adaptability ($r = .22$) and persistence/attention span ($r = .26$) correlated with general school self-concept. Hence, during middle childhood, the evidence suggested that children's academic self-concept was independent of their temperament characteristics.

Stronger and more pervasive temperament-academic self concept relations were observed during adolescence in the FLS. As shown in Table 6.06, four of the DOTS-R dimensions related significantly with general school self-concept assessed via the SDQ II averaged across the 14- and 16-year assessments: general activity level, approach, flexibility, and task orientation. Adolescents with temperaments characterized as lower in general activity, higher in approach, more flexible, and higher in task orientation had more positive self-concepts about school. Correlation coefficients tended to be higher between the SDQ II and self-reported temperament compared to parent-reported temperament. Across both informants, the temperament dimension of task orientation was correlated most strongly with general school self concept. These findings are in line with those of Klein (1995), who reported low but significant correlations between temperament and self-perceptions on the scholastic competence scale of Harter's Self-Perception Scale among college students. Klein found higher self appraisals of scholastic competence among adolescents who viewed their own temperament as

Table 6.06. Pearson Correlation Coefficients between Adolescent Temperament (Parent- and Self-Rated) and Adolescent Self Concept about School and Academic Intrinsic Motivation

Temperament dimension	General school self-concept		Intrinsic motivation	
	Parent-rated	Self-rated	Parent-rated	Self-rated
Activity-General	−.24*	−.31***	−.08	−.12
Activity-Sleep	−.04	−.10	.05	−.09
Approach	.22*	.27**	.23*	.37***
Flexibility	.24*	.41***	.20*	.35***
Positive Mood	.05	.27**	.05	.25**
Rhythmicity-Sleep	.13	.18	.09	.10
Rhythmicity-Eat	.07	.26**	−.12	.16
Rhythmicity-Habits	.03	.15	−.02	.08
Task Orientation	.41***	.48***	.34***	.43***

$N = 105$–111.
*$p < .05$. **$p < .01$. ***$p < .001$.

more positive in mood, higher in task orientation, more flexible, more approaching, and less active.

We also examined the relation between students' temperament and their level of academic intrinsic motivation, specifically their enjoyment of school in general. Academic intrinsic motivation was related to a similar cluster of temperament dimensions as that observed for general school self-concept: approach, flexibility, and task orientation. As shown in Table 6.06, both self- and parent-rated adolescent temperament related to the adolescents' perceptions of intrinsic motivation on the general school scale (aggregated across ages 13, 16, and 17), with correlation coefficients ranging to .43. Adolescents with temperament patterns characterized as more approaching, flexible, and task-oriented reported higher levels of academic intrinsic motivation during the high school years. However, no significant correlations were observed between temperament and academic intrinsic motivation during the elementary school years.

Prediction of High School Cumulative Grade Point Average

A primary, final, and global index of students' performance in high school is the cumulative grade point average, or GPA. In this section, we investigate the extent to which temperament characteristics are predictive of this index. After study participants completed high school, their cumulative files were collected and these constituted the source of GPA information. The types of schools attended by FLS participants included a full range of public, private (religious and non-sectarian), and continuation high schools in which students complete the GED rather than the diploma. As we have previously noted, the geographic location of the high schools was quite diverse. Thus, the cumulative high school GPA's were not based on students in the same high school, school district, or even the same state.

Beginning with concurrent temperament-GPA relations, parent and adolescent self-ratings on the DOTS-R were examined as predictors of cumulative high school GPA. Significant correlation coefficients ranging to .46 were observed with three dimensions of temperament: task orientation, general activity level, and flexibility. Both parent and adolescent self-ratings of task orientation ($r = .46$, $p < .001$ and $r = .27$, $p < .01$, respectively) and general activity level (both r's $= -.23$, $p < .05$) predicted cumulative high school GPA. Adolescent self-ratings of flexibility also predicted high school GPA, $r = .23$, $p < .05$. Hence, adolescents with greater task orientation, greater flexibility, and lower general activity levels earned higher GPA's in high school.

We also examined whether earlier temperament was predictive of cumulative high school GPA. Six dimensions of the MCTQ (aggregated across ages 8, 10, and 12 years) related significantly across time with GPA: persistence/attention span and distractibility (r's $= .44$ and $-.35$, p's $< .001$, respectively), adaptability, negative mood, and predictability/quality of organization (r's $= .32$, $-.31$, and $.30$, p's $< .01$, respectively), and intensity of reactions ($r = -.24$, $p < .05$). Children rated as more persistent, less distractible, quicker to adapt, more positive in mood, more predictable/organized, and less intense during the middle childhood years subsequently tended to have higher GPA's at the conclusion of their secondary school years. Even during the preschool years, parent ratings of persistence/attention span, adaptability, and approach/withdrawal on the BSQ significantly related to cumulative high school GPA, with $r = .38$, $p < .001$, and r's $= .23$, and $.26$, p's $< .05$, respectively. Hence, parent ratings of children's persistence/attention span and adaptability show long-term cross-time relations with this important measure of academic outcome. Parent ratings of temperament at 2 years on the TTS (activity level, intensity, negative mood) and at 1.5 years on the ICQ (fussy/difficult, unadaptable) showed scattered significant correlations, although none exceeded .23 in magnitude, p's $< .05$.

We conclude this chapter with a longitudinal examination of temperament as a predictor of high school cumulative GPA, after controlling for the effects of IQ and SES, two important predictors of school achievement. For each analysis, the most concurrent measures of IQ, SES, and temperament were utilized, as described below. Temperament dimensions were entered in the last step, using a stepwise procedure with a .05 p-to-enter.

Temperament dimensions measured during the preschool, middle childhood, and adolescent eras significantly improved the prediction of high school cumulative GPA, even when entered into the regression after the effects of IQ and SES. Table 6.07, which is organized in reverse chronological order from age 17 to

Table 6.07.   Multiple Regression Analyses Using Intelligence and Temperament as Predictors of Cumulative High School Grade Point Average

Age	Significant predictors	Mult R	Adj R^2	R^2 change	F	df
	Adolescent era					
17	WAIS-R Full Scale IQ	.61	.36	.37		
14, 16 Aggregated	DOTS-R Task Orientation (Parent)	.71	.50	.14		
	DOTS-R Approach (Parent)	.73	.52	.03	34.30***	3, 91
17	WAIS-R Full Scale IQ	.59	.34	.34		
14,16 Aggregated	DOTS-R Task Orientation (Teen)	.63	.39	.06		
	DOTS-R Approach (Teen)	.66	.41	.03	23.32***	3, 95
15	WISC-III Full Scale IQ	.64	.40	.40		
14, 16 Aggregated	DOTS-R Task Orientation (Parent)	.73	.52	.13		
	DOTS-R Approach (Parent)	.75	.55	.03	37.31***	3, 90
15	WISC-III Full Scale IQ	.63	.39	.39		
14, 16 Aggregated	DOTS-R Task Orientation (Teen)	.66	.43	.05		
	DOTS-R Approach (Teen)	.69	.46	.03	27.67***	3, 95
	Middle childhood era					
6, 7, 8, 12 Aggregated	WISC-R Full Scale IQ	.65	.42	.42		
12	SES	.68	.45	.04		
8, 10, 12 Aggregated	Persistence/Attention Span	.72	.51	.06	32.31***	3, 92
	Preschool era					
5	K-ABC Mental Processing Score	.52	.26	.27		
5	SES	.65	.42	.16		
3, 3.5, 5 Aggregated	Persistence/Attention Span	.69	.45	.04	27.49***	3, 96
2.5, 3, 3.5 Aggregated	McCarthy General Cognitive Index	.50	.24	.25		
2.5, 3, 3.5 Aggregated	SES	.63	.39	.15		
3, 3.5, 5 Aggregated	Persistence/Attention Span	.66	.42	.04	25.47***	3, 100
	Infant/toddler era					
2	Bayley Mental Development Index	.44	.18	.19		
2	SES	.58	.32	.14	22.15***	2, 91
1.5	Bayley Mental Development Index	.15	.14	.15		
1.5	SES	.60	.34	.21	26.29***	2, 98

*$p < .05$. **$p < .01$. ***$p < .001$.

1.5 years, displays a summary of the stepwise multiple regression analysis results. Attention span/task persistence (task orientation in adolescence) always entered first from among the temperament dimensions. During adolescence, the dimension of approach also entered into the prediction at both 15 and 17 years for both parent and self-informants. Three key points can be deduced from the findings observed across the adolescent, middle childhood, preschool, and infancy eras. First, IQ was a significant correlate of GPA in every analysis from 1.5 through 17 years, accounting for between 14.6% and 42.4% of the variance; correlations between IQ and GPA strengthened with increasing age. Second, SES contributed to the prediction of high school cumulative GPA only during the earlier ages (infancy through middle childhood) and accounted for between 3.5% and 20.8% of the variance. Finally, even when entered into the equation after these two very powerful predictors of high school academic achievement, temperament dimensions still entered as significant predictors during the preschool, middle childhood, and adolescent periods, progressively incrementing the amount of variance explained by 4.2% to 17.3%. Impressively, the multiple R resulting from these three potential predictors of high school cumulative GPA reached .73. This is particularly noteworthy when one considers that the data were derived across multiple informants, multiple methods, and indeed across a wide variation of high school types and locations. These findings provide external validity to the assessment of temperament via parent and self-ratings on standardized inventories.

Summary and Conclusions

1. *Do children with delayed school entry differ in temperament from children who entered on time?* Children whose parents delayed their kindergarten entry differed from children who entered school on time on only one temperament dimension: adaptability. As preschoolers, those with delayed entry were characterized by their parents as slower to adapt.

2. *Do children who repeat a grade differ in temperament from those who move through their school experience with no grade repetitions?* Children who repeated a grade differed in temperament from those who moved through their school experience with no grade repetitions on the dimensions of threshold of sensitivity to the environment, adaptability, and persistence. Children who repeated kindergarten or first grade demonstrated no differences in temperament as infants. However, as preschoolers they were described by their parents as less sensitive to changes in the environment and slower to adapt than were children who did not repeat kindergarten or first grade. Children who had repeated any grade from kindergarten to the end of high school displayed no differences in infant temperament from those children who did not repeat any grades. However, on measures of preschool temperament as well as middle childhood temperament, they

were evaluated by parents as less persistent/having shorter attention spans than non-repeaters.

3. *Which dimensions of temperament relate to students' academic achievement? Are the dimensions similar across various indicators of academic achievement and across the elementary and secondary school periods?* Preschool temperament predicted academic achievement levels assessed on standardized tests administered when the children were first entering elementary school. There were positive associations between the temperament dimensions of persistence, adaptability, and approach and higher academic achievement test scores. Inverse associations were observed between negative mood and academic achievement. During the adolescent years, task orientation was the dimension that pervasively related to academic achievement, measured objectively through standardized achievement tests or subjectively through parent and self-reports.

4. *Does children's temperament relate to teachers' appraisals of their pupils' classroom competence?* Children's temperament related to teachers' appraisals of their pupils' classroom behavior. High levels of persistence and adaptability as well as low levels of activity and distractibility were related to behaving appropriately, learning, and being happy in class. Temperament contributed substantially to the teachers' appraisals of children's behavior, even over and above the contribution made by children's intelligence.

5. *Do aspects of children's temperament relate to their academic intrinsic motivation and academic self-concept?* Children's temperament did not relate to their general school self-concept or their level of academic intrinsic motivation about school in general during the elementary school years. However, during adolescence, general school self-concept and intrinsic motivation toward school in general were related to both parent and self-ratings of three aspects of adolescent temperament: approach, flexibility, and task orientation. In addition, adolescents lower in general activity reported higher levels of general school self-concept.

6. *Does temperament contribute to the prediction of high school cumulative grade point average? Does temperament relate to cumulative grade point average when entered after two central correlates of academic achievement, intelligence and family socioeconomic status?* Cumulative high school grade point average was predicted by temperament measured even as early infancy, although a stable pattern of persistence/attention span and adaptability as the strongest relative predictors begins to emerge during the preschool years. Even after controlling for two potent predictors of academic success, IQ and SES, temperament variables predict high school cumulative GPA, accounting for between 4 (preschool years) and 17 percent of the variance (adolescence).

7

Temperament in the Family Context

> "He is very much a loner. He is too mature for his years. He has trouble relating to his peers—especially those who "goof off" in school. He is outgoing, polite, and caring. He always follows household rules."
>
> —Parent of Child #2, Easy Infant Temperament Group, Age 17

Issues Investigated

In this chapter, we examine the extensive FLS longitudinal data related to the participants' home and family environment, including family relationships. As we have previously reported that temperament in the FLS was not pervasively related to family socioeconomic status (A. W. Gottfried et al., 2003), we focus in this chapter on proximal variables. By proximal variables, we mean those that assess processes or specific aspects of the environment that may influence children's development. These would include, for example, language stimulation, access to toys, games, and reading materials, opportunities for variety in stimulation, etc. Keeping in mind the bidirectional and transactional traditions within developmental science perspectives, we examined child temperament as a concomitant, as a predictor, as an outcome, and as a moderator of development. Five major issues will be addressed herein:

1. *Are children's temperament characteristics related to proximal variables in their home? Are there consistent or changing patterns of relation between child temperament and proximal home environment across development from infancy through childhood?* In the FLS, homes of participants were visited during the infancy, preschool, and elementary years, and it was with these detailed and extensive data collected via the well-known HOME scales, based on both direct observation and interview methodology, that we first examined temperament-environment relations.

2. *To what extent are specific dimensions of child temperament related to concurrent and cross-time assessments of the quality of family climate? Are the strengths and patterns of relation between child temperament and*

family climate constant across development? Assessments of the family environment were regularly collected using the Family Environment Scale. These data provide another measure of proximal environment variables that may influence children's development, and the relation of child temperament to these variables across the childhood and adolescent years is assessed herein.

3. *How do individual differences in children's temperament relate to parents' and children's assessments of their relationship with each other?* Parent-child relationships, which also may be considered proximal environmental variables, are considered as a separate category. During the middle childhood and/or adolescent period, study participants and parents rated the quality of their relationship with each other, and these assessments are examined in relation to parent and adolescent assessments of the adolescents' temperament.

4. *How might variations in children's contexts influence the expression of their temperament? Which aspects of the proximal environment, if any, are predictive of children's subsequent temperament?* In this section, we examine the relation between earlier measures of home environment and subsequent measures of child/adolescent temperament.

5. *How do temperament and environment interact in influencing children's developmental outcomes?* In some cases, rather than direct main effects, individual differences in children's temperament may modify the impact of the environment on their development. In the final section, we present evidence of such temperament-environment interactions based on the FLS data. Specifically, we examine interactions between infant temperament and family conflict as predictors of behavior problems.

Description of Measures Used in the FLS

Direct Assessments of the Home Environment

A major focus of this longitudinal investigation has been an examination of environment-development relationships. Hence, over the course of investigation we have employed comprehensive and ongoing assessments of numerous aspects of the children's environment. As one component of our assessment of home environment, we administered the widely-used Home Observation for the Measurement of the Environment (HOME) inventory developed by Caldwell and Bradley (1984). The HOME was administered on three occasions to assess the environment during the developmental periods of infancy (1.25 years), the preschool years (3.25 years), and middle childhood (8 years). The HOME was administered by our staff, and in all cases both mother and child were present in the home during the visit. On the HOME, data are collected through direct observation and via semi-structured interview.

Infant HOME

This version of the HOME was used at our 1.25-year home visit. It contains 45 items assessing the following six scales: emotional and verbal responsivity of mother; avoidance of restriction and punishment; organization of the physical and temporal environment; provision of appropriate play materials; maternal involvement with the child; and opportunities for variety in daily stimulation.

Preschool HOME

When families were visited at 3.25 years, the preschool version of the HOME was used. It comprises 55 items divided into eight scales: stimulation through toys, games, and reading materials; language stimulation; physical environment: safe, clean, and conducive to development; pride, affection, and warmth; stimulation of academic behavior; modeling and encouragement of social maturity; variety of stimulation; and physical punishment.

Elementary HOME

The elementary-age version of the HOME was used at the 8-year home visit. The 59 items assess eight aspects of home environment: emotional and verbal responsivity; encouragement of maturity; emotional climate; growth fostering materials and experiences; provision for active stimulation; family participation in developmentally stimulating experiences; paternal involvement; and aspects of the physical environment.

Family Relationship Variables

Family Environment Scale

The social climate of the family was assessed by parent report using the Family Environment Scale (FES) developed by R. H. Moos and Moos (1986). The FES comprises 90 items that fall into 10 scales. Wachs (1991) recommended that future investigators focus their attention on environmental variables that directly or indirectly relate to children's transactions with their environment, particularly those that involve adult-child relations. A preliminary survey of correlation analyses between temperament and FES scales revealed, in line with Wachs' recommendations, that temperament dimensions most consistently related to three dimensions of the FES: cohesion, the help and support family members show for each other; conflict, the open expression of anger and conflict among family members; and intellectual-cultural orientation, the interest a family shows in political, social, cultural, and intellectual activities. Findings regarding these three scales are detailed herein. Expressiveness also seemed a likely candidate; however, correlations with temperament never exceeded .30 and also never related across time. Hence, in the interest of both simplification and space, findings regarding expressiveness are not reported.

Parent-Child Relationships

Children's Ratings during Middle Childhood

Children's views of the quality of their relationship with their parents were assessed using the parent relations scale of the Self Description Questionnaire-I at age 10. The Parent Relations scale consists of 8 items that reflect the child's view of how well he/she gets along with parents, likes parents, and feels parental approval. For each declarative item, the child checks one of five responses: *False, Mostly False, Sometimes, Mostly True, and True.* Marsh (1988) reported internal consistency reliability estimates exceeded .80 for all scales on the SDQ-I.

Children's Ratings during Adolescence

At ages 12, 14 and 16, adolescents completed the SDQ-II. The parent relations scale, which consists of 8 items, was used as an indicator of the quality of the adolescents' interactions with their parents. Half of the items on the SDQ-II are worded negatively to avoid response bias. To respond, the adolescent checks one of six responses: *False, Mostly False, More False Than True, More True Than False, Mostly True, True.* Marsh (1990) reports coefficient alpha of .87 for the Parent Relations scale.

Parents' Ratings when Children were Adolescents

The Parent-Child Relationship Inventory (PCRI) was completed by both parents when their children were 15 and 16 years old. Gerard (1994) described the PCRI as an instrument used to assess "parents' attitudes toward parenting and toward their children" (p. 1). The inventory comprises 78 items to which parents respond using a 4-point Likert-type response format (*Strongly Agree,*

Agree, Disagree, Strongly Disagree). Five of the seven content scales were examined: satisfaction with parenting (amount of pleasure and gratification derived from being a parent), involvement (level of interaction and knowledge about the child), communication (effectiveness in communicating with the child), limit setting (ease and effectiveness in disciplining child), and autonomy (ability to promote child's independence); parental support and role orientation scales were omitted as they did not reflect the quality of the parent-child relationship.

Findings and Discussion

HOME Inventory

Infancy

Infant temperament, assessed at 1.5 years on the ICQ, was related concurrently and across time to HOME scales assessing adult-child interactions and degree of stimulation variety in the home, both factors identified by Wachs (1991) as proximal variables most likely to relate to child temperament. Specifically, infant temperament related most pervasively to two aspects of home environment: verbal and emotional interactions with mother and opportunities for a variety of stimulation. Table 7.01 displays Pearson correlation coefficients between infant temperament and these aspects of home environment measured longitudinally. Babies displaying more challenging infant temperaments tended to experience lower levels of emotional and verbal responsiveness from their mothers on the HOME assessed during infancy, lower levels of pride and affection during the preschool years, and

Table 7.01. **Pearson Correlation Coefficients between Infant Temperament Dimensions and Specific Scales of the HOME Measured in Infancy, Preschool Years, and Elementary School Years**

Infant temperament dimension	Social-emotional interaction			Environmental enrichment		
	Infant EVR	Preschool PAW	Elementary EVR	Infant OVDS	Preschool LS	Preschool VS
Fussy/Difficult	−.18*	−.24*	−.11	−.18*	−.05	−.05
Unadaptable	−.31**	−.17	−.21*	−.22*	−.22*	−.22*
Resistant to Control	−.20*	−.23*	−.20*	−.23*	−.24*	−.30**
Unsociable	−.13	−.16	−.22*	−.35***	−.21*	−.19*

N's = 102–122.
Note: EVR = Emotional and Verbal Responsivity of Mother; PAW = Pride, Affection, and Warmth; OVDS = Opportunities for Variety in Daily Stimulation; LS = Language Stimulation; VS = Variety of Stimulation.
$p < .05.$ **$p < .01.$ ***$p < .001.$

lower levels of emotional and verbal responsivity during the elementary years, as shown in the left panel. Results in the right panel show that challenging infant temperament related inversely to opportunities for variety in daily stimulation, language stimulation, and variety of stimulation, with correlation coefficients ranging to .35 in magnitude. More challenging infant temperament related concurrently and predictively to lower levels of support in the proximal environment, including social and emotional support as well as opportunities for stimulation. Of 88 correlations examined between the ICQ factors and all of the HOME scales assessed in infancy, preschool, and elementary years, 24 correlations were significant; 18 of the 24 involved the scales displayed in Table 7.01 that pertained to these aspects of parent-child interactions and enrichment opportunities. Five of the six remaining significant correlations (out of the aforementioned 24) involved the ICQ dimension resistance to control. Infants rated as more challenging on this dimension also scored lower on maternal involvement on the infant HOME ($r = -.24$, $p < .01$), lower on stimulation through toys, games, and reading materials and lower on restriction of physical punishment on the preschool HOME ($r = -.28$, $p < .01$; $r = -.23$, $p < .05$, respectively), and lower on encouragement of maturity and emotional climate on the elementary HOME ($r = -.24$, $p < .05$ and $r = -.26$, $p < .01$, respectively). Together with the results displayed in Table 7.01, these findings show that of the four ICQ dimensions, resistance to control related most pervasively to proximal aspects of the home environment, accounting for 11 of the 18 significant correlations observed across the concurrent and predictive ICQ-HOME relations. Behaviors characterizing infants scoring high on resistance to control include negative reactions to being re-directed from a desired activity or goal, high levels of general activity, and negative reactions to being dressed or confined in other ways, for example.

Although it is instructive to identify the specific home characteristics related to infant temperament, it is also informative to identify those aspects of the home and social environment that showed no relation to infant temperament. As noted above, numerous scales of the HOME measured longitudinally bore no significant relation to temperament assessed on the ICQ at 1.5 years. Infant temperament was not significantly related to the following scales of the infant HOME: avoidance of restriction and punishment, organization of the physical and temporal environment, or provision of appropriate play materials. On the preschool HOME, no relations were observed with physical environment, stimulation of academic behavior, or modeling/encouragement of social maturity. Finally, infant temperament did not predict the following scales of the elementary HOME: growth fostering materials and experiences, provision for active stimulation, family participation in developmentally stimulating experiences, or aspects of physical environment.

Hence, infant temperament measured at 1.5 years related concurrently and across time to HOME variables associated with the quality of parent-child socio-emotional and verbal interactions and to the variety of stimulation experienced by the child, with more rewarding socioemotional parent-child relations and more enriched environmental opportunities afforded to infants with more positive temperaments (i.e., infants scored lower on the ICQ). This was particularly so for the resistant to control factor of the ICQ.

To determine whether multiple ICQ dimensions would combine to explain variance in the proximal home environment, stepwise multiple regression analyses were conducted for each of the six criterion variables displayed in Table 7.01. On only one of the six, opportunities for variety in daily stimulation on the infant HOME, did multiple temperament dimensions combine to predict HOME scores:. Resistance to control entered into the prediction after unsociability, increasing the amount of variance accounted for in the ICQ by 6.5%, to yield a multiple R of .43 and adjusted R^2 of 17%, $F(2, 121) = 13.51$, $p < .001$.

Preschool Years

Multiple dimensions of preschool-age temperament related to four dimensions of the proximal home environment during the preschool age years. Children who were adaptable and persistent were in families characterized by emotional warmth, a stimulating environment, and the use of discipline techniques other than corporal punishment. More challenging temperament related to lower scores on the HOME. More specifically, preschoolers rated by parents as more persistent and more sensitive to environmental changes (threshold) received higher levels of stimulation, such as toys, games, and reading materials, $r = .20$, $p < .05$ and $r = .28$, $p < .01$, respectively. A stepwise multiple regression analysis showed that temperamental persistence and threshold of responsiveness both contributed to the prediction of academic behavior stimulation, jointly accounting for an adjusted 9% of the variance ($R = .33$), $F(2, 114) = 6.82$, $p < .01$. Children rated as higher in approach and quicker to adapt tended to experience higher levels of affection and warmth, $r = .20$, $p < .05$ and $r = .27$, $p < .01$, respectively. Preschoolers rated as higher in approach and quicker to adapt tended to experience a wider variety of stimulation, $r = .25$, $p < .05$ and $r = .19$, $p < .05$, respectively. Parents tended to avoid restriction and punishment when children were lower in activity level and quicker to adapt (r's $= -.30$ and .33, p's $< .01$, respectively) and less negative in mood and longer in persistence/attention span (r's $= -.19$ and .19, $p < .05$, respectively). Stepwise multiple regression analysis showed that the combination of adaptability and activity level accounted for 13.8% of the variance in avoidance of physical punishment, [$R = .39$; $F(2, 114) = 10.14$, $p < .001$]. Hence, during the preschool years, numerous temperament dimensions including particularly persistence/attention span, approach/withdrawal, adaptability, and activity level, related to the nature of the child's experience in the home.

Middle Childhood

Only 5 of 72 correlations between the MCTQ and HOME during the elementary years were significant, and these were with only three scales of the HOME inventory: emotional and verbal responsivity, encouragement of maturity, and active stimulation. Children rated as quicker to adapt received higher levels of emotional and verbal responsiveness, $r = .26$, $p < .01$. This replicates findings from the BSQ. Additionally, children viewed as less active and more predictable had homes more encouraging of maturity, r's $= -.26$ and $.25$, $p < .01$, respectively. Finally, children rated lower in intensity and distractibility tended to receive higher levels of active stimulation, r's $= -.23$ and $-.25$, $p < .01$, respectively. Stepwise multiple regression analyses showed no improvement in prediction when using all dimensions to predict home environment during middle childhood. During middle childhood, temperament-environment relations were not as evident as during the infancy and preschool periods.

Family Environment Scale (FES)

Pearson correlation coefficients were used to examine the pattern of relations between aspects of the family environment and specific temperament dimensions assessed during the infancy (ICQ), preschool (BSQ), middle childhood (MCTQ), and adolescent (DOTS-R) periods of development. As described earlier in this chapter, a survey of the results of the correlation analyses showed that the most pervasive and strongest relations centered on three FES dimensions: cohesion, conflict, and intellectual-cultural orientation. These findings corroborated the recommendations of Wachs (1991), who observed that parent-child relations and degree of stimulation in the home seemed particularly sensitive to aspects of the environment. For ease of presentation, results will be reported for these dimensions of the family environment only.

By way of preview, the dimensions of child temperament that related most consistently and at highest magnitude with these three aspects of the family environment were adaptability, approach, persistence/attention span, and negative mood. Although correlations reached moderate magnitudes at best, the consistency of concurrent relations across the developmental eras investigated, and across informants, intimates the possible role of individual differences in child temperament as shapers of the family climate.

Infant Temperament

Infant temperament significantly related to cohesion, conflict, and the intellectual-cultural climate of the home through at least age 16 years. As shown

Table 7.02. **Pearson Correlation Coefficients between Infant Temperament and Aspects of the Family Environment through Adolescence**

Infant temperament dimension	Family environment scale dimension and age span aggregated								
	Cohesion			Conflict			Intellectual-cultural		
	3–5	8–12	14–16	3–5	8–12	14–16	3–5	8–12	14–16
Fussy/Difficult	−.05	−.15	−.27**	.25**	.32**	.25*	−.18	−.25**	−.31**
Unadaptable	−.23*	−.16	−.24*	.11	.13	.21*	−.23*	−.32**	−.29**
Resistant to Control	−.03	−.12	−.12	.18	.12	.09	−.18	−.22*	−.32**
Unsociable	−.30**	−.31**	−.32**	.07	.13	.15	−.23*	−.24*	−.26*

$N = 98–114$.
$*p < .05. **p < .01$.

in Table 7.02, infant unsociability related to lower family cohesion at all developmental eras. Family conflict at every developmental era was presaged by more fussy/demanding/difficult temperament during infancy. Finally higher ratings on all four dimensions of challenging temperament on the ICQ portended lower orientation toward intellectual-cultural endeavors across childhood and adolescence. Hence, variations in infant temperament related concurrently and across time to aspects of the family environment, most particularly the family's orientation toward intellectual-cultural pursuits.

Stepwise multiple regression analyses conducted to determine the amount of variance explained by infant temperament characteristics showed only two instances in which multiple temperament dimensions combined to predict family environment. First, the ICQ unsociable and fussy/difficult factors combined to account for 13% of the variance (adjusted for shrinkage) in family cohesion during adolescence, $R = .39$, $F(2, 97) = 8.29$, $p < .001$. Second, a stepwise multiple regression analysis showed that the ICQ resistant to control and unsociability factors explained 17% of the variance (adjusted for shrinkage) in the family's intellectual-cultural orientation during adolescence, $R = .32$, $F(2, 97) = 10.92$, $p < .001$. Hence, infant temperament explained a maximum of 17% of the variance in these aspects of the family environment during preschool, middle childhood, and adolescent eras.

Preschool-Age Temperament

Concurrent temperament-FES relations were observed for the cohesion, conflict, and intellectual-cultural scales; aspects of preschool-age temperament presaged intellectual-cultural orientation across all developmental eras investigated. Table 7.03 displays correlation coefficients between temperament assessed on the BSQ assessed during the preschool years and cohesion, conflict, and

Table 7.03.   Pearson Correlation Coefficients between Preschool-Age Temperament and Aspects of the Family Environment through Adolescence

Preschool-age temperament dimension	Family environment scale dimension and age span aggregated								
	Cohesion			Conflict			Intellectual-cultural		
	3–5	8–12	14–16	3–5	8–12	14–16	3–5	8–12	14–16
Activity Level	.02	.02	−.15	−.01	−.04	.01	−.11	−.02	−.25*
Rhythmicity[a]	.17	.14	.09	−.12	−.04	−.00	.16	.17	.22*
Approach[a]	.20*	.14	.08	−.10	−.15	−.12	.25**	.28**	.24*
Adaptability[a]	.24**	.04	.15	−.24**	−.13	−.18	.33***	.24*	.36***
Intensity	.08	.07	.06	.10	.08	−.02	−.04	.01	.00
Negative Mood	−.16	.01	−.10	.23*	.17	.20*	−.23*	−.16	−.18
Persistence[a]	.24**	.10	.08	−.05	−.03	.02	.42***	.35***	.36***
Distractibility	.06	.04	.06	−.04	.01	−.08	−.13	−.13	−.12
Threshold	.08	.09	.07	−.04	.00	−.03	.13	.20*	.11

[a]Signs of coefficients were reversed to facilitate interpretation.
$N = 101$–118.
$*p < .05.$ $**p < .01.$ $***p < .001.$

intellectual-cultural orientation assessed during the preschool, middle childhood, and adolescent eras. Concurrent relations only (i.e., not cross-time) were evident for family cohesion and conflict. Preschoolers whose temperaments were rated as more approaching, quicker to adapt, and more persistent tended to have more cohesive families. More conflict was reported in the families of preschoolers viewed as slower in adapting to changes and more negative in mood. Three aspects of preschoolers' temperament portended higher family orientation toward intellectual-cultural endeavors across childhood and adolescence: persistence/attention span, adaptability, and approach. Specifically, preschoolers viewed as having longer persistence/attention spans, more approaching to new experiences, and quicker to adapt to changes had families that were more oriented toward intellectual-cultural pursuits when the children were young as well as throughout childhood and adolescence.

Multiple regression analyses showed that preschool age child temperament variables combined to predict a significant amount of variance in only one FES dimension during the preschool, middle childhood, and adolescent eras: the family's intellectual cultural orientation. During preschool, 19.2% of the variance in the family's intellectual-cultural orientation was accounted for by the dimensions of persistence and approach/withdrawal, $R = .45$, $F (2, 117) = 14.86$, $p < .001$. Likewise, during middle childhood, persistence and approach/withdrawal combined to explain 15.2% of the variance, $R = .41$, $F (2, 107) = 10.56$, $p < .001$. During adolescence, adaptability and persistence combined to explain 15.4% of the variance in intellectual-cultural orientation, $R = .41$, $F (2, 100) = 10.08$,

Table 7.04.   Pearson Correlation Coefficients between Middle Childhood Temperament and Aspects of the Family Environment through Adolescence

| Childhood temperament dimension | Family environment scale dimension and age span aggregated | | | | | |
| | Cohesion | | Conflict | | Intellectual-cultural | |
	8–12	14–16	8–12	14–16	8–12	14–16
Activity Level	−.08	−.16	.14	.10	−.16	−.21*
Predictability[a]	.25*	−.15	−.29**	−.11	.19*	.14
Approach[a]	.04	−.03	−.01	.03	.21*	.17
Adaptability[a]	.25**	.26**	−.34***	−.28**	.28**	.30**
Intensity	−.25*	−.25*	.34***	.21*	−.20	−.14
Negative Mood	−.16	−.24*	.36***	.37***	−.24*	−.30**
Persistence[a]	.26**	.32**	−.20*	−.15	.36***	.35***
Distractibility	−.15	−.02	.01	−.01	−.18	−.20
Threshold	−.11	−.01	.04	−.07	−.12	−.10

[a]Signs of coefficients were reversed to facilitate interpretation.
$N = 99–107$.
$*p < .05. **p < .01. ***p < .001.$

$p < .001$. (All coefficients of determination reported above were adjusted for shrinkage.) Hence, the temperament of the study child during the preschool years explained appreciable amounts of variance in the family intellectual-cultural climate concurrently and across time.

Middle Childhood Temperament

Temperament assessed on the MCTQ between the ages of 8 and 12 years related pervasively to all three scales of the FES, both concurrently and across time. Correlation coefficients are displayed in Table 7.04, where it is evident that the temperament dimensions of adaptability, intensity, negative mood, and persistence were particularly pervasive and relatively stronger concomitants and predictors of these aspects of family climate. Adaptability and persistence related concurrently and/or across time with all three aspects of family environment, with more adaptable and persistent children experiencing more cohesive and intellectually-culturally oriented and less conflictual family environments. Negative mood also related concurrently or across-time to all three FES dimensions, with children higher in negative mood experiencing less family cohesion, greater conflict, and families less oriented toward intellectual-cultural pursuits. Although intensity of reactions related inversely to family cohesion and positively to family conflict, it did not correlate with the intellectual-cultural orientation of the family.

Multiple regression analyses showed that numerous dimensions of middle childhood temperament combined to predict only one criterion variable, family conflict during adolescence. Temperament during middle childhood explained 15.8% of the adjusted variance, $R = .42$, $F (2, 98) = 10.20$, $p < .001$.

Adolescent Temperament

Pearson correlations between parent reports of adolescents' temperament on the DOTS-R showed pervasive concurrent relations with family cohesion and intellectual-cultural orientation. Family cohesion was related most strongly to adolescents' positive mood, $r = .45$, $p < .001$, but also at low magnitudes to approach, flexibility, task orientation, and rhythmicity of eating and daily habits, r's $= .20$ to $.24$, p's $< .05$. The strongest temperamental concomitants of the family's intellectual-cultural orientation were task orientation, positive mood, and approach, r's $= .32$ to $.36$, p's $< .001$; additionally, general activity level (inverse relation), flexibility, and regularity of sleeping and eating related at low magnitudes, r's $= .24$ to $.29$, p's $< .05$. Mood was the sole correlate of family conflict during adolescence, with less conflict when adolescents were more positive in mood, $r = -.29$, $p < .01$. (Only two of 27 correlations between adolescent self-rated temperament and parent-rated family environment aggregated across ages 14 and 16 were significant).

Multiple regression analyses showed that numerous dimensions of parent ratings of temperament combined to predict intellectual-cultural orientation during adolescence. Task orientation and positive mood combined explained 19% of the variance, $R = .45$, $F (2, 103) = 12.85$, $p < .001$. Using both parent and adolescent ratings of adolescent temperament, flexibility, task orientation, and positive mood combined to explain 22% of the variance, $R = .49$, $F (3, 103) = 10.61$, $p < .001$. Hence, adolescent temperament explained approximately 20% of the variance in the intellectual-cultural climate of the family during adolescence.

Family Environment from the Adolescents' Perspective

Study children also completed the FES when they were 17 years of age. Although not a concurrent measure of temperament, the DOTS-R was completed by children and their parents at the 14 and 16 year assessments. For the next analyses, temperament scores were averaged across ages within informant. Correlations between temperament (both self- and parent-rated) and FES as reported by adolescents were computed to determine whether child temperament related across time to adolescent perceptions of the family environment at age 17. Correlation coefficients are displayed in Table 7.05; the top half displays correlations with the FES completed by study children at age 17 and their self-ratings of temperament

Table 7.05. Concurrent Pearson Correlation Coefficients between Adolescent and Parent-Rated Temperament and Adolescent-Reported Family Environment Ratings at Age 17

Temperament dimension	Family environment scale dimension		
	Cohesion	Conflict	Intellectual-cultural
Adolescent self-rated temperament ($N = 110$)			
Approach	.23*	−.16	.28**
Flexibility	.34***	−.41***	.31**
Rhythm – Eating	.26**	−.20*	.17
Rhythm – Daily	.30**	−.16	.08
Task Orientation	.21*	−.11	.25**
Parent ratings of adolescent temperament ($N = 104$)			
Approach	.28**	−.27**	.30**
Flexibility	.14	−.21*	.08
Rhythm – Eating	.18	−.21*	.13
Rhythm – Daily	.21*	−.23*	.18
Task Orientation	.15	−.11	.38***

Note: No significant correlation coefficients were observed with temperament dimensions omitted from table.
*$p < .05$. **$p < .01$. ***$p < .001$.

(14 and 16 years averaged), and the bottom half shows correlations between the FES as reported by adolescents and parent-rated adolescent temperament.

Flexibility and approach, compared to the other temperament dimensions, were relatively strong and pervasive predictors of family environment. Adolescents rating themselves as more flexible subsequently viewed their homes as higher in cohesion, lower in conflict, and higher in intellectual-cultural orientation. Additional adolescent temperament dimensions presaging family cohesiveness were approach, task orientation, and regularity of eating and daily habits. Greater family orientation toward intellectual-cultural activities was presaged by adolescent approach and task orientation.

Multiple regression analyses conducted to determine the amount of variance in family environment characteristics accounted for by adolescent temperament showed that for two FES scales, combinations of temperament dimensions accounted for approximately 10% to 20% of the variance (adjusted for inflation). Flexibility and regularity of daily habits accounted for 17% of the variance in family cohesion, $R = .43$, $F (2, 109) = 12.10$, $p < .001$. Flexibility and task orientation combined to predict 12% of the variance in the family's intellectual-cultural climate, $R = .37$, $F (2, 109) = 8.24$, $p < .001$.

Examining the lower half of Table 7.05, which displays parent ratings of temperament as predictors of their adolescents' views of the family environment, it is clear that the pattern of correlations was not as strong or pervasive as in the top half. However, six of the eight significant correlation coefficients replicate those observed in the top half: adolescents higher in approach and regularity of daily habits viewed their family as higher in cohesion; adolescents lower in flexibility and regularity of eating subsequently rated their families higher in conflict; and adolescents who were higher in approach and task orientation subsequently viewed their families as higher in intellectual-cultural orientation. In addition, adolescents viewed as more withdrawing and less regular in daily habits across ages 14 and 16 subsequently viewed their families as higher in conflict. Multiple regression analyses showed that multiple temperament dimensions joined to predict the family's intellectual-cultural climate; approach and task orientation combined to explain 18% of the variance, $R = .44$, $F (2, 103) = 11.95$, $p < .001$.

These longitudinal data spanning the years from infancy through adolescence demonstrate that, even across families with multiple children, the study child's temperament related concurrently and across-time to the levels of cohesiveness, conflict, and intellectual-cultural orientation of the family. Child temperament characteristics relating to family cohesiveness across multiple developmental eras included adaptability, persistence/attention span, and approach. For family conflict, the most consistent child temperament precursors and concomitants were adaptability and mood. Dimensions of temperament related most pervasively to the family's intellectual-cultural orientation; approach, adaptability, persistence, and mood related across numerous developmental eras. Clearly, adaptability/flexibility was the temperament dimension with the broadest relation to family climate. Families with children who were quicker to adapt to changes or more flexible had environments characterized as more cohesive, less conflictual, and more highly-oriented toward intellectual-cultural activities across childhood and adolescence.

Early Family Environment as a Predictor of Child/ Adolescent Temperament

Although temperament is linked to certain aspects of the home environment, the nature of this linkage may be bidirectional (Wachs & Kohnstamm, 2001). In order to determine the extent to which variations in family environment portended children's temperament or its expression, we examined temperamental sequelae in middle childhood and adolescence of the three FES scales (cohesion, conflict, and intellectual-cultural orientation) assessed during the preschool years. Overall, the findings revealed that variations in family environment were not as telling about children's temperament as vice versa. Correlations were neither as pervasive nor as high in magnitude as those between earlier measures of temperament and family environmental sequelae.

Middle Childhood Temperament

Family cohesiveness during the preschool years presaged only one temperament dimension during middle childhood, persistence/attention span ($r = .22$, $p < .05$). Likewise, there was only one temperamental sequela of family conflict during the preschool years, intensity of reaction ($r = .23$, $p < .01$). Although six temperamental sequelae of intellectual-cultural orientation were observed (higher intellectual-cultural orientation presaged children who were more persistent, quicker to adapt, less distractible, more approaching, less intense, and more positive in mood, magnitudes of r's = .20 to .33), multiple regression analyses showed that only one FES scale entered into the prediction of the middle childhood temperament dimensions. Hence, family environment as assessed by these three scales of the FES predicted at best 10% of the variation in children's subsequent temperament during middle childhood.

Adolescent Temperament

Family environment factors during the preschool years also showed low correlations with temperament measured during adolescence, whether temperament was rated by parents or adolescents. Two temperamental sequelae of family cohesiveness replicated across both temperament informants: families characterized as more cohesive during the preschool years tended to have adolescents who were more flexible and had more regular daily habits, r's = .22 and .21, respectively, p's < .05. No temperamental sequelae of family conflict during the preschool years were observed. Families who were higher in intellectual-cultural orientation during the preschool years had adolescents who were rated by both themselves as their parents as less active in general and higher in task orientation. As during middle childhood, multiple regression analyses failed to improve the amount of variance explained beyond the Pearson correlation coefficients observed.

Hence, family environment was not as pervasive or as strong a precursor to subsequent temperament as early temperament was to later family environment. One finding replicated across middle childhood and adolescence and across informants was that families higher in intellectual-cultural orientation tended to have children who were more persistent during middle childhood and task-oriented during adolescence. These correlations were generally the strongest, albeit .33 was the maximum magnitude observed.

Parental Assessments of Parent-Child Relationships

When the study children were 15 and 16 years of age, their parents completed the Parent Child Relationship Inventory (PCRI). This scale assesses respondents' attitudes toward the experience of parenting their children. Given high cross-time stabilities observed for mothers and fathers across the two assessments, scores were aggregated across time, but within scale and informant. Across these analyses, mothers' and fathers' ratings of their experiences as parents and the quality of their relationship with their children were related most pervasively and most strongly with two specific aspects of their children's temperament: mood and flexibility. Also, across analyses using parent and adolescent ratings of the adolescents' temperament, relations were stronger with mothers' compared to fathers' assessments of their parenting experience.

Mothers' Assessments of the Parent-Child Relationship

Mothers' ratings of their parenting experience were pervasively related to three dimensions of adolescent temperament (rated via parent report): positive mood, flexibility, and approach. As shown in Table 7.06, correlation coefficients ranged to over .50 in magnitude and, with the exception of activity level, were positive in sign indicating more positive experiences or facility in parenting adolescents with temperaments characterized by more positive mood, more flexibility, and more approaching of new experiences. General activity and task orientation also related to some PCRI scales at moderate magnitudes.

Examining the PCRI scales in turn, mothers' ratings of satisfaction derived from the parental role were higher when their child's temperament was characterized as more positive in mood, more approaching, and more flexible. Similar patterns of findings were observed for mothers' ratings of their involvement and

Table 7.06. Pearson Correlation Coefficients between Parent Ratings of Child Temperament and Parent-Child Relationship during Adolescence

| Temperament dimension | Parent-child relationship inventory scale | | | | |
	Satisfaction with parenting	Involvement	Communication	Limit setting	Autonomy
	Relationship with mother ($N = 100$)				
General Activity	−.11	−.03	−.10	−.44***	−.23*
Activity – Sleep	.15	.13	−.01	−.04	−.01
Approach	.34***	.36***	.37***	.32**	.28**
Flexibility	.24*	.30**	.27**	.41***	.35***
Positive Mood	.34**	.51***	.47***	.51***	.30**
Rhythm – Sleep	.11	.25*	.27**	.30**	.21*
Rhythm – Eating	.12	.16	.08	.29**	.30**
Rhythm – Habits	.05	.10	.10	.16	.14
Task Orientation	.16	.32**	.39***	.43***	.25*

$p < .05$. **$p < .01$. ***$p < .001$.

communication with their adolescent offspring. Specifically, mothers' ratings of their interaction with and knowledge about their child (involvement) and their perception of the efficacy of their communications with their child were more positive when adolescents were characterized as more positive in mood, higher in approach, higher in task orientation, and more flexible. The final two scales, limit setting and autonomy, shared similar patterns of relation with adolescent temperament. Mothers viewed their disciplining of their children as easier and more efficacious and found it easier to promote their child's independence when children's temperament was more positive in mood, flexible, approaching, task-oriented, and lower in activity level.

Stepwise multiple regression analyses were used to determine the amount of variance (all R^2's adjusted for shrinkage) in each of the dimensions of mother-child relationships explained by adolescent temperament; these results revealed that adolescent temperament accounted for as much as one-third of the variance in mothers' ratings of their parenting experience in relation to the study child, particularly with respect to their involvement and communication with the child. A stepwise multiple regression analysis showed that approach and mood combined to predict 16% of the variance in maternal satisfaction with the parenting role, $R = .41$, $F(2, 99) = 10.10$, $p < .001$. Positive mood and task orientation combined to yield a multiple correlation of .56, accounting for 30% of the variance in maternal involvement with the child, $F(2, 99) = 21.92$, $p < .001$. The temperament dimensions of mood, task orientation, and approach combined to predict 33% of the variance on the PCRI communication scale, $R = .59$, $F(3, 98) = 17.35$, $p < .001$. Dimensions of temperament combined to predict 15% of the variance on the autonomy scale, $R = .41$, $F(2, 99) = 9.75$, $p < .001$.

Fathers' Assessment of the Parent-Child Relationship

Fathers also completed the Parent-Child Relationship Inventory when adolescents were 15 and 16 years. Pearson correlation coefficients between fathers' ratings and parent-reported temperament were not as strong or as pervasive as those observed for mothers. Adolescent positive mood was related to fathers' ratings of involvement, communication, limit setting, and autonomy (r's ranged from .22 to .27, p's < .05). Additionally, fathers viewed it easier to promote their adolescent's autonomy when their child was more flexible ($r = .37$, $p < .001$). Multiple regression analyses using temperament to predict fathers' assessments of the parent-child relationship showed multiple dimensions of temperament predicting only one PCRI scale. Hence, adolescent temperament was not a strong predictor of fathers' assessments of the quality of their relationship with their child. In part, the weaker patterns of relation observed between adolescent temperament and the fathering experience, compared to adolescent temperament and the mothering experience, may be attributed to the fact that the mothers were the parent raters for the adolescents' temperament. However, as will be shown in the next section, when adolescents rated their own temperament, the fathers' ratings of their own parenting experience were still not as pervasively linked to adolescent temperament as were mothers' ratings of experience. Thus, the stronger mothering-adolescent temperament link cannot solely be attributed to method variance.

Relation to Adolescent Self-Ratings of Temperament

We next examined the relation between adolescents' self-reports of their own temperaments with their mothers' and fathers' views of the parent-child relationship. This removed the overlap in source variance noted above wherein mothers almost exclusively were the parents providing the temperament and the parent-child relationship rating. Although the pattern of relation was not as pervasive, the significant coefficients replicated relations observed with parent ratings of temperament. Mothers' ratings of all five aspects of their parenting experience related to their teen's flexibility; r's ranged from .24 to .37 in magnitude. Additionally, mothers' ratings of limit setting related negatively to general activity level, $r = -.32$, $p < .01$. Their autonomy, involvement, and communication ratings also related to adolescents' positive mood, r's $= .19$ to .26.

Fathers' ratings of their parenting experience on the PCRI scales of involvement and communication were significantly related to adolescents' ratings of their own positive mood, r's $= .23$ and .24, p's $< .05$, respectively. Father involvement also related to adolescent flexibility, $r = .22$, $p < .05$. Thus, as observed with parent-rated adolescent temperament, adolescent self-ratings of temperament indicated that their flexibility and positive mood were most frequently related to parents' views of aspects of the parent-child relationship. Parent ratings of their relationship with their adolescent and their experience parenting were more positive when adolescents reported temperaments characterized as more flexible and more positive in mood.

Parent-Child Relations as Predictors of Temperament

We also examined the extent to which variations in parent-child relationship explained variation in the expression of or perception of adolescent temperament. For mother reports on the PCRI and parent-reported temperament, limit setting and involvement combined to predict 26% of the adjusted variance in adolescent general activity level, $R = .52$, $F (2, 99) = 18.11$, $p < .001$. Limit setting and involvement explained 33% of the variance in adolescent positive mood, $R = .57$, $F (2, 99) = 23.66$, $p < .001$. Twenty-three percent of the adjusted variance in adolescent task orientation was explained by limit setting, communication, and satisfaction, $R = .51$, $F (3, 99) = 11.09$, $p < .001$. Hence, relations between adolescent temperament and mothers' views of the parent-child relationship were bidirectional and both variables accounted for substantial amounts of variation in the other.

Earlier Temperament as a Predictor of Parent-Child Relationships

Concurrent relations between temperament and parent-child relations leave unclear the issue of directionality. Although not eliminating the direction of effect problem, examining the relation between earlier temperament ratings and the nature of parent-child relationships in adolescence can provide evidence that is necessary but not sufficient to determine directionality. That is, finding significant correlations between earlier measures of temperament and the criterion variables of parent-child relations in adolescence does not prove that variations in parent-child relations are due to differences in child temperament. However, it is a necessary first step. Hence, we computed correlation coefficients between temperament during earlier stages of development (middle childhood and preschool years) and mothers' and fathers' reports on the PCRI to determine if individual differences in children's earlier temperament presaged parent-child relations in adolescence.

Both mothers' and fathers' reports of their relationship with their adolescent were predicted by children's temperament during middle childhood. For example, mothers' ratings of limit setting, related to the ease of and efficacy in disciplining their teen, were predicted by six dimensions of temperament during middle childhood, with significant correlation coefficients ranging from .25 to .48 in magnitude. Children rated as more positive in mood, quicker to adapt, more persistent, less intense in their reactions, less active, and more predictable or organized were subsequently, in adolescence, rated by mothers as easier to discipline. Fathers' ratings of limit setting were also predicted by multiple dimensions of middle childhood temperament, including negative mood, adaptability, and approach/withdrawal (r's = .27 to .36 in magnitude); children who were more approaching, quicker to adapt, and more positive in mood were easier to discipline as adolescents. Childhood adaptability was most pervasively related to aspects of the mother-child relationship during adolescence, whereas approach/withdrawal, negative mood, and adaptability predicted at least three of the five dimensions of the PCRI for fathers.

Ratings of temperament during the preschool years were also linked to the quality of parent-child relationships during adolescence. For example, preschoolers who were quicker to adapt, less intense, and less negative in mood were subsequently easier to discipline by mothers during adolescence, r's = .38, $-.30$, and $-.36$, respectively. Again, adaptability was the most pervasive predictor of mother-child relationships during adolescence. Relationships between preschool age temperament and fathers' ratings on the PCRI were not as pervasive or as strong as those observed for mothers' ratings. Thus, even child temperament assessed a decade earlier related to parents' future assessments of their parenting experience.

Child/Adolescent Ratings of Relations with Parents

Correlation coefficients between temperament and children's ratings of their relations with their parents on the SDQ were stronger during adolescence than during middle childhood. Relations were most pervasive with the temperament dimensions of adaptability, mood, and persistence, with more positive relations with parents enjoyed by children viewed as quicker to adapt, more positive mood, and more persistent.

Middle Childhood

At age 10, only negative mood related to children's ratings of their relations with their parents, $r = -.20, p < .05$. At age 12, five of the nine temperament dimensions related significantly to children's appraisals of their relations with their parents, although all were in the low range of magnitude, r's $= .20$ to $.23, p < .05$. Children viewed as more predictable/organized, quicker to adapt, milder in intensity, less negative in mood, and more persistent reported better relations with their parents.

Adolescence

As previously noted, correlation coefficients computed between temperament and adolescents' appraisals of their relations with their parents reached higher magnitudes during adolescence. Results of these analyses with both parent- and self-reported adolescent temperament are displayed in Table 7.07. The dimensions of flexibility, positive mood, and task orientation related to adolescents' ratings of their relations with their parents across temperament informants, with correlation coefficients ranging to .41. Hence, more positive parent relations are reported by adolescents with temperamental dispositions characterized by ready adaptation to change, positive mood, and greater task orientation.

Multiple regression analyses examining the amount of variance in adolescents' ratings of the relationship with their parents showed that parent and adolescent temperament ratings combined to explain 31% of the variance, with task orientation, mood, and flexibility as predictors, $R = .58$, $F (4, 104) = 12.55$, $p < .001$. Individually, adolescent temperament ratings explained 27% of the variance in their ratings of the quality of their relationship with parents, $R = .54$, $F (3, 104) = 13.74$, $p < .001$. Using parent-reported temperament only, 14% of the variance in adolescent ratings of their relationship with parents was explained,

**Table 7.07.   Pearson Correlation Coefficients between
Parent- and Self-Reported Temperament and
Adolescent Ratings of Relationship with Parents
on the Self Description Questionnaire**

Temperament dimension	Temperament rater	
	Self	Parent
General Activity	−20*	−.18
Activity – Sleep	−.04	−.04
Approach	.32**	.15
Flexibility	.41***	.24*
Positive Mood	.34***	.25**
Rhythmicity – Sleep	.27*	.14
Rhythmicity – Eat	.26*	.11
Rhythmicity – Habits	.18	.10
Task Orientation	.35***	.34***

$N = 111$ for self report. $N = 105$ for parent report.
*$p < .05$. **$p < .01$. ***$p < .001$.

$R = .39$, $F(2, 104) = 9.29$, $p < .001$. Hence, both parent and adolescent ratings of temperament accounted for significant amounts of variation in adolescents' ratings of their relationship with their parents.

Middle Childhood Temperament as a Predictor of Adolescent Ratings of Parent Relationships

An examination of correlation coefficients between temperament during middle childhood and adolescent ratings of their relations with parents on the SDQ II (ages 14 and 16) showed that the same temperament dimensions were predictive of adolescents' appraisals of their relations with their parents at ages 14 and 16: quicker adaptability ($r = .29$), less negative mood ($r = −.33$), and greater persistence/attention span ($r = .29$). Multiple regression analyses did not result in significant improvement in the variance explained. Hence, children were characterized with these temperament patterns several years prior to their appraisals of their relations with their parents.

Temperament X Environment Interaction: Temperament, Family Conflict, and Behavior Problems

Until this point in chapter 7, the findings we have reported described environment-organism covariance in which characteristics of the organism and characteristics of the environment vary together. Correlations may arise, for example, when children with different temperaments either select or elicit/evoke different types of experiences from their surroundings.

A temperament X environment interaction, in contrast to temperament-environment covariance, is akin to the concept of the statistical interaction wherein the effect of one variable depends upon the level of a second variable (in the case of two factors). More specifically, Wachs and Plomin (1991) defined an organism-environment interaction as "differential reactivity by different individuals to similar environmental stimulation" (p. 1). In this section, we report findings from the FLS demonstrating that the relation between family conflict and behavior problems in children depends upon the child's temperament.

The link between family conflict and externalizing or acting out types of behavior problems in children is well documented (Margolin, Oliver, & Medina, 2001). We tested the hypothesis that temperamental difficultness placed children at risk for behavior problems in families with high conflict, but not in families with low conflict. The fussy/difficult/demanding ICQ scale at 1.5 years, the conflict scale of the FES at age 8, and internalizing/externalizing scores of the CBCL at age 8 were analyzed. Because multiple informants provided family conflict and behavior problem reports at age 8, data at this age were used. Six groups of children varying on family conflict (low, high) and temperament (easy, intermediate, difficult) were formed as follows. On the FES, a median split was used to separate the FLS sample into low and high family conflict groups. On the ICQ fussy/difficult/demanding scale, the lowest 25% of scores comprised the "low" group, the centermost 50% the "intermediate" group, and the highest 25% the "high" group. Analysis of variance was used to compare average externalizing and internalizing behavior problem scores on the CBCL (age 8) and TRF (age 8). Of particular interest in each analysis was the interaction between infant temperament and family conflict; behavior problems were predicted to be higher for children with fussy/difficult temperament living in families with higher levels of conflict. In addition, main effects for family conflict and infant difficult temperament were predicted, with higher behavior problems expected among children with higher family conflict or more difficult temperament, respectively.

Parent-Reported Behavior Problems at Age 8 and Parent-Reported Family Conflict

In the first analysis, all predictor and criterion variables were assessed via mother report: infant difficult temperament (ICQ; 1.5 yrs), family conflict (FES; 8 yrs), and behavior problems (CBCL; 8 yrs). Six infant temperament-family conflict groups were designated, as described above; resultant group sizes for easy, intermediate, and difficult infant temperament groups, respectively, were as follows: for low family conflict, 23, 28, and 17; for high family conflict, 5, 19, 10.

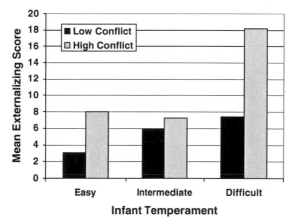

Figure 7.01. Mean externalizing behavior problems (parent report) as a function of infant temperament and family conflict (mother report) at Age 8.

Groups were compared on internalizing and externalizing behavior problems using analysis of variance.

As predicted, the combination of difficult infant temperament and high family conflict resulted in a much higher level of externalizing behavior problems than observed in the other conditions, yielding a significant interaction, $F(2, 102) = 8.46$, $p < .001$. Average externalizing behavior problems for the six groups are displayed in Figure 7.01. In addition, the main effect for family conflict was significant, with more child externalizing problems at age 8 among families with higher conflict ($M = 10.59$) than with lower conflict ($M = 5.34$), $F(1, 102) = 27.66$, $p < .001$. A significant main effect for infant difficult temperament was also evident, with higher 8-year externalizing scores associated with increasing infant temperamental difficultness, $F(2, 102) = 17.23$, $p < .001$. Means for easy, intermediate, and difficult temperament groups were 3.96, 6.47, and 11.41, respectively.

On internalizing behavior problems, significant main effects for family conflict, $F(1, 102) = 30.12$, $p < .001$ and infant difficult temperament, $F(2, 102) = 4.31$, $p < .05$, were observed; however, the interaction was not significant, $F(2, 102) = 2.25$, $p > .05$. Internalizing behavior problem scores were higher in families with higher family conflict ($M = 8.06$) than lower family conflict ($M = 3.44$) and as infant temperamental difficultness increased (M's $= 4.21$, 4.32, and 6.93 for easy, intermediate, and difficult temperament groups, respectively).

Parent-Reported Behavior Problems and Child-Reported Family Conflict

In addition to mothers' views on the family environment, we also collected children's views when they were 8 years on a children's version of the FES. Using

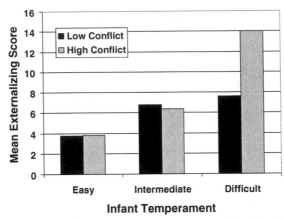

Figure 7.02. Mean externalizing behavior problems (parent report) as a function of infant temperament and family conflict (child report) at age 8.

child-reported family conflict, the following findings resulted. For externalizing behavior problems, the pattern of results (displayed in Figure 7.02) was quite similar to that observed when mothers' ratings of family conflict were examined. Externalizing behavior problem scores were markedly higher when family conflict was high and infant temperament was difficult, resulting in a significant Infant Temperament X Family Conflict interaction, F (2, 101) = 4.16, $p < .05$. The average externalizing problem scores among families with lower conflict from the children's perspective were 3.75, 6.80, and 7.62 for easy, intermediate, and difficult infant temperament groups (n's = 16, 15, and 13, respectively). In families with higher conflict from the children's perspective, average scores were 3.82, 6.36, and 14.00, respectively, for the easy, intermediate, and difficult temperament groups (n's = 11, 33, and 13, respectively). The main effect for infant temperament was also significant, F (2, 101) = 13.15, $p < .001$, with greater externalizing scores associated with increasing difficult infant temperament (M's = 3.78, 6.50, and 10.81 for easy, intermediate, and difficult temperament groups, respectively). The main effect for family conflict showed the same pattern as parents' reports, with higher externalizing scores when children viewed their family as higher in conflict ($M = 7.61$) rather than lower in conflict ($M = 5.93$), although this main effect narrowly failed to reach the customary .05 level of confidence, F (1, 101) = 3.60, $p = .06$. Neither main effects nor the interaction main effect was significant for internalizing behavior problems.

Teacher-Reported Behavior Problems at Age 8

To ascertain whether the Infant Temperament X Family Conflict interaction observed in the aforementioned analyses also predicted behavior problems in

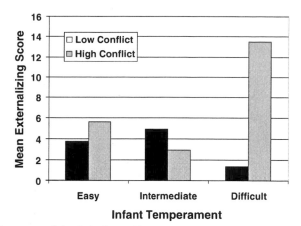

Figure 7.03. Mean externalizing behavior problems (teacher report) as a function of infant temperament and family conflict at age 8.

another setting, teacher reports of behavior problems on the TRF collected when children were age 8 were analyzed. Complete data were available for 90 families using mothers' reports on the FES; for the easy, intermediate, and difficult infant temperament groups there were 22, 23, and 15 children, respectively, in the lower family conflict groups; there were 5, 17, and 8 children, respectively, in the higher family conflict groups.

The interaction between family conflict and infant temperament was again replicated. A significant interaction between infant temperament and family conflict (mother-reported) was observed for teacher-reported externalizing behavior problems, $F(2, 90) = 8.61, p < .001$, as well as a significant main effect for family conflict, $F(2, 90) = 6.80, p < .05$. As shown in Figure 7.03, externalizing behavior problem scores averaged 13.50 for children with difficult temperament and high family conflict, compared to averages of 5.60 and 2.94 among children with easy and intermediate temperament and high family conflict, respectively. Average behavior problem scores did not differ as dramatically among children living in families with lower conflict, with means of 3.73, 4.91, and 1.33 for easy, intermediate, and difficult temperament groups, respectively. The significant main effect for family conflict showed higher levels of externalizing behavior problems among families with higher conflict ($M = 6.20$) compared to lower conflict ($M = 3.58$). The main effect for infant temperament was not significant, $F(2, 90) = 2.12$, $p > .05$. Teacher reports of internalizing behavior problems were differentiated by neither infant temperament nor family conflict, nor was the interaction of these variables significant.

We are cognizant that some researchers have expressed concerns regarding the practice of dichotomizing quantitative variables, such as the median split we utilized in the analyses just presented (MacCallum, Zhang, Preacher, & Rucker, 2002). Therefore, we used a regression approach to determine whether or not the interactions detected between child temperament and family conflict were replicated. They were. In each of the analyses, the interaction of infant temperament and family conflict added significantly to the prediction of externalizing behavior problems. For mother-reported family conflict, the interaction term increased the multiple R from .61 to .64 and the adjusted R^2 from .35 to .39, F_{Change} $(1, 98) = 7.37$, $p < .01$. For child-reported family conflict, the interaction term increased the multiple R from .47 to .53 and the adjusted R^2 from .20 to .26, F_{Change} $(1, 97) = 8.14$, $p < .01$. Finally, for teacher-reported behavior problems, the interaction term increased the multiple R from .19 to .44 and the adjusted R^2 from .02 to .16, F_{Change} $(1, 86) = 16.54$, $p < .001$. Hence, although the problem of detecting Temperament X Environment interactions using regression models has been a topic of discussion (see numerous chapters in Wachs & Plomin, 1991, for example), in these three instances all were successfully confirmed.

The finding that children who were rated as having a more difficult temperament at 1.5 years and who were in high conflict homes had more behavior problems was a robust finding, across context and reporter. The mechanism by which environment and temperament interact in relation to externalizing behavior problems has not been determined. Grych and Fincham (1990) detailed three possible mechanisms to explain why children in families with high conflict exhibit elevated behavior problems. These were modeling, stress, and disrupted parent-child interactions and discipline. The strong evidence reported here concerning the environment-temperament interaction warrants further investigation into the mechanisms through which the interaction occurs.

Summary and Conclusions

1. *Are children's temperament characteristics related to proximal variables in their home environment? Are there consistent or changing patterns of relation between child temperament and proximal home environment across the developmental eras from infancy through adolescence?* Infants with challenging temperament characteristics, particularly resistance to control or unmanageability, tended to experience less verbal and emotional interactions with mothers, receive fewer opportunities for variety of stimulation, and were more likely to be punished physically. Infant temperament explained about 10% to 15% of the variance in aspects of the home environment. During the preschool years, child temperament, particularly adaptability and persistence, related to similar aspects of the home environment; preschoolers who were slower to adapt and had shorter attention spans tended to experience less maternal pride, affection, and warmth,

less work on academics, less variety in stimulation, and more physical punishment. Preschool temperament accounted for at most 10% to 15% of the variance in home environment. Infant temperament continued to relate across time to similar aspects of the home environment at age 8; however, the amount of variance in the home environment explained by infant temperament was 5% or less.

2. *To what extent are specific dimensions of child temperament related to concurrent and cross-time assessments of the quality of family relationships? Is the strength of relation between child temperament and family relationships constant across development?* Aspects of infant temperament related across time to the cohesion, conflict, and intellectual-cultural climate of the home. Correlations were low at best, but consistent across time. Infants who were more unsociable subsequently lived in families characterized as less cohesive, whereas infants who were more fussy had families characterized by more conflict during childhood and adolescence. Lower intellectual-cultural climate in the home was presaged by all four aspects of challenging infant temperament.

   Among the nine NYLS temperament dimensions measured during childhood and adolescence, adaptability/flexibility and mood were most consistently and strongly related to aspects of family climate, especially the intellectual-cultural orientation of the family. Aspects of child temperament explained between 15% and 20% of the variance in this aspect of family climate during childhood and adolescence.

3. *How do individual differences in children's temperament relate to parents' and children's assessments of their relationship with each other?* Mothers' and fathers' ratings of their parent-child relationship and parenting experience when their children were adolescents were significantly predicted by and concurrently related to aspects of their children's temperament including most often mood, adaptability/flexibility, and persistence/task orientation. The amount of variance explained by child temperament ranged to 30%. Relations were stronger between child temperament and mothers' assessments than fathers' assessments; this was true across temperament informant. Child flexibility, positive mood, and task orientation also related to the adolescents' own assessments of their relationship with their parents, although correlations were weak at best between concurrent measures during middle childhood. During adolescence, child flexibility, mood, and task orientation related to the adolescents' appraisals of their relationship with parents, explaining between 15% and 30% of the variance (depending upon temperament informant). Thus, both parent and child ratings of their relationship with each other were related to the child's temperament, and earlier ratings of child temperament related across time to later assessments of parent-child relations.

4. *How might variations in children's contexts influence the expression of their temperament? Which aspects of the proximal environment, if any, are predictive of children's subsequent temperament?* Early measures of family environment were not as pervasive nor as strong in predicting children's subsequent temperament as vice versa. One finding replicated across developmental eras was that family intellectual-cultural orientation related across time to the child's persistence or task orientation, albeit at low levels. At best, family environment during the preschool years predicted approximately 10% of the variance in subsequent child or adolescent temperament.

5. *How do temperament and environment interact in influencing children's developmental outcomes?* One example of how child temperament and family environment interact in influencing children's outcomes was replicated across three combinations of informants. Specifically, fussy/difficult/demanding temperament as measured in infancy interacted with the level of conflict reported in the family at age 8 in explaining the child's number of externalizing behavior problems at age 8. The combination of high infant fussiness and high conflict in the home was associated with markedly higher levels of externalizing behavior problems at age 8 compared to all other combinations of infant temperament (easy, intermediate, difficult) and family conflict (lower, higher). The level of externalizing behavior problems at age 8 depended upon both the child's temperamental history and the level of conflict in the home.

8

Temperament in the Extremes–Developmental Trajectories of Infants in Three Temperament Groups

"He seems angry a lot lately. He needs to lighten up and enjoy life instead of finding fault in all areas. He has a quick temper... He's very aware of other peoples' feelings. When he does a job, he does a good job. He has a good sense of humor."
—Parent of Child #13, Difficult Infant Temperament Group, Age 11

Issues Investigated

At this point in the course of the FLS, comprehensive data detailing the development of over 100 children and their families have been collected from infancy through high school completion. In this chapter, we examine the FLS data to determine whether unique and differentiated long-term sequelae of the earliest measure of temperament employed in the FLS are evident. As noted in chapters 1 and 2, many researchers have suggested the potential benefit of employing an extreme groups approach. Hence, for each factor of challenging infant temperament assessed via the Infant Characteristics Questionnaire at 1.5 years, three groups were formed: low, intermediate, and high. The "low" group comprised infants scoring in the bottom quartile and viewed by parents as exhibiting the least challenging temperament features, the "intermediate" group comprised infants scoring in the center two quartiles and served as a baseline for comparison, and the "high" group comprised infants in the top quartile representing infants rated as displaying the most challenging temperament characteristics.

Using these three groups on each ICQ factor, we compared the developmental and environmental sequelae of challenging infant temperament throughout the childhood and adolescent eras. In view of the large number of comparisons, we looked for cross-time patterns of significant results when possible to reduce the potential for Type I errors. When a significant omnibus F test was obtained, post hoc comparisons (Tukey's HSD) were conducted to determine the pattern of group differences in that situation. Each statistically significant outcome was classified as exemplifying one or more of the following temperament influences:

- *generalized risk/protective factor* (GRPF) – when low and high groups differed from each other, but neither differed from the intermediate group;
- *developmental asset* (DA) – when an extreme infant temperament group, either low or high, was associated with advantaged outcome and differed significantly from both the intermediate and other extreme group;
- *developmental liability* (DL) – when an extreme infant temperament group, either low or high, was associated with a compromised outcome and differed significantly from both the intermediate and other extreme group; and/or
- developmental asset and liability (DA, DL) – when the outcome was significantly different among all infant temperament groups.

Working within this framework in this chapter, we examined the following issues:

1. *Are there gender differences in extreme temperament group membership?* Although the consensus is that the genders are more alike than different on aspects of temperament (Guerin & Gottfried, 1994a, 1994b), we analyzed group membership by gender to determine whether this general finding also holds for extreme temperament group membership.

2. *Do infants classified as challenging or easy on one temperament factor tend to be extreme on other ICQ factors, or is group membership on any given factor independent of the others?* Given that the continuous dimensions on the ICQ are intercorrelated (see chapter 2 and Guerin & Gottfried, 1994b), it seems likely that overlap will exist among extreme temperament groups. For example, given that fussy/difficult/demanding and unadaptability are correlated at a moderate level, it is likely that infants high on one of these two factors will also be high on the other.

3. *Is there evidence of short and/or long-term temperamental and personality sequelae for any of the four ICQ factors, or are these aspects of behavioral style specific to the infant period?* Here, we compare the low, intermediate, and high groups for each dimension on all dimensions in subsequent developmental eras, limiting our attention to patterns replicated across a minimum of two consecutive developmental eras.

4. *Are there systematic and unique outcomes in the domains of intelligence, school functioning, behavioral adjustment, and home/family environment for each of the four ICQ factors of challenging infant temperament?* As described in the prior issue, the low, intermediate, and high infant temperament groups were compared across developmental eras. When possible (i.e., when variables were assessed across multiple developmental eras), patterns replicated across two consecutive domains were of most interest.

5. *Finally, is there evidence supporting the role of extreme temperament as an asset or liability to the process of development?* That is, across all reliable differences, how often are each of the specified patterns (general risk/protective factor, developmental asset, developmental liability, combined developmental asset/liability) observed?

Description of Measures Used in the FLS

Formation of Low, Intermediate, and High Challenging Temperament Groups

The Infant Characteristics Questionnaire was completed by mothers when babies were 1.5 years old. Scores on the four dimensions of the ICQ (fussy/difficult, unadaptable, resistant to control, and unsociable) were used to form low, intermediate, and high infant temperament groups for each of the four ICQ factors. Separate frequency distributions were created for the four ICQ factors; cut-offs at the first and third quartiles were established. Scores at or below the 25th percentile delineated the low infant temperament group, comprising infants rated with the fewest challenging temperament features. Scores at or above the 75th percentile designated the high infant temperament group, encompassing the infants rated as presenting the most challenging temperament characteristics. Those in the center two quartiles represented the moderate temperament or intermediate group.

Group sizes for the four factors varied slightly due to differences in the distribution of scores. Following the procedure described, the low, intermediate, and high groups for the fussy/difficult/demanding factor comprised 33, 55, and 35 children, respectively; the cut-off scores were 2.69 and 3.56. For ICQ unadaptability, the low, intermediate, and high groups consisted of 32, 60, and 31 babies, respectively, and the cut-off scores were 2.20 and 3.60. Using cut-offs of 3.67 and 4.83, there were 32, 54, and 37 children in the low, intermediate, and high ICQ resistant to control groups. Finally, for ICQ unsociability, the low, intermediate, and high groups had 30, 55, and 38 children, respectively, and cut-off scores of 1.60 and 2.60.

Temperament

Temperament measures were described in detail in chapter 3. Temperamental consequences of the four ICQ factors were examined using the Toddler Temperament Scale at 2 years, the Behavioral Style Questionnaire (ages 3, 3.5, and 5 years, averaged), the Middle Childhood Temperament Questionnaire (ages 8, 10,

and 12, averaged), and the Dimensions of Temperament Survey – Revised (parent-
and self-report; 14 and 16 years, averaged within informant).

Personality

Also described more fully in chapter 3, the NEO-FFI was used to assess the
"Big Five" dimensions of personality when study cohort was 17 years.

Behavior Problems

Behavioral adjustment measures were described in detail in chapter 4. The
measures examined in this chapter include the intensity and problem scores of the
Eyberg Child Behavior Inventory administered at 3.25 years and the total behavior
disturbed, hostile-aggressive, anxious, and hyperactive-distractible scores of the
Preschool Behavior Questionnaire (3.5 years). Narrow band scores were analyzed
on the Child Behavior Checklist (ages 4 and 5, averaged; ages 6 through 12,
averaged; and ages 13–17, averaged), Teacher Report Form (ages 6 through 11,
averaged), and YSR (age 17). The narrow band scores assess behavior problems
in the following categories: withdrawn, somatic complaints, anxious/depressed,
social problems, thought problems, attention problems, delinquency behaviors,
and aggressive behaviors.

Intelligence

Additional details concerning the measures of intelligence used in the FLS
were presented in chapter 5. In this chapter, the general cognitive index of the
McCarthy Scales of Children's Abilities, averaged across ages 2.5, 3, and 3.5 years,
was examined. At age 5, the mental processing scale of the Kaufman Assessment
Battery for Children was analyzed. The full scale IQ of the Wechsler Intelligence
Scale for Children – Revised was averaged across ages 6, 7, 8, and 12 years.
The full scale IQ score of the Wechsler Intelligence Scale for Children – III, was
examined at age 15. At age 17, the full scale IQ of the Wechlser Adult Intelligence
Scale – Revised was used.

School Functioning

Measures of achievement commenced at age 5 and were described in detail in chapter 6. The achievement scale of the Kaufman Assessment Battery for
Children was examined at age 5. At age 6, the reading and arithmetic scales of the

Wide Range Achievement Test – Revised were analyzed. The Woodcock-Johnson Psychoeducational Battery was administered annually from age 7 through 12 years; reading and math scores based on grade norms were used. From ages 13 through 17, reading and math scores based on grade norms on the Woodcock-Johnson Psychoeducational Battery – Revised were analyzed.

Home and Family Environment

Detailed descriptions of the home and family environment measures used in the FLS are provided in chapter 7. The scales of the HOME Inventory administered at ages 1.25, 3.25, and 8 years were analyzed. The cohesion, conflict, and intellectual-cultural scales of the Family Environment Scale completed by mothers were analyzed during the preschool years (ages 3 and 5 years, averaged), middle childhood years (ages 8, 10, 12 years, averaged), and adolescence (ages 14 and 16, averaged; age 17 years). Child and father reports on the FES were also analyzed at age 17 years. The satisfaction, involvement, communication, limit setting, and autonomy scales of the Parent-Child Relationship Inventory completed independently by mothers and fathers when children were 15 and 16 years were analyzed, averaging across age. Ratings by the study children on the parent relations scale of the Self Description Questionnaire I (age 10) and the Self Description Questionnaire II (age 12; ages 14 and 16 years, averaged) were examined.

Findings and Discussion

Gender Distribution

No gender differences were detected in any of the four ICQ temperament variables in terms of infant temperament group membership (low, intermediate, or high). On the fussy/difficult/demanding factor, the numbers of boys in the low, intermediate, and high groups were 18, 27, and 19, respectively; girls showed a similar pattern, with 15, 28, and 16, respectively, *Chi-square* $(N = 123, df = 2) = 0.35$, $p > .05$. For the unadaptability factor, there were 19, 29, and 16 boys, in the low, intermediate, and high groups, and 13, 31, and 15 girls, respectively, *Chi-square* $(N = 123, df = 2) = 1.02, p > .05$. On the variable of resistance to control, the number of boys in the low, intermediate, and high groups were 14, 27, and 23, respectively, with 18, 27, and 14 girls correspondingly, *Chi-square* $(N = 123, df = 2) = 2.49, p > .05$. Finally, for the unsociability factor, a similar pattern of no gender differences prevailed: 13, 33, 18 boys were in the low, intermediate, and high groups compared to 17, 22, and 20 girls, respectively, *Chi-square* $(N = 123, df = 2) = 2.64, p > .05$.

These findings are consistent with several prior studies, as reported by Guerin and Gottfried (1994a, 1994b). Lee and Bates (1985), who used $+/-1$ SD as cut-points to create three groups based on infant difficultness, noted a lack of gender differences at 6 and 13 months of age, although they found the difficult temperament group at age 2 comprised mostly boys (13 out of 17).

Independence/Overlap of Group Membership

We have previously reported that the ICQ factors are not orthogonal to each other. Hence, we expected some degree of overlap among the infants in terms of temperament group membership. Chi-square analyses showed that extreme group membership overlapped significantly ($p < .05$) on three combinations of ICQ factors: unadaptability and unsociability, unadaptability and fussy/difficult/demanding, and finally fussy/difficult/demanding and resistant to control. Chi-square test values were 12.91, 23.02, and 24.31, respectively, with $N = 123$ and $df = 4$, indicating a lack of independence. Membership in the extreme groups on these dimensions overlapped approximately 50%. For example, 16 of 31 infants who were in the high group on unadaptability were also in the high fussy/difficult/demanding group; 16 of 35 infants who were in the high fussy/difficult/demanding group were also in the high group for unadaptability. The remaining three combinations of ICQ factors (resistant to control and unsociable, fussy/difficult/demanding and unsociable, unadaptable and resistant to control) did not show statistically significant overlap, however, extreme groups on these paired factors overlapped 25% to 35%. Hence, a substantial percentage of infants rated in the extreme on one ICQ factor were also rated in the extreme on a second factor. In chapter 2 we noted the intercorrelations among the ICQ factors were strongest between fussy/difficult demanding and unadaptability, fussy/difficult/demanding and unsociability, and unadaptability and resistance to control, with all r's in the .40 to .50 range. Only one of these pairs showed significant overlap in extreme group membership, fussy/difficult/demanding and unadaptable. Hence, factors with the strongest overlap in extreme group membership did not show a one-to-one correspondence to factors with the highest linear relationship.

Temperamental and Personality Consequences of Challenging Infant Temperament

Temperamental Sequelae

Long-term and differentiated temperamental sequelae were evident for all four temperament factors of the ICQ. Analysis of variance results comparing the high, intermediate, and low groups for each temperamental factor are displayed in Table 8.01. Findings (significant omnibus F tests) that were not replicated on the same dimension in two consecutive developmental eras were dropped from Table 8.01. These findings demonstrated that infants' temperamental characteristics at 1.5 years prognosticated temperamental patterns across several eras of development.

Four major conclusions can be drawn from an examination of the results displayed in Table 8.01. First, slower adaptability and more negative mood were characteristic and long-term sequelae of three infant temperament factors: fussy/difficult/demanding, unadaptable, and resistant to control. Infants rated as more challenging on the ICQ were subsequently rated as less adaptable/flexible and more negative/less positive in mood throughout childhood, almost consistently, and sometimes through adolescence.

To facilitate comparison across temperament scales, all temperament scores were transformed to z-scores and coded so that higher scores were consistent with the temperament dimension labels shown along the abscissa of each figure. Mean z-scores are plotted on Figure 8.01 for sequelae of infant fussy/difficult/demanding infant temperament, Figure 8.02 for resistance to control, and Figure 8.03 for unadaptability. Across these three figures, an almost consistent pattern showing the high infant temperament groups as slower to adapt and more negative in mood from 2 years through at least childhood on the MCTQ is evident.

Second, temperamental sequelae were most pervasive for babies with fussy/difficult/demanding and resistant to control temperaments. In addition to the aforementioned characteristics of slower adaptability and more frequent negative mood, infants in the high groups on fussy/difficult/demanding and resistance to control were also subsequently rated as higher in activity level (at every developmental era), and lower in persistence/task orientation during the later years (not shown on figures). These two groups diverged, however, on other temperamental sequelae. Infants in the fussy/difficult/demanding group showed a tendency to be withdrawing, whereas infants in the resistant to control group were consistently more intense from age 2 through childhood. Thus, infants whose temperament was more fussy/difficult/demanding and resistant to control at 1.5 years showed similar sequelae in that they were subsequently viewed as slower to adapt, more negative in mood, higher in activity level, and lower in attention span/persistence. These groups of infants were different, however, in that those high on fussy/difficult/demanding were subsequently more withdrawing, whereas those high on the resistant to control factor were characterized by intense reactions to their environment.

Third, infants in the high group on the unadaptable factor, while sharing the characteristics of slower adaptability and more negative mood also common to the high groups on the fussy/difficult/demanding and resistant to control factors, also showed a greater tendency to withdraw rather than approach their environment during childhood. Their subsequent temperament patterns were characterized by more reticence or fearfulness to novel conditions.

Table 8.01. Temperamental Sequelae of Four Challenging Infant Temperaments: Fussy/Difficult/Demanding, Unadaptable, Resistant to Control, and Unsociable

		Temperament group			F	df	Post test[e]
		Low	Inter	High			
		Fussy/difficult/demanding					
TTS	Activity	3.59	3.84	4.13	5.35**	2, 110	GRPF
	Approach[a]	2.42	3.08	3.20	6.93**	2, 110	DA, GRPF
	Adaptability[b]	2.58	2.91	3.13	4.82*	2, 110	GRPF
	Neg. Mood	2.43	2.65	3.06	11.73***	2, 110	GRPF, DL
BSQ	Activity	3.51	3.60	3.98	6.89	2, 114	GRPF,DL
	Approach[a]	2.45	2.92	3.11	7.09**	2, 114	DA, GRPF
	Adaptability[b]	2.13	2.59	2.77	14.92***	2, 114	DA, GRPF
	Neg. Mood	2.73	3.02	3.29	10.17***	2, 114	DA, DL
MCTQ	Activity	2.41	2.74	3.38	15.90***	2, 103	GRPF, DL
	Adaptability[b]	2.06	2.40	2.84	15.17***	2, 103	DA, DL
	Neg. Mood	2.39	2.71	3.04	8.80***	2, 103	GRPF, DL
	Persistence[c]	2.12	2.39	2.74	7.45**	2, 103	GRPF, DL
DOTS-R (Parent)	Gen. Activity	1.61	1.91	2.44	12.40***	2, 99	GRPF, DL
	Approach	3.27	2.96	3.19	4.52*	2, 99	DA
	Flexibility	3.54	3.38	3.20	4.71*	2, 99	DL
	Task Orient.	2.93	2.66	2.61	3.40*	2, 99	DL
		Unadaptable					
TTS	Approach[a]	2.38	2.97	3.45	10.92***	2, 110	DA, DL
	Neg. Mood	2.54	2.64	3.02	6.45**	2, 110	GRPF, DL
BSQ	Approach[a]	2.42	2.86	3.25	10.05***	2, 114	DA, DL
	Adaptability[b]	2.17	2.57	2.74	10.08***	2, 114	DA, GRPF
	Neg. Mood	2.63	3.11	3.19	11.74***	2, 114	DA, GRPF

					F	df	
MCTQ	Approach[a]	1.97	2.31	2.43	4.40*	2, 103	DA, GRPF
	Adaptability[b]	2.11	2.52	2.59	5.83**	2, 103	DA, GRPF
	Neg. Mood	2.34	2.87	2.79	7.42**	2, 103	DA, GRPF
DOTS-R (Parent)	Flexibility	3.57	3.34	3.24	4.22*	2, 99	DL
			Resistant to control				
TTS	Activity	3.46	3.90	4.12	8.50***	2, 110	DA, GRPF
	Adaptability[b]	2.53	2.88	3.17	6.57**	2, 110	DL
	Intensity	3.33	3.70	4.15	10.33***	2, 110	DA, GRPF
	Neg. Mood	2.46	2.67	2.98	7.23**	2, 110	DA, GRPF
BSQ	Activity	3.34	3.77	3.86	9.10***	2, 114	DA, GRPF
	Adaptability[a]	2.26	2.56	2.70	6.10**	2, 114	DA, GRPF
	Intensity	4.09	4.22	4.47	4.89**	2, 114	DL
	Neg. Mood	2.81	3.04	3.18	4.13*	2, 114	DL
MCTQ	Activity	2.46	2.81	3.18	7.74***	2, 103	DL
	Adaptability[b]	2.21	2.45	2.61	3.55*	2, 103	DL
	Intensity	3.01	3.30	3.64	4.82*	2, 103	DL
	Neg. Mood	2.51	2.63	3.02	6.07**	2, 103	GRPF, DL
	Persistence[c]	2.29	2.30	2.69	4.31*	2, 103	GRPF, DL
DOTS-R (Parent)	Gen. Activity	1.55	1.98	2.37	11.46***	2, 99	DA, DL
	Task Orient.	2.85	2.77	2.52	3.34*	2, 99	DL
			Unsociable				
TTS	Threshold[d]	4.26	3.96	3.77	3.21*	2, 110	DL
BSQ	Threshold[d]	3.95	3.89	3.70	3.15*	2, 114	DL

[a] Higher mean scores indicate withdrawal.
[b] Higher mean scores indicate slower adaptability.
[c] Higher mean scores indicate shorter attention span/lack of persistence.
[d] Higher mean scores indicate greater sensitivity/reactivity.
[e] DA = Developmental asset; DL = Developmental liability; GRPF = General risk/protective factor. Labels based on results of post-test comparisons.
*$p < .05$. **$p < .01$. ***$p < .001$.

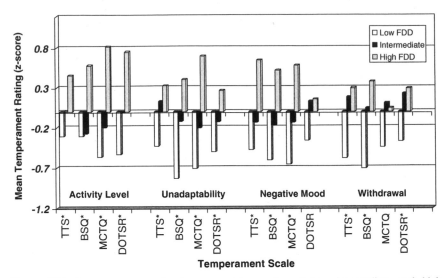

Figure 8.01. Average *z*-scores for temperamental sequelae of low, intermediate, and high fussy/difficult/demanding infant temperament groups on four measures of temperament across childhood and adolescence. Asterisks indicate significant omnibus *F* test results.

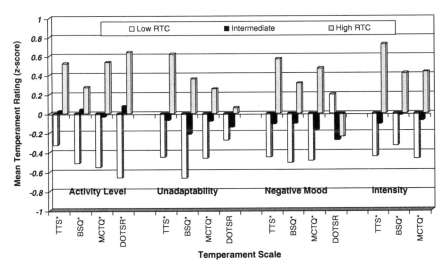

Figure 8.02. Average *z*-scores for temperamental sequelae of low, intermediate, and high resistant to control infant temperament groups on four measures of temperament across childhood and adolescence. Asterisks indicate significant omnibus *F* test results.

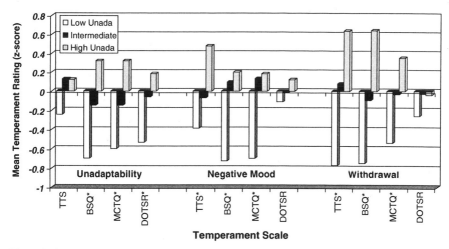

Figure 8.03. Average z-scores for temperamental sequelae of low, intermediate, and high unadaptability infant temperament groups on four measures of temperament across childhood and adolescence. Asterisks indicate significant omnibus F test results.

Finally, infants in the high unsociable group showed only one replicated temperamental sequela: they were rated as less sensitive or reactive on the threshold of responsiveness dimension at age 2 and during the preschool years.

Clearly, the infants with high fussy/difficult/demanding and resistant to control temperaments had the most pervasive and consistent patterns of temperamental sequelae across the childhood and adolescent years, including higher activity level, slower adaptability, more negative mood, greater withdrawing tendencies during the toddler and early childhood years, and lower persistence during middle childhood and adolescence. Infants who were high on unadaptability subsequently showed similar patterns of slower adaptability, more negative mood, and greater withdrawal through early childhood. Hence, challenging temperament characterized the development of infants over several developmental eras and was not something they quickly "grew out of."

Personality Sequelae

Given the widespread interest in temperament as a precursor of the "Big Five" personality traits, the relation of ICQ extreme temperament groups to adolescents' self-reports on the NEO were examined. Although these findings did not reach the criteria set for inclusion on Table 8.01, we report them here for those interested in these long-term data. Omnibus F test results, significant at the $p = .05$ level, were observed for the fussy/difficult/demanding dimension and neuroticism, F (2, 105)

$= 3.16$, $p = .05$, and agreeableness, $F(2, 105) = 3.11$, $p = .05$. In both cases, no significant post-test comparisons were observed. Visual inspection of the group means showed that in both cases, the low group, comprising infants who were the least fussy, subsequently showed relatively lower neuroticism ($M = 48.10$) than the intermediate and high groups (M's $= 53.29$ and 53.57, respectively) and higher agreeableness ($M_{Low} = 49.17$, $M_{Intermediate} = 43.46$, $M_{High} = 43.89$). These findings did not replicate those reported by Lanthier and Bates (1997), who examined linear correlations between infant temperament and personality at age 17 (see page 50).

Behavioral Sequelae

Next to temperament, the strongest evidence of developmental sequelae of infant temperament was in the domain of behavioral adjustment. All four factors of infant temperament showed significant differences among the low, intermediate, and/or high groups on average behavior problem indices across childhood and adolescence, generally with higher average behavior problem scores characterizing children in the high infant temperament group. As with temperamental sequelae, findings that were not replicated on the same dimension across two consecutive developmental eras from age 4 onward were not listed.

As shown in Table 8.02, the largest numbers of significant behavioral sequelae were observed for the fussy/difficult/demanding factor of the ICQ. Significant group differences among the groups of the fussy/difficult temperament factor were evident in the preschool, middle childhood, and adolescent years and across informants. During the preschool and middle childhood years, differences more often showed that the fussy/difficult infants had higher scores than the low and intermediate groups; this pattern was evident on the ECBI, total behavior disturbed scale of the PBQ, and on several scales of the CBCL at ages 4–5 and 6–12. However, in adolescence on the CBCL and YSR, differences between the easy and intermediate groups were observed, with the easy infant temperament group reporting significantly fewer problems than the intermediate group.

With respect to the nature of problems observed, behavioral adjustment sequelae of fussy/difficult/demanding infant temperament that replicated across developmental era (and often across informant, as well) included attention problems, delinquent behavior, and aggressive behavior. On parent report measures of behavior problems, average behavior problem scores were highest for those who had as infants been in the high fussy/difficult/demanding group and lowest for those in the low group. On the YSR, differences emerged due to significantly lower scores characterizing the low versus the intermediate and high infant temperament groups. These results coincide with those previously reported by Guerin et al. (1997) in which the percentage of clinically-elevated behavior problem scores were compared in FLS participants with difficult versus intermediate or low fussy/difficult temperament scores. They also dovetail with the aforementioned temperamental consequences of fussy/difficult temperament with respect to attentional issues characterizing the subsequent temperaments of the most fussy/difficult infants; group differences in attention span/persistence, distractibility, and task orientation were temperamental sequelae of the fussy/difficult/demanding factor.

As noted by Bates (1989), infant fussy/difficult/demanding temperament related to a wide range of behavior problems in subsequent development, including those of both an internalizing and externalizing nature. With increasing age beyond the preschool years, differences among extreme groups were more consistent among the externalizing types of problems.

Long-term behavioral sequelae of infants rated as more unadaptable were also evident. As shown in Table 8.02, across all age periods in which the CBCL was completed, infants in the low versus high unadaptable groups differed significantly on two narrow band categories: delinquent and aggressive behavior, with those in the high unadaptable group averaging higher problem scores. These results did not corroborate the suggestion by Bates (1989) that early unadaptability will presage internalizing types of problems more than externalizing problems.

Infants in the extreme groups of the resistant to control factor also evidenced significant differences in behavior problems throughout childhood and adolescence. As shown in Table 8.02, consistent differences in attention problems and aggressive behaviors emerged during the preschool years and persisted throughout adolescence. Beginning in the elementary school period, delinquent behaviors were also significantly different across the three temperament groups. These findings are consistent with the suggestion by Bates (1989) that early resistance to control was a better predictor of externalizing compared to internalizing types of behavior problems. In all cases, behavior scores were higher for infants in the high resistant to control group; these differences were present in both parent and teacher reports.

Infants in the high unsociable infant temperament group were rated higher by parents and teachers during the preschool and elementary school years on the social problems scale of the CBCL or TRF. These results are displayed in Table 8.02. During the preschool and elementary school years, parents also reported higher scores on the somatic complaints scale. Bates (1989) noted that unsociability was a precursor of anxiety more so than acting-out types of problems; findings during the preschool and middle childhood years in the FLS support Bates' contention. Parents also reported higher scores on the delinquent behavior scale at all ages on the CBCL. In all cases, higher scores were characteristic of infants in the high versus low unsociable infant temperament group.

Table 8.02. Behavioral Adjustment Sequelae of Four Infant Temperament Groups from Age 2 through 17 Years

		Temperament group			F	df	Post test
		Low	Intermediate	High			
		Fussy/difficult/demanding					
ECBI	Intensity	101.62	111.16	122.91	9.08***	2, 110	GRPF, DL
	Problem	3.48	5.08	7.47	6.37**	2, 110	GRPF, DL
PBQ	Total Behavior Disturbed	13.00	15.58	18.81	7.84**	2, 100	GRPF, DL
	Hostile-Aggressive	5.23	6.21	7.70	5.80**	2, 105	GRPF
	Anxious	2.93	3.88	4.93	6.36**	2, 109	GRPF
	Hyperactive-Distractible	2.66	2.98	3.84	4.00*	2, 109	GRPF
CBCL 4, 5	Anxious/Depressed	1.43	2.05	3.26	7.22**	2, 111	GRPF, DL
	Social Problems	1.35	2.03	2.85	7.22**	2, 111	GRPF
	Attention Problems	2.08	2.61	4.11	8.61***	2, 111	GRPF, DL
	Delinquent Behavior	1.27	1.43	2.60	12.55***	2, 111	GRPF, DL
	Aggressive Behavior	5.83	7.48	12.42	19.57***	2, 111	GRPF, DL
CBCL 6–12	Anxious/Depressed	1.81	2.53	4.29	7.39**	2, 107	GRPF, DL
	Social Problems	1.08	1.54	2.20	3.75*	2, 107	GRPF
	Thought Problems	0.17	0.40	0.78	4.96**	2, 107	GRPF, DL
	Attention Problems	1.26	2.38	4.06	11.31***	2, 107	GRPF, DL
	Delinquent Behavior	0.63	1.11	1.87	9.58***	2, 107	GRPF, DL
	Aggressive Behavior	3.33	6.09	9.91	18.89***	2, 107	DA, DL
CBCL 13–17	Thought Problems	0.16	0.25	0.65	5.46**	2, 108	DA, GRPF
	Attention Problems	0.94	1.89	3.56	9.99***	2, 108	GRPF, DL
	Delinquent Behavior	0.41	1.37	1.99	9.02***	2, 108	DA, GRPF
	Aggressive Behavior	2.16	4.58	7.86	15.82***	2, 108	DA, DL
YSR 17	Attention Problems	5.52	8.06	7.68	5.16**	2, 105	DA
	Delinquent Behavior	4.86	6.92	6.11	5.22**	2, 105	DA
			Unadaptable				
PBQ	Total Behavior Disturbed	13.00	15.96	17.64	4.32**	2, 100	GRPF
	Anxious	3.37	3.58	5.11	5.50**	2, 109	GRPF, DL

					F	df	
CBCL 4, 5	Delinquent Behavior	1.09	1.74	2.26	6.53**	2, 111	GRPF
CBCL 6–12	Aggressive Behavior	6.18	8.32	10.74	6.45**	2, 111	GRPF
	Delinquent Behavior	0.80	1.16	1.60	3.29*	2, 107	GRPF
CBCL 13–17	Aggressive Behavior	4.16	6.59	8.04	5.14**	2, 107	GRPF
	Delinquent Behavior	0.78	1.26	1.82	3.27*	2, 108	GRPF
	Aggressive Behavior	3.44	4.69	6.47	3.43*	2, 108	GRPF
			Resistant to control				
ECBI	Intensity	101.90	112.83	120.21	7.17**	2, 110	DA, GRPF
PBQ	Problem	3.27	5.17	7.52	7.49**	2, 110	GRPF, DL
	Hyperactive-Distractible	2.34	3.31	3.61	4.64**	2, 109	DA, GRPF
CBCL 4, 5	Attention Problems	1.87	3.22	3.33	5.01**	2, 111	DA, GRPF
	Aggressive Behavior	5.80	8.33	10.91	9.34***	2, 111	GRPF, DL
CBCL 6–12	Attention Problems	1.35	2.71	3.34	5.82**	2, 107	DA, GRPF
	Delinquent Behavior	0.67	1.29	1.51	4.66**	2, 107	GRPF
	Aggressive Behavior	4.18	6.50	8.19	6.14**	2, 107	GRPF
CBCL 13–17	Attention Problems	1.19	2.22	2.77	3.29*	2, 108	GRPF
	Delinquent Behavior	0.64	1.32	1.82	4.70*	2, 108	GRPF
	Aggressive Behavior	3.22	4.82	6.39	4.08*	2, 108	GRPF
TRF 6–11	Attention Problems	3.65	6.18	6.83	3.15*	2, 106	GRPF
	Delinquent Behavior	0.44	0.49	0.90	3.24*	2, 106	GRPF
	Aggressive Behavior	3.65	6.18	6.83	3.15*	2, 106	GRPF
			Unsociable				
CBCL 4, 5	Somatic Complaints	0.71	0.46	0.99	3.75*	2, 111	DL
	Social Problems	1.31	2.09	2.61	5.15**	2, 111	GRPF
	Delinquent Behavior	1.17	1.61	2.24	5.93**	2, 111	GRPF
TRF 6–11	Social Problems	0.93	1.24	1.87	3.59*	2, 106	GRPF
CBCL 6–12	Somatic Complaints	0.71	0.74	1.37	5.16**	2, 107	GRPF, DL
	Social Problems	0.75	1.80	1.92	4.95**	2, 107	DA, GRPF
	Delinquent Behavior	0.73	1.19	1.50	3.27*	2, 107	GRPF
CBCL 13–17	Delinquent Behavior	0.76	1.16	1.84	3.99*	2, 108	GRPF

*$p < .05.$ **$p < .01.$ ***$p < .001.$

221

Intellectual Sequelae

Although prior studies spanning the infancy and school entry years (Anders-son & Sommerfelt, 1999; Olson et al., 1992) failed to find a relation between infant temperament and subsequent intelligence, findings from the FLS revealed two of the four ICQ factors showed intellectual sequelae that replicated across more than one developmental era: fussy/difficult/demanding and unadaptable. The results of the analysis of variance comparing the subsequent intellectual performance of infants in the low, intermediate, and high infant temperament groups are displayed in Table 8.03.

The findings suggest differential significance of these two aspects of infant temperament with respect to the development of intellectual outcomes. To facilitate comparisons across intelligence tests and among temperament groups, IQ scores were transformed to z-scores; these are displayed in Figure 8.04 for infant temperament groups based on the fussy/difficult demanding factor. Infants rated low on the fussy/difficult/demanding temperament factor subsequently scored higher on intellectual tests compared to those rated intermediate or high on infant fussiness. Compare the group patterns displayed in Figure 8.04 for fussy/difficult/demanding infant temperament to those displayed in Figure 8.05 for unadaptable infant temperament groups. Infants who were in the high group of the unadaptable factor during infancy subsequently scored lower on intellectual tests compared to the intermediate and low groups. Hence, particularly easy temperament at 1.5 years was predictive of relatively higher performance on intelligence tests at school entry and during adolescence, whereas infants who were slower in adaptability at the same age subsequently scored relatively lower (but still in the average range) performance on intellectual tests during childhood and adolescence. Although

Table 8.03.   Intellectual Sequelae of Fussy/Difficult and Unadaptable Infant Temperament

		Temperament group			F	df	Post test
		Low	Inter	High			
		Fussy/difficult/demanding					
KABC	MPC	119.69	112.20	109.48	6.13**	2, 108	DA, DL
WISC-III	Full Scale IQ	114.04	106.54	105.93	3.51*	2, 102	DA
WAIS-R	Full Scale IQ	115.96	108.40	109.57	3.58*	2, 103	DA
		Unadaptable					
MSCA	GCI	113.76	111.24	105.93	3.73*	2, 118	DL
KABC	MPC	116.50	114.69	108.21	3.93*	2, 108	DA
WAIS-R	Full Scale IQ	114.38	111.51	105.73	3.48*	2, 103	DL

$^*p < .05.$ $^{**}p < .01.$ $^{***}p < .001.$

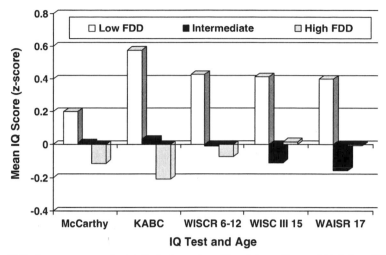

Figure 8.04. Average *z*-scores for intellectual sequelae of low, intermediate, and high fussy/difficult/demanding infant temperament groups across childhood and adolescence.

concurrent temperament-intelligence correlations were not generally above .40 in magnitude, group differences of 7 to 10 points (as shown in Table 8.03) between the low and high infant temperament groups reflected a meaningful difference in intellectual performance as a function of infant temperament.

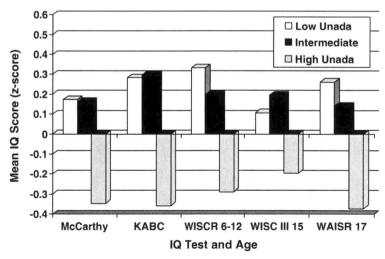

Figure 8.05. Average *z*-scores for intellectual sequelae of low, intermediate, and high unadaptability infant temperament groups across childhood and adolescence.

Table 8.04. **Academic Achievement Sequelae of Fussy/Difficult and Unadaptable Infant Temperament**

		Temperament group			F	df	Post test
		Low	Inter	High			
		Fussy/difficult/demanding					
WRAT-R	Arithmetic	64.07	51.50	43.39	3.31*	2, 102	DL
WJ-R	Reading	85.51	79.59	74.86	4.59*	2, 107	DL
13–17	Math	82.56	70.18	69.28	3.22*	2, 107	DA
		Unadaptable					
KABC	Achievement	115.64	112.14	106.54	4.74*	2, 108	DL
WRAT-R	Reading	58.40	47.48	36.37	3.73*	2, 102	DL
WJ-R 13–17	Reading	86.95	81.42	74.14	3.08 = .05*	2, 107	DL

$*p < .05.$ $**p < .01.$ $***p < .001.$

Academic Achievement Sequelae

Academic achievement scores also showed significant differences among infant temperament groups replicated across developmental eras for the only two factors: fussy/difficult/demanding and unadaptable. Analysis of variance results are displayed in Table 8.04. Babies in the high challenging temperament groups (fussier, slower to adapt) scored lower on tests of academic achievement administered during childhood and adolescence compared to those in the intermediate and/or low challenging temperament groups. On the Woodcock-Johnson reading and math scales, differences between these two groups exceeded 10 percentile points using norms based on grade level to control for grade differences among children. (Grade levels among participants in the FLS resulted from either different school entry ages or grade repetition; see chapter 6 for additional information.) Hence, both intellectual and achievement sequelae were associated with fussy/difficult/demanding and unadaptable infant temperament. Although Olson et al. (1992) did not find infant temperament related to teacher ratings of academic competence on the TRF at ages 6 or 8, in the FLS differences were revealed when comparing the extreme and intermediate temperament groups on two factors, fussy/difficult/demanding and unadaptable.

Home and Family Environment Sequelae of Challenging Infant Temperament

Long-term differences in both home and family environment were evident as a function of infant temperament group. At three points during the FLS, investigators visited the homes of study participants and administered the HOME Inventory. Comparisons of the low, intermediate, and high infant temperament groups revealed significant differences in the types of experiences and interchanges afforded to children. As shown in Table 8.05, differences in the variety and amount of stimulation and/or verbal/emotional responsivity were evident for all four of the ICQ factors, particularly for the fussy/difficult/demanding, resistant to control, and unsociable factors and less so for the unadaptable factor. In almost every instance (all save one), when significant differences in home environment were detected, the difference favored infants in the low compared to the high infant temperament group. That is, children who had been rated as less fussy, quicker to adapt, less resistant to control, and more sociable subsequently experienced more stimulating and/or responsive home environments.

The Family Environment Scale was administered throughout the FLS, beginning at the 3-year assessment and continuing through the 17-year assessment. Differences among the infant temperament groups on the FES were evident across the preschool, childhood, and adolescent eras; those replicated across developmental eras are displayed in Table 8.05. The largest number of differences in family environment were observed as sequelae of the fussy/difficult factor. Children in the low fussy/difficult/demanding infant temperament group compared to the high group subsequently had family environments characterized as lower in conflict, higher in cohesiveness, and higher in intellectual-cultural orientation across multiple eras of development and informants, especially during adolescence. Additionally, their mothers reported greater satisfaction, involvement, and ease in disciplining related to their parenting experience. Finally, when adolescents, those in the low fussy/difficult infant temperament group reported more positive parent relations compared to those in the high fussy/difficult group. Hence, variations in fussy/difficult infant temperament presaged differences in family relations that were most striking several years later, especially portending more positive relations for infants rated as low in fussy/difficult behavioral style.

Sequelae of unadaptable infant temperament on the FES were almost exclusively limited to differences in the subsequent orientation toward intellectual-cultural pursuits. Quick adaptability during infancy prophesied a higher orientation to these interests and slow adaptability a lower orientation to them during childhood and adolescence.

Although no differences in family environment that replicated across developmental era or informant were evident for the resistant to control infant temperament groups, differences in cohesiveness and expressiveness were evident among the infant temperament groups based on the unsociable factor. Infants in the high unsociable infant temperament group subsequently had family environments characterized as less cohesive and also less expressive than those in the low unsociable infant temperament group. Mothers also reported less involvement with infants in the high unsociable infant temperament group compared to the low unsociable

Table 8.05. Home and Family Environment Sequelae of Infant Temperament Groups

		Temperament group			F	df	Post test
		Low	Intermediate	High			
		Fussy/difficult/demanding					
Infant HOME	VI. Variety of Stimulation	3.85	3.28	3.31	3.17*	2, 122	DA
Preschool HOME	IV. Pride, Affection	5.33	5.04	4.41	3.13*	2, 112	GRPF
Elem. HOME	IV. Materials, Experiences	6.26	5.82	6.54	3.28*	2, 102	DA
FES (M) 3–5	Conflict	1.82	3.06	3.11	7.08**	2, 114	DA, GRPF
FES (M)	Cohesion	8.09	7.27	6.86	3.97*	2, 98	GRPF
14–16	Conflict	1.85	2.83	3.27	4.16*	2, 98	GRPF
	Intellectual-Cultural	7.72	6.34	6.18	6.07**	2, 98	DA, GRPF
FES (M) 17	Cohesion	8.15	6.85	7.09	3.51*	2, 89	DA
	Conflict	1.65	2.95	3.35	5.11**	2, 89	DA, GRPF
	Intellectual-Cultural	7.81	6.00	6.52	5.69**	2, 89	DA, GRPF
FES (C) 17	Conflict	2.14	3.66	3.61	4.86*	2, 104	DA, GRPF
	Intellectual-Cultural	6.66	4.77	5.50	7.85**	2, 104	DA
PCRI	Mother Satisfaction	48.95	43.88	46.77	4.63*	2, 98	DA
	Mother Involvement	50.38	45.57	46.44	3.46*	2, 98	DA
	Mother Limit Setting	51.38	46.00	45.12	5.38**	2, 98	DA, GRPF
SDQ II 14, 16	Parent Relations	5.12	4.73	4.64	3.81*	2, 105	GRPF
		Unadaptable					
Infant HOME	I. Emot. & Verbal Resp.	9.06	8.85	8.00	4.70	2, 122	GRPF, DL
FES (M) 8–12	Intellectual-Cultural	8.00	6.93	6.46	6.66**	2, 104	DA, GRPF
FES (M) 14–16	Intellectual-Cultural	7.60	6.47	6.10	4.61*	2, 98	DA, GRPF
FES (F) 17	Intellectual-Cultural	7.72	6.51	5.71	5.17**	2, 89	GRPF

		Resistant to control					
Infant HOME	VI. Opp. Var. Daily Stim.	3.87	3.31	3.27	3.25*	2, 122	DA, GRPF
Preschool HOME	I. Stim. Games, Reading	9.57	8.71	8.58	3.12*	2, 112	GRPF
	II. Language Stimulation	6.00	5.86	5.12	6.28**	2, 112	GRPF, DL
	VII. Variety of Stimulation	7.37	6.61	6.21	6.12**	2, 112	DA, GRPF
Elem. HOME	III. Emotional Climate	6.48	5.95	5.70	3.36*	2, 102	GRPF
		Unsociable					
Infant HOME	VI. Opp. Var. Daily Stim.	4.10	3.43	2.95	10.55***	2, 122	DA, GRPF
Preschool HOME	II. Language Stimulation	5.88	5.86	5.28	3.42*	2, 112	DL
	VII. Variety of Stimulation	6.68	7.04	6.22	3.85*	2, 112	DL
Elem. HOME	IV. Materials, Experiences	5.75	6.47	5.87	3.76*	2, 102	DA
FES (M) 3–5	Cohesion	8.48	8.14	7.67	3.50*	2, 114	GRPF
FES (M) 8–12	Cohesion	7.96	8.11	7.25	4.14*	2, 104	DL
FES (M) 17	Cohesion	8.05	7.54	6.05	6.53**	2, 89	DA, GRPF
PCRI	Mother Involvement	51.61	47.20	44.05	6.27**	2, 98	GRPF
	Father Involvement	40.73	46.18	40.83	3.70*	2, 88	DL

*$p < .05.$ **$p < .01.$ ***$p < .001.$

group; however, father reports of involvement revealed more involvement with infants in the intermediate group compared to either low or high infant unsociability.

Uniqueness or Specificity of Sequelae for Four ICQ Temperament Factors

Babies rated as least challenging in infant temperament as assessed via the ICQ at 1.5 years evidenced different developmental paths in the FLS compared to babies rated highest. Across all categories of sequelae examined, including temperament, behavioral adjustment, intelligence, achievement, and home/family environment, differences among the extreme groups on the fussy/difficult/demanding aspect of infant temperament were evident. For example, across the aforementioned categories of sequelae, 36%, 50%, 60%, 43%, and 35% of comparisons, respectively, resulted in significant omnibus F tests. Almost without exception, outcomes were more positive for the infants who were low on fussy/difficult/demanding temperament compared to those who were high. The fussy/difficult/demanding factor of infant temperament was unique in that it was the only one of the four ICQ factors with clear and consistent sequelae across all five categories.

The resistant to control dimension showed specificity with respect to developmental sequelae. Over one-third of the omnibus F tests of the temperamental and behavioral adjustment sequelae of the resistance to control factor were significant. Again, differences were consistently in the direction of "easier" temperament and lower behavior problems among those who had been lower on resistance to control as infants compared to those who were high. No differences in subsequent IQ or achievement were evident among the infant resistance to control extreme groups, nor was there a great preponderance of significant tests in the home/environment domain (10% of comparisons). The sequelae of resistance to control in infancy appeared quite specific to the behavioral domain.

Unadaptability during infancy resulted in three to four times more significant F tests in the temperament and behavioral domains than expected by chance, with 20% and 17% of tests significant, respectively. However, unadaptability was the sole factor besides fussy/difficult/demanding that showed repeated differences in the IQ and achievement domans, in which 60% and 43% of F tests were significant, respectively. The frequency of significant F tests at 8% was similar to that expected by chance with respect to sequelae in home/family environment. Thus, infants who were highly unadaptable/slowest to adapt showed lower intelligence and achievement during childhood and adolescence compared to those who were quickest to adapt; the quickest to adapt also had fewer subsequent behavior problems and easier adjustment.

Extreme unsociability during infancy showed the most pervasive sequelae in the areas of behavioral adjustment and home/family environment relative to the other categories of sequelae. For each, just under 20% of *F* tests were significant, indicating in those cases that the most unsociable infants subsequently had higher levels of behavior problems and less engaging home/family environments than infants who were viewed low on unsociability. Unsociability in infancy showed no pervasive sequelae in the domains of temperament, intelligence, or achievement.

Hence, patterns of specificity in terms of the categories of sequelae investigated were evident. Although high fussy/difficult/demandingness during infancy showed significant consequences in all five domains, the consequences of unadaptability in infancy were most evident in intelligence and achievement domains, followed by temperament and behavioral adjustment. The developmental consequences of extreme resistance to control in infancy were quite specific to the domains of temperament and behavioral adjustment, whereas the sequelae of extreme unsociability in infancy were restricted to the domains of behavioral adjustment and home/family environment.

Temperament as a Developmental Asset, Developmental Liability, and General Risk/Protective Factor

We were especially interested in ascertaining the pattern of differences among the three infant temperament groups as one way to understand the possible mechanisms by which temperament and developmental outcomes were related. When only two extreme groups are compared, one cannot distinguish among the following four patterns of results:

1. *Developmental asset:* Babies rated as lowest on challenging temperament were developmentally advantaged compared to most other babies;
2. *Developmental liability:* Babies rated with the most challenging temperaments were compromised in their subsequent development compared to most other babies;
3. *Generalized risk/protective factor:* Babies rated as lowest and highest in challenging infant temperament differed significantly from each other in their developmental outcomes, but not significantly from most other babies; or
4. *Developmental asset and liability:* Babies rated as lowest and highest in challenging infant temperament differed not only significantly from each other, but also differed significantly from the comparison group of babies.

To differentiate between these four possibilities, we included the centermost fifty percent of babies in the FLS in our analyses as a reference comparison group, rather than comparing only the lowest and highest groups. Although we recognize the arbitrary nature of cut-off points, we believed this strategy might serve as a starting point to investigate the possibility that temperament characteristics may provide developmental advantage to children. In our view, past research has instead highlighted the developmental disadvantage associated with challenging temperament features, particularly the difficult constellation identified. By including the centermost fifty percent or intermediate temperament group for each ICQ factor, we could then ascertain which of the four possible outcomes delineated above characterized the relation between infant temperament and its developmental sequelae. Examining the pattern of post-test comparisons, the label of "developmental asset," or DA, was assigned when an extreme group differed from the intermediate group and the development of the extreme group was more desirable. When post-test results indicated that the two extreme groups differed from each other, but neither differed significantly from the intermediate group, the label "general risk/protective factor," or GRPF, was assigned. Finally, when post-test results showed less desirable sequelae for an extreme group and the extreme group differed from the intermediate group, the label of "developmental liability," or DL, was given. These labels are shown in the last columns of Tables 8.01 through 8.05.

In Table 8.06, we summarize the number of times each of these ascriptions were made by category of sequelae examined. Using this strategy, approximately 50% of the post-tests suggested temperament acted as a generalized risk/protective factor. Examining the patterns of inter-group differences summarized in Table 8.06 across all sequelae examined, the most prevalent result of the four aforementioned patterns was case 3, in which the outcomes of low and high infant temperament groups differed significantly from each other, but neither significantly differed from the intermediate group. Figure 8.06 illustrates this pattern of results in terms of the achievement sequelae of quick versus slow infant adaptability. The subsequent achievement test performance of infants in the slow and quick adaptability extreme groups differed significantly from each other, but neither differed significantly from the intermediate infants. Hence, a small developmental advantage in the area of achievement was observed for the babies quickest to adapt and a small developmental disadvantage was associated with babies who were slowest to adapt; although neither extreme temperament group differed from the comparison group, on average these groups evinced significantly different developmental outcomes from each other.

Evidence of temperament serving as a developmental advantage was also evident. In approximately 25% of the analyses summarized across sequelae in Table 8.06, the pattern of inter-group differences showed that babies in the least challenging infant temperament group displayed significantly more positive outcomes than either babies in the intermediate or the highest groups. For example, as depicted in Figure 8.07, babies who were quickest to adapt subsequently had families characterized as higher in orientation to intellectual-cultural activities. Another example is displayed in Figure 8.08, which shows that babies lowest in resistance to control received significantly greater variety of stimulation in their home environments compared to babies rated as intermediate or high in resistance to control.

Table 8.06. **Summary of Patterns of Results Observed Among Low, Intermediate, and High Infant Temperament Groups in Each Category of Sequelae Examined**

	Infant temperament factor				
	Fussy/ difficult	Unadaptable	Resistant to control	Unsociable	Total (%)
Temperamental sequelae					
Developmental Asset	6	7	6	0	19 (27.5)
Developmental Liability	10	4	10	2	26 (37.7)
Generalized Risk/ Protective Factor	11	6	7	0	24 (34.8)
Both Asset and Liability	(2)	0	(1)	0	(3) (4.3)
Total	27	17	23	2	69
Behavioral adjustment sequelae					
Developmental Asset	6	0	4	1	11 (14.1)
Developmental Liability	14	1	2	2	19 (24.4)
Generalized Risk/ Protective Factor	19	8	14	7	48 (61.5)
Both Asset and Liability	(2)	0	0	0	(2) (2.6)
Total	39	9	20	10	78
Intelligence					
Developmental Asset	3	1	0	0	4 (57.1)
Developmental Liability	1	2	0	0	3 (42.8)
Generalized Risk/ Protective Factor	0	0	0	0	0 (0.0)
Both Asset and Liability	(1)	0	0	0	(1) (14.3)
Total	4	3	0	0	7
Academic achievement					
Developmental Asset	1	0	0	0	1 (16.7)
Developmental Liability	2	3	0	0	5 (83.3)
Generalized Risk/ Protective Factor	0	0	0	0	0 (0.0)
Both Asset and Liability	0	0	0	0	0 (0.0)
Total	3	3	0	0	6
Home and family environment					
Developmental Asset	12	2	2	3	19 (40.4)
Developmental Liability	0	1	1	4	6 (12.7)
Generalized Risk/Protective Factor	9	4	5	4	22 (46.8)
Both Asset and Liability	(1)	0	0	0	(1) (2.1)
Total	22	7	7	11	47

Finally, in approximately 25% of outcomes, the pattern of results supported the interpretation that infant temperament was a developmental liability. In these cases, babies with high levels of challenging infant temperament showed compromised development or environments during childhood or adolescence.

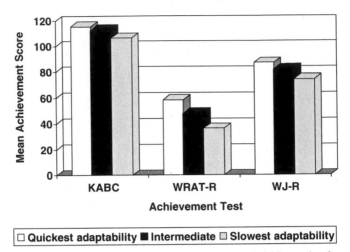

Figure 8.06. Example of temperament operating as a generalized risk/protective factor; average achievement of extreme groups differs from each other, but not from intermediate temperament group.

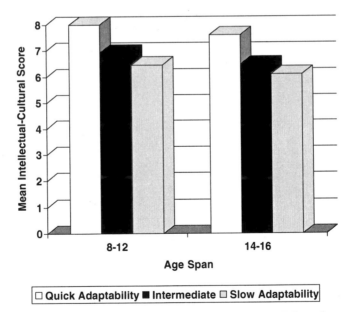

Figure 8.07. Example of temperament operating as a developmental asset; infants who were quickest to adapt subsequently experienced family environments characterized as more intellectually and culturally stimulating compared to infants who were average or slower in adaptability.

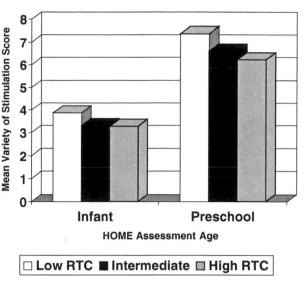

Figure 8.08. Example of temperament serving as a developmental asset; infants who were lower in resistance to control received more variety in daily stimulation than those who were intermediate or high in resistance to control.

For example, as displayed in Figure 8.09, infants who were the most fussy/difficult/demanding in temperament showed higher levels of attention problems compared to both those intermediate or lowest in fussiness.

Finally, in only a few cases were all three infant temperament groups different from each other on the post-tests, supporting the notion that temperament served as both a developmental asset and liability. For example, this pattern of results is displayed in Figure 8.10, which shows the average aggressive behavior score on the CBCL at ages 4–5 and 6–12 for babies in the low, intermediate, and high fussy/difficult temperament groups. As shown, a positive linear relation emerged. Babies with the easiest temperament showed the least number of aggressive behaviors. Those in the intermediate group showed a higher average that differed significantly from that of the easiest group, whereas babies in the highest fussy/difficult temperament group averaged highest in aggressive behavior problems, significantly higher than both of the other infant temperament groups.

Thus, all four patterns of outcomes were observed in the developmental sequelae of challenging infant temperament. Although the emphasis in the literature to date has tended to focus upon temperament as a risk factor in development, in about 25% of the significant outcomes examined herein, results suggested that infants with the least challenging temperament subsequently enjoyed enhanced developmental or environmental contexts compared to infants with intermediate or highly challenging temperaments.

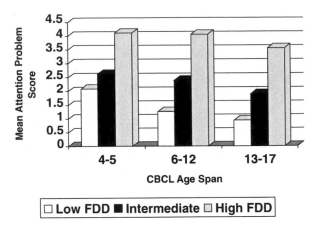

Figure 8.09. Example of temperament operating as a developmental liability; infants who were high-est in fussy/difficult/demanding temperament subsequently exhibited significantly higher levels of attention problems compared to infants who were average or lowest in fussiness.

These findings reveal divergent patterns of developmental and environ-mental outcomes among infants with different temperament characteristics. Al-though the causal relation between infant temperament and these outcomes cannot be demonstrated with certainty, the patterns were replicated in all domains across developmental eras through adolescence. Additionally, some outcomes were assessed across informants and in many cases outcomes were replicated

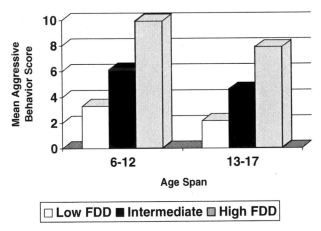

Figure 8.10. Example of temperament serving as both a developmental asset and developmental liability; all three fussy/difficult/demanding infant temperament groups differ in the level of aggressive behavior exhibited during childhood and adolescence.

across informants. Furthermore, in a significant proportion of the outcomes, the pattern of differences among low, intermediate, and high temperament groups suggested that temperament served as a developmental asset: those infants with the least challenging temperament styles showed superior outcomes to infants in the intermediate or highly challenging temperament groups. Hence, in addition to placing children at risk, certain temperament styles may serve to enhance development.

Summary and Conclusions

1. *Are there gender differences in extreme temperament group membership?* Boy and girl infants at 1.5 years were equally likely to be rated as extreme in temperament by their parent. This was true for all four aspects of challenging temperament assessed on the ICQ.
2. *Do infants classified as challenging or easy on one temperament factor tend to be extreme on other ICQ factors, or is group membership on any given factor independent of the others?* There was significant overlap in extreme temperament group membership for three combinations of infant temperament: fussy/difficult demanding and resistant to control, fussy/difficult/demanding and unadaptability, and unadaptability and unsociability. For example, in these three combinations of ICQ factors, about 50% of infants in the high group on one were also in the high group of the other.
3. *Is there evidence of short and/or long-term temperamental sequelae for any of the four ICQ factors, or are these aspects of behavioral style specific to the infant period?* Three of the four ICQ factors showed temperamental differences that replicated across at least two developmental eras. Across the groups highest on the fussy/difficult/demanding, resistant to control, and unadaptable factors, negative mood and slow adaptability were long-lasting temperamental sequelae. Additional temperamental sequelae showed divergence or specificity among these three ICQ factors. For example, the former two dimensions showed higher activity level across the childhood and adolescent years, whereas the latter did not.
4. *Are there systematic and unique outcomes in the domains of intelligence, school functioning, behavioral adjustment, and home/family environment for each of the four ICQ factors of challenging infant temperament?* Fussy/difficult/demanding infant temperament was associated with compromised outcomes in all domains. Unique patterns or specificity of outcomes were also observed. Differences in intelligence and achievement throughout childhood and adolescence outcomes of fussy/difficult/demanding and unadaptability in infancy, whereas

unsociability in infancy presaged lower parental involvement and family cohesion during childhood and adolescence. The types of behavior problem outcomes also showed specificity to the nature of infant temperament.

5. *Finally, is there evidence supporting the role of extreme temperament as an asset or liability to the process of development?* Findings from the FLS support the conclusion that temperament most often operated as a general risk/protective factor, in which the outcomes of the extreme groups differ significantly from each other but not from the intermediate or moderate temperament group. In about 25% of outcomes in the FLS, temperament served as a developmental asset, in which extreme temperament was associated with enhanced development compared to the outcome associated with moderate temperament. In the remaining 25% of outcomes in the FLS, temperament operated as a developmental liability. In these cases, the outcome of the extreme temperament group was compromised in comparison to the intermediate or moderate temperament group.

9

Synthesis and Implications

"She is so perfect—can she really be mine?"
—Parent of Child #6, Easy Infant Temperament Group, Age 17

We conclude this volume by synthesizing the body of findings resulting from the Fullerton Longitudinal Study with respect to numerous issues. Findings germane to the understanding of the developmental course of temperament and the significance of individual differences in youngsters temperament for their development in the domains of personality, behavioral adjustment, intelligence, and school functioning are first addressed. Individual differences in children's temperament interface with their home and family contexts of development, yielding additional clues as to the mechanisms by which temperament and developmental outcomes may come to be related. In support of the parental report methodology, results from the FLS yielded strong evidence regarding the predictive and construct validity of parent reports of children's temperament. The interaction of individual differences in temperament with contexts of development, subject variables, and developmental differences in other domains have only begun to be examined. However, findings from the FLS demonstrate that even aspects of temperament assessed as early as 1.5 years have long-term sequelae, both through direct main effects and also through interactions with developmental contexts, and that early differences in temperament are associated not only with developmental risk, but also can serve as assets that may facilitate or enhance not only the children's context of development but also their developmental trajectory.

Temperament from Infancy through Adolescence:
Pathways and Trajectories

The FLS is one of a handful of studies that has charted the temperament of children from infancy through adolescence. Canonical correlations showed that the four temperament characteristics measured during infancy correlated with temperament measured during the preschool, middle childhood, and adolescent eras at a relatively stable and moderate level. After infancy, measures based on the NYLS model were used, and in the next several sections we summarize the stability and continuity of each of the NYLS dimensions of temperament. Implications are then discussed.

Activity Level

Among the temperament dimensions investigated in the FLS, activity level showed the highest stability from age 2 years through mid-adolescence. Precursors of activity level in childhood and adolescence were the fussy/difficult/demanding and resistance to control factors of the ICQ at 1.5 years. Both of these factors correlated in the low to moderate range (i.e., .3 to .5) with activity level at age 2, in the preschool years, middle childhood, and adolescence. Stability of activity level from age 2 and the preschool period across middle childhood and adolescence was also in the moderate range. During middle childhood, average ratings of activity level across the participants in the FLS dropped significantly, indicating a shift toward lower activity level with increasing age from 8 to 12 years. From middle childhood to and through adolescence, stability coefficients exceeded .70. Thus, although average activity level decreased during middle childhood, the relative standing of children compared to the cohort remained similar.

Biological Rhythmicity/Predictability or Quality of Organization

Rhythmicity, as defined in the NYLS model, refers to the regularity of the individual's biological functioning. The items of the TTS and BSQ during the preschool years and of the three rhythmicity scales of the DOTS-R during adolescence clearly reflect this aspect of individuality. However, during middle childhood, this dimension was replaced by the conceptually-related dimension of predictability/quality of organization on the MCTQ. Given these comments, the stability of this dimension in the FLS was as follows. First, fussy/difficult/demanding infant temperament presaged toddler biological irregularity; although coefficients were low in magnitude, this aspect of infant temperament presaged all subsequent measures of rhythmicity, including all three aspects of rhythmicity assessed during adolescence (eating, daily habits, sleeping). Across the toddler to preschool period, a moderate level of stability was evident; average ratings across the ages from 3 to 5 showed a trend toward greater regularity with increasing age. Perhaps reflecting the shift from biological to social predictability on the preschool versus middle childhood measures of temperament, stability from the preschool to middle childhood years was low, whereas stability from age 2 to adolescence reached moderate magnitude. Stability from the preschool and middle childhood years to adolescence was also in the moderate range. During adolescence, both parent and adolescent reports showed moderately strong stability from 14 to 16 years.

Adaptability – Flexibility

The temperamental dimension of adaptability reflects the sequential course of the individual's responses to new stimuli, changes in routine, alterations in plans, or redirection by parents. For example, some children may adjust to a new routine quickly and without fuss, whereas others may require several days before they transition smoothly. During adolescence, this disposition was reflected in the flexibility dimension of the DOTS-R. In the FLS, slow adaptability during childhood and adolescence was presaged by higher scores on two of the four ICQ factors during infancy: fussy/difficult/demanding and resistant to control. Babies who fussed and cried frequently and who were difficult to redirect were subsequently slower to adapt as children and adolescents. Adaptability showed low stability from age two to either the childhood or adolescent periods, however it showed moderately high stability from the preschool years to middle childhood, and also from middle childhood to adolescence. Stability was high across the ages of 14 to 16.

Approach/Withdrawal

This dimension refers to the individual's initial reaction to novel people, places, foods, and so on, ranging from acceptance and easy tolerance to initial rejection and withdrawal. Approach/withdrawal during the preschool and middle childhood years was presaged by unadaptability during infancy, with correlations generally in the moderate range. Stability of approach/withdrawal from age 2 years through the preschool and middle childhood years was moderate, reaching high levels from the preschool through adolescent years. During middle childhood, significant changes in average ratings across the FLS cohort suggested a tendency for children to become more approaching with increasing age from 8 to 12. Stability across the ages from 14 to 16 years was high.

Intensity of Reaction

Intensity of reaction refers to the strength of the individual's responses and ranges from mild to strong in magnitude; it was assessed during the toddler, preschool, and middle childhood eras in the FLS. Infants viewed as more fussy/difficult/demanding and more resistant to control tended to be more intense in their reactions during the toddler, preschool, and middle childhood periods, with correlation coefficients in the low range. Stability was moderate across the period from age 2 through the preschool years and also through middle childhood. Intensity during the preschool years correlated in the low range with intensity during middle childhood. Across the preschool and middle childhood periods, children tended to become milder in their reactions with increasing age.

Quality of Mood

This aspect of individuality ranges from predominantly positive, joyful, and friendly to predominantly negative, crying, and unfriendly. In adolescence, the measure of temperament employed in the FLS assessed positive rather than negative mood. Quality of mood throughout childhood and adolescence was presaged virtually uniformly by three dimensions of challenging temperament during infancy: fussy/difficult/demanding, unadaptability, and resistance to control. From toddlerhood to the preschool and middle childhood periods, stability was moderate to low in magnitude. During the preschool years, age-related changes in means indicated a trend toward more positive mood with increasing age from 3 to 5. Although stability from the preschool to middle childhood years was moderately strong, stability from the preschool or middle childhood years to adolescence was low. This may be due in part to a shift from assessing negative mood on the earlier temperament measures to assessing positive mood on the DOTS-R. Stability across the ages of 14 to 16 years was moderately high.

Persistence/Attention Span – Task Orientation

This aspect of temperament refers to the length of time the individual stays on tasks, even when interrupted. No consistent infant temperament antecedents of childhood persistence were evident in the FLS. Across the toddler to preschool years, high stability of persistence/attention span was evident; however, stability was low across longer intervals. During the preschool years, changes in mean ratings suggested increasing persistence/attention span with increasing age from 3 to 5. Stability was high from the middle childhood to adolescent era (this dimension is reflected in the DOTS-R scale of task orientation), and also high from age 14 to 16.

Distractibility

In the NYLS model, the dimension of distractibility relates to the propensity of extraneous environmental stimuli to interfere with or alter the child's ongoing activities. No precursors of distractibility during childhood were evident in infancy. Stability was in the moderate range across the toddler period to the preschool and middle childhood periods, and also from the preschool to the middle childhood periods. However, distractibility during the preschool years was not predictive of task orientation during adolescence; from middle childhood to adolescence stability was low. Developmental changes in mean level of distractibility were not evident during the preschool or middle childhood periods.

Threshold of Responsiveness

Threshold of responsiveness, referring to the level of extrinsic stimulation that is necessary to evoke a perceptible response from the individual, showed the least evidence of developmental stability in the FLS. Threshold of responsiveness during the toddler and preschool years was predicted at low levels by unsociability during infancy. Cross-time correlations from the toddler, preschool, and middle childhood periods reached the moderate range at only one age combination, from preschool to middle childhood. This dimension showed different trajectories during the preschool and middle childhood eras, with children viewed as more reactive with increasing age from 3 to 5 years and less reactive to environmental stimulation with increasing age from 8 to 12 years.

Differential Developmental Significance of Temperament Dimensions

A major goal of this research effort was to determine the pattern of relations between NYLS dimensions of temperament and developmental outcomes across childhood and adolescence. An appraisal of the accumulated findings revealed that the developmental significance of the NYLS dimensions varied considerably. The dimensions that showed the strongest and most pervasive relations to the range of environmental concomitants and developmental outcomes examined were adaptability and persistence/attention span. Individual differences on these dimensions were particularly relevant with respect to outcomes across the behavioral, intellectual, and academic domains, as well as with respect to the nature of the family environment experienced. On the opposite extreme, intensity of reactions, distractibility, and threshold of responsiveness showed fewer and lower relationships with the outcomes examined in the FLS.

The remaining four dimensions (activity level, approach/withdrawal, quality of mood, and biological rhythmicity) showed relations with some outcomes, but few or none with other outcomes, or a low pattern of relations across numerous outcomes. For example, activity level was a concomitant and precursor of externalizing behavior problems and related inversely to performance in the academic domain, but did not relate pervasively or strongly with any other domains investigated. Quality of mood related to all categories of outcomes examined, but especially to externalizing behaviors and family relations. Approach/withdrawal showed modest relations with outcomes of all types examined, especially early behavior problems. Finally, biological rhythmicity also showed low correlations with all outcomes investigated. In the following sections, more detailed descriptions of the sequelae of each temperament dimension are reviewed.

Adaptability – Flexibility

Variability on the temperament dimension of adaptability showed the widest range of environmental and developmental concomitants and sequelae. The speed with which children adjusted to changes related concurrently and/or across time to their behavioral adjustment, their intellectual development, how they functioned in the school setting, and characteristics of their family relations.

Slower adaptability during and after the preschool period presaged higher levels of behavior problems, especially externalizing problems (but also internalizing problems to a lower degree), during middle childhood and adolescence. Concurrent relations between adaptability and behavior problems were in the moderate range during the preschool and middle childhood periods, ranging to .60 in magnitude, but low to moderate during adolescence, ranging to .40 in magnitude. Significant correlations were also observed across the informants on behavior problems (teachers during middle childhood; adolescents and parents in adolescence). In all cases, slower adaptability/lower flexibility portended higher behavior problem scores, and correlations were stronger with externalizing than internalizing problems.

Adaptability also related to intellectual development and academic performance. After age two, slower adaptability related concurrently and across time to lower intelligence, although correlations were low in magnitude. Age-eligible children whose parents voluntarily delayed their entry into kindergarten were as a group slower to adapt than those who entered on time, and slower adaptability also characterized children who repeated kindergarten or first grade. Additionally, slower adaptability also portended lower standardized achievement test scores during the early years of school, lower teacher assessments of classroom competence during middle childhood, and lower self-perceptions of competence in school and motivation toward academics in adolescence, with correlation coefficients in the low range (i.e., .40 maximum). Lower flexibility in adolescence related concurrently to lower cumulative high school grade point average. Hence, variation in adaptability-flexibility related to a wide range of outcomes in the academic arena, including when the child entered the formal educational process, how the child progressed through grades, levels of achievement, classroom behavior, and self perceptions of competence and motivation in adolescence.

Adaptability-flexibility also related pervasively to aspects of the home and family environment experienced by children. As preschoolers, children who were slower to adapt lived in families characterized with lower levels of affection and warmth, less variety of stimulation, and greater levels of restriction and punishment compared to those who were quicker to adjust. During middle childhood, they continued to experience relatively lower levels of emotional and verbal responsiveness in their family. Slower adaptability in the preschool years foretold a lower family orientation toward intellectual-cultural interests/activities across childhood and adolescence. During middle childhood, those who were slower to adjust experienced family environments characterized by less cohesion and greater conflict; these differences persisted throughout adolescence. At age 17, the adolescents' own assessments of their family environment reflected these characteristics; adolescents viewing themselves as lower flexibility also viewed their family environment as lower in cohesion, expressiveness, and intellectual-cultural orientation, as well as higher in conflict. During adolescence, flexibility related to both parent and adolescent assessments of the parent-child relationship, across informant, and at low to moderate levels. Slower adaptability/flexibility was associated with less positive parent-child relations.

Hence, adaptability/flexibility related concurrently and across time to a wide range of important developmental outcomes and to the nature of the family context in which children developed through at least adolescence. Martin et al. (1983) noted that some temperamental theorists consider adaptability to be the most general temperament factor. These findings support this supposition.

Persistence/Attention Span – Task Orientation

Persistence/attention span reflects the length of time a particular activity is pursued, in spite of obstacles to its continuation. In adolescence, this dimension was assessed via the task orientation dimension of the DOTS-R. This dimension related at low to moderately high levels with a wide range of developmental outcomes, including behavioral adjustment, intelligence, academic functioning, and family relationships. Relations were evident across time, across informant, across context, and across method.

With respect to behavioral adjustment, correlations reached moderate magnitudes and indicated greater persistence/attention span was associated with lower internalizing and externalizing behavior problem scores. Significant relations were observed in all age eras examined from preschool through adolescence, and became stronger with externalizing compared to internalizing problems with increasing age. Even across informant and context, correlation coefficients were impressive in magnitude. For example, during middle childhood parent ratings of persistence correlated $-.49$ with teacher ratings of externalizing problems in the classroom. That persistence is a particularly salient individual difference variable in the academic setting was also supported by significant correlations ranging to moderate magnitudes with a wide range of academic outcomes, including achievement, classroom behavioral competence, academic self-concept, and academic intrinsic motivation. Persistence/attention span also related concurrently and across time with intelligence; correlations ranged to .40 in magnitude. Concurrent, cross-time, and cross-informant relations were also observed between persistence and family environment variables; children and adolescents who were more persistent had families characterized as high in cohesion and intellectual-cultural orientation. Additionally, parents and adolescent's assessments of the parent-child relation related to persistence, with more positive relations associated with greater task orientation.

Activity Level

Activity level related most strongly to externalizing behavior problems, and this relation existed across the preschool, middle childhood, and adolescent periods. Correlations reached moderate magnitudes when measured concurrently, and reached .40 when measured across time and across informant. Although higher activity level related at low magnitudes to lower intelligence during the preschool period, it was not related to intelligence during middle childhood or adolescence. Higher intelligence during the preschool years, however, did predict lower activity levels during adolescence. Activity level was also associated with academic achievement during elementary school, although correlations were low in magnitude. Higher levels of activity level related to lower levels of achievement. During adolescence, activity level related at a low magnitude to academic self-concept. Children with lower activity levels during the preschool and middle childhood years had families characterized as more oriented toward intellectual-cultural pursuits. During adolescence, lower activity was associated with more positive parent-child interactions, across both parent and adolescent informants. Parental perceptions of the ease and effectiveness of limit setting related particularly strongly to their teen's activity level; adolescents who were more active were more challenging to discipline.

Approach/Withdrawal

The tendency of the child to approach or withdraw from novel people, places, and experiences related concurrently and across time to developmental outcomes in the domains of behavior, intelligence, and family relations. In the behavioral domain, children who were predisposed to withdraw from novel experiences tended toward higher levels of behavior problems, particularly internalizing types of problems; children with more behavior problems during the preschool years also tended toward withdrawal from novelty during middle childhood and adolescence. Approach/withdrawal also related across age to intelligence, with children more approaching to new people, places, and experiences scoring higher on intelligence; correlations were limited to the low range. In terms of academic performance, children who were more approaching during the preschool years tended to score higher in academic achievement during the early elementary school years and, in high school, to have higher self-concept related to school and greater academic intrinsic motivation. Their home environments tended to be more oriented toward intellectual-cultural pursuits across the preschool, middle childhood, and adolescent periods and, during adolescence, also as more cohesive. Within parent and adolescent informants, but not across, approach in adolescence related to assessments of the parent-child relationship (more positive assessments related to greater tendency to approach). Hence, the dimension of approach/withdrawal demonstrated both concurrent and cross-time relations with behavioral, intellectual, academic, and social aspects of functioning during childhood and adolescence.

Quality of Mood

Quality of mood related most strongly to the domain of behavior problems. Correlations with behavior problems ranged to .60 during the preschool, middle childhood, and adolescent eras. Even when mood and behavior problems were assessed across time and across informants, correlations were generally in the .30 to .40 range. Higher behavior problem scores were related to more negative mood. Quality of mood also related concurrently and across time to intelligence, with correlations in the low range and indicative of lower intelligence associated with negative mood. Negative mood also related to academic achievement, classroom behavior, academic self-concept, and academic intrinsic motivation, albeit at low levels; more negative mood was associated with poorer achievement, less classroom competence, and lower academic self-concept and motivation. Positive mood during the preschool and middle childhood years was related concurrently and across time to lower levels of family conflict and higher levels of intellectual-cultural orientation. During adolescence, both adolescents and parents reported more positive parent-child relations when the adolescents' mood was more positive in quality; correlations were low in magnitude. Maternal ratings of parent-child relations, especially involvement, communication, and limit setting, were related to parental assessments of adolescent mood.

Biological Rhythmicity – Quality of Organization

Items on the temperament measures employed in the FLS during the toddler, preschool, and adolescent eras focused on the regularity of biological functioning, whereas the measure during middle childhood assessed the quality of the child's social predictability/quality of organization. Given the slightly different focus of these scales, developmental outcomes associated with each will be addressed separately.

Biological rhythmicity related concurrently to both internalizing and externalizing behavior problem scores during the preschool and adolescent periods; correlations were low and indicated higher numbers of problems when regularity was lower. During middle childhood, predictability/quality of organization related concurrently to both parent and teacher reports of behavior problems and teacher reports of classroom competence, with correlations ranging to moderate magnitudes, and also across time to behavior problems in adolescence, with correlations in the range of .30 to 40. Biological regularity was not related to intelligence across the ages investigated. During middle childhood, predictability/quality of organization related at low magnitudes with standardized achievement tests, as well as parent and teacher ratings of academic performance in reading and/or math. During adolescence, aspects of rhythmicity related concurrently to family cohesion and conflict at low levels, with regularity of functioning associated with greater family cohesion and lower family conflict (all at low magnitude). Additionally, both adolescents and parents rated their relationships more favorably when the adolescents' rhythmicity was higher, again with coefficients in the low range.

Intensity of Reactions

The dimension of intensity of reactions related almost exclusively to developmental outcomes in the behavioral domain. Individual differences in intensity showed repeated but generally low correlations with behavior problems, more so externalizing types than internalizing types, across the preschool and middle childhood periods. Intensity in middle childhood also related across time to behavior problems during adolescence. Very few significant correlations were observed with intelligence and achievement or other aspects relating to the academic setting aside from low correlations with specific aspects of teacher-reported classroom behavior. Intensity during middle childhood related concurrently and across time at low levels with the amount of cohesion and conflict in the family; children with more intense reactions lived in family environments characterized as lower in cohesion and higher in conflict. Hence, individual differences in reactivity had developmental significance that was somewhat restricted to the domain of behavioral adjustment.

Distractibility

Distractibility refers to the effectiveness of extraneous environmental stimuli in interfering with, or in altering the direction of, the child's ongoing behavior; it was assessed during the toddler, preschool and middle childhood eras in the FLS. Across these eras of development, distractibility related at low levels concurrently and across time with behavior problems, almost exclusively externalizing types. Distractibility also related concurrently and across time with intelligence, again at low magnitudes, with higher distractibility relating to lower intelligence. In the academic setting, distractibility related concurrently, inversely, and at low levels with achievement as measured by standardized tests, parent reports, and teacher ratings, as well as with teacher ratings of classroom behavior. Distractibility was not related to family environment.

Threshold of Responsiveness

Threshold of responsiveness refers to the amount of extrinsic stimulation that is necessary to evoke a noticeable reaction from the child. Threshold failed to relate systematically with any behavioral, intellectual, academic, or family/environmental variable, and the correlations that were observed rarely reached magnitudes in excess of .30. Although the infant's sensitivity to environmental stimulation may be of significance to parents or other caregivers, variability on this dimension demonstrated little evidence of developmental sequelae in the FLS.

Implications of Findings Regarding Temperamental Continuity/Stability

The mechanism or mechanisms by which temperament and developmental outcomes come to be associated remain to be elucidated. Genetic and biological underpinnings of temperament continue to be explored, and data are accumulating as to their contributions. Results from the FLS, however, are more useful in illuminating the possible role of environment and developmental progress in other domains as potential mechanisms. The aforementioned results showed that variation in temperament is a precursor, concomitant, and sequela of developmental outcomes across a range of domains as well as factors in the home and family environment. These extensive data thus support the conclusions of other researchers that temperament operates through bidirectional, transactional processes that result in both main effects and interactions with other developmental and contextual variables. Across the chapters in this book, findings indicated that individual differences in temperament related both to the environments that children experienced as well as to the environments they selected or elicited. For example, family conflict related to children's externalizing behavior problems at age 8 much more potently if children had difficult as opposed to easy temperament as infants. Even when family conflict was high, children who had easy infant temperament showed behavior problems at a level similar to those who lived in families characterized as low in conflict. Children higher on the approach dimension requested more and different extracurricular activities compared to those who were low in approach. They were also higher in academic intrinsic motivation during adolescence. Findings such as these highlight the need for additional detailed process-oriented research for a full explanation of how covariation between temperament and developmental outcomes emerge.

Findings with respect to continuity provide evidence of the criterion validity of parent ratings of temperament. Trends that emerged from parent reports of temperament are consistent with the body of accruing data on development patterns. For example, across the preschool period from 3 to 5 years, parents reported that the cohort became more predictable in biological functions, more persistent/longer in attention span, more positive in mood, and increasingly sensitive to their environment. With increasing age in middle childhood, parents rated the cohort on average as becoming lower in activity level, milder in intensity of reactions, and more approaching of new people, places, and things. Trends such as these mirror expected trends and, together with data collected across informants and contexts that will be elucidated below, support the use of parent reports of temperament in developmental research.

Parent perceptions of their children's temperament showed significant cross-time stability. This finding suggests that temperament may have utility as an early indicator of developmental risk. Because the FLS is a non-intervention study, the outcomes reported are indicative of the course of normal development for infants and children with varying temperamental characteristics. In the absence of intervention, different developmental trajectories were evident for children who were "temperamentally challenged." Fussy/difficult/demanding infant temperament as assessed by the ICQ developed by Bates and colleagues, and, later, slow adaptability and low persistence/attention span as measured on the scales developed by Carey and colleagues seem particularly likely candidates as early indicators of risk. They showed significant and moderate relations with a range of developmental outcomes across the long term and a tendency to remain stable across time. The efficacy of recently developed temperament-based parent-education programs or other temperament-focused therapeutic interventions in altering the long-term trajectories observed in the FLS is important to evaluate. Results from an intervention during infancy with mothers of extremely irritable infants show promise in short-term longitudinal evaluations (van den Boom, 1994; 1995).

Temperament as a Precursor of Personality

Recent interest in child temperament as a predictor of the "Big Five" personality factors led us to examine the relation between the early measures of temperament collected in the FLS and personality as assessed by self-report when the
cohort was 17 years of age. Although scattered correlations were evident across the
several assessments of child temperament collected via parent report in the infancy,
preschool, and middle childhood eras and the adolescents' self-reported personality at age 17, correlations were neither impressive in magnitude nor replicated
across eras. Multiple regression analyses between adolescent self-rated temperament aggregated across ages 14 and 16 years and their self-reported personality
at age 17 showed significant multiple correlations, with the amount of variance
explained by temperament (adjusted for shrinkage) in neuroticism, extraversion,
openness to experience, agreeableness, and conscientiousness equal to 24%, 29%,
7%, 14%, and 18%, respectively. Combining both parent and adolescent reports of
adolescent temperament did not improve the amount of adjusted variance in personality explained by any appreciable amount. Hence, impressive links between
temperament assessed a few years earlier and personality assessed at age 17 were
evident, but not between earlier measures of temperament and personality at 17.

Thus, there was not a direct and linear mapping of childhood temperament
dimensions to personality traits in adolescence. Given the high stability of temperament during childhood and adolescence, we considered it likely that age-to-age
links between personality at 17 and temperament could be traced backward in
age. However, significant linkages (i.e., correlation coefficients) between parent
reports of temperament and adolescent reports of temperament and personality
were sparse and thus created breaks in the chain. Unfortunately, parent assessments of their adolescent children's personality were not collected at age 17; these
data may have provided more encouraging evidence of temperament-personality
linkages beyond those observed within the adolescent period only. We intend to
use additional multivariate methods to continue our examination of these data.
Additionally, it may be that age 17 is not the best age to use as the criterion variable to answer the question of temperament-personality linkages. That is, perhaps
personality in adulthood may be a superior outcome indicator, given that personality has been shown to show impressive stability in adulthood (Costa & McCrae,
1988). Finally, perhaps the relation between early temperament and later personality is simply not linear; examination of typologies or extreme groups may prove
to be more useful approaches.

In chapter 5, we noted that early measures of intelligence related consistently
across several developmental eras and at low magnitudes to personality at age 17.
In particular, intelligence measures from infancy and/or preschool years onward
related positively to openness to experience and agreeableness. Hence, it may be
that early intelligence is a useful harbinger of some aspects of personality. As

noted by Hart, Hofmann, Edelstein, and Keller (1997, p. 203), personality is likely a result of development in multiple domains: "... there are no findings in the behavioral-genetic literature that would suggest that personality type is wholly a product of temperament. There will be no single, simple answer to the question of the sources of personality type."

Temperamental Dimensions as Sequelae of Earlier Development

Wachs and Kohnstamm (2001) noted that temperament may be an outcome or sequela of earlier development, although it is usually treated as a predictor of developmental outcomes. Given that behavioral adjustment, intelligence, and family environment were repeatedly assessed throughout the course of the FLS, as well as temperament, we were able to assess the bi-directionality of the relation between temperament and these aspects of development. Thus, early measures of behavioral adjustment, intelligence, and family environment were examined as cross-time predictors of temperament during middle childhood and adolescence.

With respect to behavioral adjustment, bidirectional relations were evident between the preschool behavior problem scores and almost all dimensions of temperament during middle childhood, and also with a more restricted set of temperament dimensions during adolescence (flexibility, task orientation, general activity level, and approach). Correlations reached moderate high magnitudes, even between preschool behavior problems and temperament assessed a decade later. Hence, clear evidence of bidirectional relationships between early and later measures of temperament and behavioral adjustment were in evidence.

In the intellectual domain, intelligence test scores from the infancy, preschool, and middle childhood years significantly and consistently related to subsequent measures of one temperament dimension: persistence/attention span-task orientation. Correlations at every age ranged from .25 to .39 and were positive, indicating children scoring higher on earlier tests of intelligence were subsequently viewed as more persistent. In fact, in the FLS intelligence was a more consistent predictor of later persistence than earlier persistence was of later intelligence. In terms of temperamental predictors of intelligence, a different dimension was a more consistent predictor of intelligence: approach/withdrawal. Hence, bidirectional relations between temperament and intelligence were evident, although the specific dimensions of temperament emerging as correlates varied depending on the directionality: earlier approach/withdrawal was a consistent predictor of intelligence, although early intelligence was a consistent predictor of persistence-task orientation.

Early assessments of family environment were not as consistent in predicting the temperament of children within the family as early child temperament was in predicting subsequent family environment. Hence, bidirectional relationships

between temperament and outcomes are evident, although the pattern is not necessarily a reciprocal one. Different temperament dimensions emerged as precursors
and sequelae and the magnitude of relation was not equal in degree when variables
were reversed as predictors and outcomes.

Evidence that Temperament is a Useful Construct Beyond Parent-Child Interactions/Relationship

Some have questioned the validity of parent reports of temperament beyond
indicating the parents' perception of the quality of interactions or relationships
with their child. Evidence from the FLS provides strong evidence that parent
ratings of temperament show conceptually meaningful patterns of relation with
aspects of child development measured by other informants, in developmental
contexts outside the home, across time, and across methods. The most extensive
evidence supporting the external validity of parent reports of temperament are
those regarding the child's performance in the academic setting.

During the elementary years, parent reports of children's behavioral styles
related at moderate levels to teacher reports of children's classroom behavior and
adjustment. Teacher reports of children's classroom behavior (the extent to which
the child worked hard, behaved appropriately, was learning, and was happy) related
pervasively and to moderate magnitudes with parent reports of their children's
temperament. The child's persistence/attention span was an especially consistent
and moderately strong correlate; however, the child's adaptability, distractibility,
predictability and also negative mood, activity level, and intensity also related to
teachers' reports of classroom functioning.

Multiple regression analyses, entering parent ratings of temperament after
child intelligence in predicting teacher ratings of classroom behavior, also attested
to the external validity of parent ratings of children's temperament. Even after
controlling for children's intelligence (which explained 9 to 41% of the variance in
teacher ratings of children's classroom behavior), parent ratings of temperament
significantly improved the prediction of classroom behavior. For example, the
strongest multiple correlation was observed between the predictor variables of child
intelligence and temperament and the criterion variable of how much the child was
learning. Results showed that including temperament in the prediction equation
increased the variance explained from 41% to 58% (adjusted for shrinkage). Even
larger increments in the variance explained occurred in the criterion variables
reflecting the teacher's assessment of how hard the child worked in class and the
appropriateness of the child's behavior. On these variables, child temperament
increased the variance explained beyond that explained by child intelligence by
26 and 27%, respectively. The fourth aspect of classroom behavior, how happy the
child was compared to other pupils, was also predicted by child intelligence (which

accounted for 9% of the variance) and child temperament; child temperament explained an additional 20% of the variation in teacher ratings of pupil happiness. Hence, parent ratings of child temperament were predictive of teacher ratings of the child's classroom behavior and increased the variance explained beyond child intelligence between approximately 15 and 30 percent, depending upon the specific classroom behavior. These findings are particularly impressive given that children participating in the FLS were not selected from particular classrooms, but instead attended a wide range of schools across diverse geographic locales.

Parent ratings of child temperament also related across time to teacher reports of externalizing behavior problems and concurrently with teacher reports of both internalizing and externalizing behavior problems. Ratings of temperament assessed in the preschool years predicted 7% of the variance in teacher reports of externalizing problems during the elementary school years. Parent assessments of temperament and teacher reports and internalizing and externalizing behavior problems showed an overlap of 31% and 53% of the variance, respectively.

Parent ratings of temperament also related to other aspects of children's functioning than behavioral adjustment when assessed via different informants or in different contexts. For example, parent reports of temperament related to both standardized tests and teacher ratings of student achievement during the elementary school years. During adolescence, parent reports of their child's temperament predicted their child's cumulative high school grade point average. Even when entered after intelligence, temperament captured 17% of the variance in cumulative high school grade point average, increasing the adjusted multiple correlation from .61 to .73. Additionally, parent reports of child temperament from earlier eras also increased the amount of variance explained in cumulative grade point average beyond that explained by child intelligence. Hence, parent ratings of temperament related to both behavioral and academic achievement when assessed concurrently and also, to a lesser extent, when temperament ratings preceded behavior and achievement outcomes. The external validity of parent ratings of their children's temperament is supported by data collected across informant, across setting, and across methods. These data support the validity of parent reports of their children's temperament as reflecting more than just the quality of the parent-child relationship.

Temperament in the Classroom

The aforementioned results detailing the relation of temperament to school entry and progress through grades, academic achievement, classroom behavior and adjustment, and, during adolescence, student self-perceptions of academic competence and academic intrinsic motivation, reinforce and amplify the call of previous researchers, including Keogh (2003), Rothbart and Jones (1998), and Carey and

McDevitt (1995), for temperament to be included in professional development and teacher preparation programs. Additionally, writing from an applied clinical perspective, Kurcinka (1990) discussed interventions for parents and teachers to incorporate when working with temperamentally "spirited" children.

Additionally, there has been widespread renewed interest in school readiness and its assessment over the past decade (e.g., U.S. Department of Education, National Center for Education Statistics, 2001). Data from the FLS suggest that child temperament may be a useful indicator to include in the set of predictors of readiness for school, particularly adaptability.

Temperament-Environment Interactions

Analyses reported herein focused almost exclusively on examining the main effects of temperament rather than how temperament interacts with other child or environmental variables. In chapter 7, however, an interaction between infant temperament and childhood family environment in explaining externalizing behavior problems at age 8 was replicated consistently across informants. Results clearly supported the notion that the externalizing behavior problem scores of children depended upon both the child's infant temperament and the family environment in which the child lived. Difficult infant temperament was associated with higher behavior problem scores at age 8 when family environment was characterized as higher in conflict; infants with difficult temperament whose family environment was characterized as lower in conflict exhibited significant lower behavior problem scores—levels more similar to those of children who had been low or intermediate in fussy/difficult/demanding temperament as infants. Although initially analyzed by comparing mean behavior problems of groups created by a median split (family conflict) and analysis of highest, centermost, and lowest quartiles (infant temperament), similar results were replicated treating these predictors as continuous variables using a regression approach. Depending upon the sources (informants) of data examined, the interaction between infant temperament and family conflict explained an additional 4% to 14% in the variation of externalizing behavior problems. Hence, identifying variables that moderate relations between temperament and criterion variables may markedly improve our ability to understand the ways that temperament is related to child/adolescent development.

Temperament as an Asset and Liability in Development

Evidence that temperament can serve as both an asset and a liability in development during childhood and adolescence was presented in chapter 8. Although the focus in the research literature as well as in publications directed toward parents and applied professionals has been children with more challenging aspects of temperament, data from the FLS demonstrated evidence that infants low on challenging temperamental characteristics subsequently enjoyed more positive developmental and environmental outcomes that did infants who were intermediate or high on aspects of temperament that parents find challenging (fussy/difficult/demanding, slow adaptability, resistance to control, and/or unsociability). Comparing the domains investigated herein, infants with more positive temperament more often enjoyed significantly higher intelligence and more positive family environments (including, for example, greater family cohesiveness and intellectual-cultural orientation).

Evidence of temperament acting as a developmental liability, in which infants who were high on challenging temperament subsequently exhibited compromised development compared to their cohort comparisons with intermediate infant temperament scores, occurred primarily in the areas of academic achievement and behavior problem scores. However, the behavioral adjustment outcomes of infant temperament were most frequently categorized as a generalized risk/protective factor, wherein the extreme groups differed from each other but neither differed from the intermediate infant temperament group. The temperamental outcomes of infant temperament were approximately evenly divided among the asset, liability, and generalized risk/protective categories.

In a clinical setting, it may be useful to identify both temperamental strengths/assets as well as temperamental liabilities/risks during the initial assessment. The identification of temperament assets may prove a useful starting point for building on the strengths of children to meet current and future stresses. As noted by Carey and McDevitt (1995), the identification of temperamental liabilities/risks when concerns have emerged may point to additional intervention strategies that can be implemented in concert with parents, caregivers, teachers, or the child/adolescent directly.

Long-Term Developmental Sequelae of Temperament Assessed in Infancy

Analyzing the developmental and environmental consequences of our earliest measure of temperament, the Infant Characteristics Questionnaire collected at 1.5 years, using an extreme groups comparison approach revealed substantial evidence of both short- and long-term sequelae of specific aspects of infant temperament. The developmental trajectories of children in the low, intermediate, and high challenging infant temperament groups differed across childhood and throughout adolescence in the behavioral, intellectual, and academic achievement domains; the nature of their home and family environment also diverged in the short term and continued to show differences throughout at least age 17 years. Additionally, differences were evident across informant and/or across context. Variations in infant temperament were followed by developmental and environmental differences. Although these longitudinal data are not sufficient to conclude that variations in infant temperament caused these different trajectories, they can provide a rich description of the developmental course that infants varying in temperament followed throughout childhood and adolescence. We focus this description on the sequelae of fussy/difficult/demanding aspect of challenging infant temperament; to facilitate the description, we use the term "fussy/difficult temperament" as a moniker for the high fussy/difficult/demanding temperament group and the term "easy temperament" for the low fussy/difficult/demanding temperament group.

Babies whose temperament was characterized as most fussy/difficult had home environments during the infancy and preschool years that were less varied and stimulating and also lower in pride, affection, and warmth compared to babies with the easiest temperament. During childhood and/or adolescence, the family environments of the most fussy/difficult versus easiest infant temperament groups differed on the level of conflict, cohesion, and intellectual-cultural orientation in the family, with the easiest infant temperament group experiencing less conflict, greater family cohesion, and higher levels of intellectual-cultural orientation compared to those who had been most fussy/difficult as infants. During adolescence, those who had been easiest in temperament as infants experienced family environments that were also less conflictual than adolescents who were, as infants, in the intermediate temperament group. Likewise, those adolescents who had been especially easy-going in temperament as infants had parents who reported more positive parent-child relations in the areas of satisfaction with the parental role, involvement, and limit-setting; these adolescents also rated their parent-child relations as more positive. Hence, different trajectories, both short-term and long-term, were evident as a function of fussy/difficult infant temperament; these trajectories indicated home/family environments generally considered as more favorable for those who had, as infants, been characterized as less fussy/difficult. It was more often the case that temperamental easiness in infancy was associated with more auspicious family environment and parent relations during adolescence than the case that fussy/difficult temperament was associated with less favorable environment/relations compared to the intermediate infant temperament group (which we treated as a baseline comparison group).

Long-term differences in trajectory were also evident in the domain of behavioral adjustment, where, especially during the preschool and childhood years, babies who had been the fussiest/most temperamentally difficult were subsequently those with the highest average behavior problem scores, often showing significantly higher behavior problem scores than those who had been in the intermediate temperament group as infants. By adolescence, those who had been easiest in infant temperament also showed significantly lower behavior problem scores than the baseline comparison group. Hence, fussy/difficult infant temperament was associated with significantly higher behavior problem scores over several years, and easy infant temperament, in late adolescence, was associated with significantly lower levels of behavior problems than those in the baseline comparison group. These data mirror those observed in the family environment domain.

In the intellectual domain, adolescents who had, as infants, been particularly easy-going in their temperament were also advantaged. On both the WISC-III and WAIS-R tests administered during the adolescent era, those who had been in the easiest infant temperament group scored significantly higher than the baseline comparison group, with differences in the magnitude of 7 IQ points. At age 17, their average math score on the Woodcock-Johnson was 12 percentage points higher than the baseline comparison group.

Although challenging temperament has been reported in a limited number of studies to operate in some settings to protect or enhance development, this trend was not observed in this cohort consisting of children from a wide range of middle class families. In our sample, infants with particularly easy temperament enjoyed developmental advantage; the trajectory of infants with particularly challenging temperament was indicative of compromised normative progress in development, not superior.

Temperament from Infancy through Adolescence

At this point, we do not know what trajectories the infants in the easy, intermediate, and fussy/difficult temperament groups will follow beyond their high school completion. However, we can conclude that as the FLS cohort begins its transition from adolescence to early adulthood, those with easier temperaments as infants subsequently showed more optimal development across behavioral, intellectual, and academic domains. They had a family environment that was more stimulating and cohesive, had mothers who were more satisfied with being a parent, and enjoyed more positive relations with their parents during adolescence.

Scientific, clinical, and lay communities have focused a considerable amount of attention on aspects of temperament associated with compromised adjustment and development, and data from the FLS corroborate that there are temperament traits that are clearly associated with less optimal development. However, data from the FLS also show that specific aspects of early temperament were associated with more optimal developmental outcomes, benefits that were not necessarily evident in childhood but that emerged during the adolescent era.

Individual differences in temperament have clear developmental and environmental concomitants across both the short- and long-term, perhaps due in part to the impressive stability observed in numerous temperament dimensions from preschool through childhood and into adolescence. The relation between temperament and developmental outcomes is sometimes dependent upon other child or family characteristics, as in the case of externalizing behavior problems, which were significantly higher when difficult infant temperament was paired with a family environment characterized as higher in conflict. In virtually every instance, however, when significant effects were observed it was the case that youngsters with what have been widely considered as more temperamentally challenging characteristics (slower adaptability, more negative mood, more withdrawing, less persistent, etc.) experienced less optimal home/family environmental circumstances and also less optimal development than those who were more moderate in temperament and/or those with extremely positive temperamental characteristics (quick adaptability, positive mood, persistence, approach to novelty, etc.). In contrast, fully one-quarter of the findings of significant long-term sequelae of infant temperament showed that infants with the easiest temperament characteristics showed superior development compared to either those with the most challenging temperament or those in the average group, with sequelae spanning over a 15-year interval.

Evidently, the prophecy in the fortune cookie at the beginning of this book was right: "Your good nature will bring you much happiness."

References

Achenbach, T. M. (1991a). *Manual for the Child Behavior Checklist and 1991 Profile*. Burlington, VT: University of Vermont Department of Psychiatry.

Achenbach, T. M. (1991b). *Manual for the Teacher's Report Form and 1991 Profile*. Burlington, VT: University of Vermont Department of Psychiatry.

Achenbach, T. M. (1991c). *Manual for the Youth Self-Report and 1991 Profile*. Burlington, VT: University of Vermont Department of Psychiatry.

Achenbach, T. M., Howell, C. T., McConaughy, S. H. (1987). Child/adolescent behavioral and emotional problems: Implications of cross-informant correlations for situational specificity. *Psychological Bulletin, 101*, 213–232.

Ahadi, S. A., & Rothbart, M. K. (1994). Temperament, development, and the Big Five. In C. F. Halverson, G. A. Kohnstamm, & R. P. Martin (Eds.), *The developing structure of temperament and personality from infancy to adulthood* (pp. 189–207). Hillsdale, NJ: Lawrence Erlbaum Associates.

Andersson, H. W., & Sommerfelt, K. (1999). Infant temperamental factors as predictors of problem behavior and IQ at age 5 years: Interactional effects of biological and social risk factors. *Child Study Journal, 29*, 207–226.

Angleitner, A., & Ostendorf, F. (1994). Temperament and the Big Five factors of personality. In C. F. Halverson, G. A. Kohnstamm, & R. P. Martin (Eds.), *The developing structure of temperament and personality from infancy to adulthood* (pp. 69–90). Hillsdale, NJ: Lawrence Erlbaum.

Angleitner, A., & Riemann, R. (1991). What can we learn from the discussion of personality questionnaires for the construction of temperament inventories? In J. Strelau & A. Angleitner (Eds.), *Explorations in temperament: International perspectives on theory and measurement* (pp. 191–204). New York: Plenum Press.

Baron, R. M., & Kenny, D. A. (1986). The moderator-mediator variable distinction in social psychological research: Conceptual, strategic, and statistical considerations. *Journal of Personality and Social Psychology, 51*, 1173–1182.

Barron, A. P., & Earls, F. (1984). The relation of temperament and social factors to behavior problems in three-year-old children. *Journal of Child Psychology and Psychiatry, 25*, 23–33.

Basic Behavioral Science Task Force of the National Advisory Mental Health Council. (1996). Vulnerability and reslience. *American Psychologist, 51*, 22–28.

Bates, J. E. (1989). Concepts and measures of temperament. In G. A. Kohnstamm, J. E. Bates, & M. K. Rothbart (Eds.), *Temperament in childhood* (pp. 3–26). New York: John Wiley & Sons.

Bates, J. E. (1990). Conceptual and empirical linkages between temperament and behavior problems: A commentary on the Sanson, Prior, and Kyrios Study. *Merrill-Palmer Quarterly, 36*, 193–199.

Bates, J. E. (1980). The concept of difficult temperament. *Merrill-Palmer Quarterly, 26*, 299–319.

Bates, J. E., Freeland, C. A. B., & Lounsbury, M. L. (1979). Measurement of infant difficultness. *Child Development, 50*, 794–803.

Bates, J. E., Maslin, C. A., & Frankel, K. A. (1985). Attachment security, mother-child interaction, and temperament as predictors of behavior-problem ratings at age three years. *Monographs of the Society for Research in Child Development, 50*, 167–193.

Bates, J. E., & McFayden-Ketchum, S. (2000). Temperament and parent-child relations as interacting factors in children's behavioral adjustment. In V. J. Molfese & D. Molfese (Eds.), *Temperament and personality development across the lifespan* (pp. 141–176). Mahwah, NJ: Lawrence Erlbaum.

Bates, J. E., Pettit, G. S., Dodge, K. A., & Ridge, B. (1998). Interaction of temperamental resistance to control and restrictive parenting in the development of externalizing behavior. *Developmental Psychology, 34*, 982–995.

Bates, J. E. & Wachs, T. D. (Eds.) (1994). *Temperament: Individual differences at the interface of biology and behavior.* Washington, D.C.: American Psychological Association.

Bathurst, K., & Gottfried, A. W. (1987). Untestable subjects in child development research: Developmental implications. *Child Development, 58*, 1135–1144.

Bayley, N. (1969). *Bayley Scales of Infant Development.* New York: Psychological Corp.

Beck, C. T. (1996). A meta-analysis of the relationship between postpartum depression and infant temperament. *Nursing Research, 45*, 225–230.

Behar, L., & Stringfield, S. (1974). A behavior rating scale for the preschool child. *Developmental Psychology, 10*, 601–610.

Benson, J. B., Cherny, S. S., Haith, M. M., & Fulker, D. W. (1993). Rapid assessment of infant predictors of IQ: Midtwin-midparent analyses. *Developmental Psychology, 29*, 434–447.

Bernstein, G. A., Borchardt, C. M., & Perwien, A. R. (1996). Anxiety disorders in children and adolescents: A review of the past 10 years. *Journal of the American Academy of Child and Adolescent Psychiatry, 35*, 1110–1119.

Blum, J. S., & Mehrabian, A. (1999). Personality and temperament correlates of marital satisfaction. *Journal of Personality, 67*, 93–125.

Bulik, C. M., Sullivan, P. F., Carter, F. A., & Joyce, P. R. (1997). Lifetime comorbidity of alcohol dependence in women with bulimia nervosa. *Addictive Behaviors, 22*, 437–446.

Burns, G. L., & Patterson, D. R. (1990). Conduct problem behaviors in a stratified sample of children and adolescents: New standardization data on the Eyberg Child Behavior Inventory. *Psychological Assessment, 2*, 391–397.

Burns, G. L., Patterson, D. R., Nussbaum, B. R., & Parker, C. M. (1991). Disruptive behaviors in an outpatient pediatric population: Additional standardization data on the Eyberg Child Behavior Inventory. *Psychological Assessment, 3*, 202–207.

Buss, A. H. (1991). The EAS theory of temperament. In J. Strelau & A. Angleitner (Eds.), *Explorations in temperament: International perspectives on theory and measurement* (pp. 43–60). New York: Plenum Press.

Buss, A. H., & Plomin, R. (1984). *Temperament: Early developing personality traits.* Hillsdale, NJ: Lawrence Erlbaum Associates.

Cameron, J. R., Hansen, R., & Rosen, D. (1991). Preventing behavioral problems in infancy through temperament assessment and parental support programs within health maintenance organization. In J. H. Johnson & S. B. Johnson (Eds.), *Advances in child health psychology.* University of Florida Press: Gainesville.

Cameron, J. R., & Rice, D. C. (1986). Developing anticipatory guidance programs based on early assessment of infant temperament: Two tests of a prevention model. *Journal of Pediatric Psychology, 11*, 221–234.

Caldwell, B. M., & Bradley, R. H. (1984). *Administration manual (revised edition) of the Home Observation for Measurement of the Environment.* Little Rock: University of Arkansas.

Carey, W. B. (with Jablow, M. M.) (1997). *Understanding your child's temperament.* New York: Macmillan.

Carey, W. B., & McDevitt, S. C. (1995). *Coping with children's temperament: A guide for professionals.* New York: Basic Books.

Caspi, A. (1998). Personality development across the life course. In W. Damon & N. Eisenberg (Eds.), *Handbook of child psychology, Vol. 3: Social, emotional, and personality development* (5th ed., pp. 311–388). New York: John Wiley & Sons.

Caspi, A., Begg, D., Dickson, N., Harrington, H., Langley, J., Moffitt, T. E., et al. (1997). Personality differences predict health-risk behaviors in young adulthood: Evidence from a longitudinal study. *Journal of Personality and Social Psychology, 73*, 1052–1063.

Caspi, A., Henry, B., McGee, R. O., Moffitt, T. E., & Silva, P. A. (1995). Temperamental origins of child and adolescent behavior problems: From age three to age fifteen. *Child Development, 66*, 55–68.

Chess, S., & Thomas, A. (1984). *Origins and evolution of behavior disorders*. New York: Brunner/Mazel.

Chess, S., & Thomas, A. (1986). *Temperament in clinical practice*. New York: Guilford Press.

Chess, S., & Thomas, A. (1996). *Temperament: Theory and practice*. New York: Brunner/Mazel.

Collis, J. M., & Messick, S. (Eds.) (2001). *Intelligence and personality: Bridging the gap in theory and measurement*. Mahwah, NJ: Lawrence Erlbaum.

Costa, P. T., & McCrae, R. R. (1985). *The NEO Personality Inventory manual*. Odessa, FL: Psychological Assessment Resources.

Costa, P. T., & McCrae, R. R. (1989). *NEO PI/FFI manual supplement*. Odessa, FL: Psychological Assessment Resources.

Costa, P. T., & McCrae, R. R. (1988). Personality in adulthood: A six-year longitudinal study of self-reports and spouse ratings on the NEO Personality Inventory. *Journal of Personality and Social Psychology, 54*, 853–863.

Crockenberg, S. B. (1986). Are temperamental differences in babies associated with predictable differences in care giving? In J. V. Lerner & R. M. Lerner (Eds.), *Temperament and social interaction in infants and children* (pp. 53–73). San Francisco: Jossey-Bass.

Czeschlik, T. (1993). General intelligence, temperament, and the Matching Familiar Figures Test. *European Journal of Personality, 7*, 379–386.

Daniels, D., Plomin, R., & Greenhalgh, J. (1984). Correlates of difficult temperament in infancy. *Child Development, 55*, 1184–1194.

Dean, R. S., & Steffen, J. E. (1984). Direct and indirect pediatric screening measures. *Journal of Pediatric Psychology, 9*, 65–75.

DeVries, M. W. (1984). Temperament and infant mortality among the Masai of East Africa. *American Journal of Psychiatry, 141*, 1189–1194.

DiPietro, J. A., Hodgson, D. M., Costigan, K. A., & Johnson, T. R. B. (1996). Fetal antecedents of infant temperament. *Child Development, 67*, 2568–2583.

Eaton, W. O. (1994). Temperament, development, and the five-factor model: Lessons from activity level. In C. F. Haverson, G. A. Kohnstamm, & R. P. Martin (Eds.), *The developing structure of personality from infancy to adulthood* (pp. 173–187). Hillsdale, NJ: Lawrence Erlbaum Associates.

Earls, F. (1981). Temperamental characteristics and behavior problems in three-year-old children. *Journal of Nervous and Mental Disease, 169*, 367–373.

Eisenberg, N., Shepard, S. A., Fabes, R. A., Murphy, B. C., & Guthrie, I. K. (1998). Shyness and children's emotionality, regulation, and coping: Contemporaneous, longitudinal, and across-context relations. *Child Development, 69*, 767–790.

Epstein, S. (1979). The stability of behavior: I. On predicting most of the people much of the time. *Journal of Personality and Social Psychology, 37*, 1097–1126.

Escalona, S. A. (1968). *The roots of individuality: Normal patterns of development in infancy*. Chicago: Aldine.

Eyberg, S. M. (1980). Eyberg Child Behavior Inventory. *Journal of Clinical Child Psychology, 9*, 29.

Fabes, R. A., Shepard, S. A., Guthrie, I. K., & Martin, C. L. (1997). Roles of temperamental arousal and gender-segregated play in young children's social adjustment. *Developmental Psychology, 33*, 693–702.

Fagan, J. (1990). The interaction between child sex and temperament in predicting behavior problems of preschool-age children in day care. *Early Child Development and Care, 59*, 1–9.

Fullard, W., McDevitt, S. C., & Carey, W. B. (1984). Assessing temperament in one-to three-year-old children. *Journal of Pediatric Psychology, 9*, 205–217.

Garrison, W. T., & Earls, F. J. (1987). *Temperament and child psychopathology.* Newbury Park, CA: Sage.

Garrison, W., Earls, F., & Kindlon, D. (1984). Temperament characteristics in the third year of life and behavioral adjustment at school entry. *Journal of Clinical Child Psychology, 13*, 298–303.

Gerard, A. B. (1994). *Parent Child Relationship Inventory (PCRI) manual.* Los Angeles: Western Psychological Services.

Gibbs, M. V., Reeves, D., & Cunningham, C. C. (1987). The application of temperament questionnaires to a British sample: Issues of reliability and validity. *Journal of Child Psychology and Psychiatry and Allied Disciplines, 28*, 61–77.

Glutting, J. J., & Oakland, T. (1992). *Guide to the assessment of test session behavior for the WISC-III and WIAT (Manual).* San Antonio, TX: The Psychological Corp.

Goldsmith, H. H., Buss, A. H., Plomin, R., Rothbart, M. K., Thomas, A., Chess, S., Hinde, R. A., & McCall, R. B. (1987). Roundtable: What is temperament? Four approaches. *Child Development, 58*, 505–529.

Goldsmith, H. H., & Gottesman, I. I. (1981). Origins of variation in behavioral style: A longitudinal study of temperament in young twins. *Child Development, 52*, 91–103.

Gordon, B. N. (1981). Child temperament and adult behavior: An exploration of "goodness of fit." *Child Psychiatry and Human Development, 11*, 167–178.

Gottfried, A. E. (1985). Academic intrinsic motivation in elementary and junior high school students. *Journal of Educational Psychology, 77*, 631–645.

Gottfried, A. E. (1986). *Children's Academic Intrinsic Motivation Inventory.* Odessa, FL: Psychological Assessment Resources.

Gottfried, A. E. (1990). Academic intrinsic motivation in young elementary school children. *Journal of Educational Psychology, 82*, 525–538.

Gottfried, A. E., Bathurst, K., & Gottfried, A. W. (1994). Role of maternal and dual-earner employment status in child development. In A. E. Gottfried & A. W. Gottfried (Eds.), *Redefining families: Implications for children's development* (pp. 55–97). New York: Plenum.

Gottfried, A. E., Fleming, J. S., & Gottfried, A. W. (2001). Continuity of academic intrinsic motivation from childhood through late adolescence: A longitudinal study. *Journal of Educational Psychology, 93*, 3–13.

Gottfried, A. E., Fleming, J. S., & Gottfried, A. W. (1994). Role of parental motivational practices in children's academic intrinsic motivation and achievement. *Journal of Educational Psychology, 86*, 104–113.

Gottfried, A. E. & Gottfried, A. W. (1996). A longitudinal study of academic intrinsic motivation in intellectually gifted children: Childhood through early adolescence. *Gifted Child Quarterly, 40*, 179–183.

Gottfried, A. E., & Gottfried, A. W. (1994). *Redefining families: Implications for children's development.* New York: Plenum.

Gottfried, A. E., Gottfried, A. W., & Bathurst, K. (2002). Maternal and dual-earner employment status and parenting. In M. H. Bornstein (Ed.), *Handbook of parenting: Vol. 2: Biology and ecology of parenting* (2nd ed., pp. 207–229). Mahwah, NJ: Lawrence Erlbaum.

Gottfried, A. E., Gottfried, A. W., & Bathurst, K. (1995). Maternal and dual-earner employment status and parenting. In M. H. Bornstein (Ed.), *Handbook of parenting: Vol. 2: Biology and ecology of parenting* (pp. 139–160). Mahwah, NJ: Lawrence Erlbaum.

Gottfried, A. E., Gottfried, A. W., & Bathurst, K. (1988). Maternal employment, family environment, and children's development: Infancy through the school years. In A. E. Gottfried and A. W. Gottfried (Eds.), *Maternal employment and children's development: Longitudinal research* (pp. 11–58). New York: Plenum.

Gottfried, A. E., Gottfried, A. W., Bathurst, K., & Killian, C. (1999). Maternal and dual-earner employment: Family environment, adaptations, and the developmental impingement perspective. In M. E. Lamb (Ed.), *Parenting and child development in "nontraditional" families* (pp. 15–37). Mahwah, NJ: Lawrence Erlbaum.

Gottfried, A. W. (1973). Intellectual consequences of perinatal anoxia. *Psychological Bulletin, 80*, 231–242.

Gottfried, A. W., & Gottfried, A. E. (1984). Home environment and cognitive development in young children of middle-socioeconomic-status families. In A. W. Gottfried (Ed.), *Home environment and early cognitive development: Longitudinal research* (pp. 57–115). New York: Academic Press.

Gottfried, A. W. (1985). Measures of socioeconomic status in child development research: Data and recommendations. *Merrill-Palmer Quarterly, 31*, 85–92.

Gottfried, A. W., Gottfried, A. E., Bathurst, K., & Guerin, D. W. (1994). *Gifted IQ: Early developmental aspects.* New York: Plenum.

Gottfried, A. W., Gottfried, A. E., Bathurst, K., Guerin, D. W., & Parramore, P. (2003). Socioeconomic status in children's development and family environment: Infancy through adolescence. In M. H. Bornstein & R. H. Bradley (Eds.), *Socioeconomic status, parenting, and child development.* Mahwah, NJ: Lawrence Erlbaum.

Gottfried, A. W., Guerin, D. W., Spencer, J. E., & Meyer, C. (1983). Concurrent validity of the Minnesota Child Development Inventory in a nonclinical sample. *Journal of Consulting and Clinical Psychology, 51*, 643–644.

Gottfried, A. W., Guerin, D. W., Spencer, J. E., & Meyer, C. (1984). Validity of Minnesota Child Development Inventory in screening young children's developmental status. *Consulting and Clinical Psychology, 51*, 643–644.

Grych, J. H., & Fincham, F. (1990). Marital conflict and children's adjustment: A cognitive-contextual framework. *Psychological Bulletin, 108*, 267–290.

Guerin, D., & Gottfried, A. W. (1987). Minnesota Child Development Inventories: Predictors of intelligence, achievement, and adaptability. *Journal of Pediatric Psychology, 12*, 595–609.

Guerin, D. W., & Gottfried, A. W. (1994a). Developmental stability and change in parent reports of temperament: A ten-year longitudinal investigation from infancy through preadolescence. *Merrill-Palmer Quarterly, 40*, 334–355.

Guerin, D. W., & Gottfried, A. W. (1994b). Temperamental consequences of infant difficultness. *Infant Behavior and Development, 17*, 413–421.

Guerin, D. W., Gottfried, A. W., Oliver, P. H., & Thomas, C. W. (1994). Temperament and school functioning during early adolescence. *Journal of Early Adolescence, 14*, 200–225.

Guerin, D. W., Gottfried, A. W., & Thomas, C. W. (1997). Difficult temperament and behaviour problems: A longitudinal study from 1.5 to 12 years. *International Journal of Behavioural Development, 21*, 71–90.

Guerin, D. W., Griffin, J. R., Gottfried, A. W., & Christenson, G. N. (1993a). Concurrent validity and screening efficiency of The Dyslexia Screener. *Psychological Assessment, 5*, 369–373.

Guerin, D. W., Griffin, J. R., Gottfried, A. W., & Christenson, G. N. (1993b). Dyslexia subtypes and severity levels: Are there gender differences? *Optometry & Vision Science, 70*, 348–351.

Guerin, D. W., Sandwell, J. C., & Lovil, L. T. (1998). Kindergarten policies: Another look at the research. *Kindergarten Education: Theory, Research, and Practice, 3*, 29–45.

Hagekull, B. (1994). Infant temperament and early childhood functioning: Possible relations to the five-factor model. In C. F. Haverson, G. A. Kohnstamm, & R. P. Martin (Eds.), *The developing structure of personality from infancy to adulthood* (pp. 227–240). Hillsdale, NJ: Lawrence Erlbaum Associates.

Hagekull, B., & Bohlin, G. (1998). Preschool temperament and environmental factors related to the five-factor model of personality in middle childhood. *Merrill-Palmer Quarterly, 44*, 194–215.

Harrington, D., Black, M. M., Starr, R. H., Jr., & Dubowitz, H. (1998). Child neglect: Relation to child temperament and family context. *American Journal of Orthopsychiatry, 68*, 108–116.

Hart, D., Hofmann, V., Edelstein, W., & Keller, M. (1997). The relation of childhood personality types to adolescent behavior and development: A longitudinal study of Icelandic children. *Developmental Psychology, 33*, 195–205.

Hegvik, R. L., McDevitt, S. C., & Carey, W. B. (1982). The Middle Childhood Temperament Questionnaire. *Developmental and Behavioral Pediatrics, 3*, 197–200.

Henry, B., Caspi, A., Moffitt, T., & Silva, P. (1996). Temperamental and familial predictors of violent and nonviolent criminal convictions. *Developmental Psychology, 32*, 614–623.

Hofstee, W. K. B. (1991). The concepts of personality and temperament. In J. Strelau & A. Angleitner (Eds.), *Explorations in temperament: International perspectives on theory and measurement* (pp. 177–188). New York: Plenum Press.

Hollingshead, A. B. (1975). *Four Factor Index of Social Status.* Unpublished manuscript, Yale University, Department of Sociology.

Honjo, S., Mizuno, R., Ajiki, M., Suzuki, A., Nagata, M., Goto, Y., et al. (1998). Infant temperament and child-rearing stress. *Early Human Development, 51*, 123–135.

Hubert, N. C., Wachs, T. D., Peters-Martin, P., & Gandour, M. J. (1982). The study of early temperament: Measurement and conceptual issues. *Child Development, 53*, 571–600.

Huttunen, M. O., & Nyman, G. (1982). On the continuity, change, and clinical value of infant temperament in a prospective epidemiological study. In R. Porter & G. M. Collins (Eds.), *Temperamental differences in infants and young children.* London: Pitman.

Ireton, H., & Thwing, E. (1972–1974). *Manual for the Minnesota Child Development Inventory.* Minneapolis: Behavioral Science Systems.

Ireton, H., & Thwing, E. (1979). *Manual for the Minnesota Preschool Inventory.* Minneapolis: Behavioral Science Systems.

Ireton, H., Thwing, E., & Currier, S. K. (1977). Minnesota Child Development Inventory: Identification of children with developmental disorders. *Journal of Pediatric Psychology, 2*, 18–22.

Jansen, R. E., Fitzgerald, H. E., Harn, H. P., & Zucker, R. A. (1995). Pathways into risk: Temperament and behavior problems in three- to five-year-old sons of alcoholics. *Alcoholism: Clinical and Experimental Research, 19*, 501–509.

Jastak, S., & Wilkinson, G. S. (1984). *Wide Range Achievement Test – Revised.* Wilmington, DE: Jastak Associates.

Jewsuwan, R., Luster, T., & Kostelnik, M. (1993). The relation between parents' perceptions of temperament and children's adjustment to preschool. *Early Childhood Research Quarterly, 8*, 33–51.

John, O. P. (1989). Towards a taxonomy of personality descriptors. In D. M. Buss & N. Cantor (Eds.), *Personality psychology: Recent trends and emerging directions* (pp. 261–271). New York: Springer.

John, O. P., Caspi, A., Robins, R. W., Moffitt, T. E., & Stouthamer-Loeber, M. (1994). The "little five:" Exploring the nomological network of the five-factor model of personality in adolescent boys. *Child Development, 65*, 160–178.

John, O. P. (1990). The "big five" factor taxonomy: Dimensions of personality in the natural language and in questionnaires. In L. A. Pervin (Ed.), *Handbook of personality: Theory and research* (pp. 66–100). New York: Guilford.

Kagan, J. (with Snidman, N., Arcus, D., & Reznick, J. S.) (1994). *Galen's prophecy: Temperament in human nature.* New York: BasicBooks.

Kagan, J., Reznick, J. S., & Snidman, N. (1989). Issues in the study of temperament. In G. A. Kohnstamm, J. E. Bates, & M. K. Rothbart (Eds.), *Temperament in childhood* (pp. 133–144). New York: John Wiley & Sons.

Kagan, J., Snidman, N., & Arcus, D. (1998). The value of extreme groups. In R. B. Cairns, L. R. Bergman, & J. Kagan (Eds.), *Methods and models for studying the individual.* Thousand Oaks, CA: Sage.

Katainen, S., Raeikkoenen, K., & Keltikangas-Jaervinen, L. (1998). Development of temperament: Childhood temperament and the mother's childrearing attitudes as predictors of adolescent temperament at a 9-yr follow-up study. *Journal of Research on Adolescence, 8*, 485–509.

Kaufman, A. S., & Kaufman, N. L. (1983). *Kaufman Assessment Battery for Children: Adminstration and scoring manual.* Circle Pines, MN: American Guidance Service.

Kawaguchi, M., Welsh, D. P., Powers, S. I., & Rostosky, S. S. (1998). Mothers, fathers, sons, and daughters: Temperament, gender, and adolescent-parent relationships. *Merrill-Palmer Quarterly, 44*, 77–96.

Keogh, B. K. (1989). Applying temperament research to school. In G. A. Kohnstamm, J. E. Bates, & M. K. Rothbart (Eds.), *Temperament in childhood* (pp. 437–450). New York: Wiley & Sons.

Keogh, B. K. (1982). Children's temperament and teachers' decisions. In R. Porter & G. M. Collins (Eds.), *Temperamental differences in infants and young children* (pp. 269–285). London: Pitman Books.

Keogh, B. K. (1986). Temperament and schooling: Meaning of "goodness of fit". Lerner, J. V. & R. M. Lerner (Eds.) *Temperament and social interaction in infants and children* (pp. 89–108). San Francisco: Jossey-Bass.

Keogh, B. K. (2003). *Temperament in the classroom: Understanding individual differences.* Baltimore, MD: Paul H. Brookes.

Klein, H. A. (1995). Self-perception in late adolescence: An interactionist perspective. *Adolescence, 30*, 579–591.

Kochanska, G. (1998). Mother-child relationship, child fearfulness, and emerging attachment: A short-term longitudinal study. *Developmental Psychology, 34*, 480–490.

Kochanska, G. (1997). Multiple pathways to conscience for children with different temperaments: From toddlerhood to age 5. *Developmental Psychology, 33*, 228–240.

Kurcinka, M. S. (1991). *Raising your spirited child.* New York: Harper.

Lanthier, R. P., & Bates, J. E. (1997, April). *Do early temperament and parenting characteristics predict personality in adolescence?* Paper presented at the biennial meeting of the Society for Research, Child Development, Washington, DC.

Lee, C. L., & Bates, J. E. (1985). Mother-child interaction at age two years and perceived difficult temperament. *Child Development, 56*, 1314–1325.

Lemery, K. S., Essex, M. J., & Smider, N. A. (2002). Revealing the relation between temperament and behavior problem symptoms by eliminating measurement confounding: Expert ratings and factor analyses. *Child Development, 73*, 867–882.

Lengua, L. J., West, S. G., & Sandler, I. N. (1998). Temperament as a predictor of symptomatology in children: Addressing contamination of measures. *Child Development, 69*, 164–181.

Lerner, J. V., Lerner, R. M., & Zabski, S. (1985). Temperament and elementary school children's actual and rated academic performance: A test of a 'goodness-of-fit' model. *Journal of Child Psychology and Psychiatry, 26*, 125–136.

Lewis, K. E., & Goldberg, L. L. (1997). Measurements of temperament in the identification of children who stutter. *European Journal of Disorders of Communication, 32*, 441–448.

MacCallum, R. C., Zhang, S., Preacher, K. J., & Rucker, D. D. (2002). On the practice of dichotomization of quantitative variables. *Psychological Methods, 7*, 19–40.

Margolin, G., Oliver, P. H., & Medina, A. M. (2001). Conceptual issues in understanding the relation between interparental conflict and child adjustment: Integrating developmental psychopathology and risk/resilience perspectives. In J. H. Grych & F. D. Fincham (Eds.), *Child development and interparental conflict.* Cambridge: Cambridge University Press.

Marsh, H. W. (1988). *Self-Description Questionnaire-I: Manual.* San Antonio, TX: Psychological Corporation.

Marsh, H. W. (1990). *Self-Description Questionnaire-II: Manual and research monograph.* San Antonio, TX: Psychological Corporation.

Martin, R. P. (1989). Activity level, distractibility, and persistence: Critical characteristics in early schooling. In G. A. Kohnstamm, J. E. Bates, & M. K. Rothbart (Eds.), *Temperament in childhood* (pp. 451–461). Chichester, England: Wiley & Sons.

Martin, R. P., Drew, K. D., Gaddis, L. R., & Moseley, M. (1988). Prediction of elementary school achievement from preschool temperament: Three studies. *School Psychology Review, 17,* 125–137.

Martin, R. P., Nagle, R., & Paget, K. (1983). Relationships between temperament and classroom behavior, teacher attitudes, and academic achievement. *Journal of Psychoeducational Assessment, 1,* 377–386.

Martin, R. P., & Holbrook, J. (1985). Relationship of temperament characteristics to the academic achievement of first-grade children. *Journal of Psychoeducational Assessment, 3,* 131–140.

Martin, R. P., Wisenbaker, J., & Huttunen, M. (1994). Review of factor analytic studies of temperament measures based on the Thomas-Chess structural model: Implications for the Big Five. In C. F. Halverson, G. A. Kohnstamm, & R. P. Martin (Eds.), *The developing structure of temperament and personality from infancy to adulthood* (pp. 157–172). Hillsdale, NJ: Lawrence Erlbaum Associates.

Matheny, A. P. (1980). Bayley's Infant Behavior Record: Behavioral components and twin analyses. *Child Development, 51,* 1157–1167.

Matheny, A. P. (1989). Temperament and cognition: Relations between temperament and mental test scores. In G. A. Kohnstamm, J. E. Bates, & M. K. Rothbart (Eds.), *Temperament in childhood* (pp. 263–282). New York: Wiley & Sons.

Matheny, A. P., Jr., & Phillips, K. (2001). Temperament and context: Correlates of home environment with temperament continuity and change, newborn to 30 months. In T. D. Wachs & G. A. Kohnstamm (Eds.), *Temperament in Context* (pp. 81–101). Mahwah, NJ: Lawrence Erlbaum.

Matheny, A. P., Wilson, R. S., & Thoben, A. S. (1987). Home and mother: Relations with infant temperament. *Developmental Psychology, 23,* 323–331.

Maziade, M., Boutin, P., Cote, R., & Thivierge, J. (1986c). Empirical characteristics of the NYLS temperament in middle childhood: Congruities and incongruities with other studies. *Child Psychiatry and Human Development, 17*(1), 38–52.

Maziade, M., Caperaa, P., Laplante, B., Boudreault, M., Thivierge, J., Cote, R., et al. (1985). Value of difficult temperament among 7-year-olds in the general population for predicting psychiatric diagnosis at age 12. *American Journal of Psychiatry, 142,* 943–946.

Maziade, M., Cote, R., Boudreault, M., Thivierge, J., & Boutin, P. (1986) Family correlates of temperament continuity and change across middle childhood. *American Journal of Orthopsychiatry, 56,* 195–203.

Maziade M., Cote, R., Bernier, H., Boutin, P., & Thivierge, J. (1989a). Significance of extreme temperament in infancy for clinical status in pre-school years I. Value of extreme temperament at 4–8 months for predicting diagnosis at 4.7 years. *British Journal of Psychiatry, 154,* 535–543.

Maziade, M., Cote, R., Bernier, H., Boutin, P., & Thivierge, J. (1989b). Significance of extreme temperament in infancy for clinical status in pre-school years II: Patterns of temperament change and implications for the appearance of disorders. *British Journal of Psychiatry, 154,* 544–551.

Maziade, M., Cote, R., Boutin, P., Bernier, H., & Thivierge, J. (1987). Temperament and intellectual development: A longitudinal study from infancy to four years. *American Journal of Psychiatry, 144,* 144–150.

Maziade, M., Cote, R., Boutin, P., Boudreault, M., & Thivierge, J. (1986). The effect of temperament on longitudinal academic achievement in primary school. *Journal of the American Academy of Child Psychiatry, 25,* 692–696.

McCarthy, D. (1972). *Manual for the McCarthy Scales of Children's Abilities.* New York: Psychological Corporation.

McClowry, S. G. (1998). The science and art of using temperament as the basis for intervention. *School Psychology Review, 27,* 551–563.

McDevitt, S. C., & Carey, W. B. (1978). The measurement of temperament in 3–7 year old children. *Journal of Child Psychology and Psychiatry, 19,* 245–253.

McIntosh, D. E., & Cole-Love, A. S. (1996). Profile comparisons between ADHD and non-ADHD children on the Temperament Assessment Battery for Children. *Journal of Psychoeducational Assessment, 14*, 362–372.

Mettetal, G. (1996). Non-clinical interventions for families with temperamentally difficult children. *Early Child Development and Care, 121*, 119–133.

Miller, P. A., & Jansen-op-de-Haar, M. A. (1997). Emotional, cognitive, behavioral, and temperament characteristics of high-empathy children. *Motivational and Emotion, 21*, 109–125.

Moos, R. H., & Moos, B. S. (1986). *Family Environment Scale manual* (2nd ed.). Palo Alto: CA: Consulting Psychologists Press.

Neville, H., & Johnson, D. C. (1997). *Temperament tools: Working with your child's inborn traits.* Seattle: Parenting Press.

Newman, D. L., Caspi, A., Moffitt, T. E., & Silva, P. A. (1997). Antecedents of adult interpersonal functioning: Effects of individual differences in age 3 temperament. *Developmental Psychology, 33*, 206–217.

Nordstroem, P., Gustavsson, P., Edman, G., & Asberg, M. (1996). Temperamental vulnerability and suicide risk after attempted suicide. *Suicide and Life-Threatening Behavior, 26*, 380–394.

Olson, S. L., Bates, J. E., & Kaskie, B. (1992). Caregiver-infant interaction antecedents of children's school-age cognitive ability. *Merrill-Palmer Quarterly, 38*, 309–330.

Palisin, H. (1986). Preschool temperament and performance on achievement tests. *Developmental Psychology, 22*, 766–770.

Paul, R., & Kellogg, L. (1997). Temperament in late talkers. *Journal of Child Psychology and Psychiatry and Allied Disciplines, 38*, 803–811.

Petrill, S. A., & Thompson, L. A. (1993). The phenotypic and genetic relationships among measures of cognitive ability, temperament, and scholastic achievement. *Behavior Genetics, 23*, 511–518.

Pettit, G. S., & Bates, J. E. (1984). Continuity of individual differences in the mother-infant relationship from six to thirteen months. *Child Development, 55*, 729–739.

Pettit, G. S., & Bates, J. E. (1989). Family interaction patterns and children's behavior problems from infancy to 4 years. *Developmental Psychology, 25*, 413–420.

Phares, V., Compas, B. E., & Howell, D. C. (1989). Perspectives on child behavior problems: Comparisons of children's self-reports with parent and teacher reports. *Psychological Assessment, 1*, 68–71.

Plumert, J., & Schwebel, D. C. (1997). Social and temperamental influences on children's overestimation of their physical abilities: Links to accidental injuries. *Journal of Experimental Child Psychology, 67*, 317–337.

Prior, M. (1992). Childhood temperament. *Journal of Child Psychology and Psychiatry, 33*, 249–279.

Prior, M. R., Sanson, A. V., & Oberklaid, R. (1989). The Australian Temperament Project. In G.A. Kohnstamm, J. E. Bates, & M. K. Rothbart (Eds.), *Temperament in childhood* (pp. 537–554). New York: John Wiley & Sons.

Putnam, S. P., Sanson, A. V., & Rothbart, M. K. (2002). Child temperament and parenting. In M. H. Bornstein (Ed.), *Handbook of parenting* (2nd ed., pp. 255–277). Mahwah, NJ: Lawrence Erlbaum.

Radke-Yarrow, M. (1998). Comments on chapter 4. In R. B. Cairns, L. R. Bergman, & J. Kagan (Eds.), *Methods and models for studying the individual.* Thousand Oaks, CA: Sage.

Raine, A., Reynolds, C., Venables, P. H., & Mednick, S. (2002). Stimulation seeking and intelligence: A prospective longitudinal study. *Journal of Personality and Social Psychology, 82*, 663–674.

Rende, R. D., & Plomin, R. (1992). Relations between first grade stress, temperament, and behavior problems. *Journal of Applied Developmental Psychology, 13*, 435–446.

Robinson, E. A., Eyberg, S. M., & Ross, A. W. (1980). The standardization of an inventory of child conduct problem behaviors. *Journal of Clinical Child Psychology, 9*, 22–29.

Rothbart, M. K. (1989). Temperament and development. In G. A. Kohnstamm, J. E. Bates, & M. K. Rothbart (Eds.), *Temperament in childhood* (pp. 187–247). New York: John Wiley & Sons.

Rothbart, M. K., & Bates, J. E. Temperament. (1998). In W. Damon & N. Eisenberg (Eds.), *Handbook of child psychology, Vol. 3: Social, emotional, and personality development* (Fifth ed.; pp. 105–176). New York: John Wiley & Sons.

Rothbart, M. K., & Jones, L. B. (1998). Temperament, self regulation, and education. *School Psychology Review, 27*, 479–491.

Rushton, J. P., Brainerd, C. J., & Pressley, M. (1983). Behavioral developmental and construct validity: The principle of aggregation. *Psychological Bulletin, 94*, 18–38.

Sanson, A., Prior, M., & Kyrios, M. (1990). Contamination of measures in temperament research. *Merrill-Palmer Quarterly, 36*, 179–192.

Sattler, J. M. (1982). *Assessment of children's intelligence and special abilities* (2nd ed.). Boston: Allyn & Bacon.

Saylor, C. F., & Brandt, B. (1986). The Minnesota Child Development Inventory: A valid maternal report form for screening development in infancy. *Journal of Developmental and Behavioral Pediatrics, 7*, 308–311.

Scarr, S., & McCartney, K. (1983). How people make their own environments: A theory of genotype → environment effects. *Child Development, 54*, 424–435.

Schoen, M. J., & Nagle, R. J. (1994). Prediction of school readiness from kindergarten temperament scores. *Journal of School Psychology, 32*, 135–147.

Sellman. J. D., & Joyce, P. J. (1996). Phobic disorders are associated with temperament in alcoholic men. *Australian and New Zealand Journal of Psychiatry, 30*, 110–113.

Sheeber, L. B. (1995). Empirical dissociations between temperament and behavior problems: A response to the Sanson, Prior, and Kyrios study. *Merrill-Palmer Quarterly, 41*, 554–561.

Sheeber, L. B., & Johnson, J. H. (1994). Evaluation of a temperament-focused, parent-training program. *Journal of Clinical Child Psychology, 23*, 249–259.

Sheeber, L. B., & McDevitt, S. C. (1998). Temperament-focused parenting program. In J. M. Briesmeister & C. E. Schaefer (Eds.), *Handbook of parent training: Parents as co-therapists for children's behavior problems* (2nd ed.) (pp. 479–507). New York: John Wiley & Sons.

Shoemaker, O., Saylor, C. F., & Erikson, M.T. (1993). Concurrent validity of the Minnesota Child Development Inventory with high-risk infants. *Journal of Pediatric Psychology, 18*, 377–388.

Silva, P. A. (1990). The Dunnedin multidisciplinary health and development study: A fifteen year longitudinal study. *Paediatric and Perinatal Epidemiology, 4*, 96–127.

Slabach, E. H., Morrow, J., & Wachs, T. D. (1991). Questionnaire measurement of infant and child temperament: Current status and future directions. In J. Strelau & A. Angleitner (Eds.), *Explorations in temperament: International perspectives* (pp. 205–234). New York: Plenum.

Strelau, J. (1998). *Temperament: A psychological perspective.* New York: Plenum.

Strelau, J., & Angleitner, A. (1991). Temperament research: Some divergences and similarities. In J. Strelau & A. Angleitner (Eds.), *Explorations in temperament: International perspectives on theory and measurement* (pp. 1–12). New York: Plenum Press.

Strelau, J., Zawadzki, B., & Piotrowska, A. (2001). Temperament and intelligence: A psychometric approach to the links between both phenomena. In J. M. Collis & S. Messick (Eds.), *Intelligence and personality: Bridging the gap in theory and measurement*. Mahwah, NJ: Lawrence Erlbaum.

Tabachnick, B. G., & Fidell, L. S. (2001). *Using multivariate statistics.* (4th ed.). Boston: Allyn & Bacon.

Talwar, R., Schwab, J., & Lerner, R. M. (1989). Early adolescent temperament and academic competence: Tests of "direct effects" and developmental contextual models. *Journal of Early Adolescence, 9*(3), 291–309.

Teglasi, H., & MacMahon, B. H. (1990). Temperament and common behaviors of children. *Journal of Applied Developmental Psychology, 11*, 331–349.

Terestman, N. (1980). Mood quality and intensity in nursery school children as predictors of behavior disorder. *American Journal of Orthopsychiatry, 50*, 125–138.

Thomas, A., & Chess, S. (1977). *Temperament and development*. New York: Bruner/Mazel.

Thomas, A., & Chess, S. (1986). The New York Longitudinal Study: From infancy to early adult life. In R. Plomin & J. Dunn (Eds.), *The study of temperament: Changes, continuities, and challenges* (pp. 39–52). Hillsdale, NJ: Lawrence Erlbaum Associates.

Thomas, A., Chess, S., & Birch, H. G. (1968). *Temperament and behavior disorders in children*. New York: New York University Press.

Thomas, A., Chess, S., Birch, H. G., Hertzig, M. E., & Korn, S. (1963). *Behavioral individuality in early childhood*. New York: New York University Press.

Turecki, S. & Tonner, L. (1985). *The difficult child*. New York: Bantam Books.

U.S. Department of Education, National Center for Education Statistics. (2001). *Entering kindergarten: A portrait of American children when they begin school: Findings from the condition of education 2000, NCES 2001–025*. Washington, DC: U.S. Government Printing Office.

van den Boom, D. C. (1994). The influence of temperament and mothering on attachment and exploration: An experimental manipulation of sensitive responsiveness among lower-class mothers with irritable infants. *Child Development, 65*, 1457–1477.

van den Boom, D. C. (1995). Do first-year intervention effects endure? Follow-up during toddlerhood of a sample of Dutch irritable infants. *Child Development, 66*, 1798–1816.

Wachs, T. D. (1991). Environmental considerations in studies with nonextreme groups. In T. D. Wachs & R. Plomin (Eds.), *Conceptualization and measurement of the organism-environment interaction* (pp. 44–67). Washington, DC: American Psychological Association.

Wachs, T. D. (1994). Fit, context, and the transition between temperament and personality. In C. F. Halverson, G. A. Kohnstamm, & R. P. Martin (Eds.), *The developing structure of temperament and personality from infancy to adulthood* (pp. 209–220). Hillsdale, NJ: Lawrence Erlbaum Associates.

Wachs, T. D., & Gandour, M. J. (1983). Temperament, environment, and six-month cognitive-intellectual development: A test of the organismic specificity hypothesis. *International Journal of Behavioral Development, 6*, 135–152.

Wachs, T. D., & Gruen, G. (1982). *Early experience and human development*. New York: Plenum.

Wachs, T. D., & Kohnstamm, G. A. (2001). The bidirectional nature of temperament-context links. In T. D. Wachs & G. A. Kohnstamm (Eds.), *Temperament in context*, (pp. 201–222). Mahwah, NJ: Lawrence Erlbaum.

Wachs, T. D. & Plomin, R. (Eds.) (1991). *Conceptualization and measurement of the organism-environment interaction*. Washington, DC: American Psychological Association.

Webster-Stratton, C., & Eyberg, S. M. (1982). Child temperament: Relationship with child behavior problems and parent-child interactions. *Journal of Clinical Child Psychology, 11*, 123–129.

Wechsler, D. (1974). *Manual for the Wechsler Intelligence Scale for Children*. San Antonio, TX: Psychological Corporation.

Wechsler, D. (1991). *WISC-III. Wechsler Intelligence Scale for Children – Third Edition*. San Antonio, TX: Psychological Corporation.

Wechsler, D. (1981). *WAIS-R manual*. New York: The Psychological Corporation.

Wills, T. A., Windle, M., & Cleary, S. D. (1998). Temperament and novelty seeking in adolescent substance abuse: Convergence of dimensions of temperament with constructs from Cloninger's theory. *Journal of Personality and Social Psychology, 74*, 387–406.

Windle, M., & Lerner, R. M. (1986). Reassessing the dimensions of temperamental individuality across the life span: The Revised Dimensions of Temperament Survey (DOTS-R). *Journal of Adolescent Research, 1*, 213–229.

Woodcock, R. W., & Johnson, M. B. (1977). *Woodcock-Johnson Pscho-Educational Battery*. Hingham, MA: Teaching Resources Corporation.

Woodcock, R. W., & Johnson, M. B. (1989). *Woodcock-Johnson Psycho-Educational Battery – Revised*. Allen, TX: DLM.

Author Index

Subject Index